ANTHROPOLOGIES OF UNEMPLOYMENT

ANTHROPOLOGIES OF UNEMPLOYMENT

New Perspectives on Work
and Its Absence

**Edited by Jong Bum Kwon and
Carrie M. Lane**

ILR PRESS

AN IMPRINT OF

CORNELL UNIVERSITY PRESS   ITHACA AND LONDON

First published 2016 by Cornell University Press
First printing, Cornell Paperbacks, 2016
Printed in the United States of America

Library of Congress Cataloging-in-Publication Data

Names: Kwon, Jong Bum, 1971– editor. | Lane, Carrie M., 1974– editor. |
    Container of (work): Lane, Carrie M., 1974– Limits of liminality.
    Title: Anthropologies of unemployment : new perspectives on work and
    its absence / edited by Jong Bum Kwon and Carrie M. Lane.
Description: Ithaca : Cornell University Press, 2016. | Includes bibliographical
    references and index.
Identifiers: LCCN 2016016169
ISBN 9781501704659 (cloth : alk. paper)
ISBN 9781501704666 (pbk.)
Subjects: LCSH: Unemployment—Social aspects. | Unemployed—Social
    conditions. | Economic anthropology.
Classification: LCC HD5708 .A58 2016 | DDC 331.13/7—dc23
LC record available at https://lccn.loc.gov/2016016169

Cornell University Press strives to use environmentally responsible suppliers and materials to the fullest extent possible in the publishing of its books. Such materials include vegetable-based, low-VOC inks and acid-free papers that are recycled, totally chlorine-free, or partly composed of nonwood fibers. For further information, visit our website at www.cornellpress.cornell.edu.

Cloth printing   10 9 8 7 6 5 4 3 2 1
Paperback printing   10 9 8 7 6 5 4 3 2 1

This book is dedicated to all people engaged in the daily work of producing meaning, community, security, and livelihood.

Contents

Acknowledgments

This volume exists because countless people in more than half a dozen countries agreed to share their thoughts and stories with the anthropologists whose work is featured herein. Those people are the protagonists of this book, and it is they who give it whatever heart and import it possesses. We are grateful to them for their trust and candor. We hope that we have lived up to the task of representing their perspectives and experiences as accurately as possible within these pages.

The editors would also like to thank our wonderful team of contributors, whose creativity and collegiality made this project a pleasure from start to finish. This book is the result of many conversations and shared meals, and it has been a joy to get to know you all, as scholars and as people, throughout this long process. We are grateful to the Society for the Anthropology of Work for sponsoring the original American Anthropological Association conference session on which this volume is based. We also thank the panelists, discussants, and audience members whose contributions enlivened that session and inspired us to compile this volume.

Fran Benson provided unflagging support and encouragement from the first moment we told her of our plans to assemble this volume. We are grateful to her and to the editorial and design teams at Cornell University Press, as well as an anonymous reviewer, who helped shepherd this manuscript to its published form.

The editors thank our universities—Webster University and California State University, Fullerton—for providing grants and other resources that helped support us during the preparation of this volume. We are also grateful to the many colleagues and friends who encouraged us onward as we tackled each phase of this process. Thanks especially to Caitrin Lynch for her excellent advice on our introductory chapter. Carrie Lane would like to thank Matt Sterling for reminding her that life is much bigger than work, and Frank Sterling for taking really long naps that allowed her to work on this volume. Jong Bum Kwon would like to thank Elaine Cha for her unwavering faith. He would also like to express his gratitude to Dr. Laurel Kendall, who has patiently guided his work, and to his mentor Dr. Owen Lynch, whose care was invaluable to his becoming a working anthropologist.

ANTHROPOLOGIES OF UNEMPLOYMENT

INTRODUCTION

Jong Bum Kwon and Carrie M. Lane

In the cartoon by Jimmy Margulies depicted below, which ran in U.S. newspapers in 2014, we see a baffled-looking, middle-aged white man sitting beneath a version of the *American Idol* logo that has been revised to read "American Idle." Holding a newspaper announcing that jobless benefits will not be extended for U.S. workers, the man, whose shirt identifies him as a representative of the "long-term unemployed," says, "We've been renewed for another season." On one level, the cartoon sends a straightforward, if humorous, message about the continuing plight of the American unemployed, whose situation seems unlikely to improve any time soon. On other levels, the cartoon offers us a great deal more to consider.

For instance, what should we make of the choice to represent the long-term unemployed as a white male in a white-collared shirt, clothing traditionally associated with middle-class occupations? If the character pictured were a white woman, for instance, the cartoon's message would be reshaped by long-standing assumptions about the appropriate role of white women relative to paid employment in the United States. Some might brand it a sexist commentary on the inability of women to keep up in the labor force; others might celebrate the cartoon for bringing attention to the plight of unemployed females.

Alternately, attaching the caption "American Idle" to an image of an African American male could be perceived as racially inflammatory in light of pejorative stereotypes of the work ethic and employability of black American men. Yet that version would arguably be more accurate, as African American men not only have been historically marginalized from employment but also continue to

FIGURE 1. "American Idle." Reprinted with permission from Cagle Cartoons, Inc.

experience the highest rates of chronic unemployment. With that in mind, we might now see the choice to represent the jobless with a white man as a politically charged attempt to position white American men as the primary victims of the recession.

We could continue this thought exercise indefinitely. What if the character were Asian American or Latina, teenaged or elderly, clothed in a turban or a military uniform? How would each of those variables change the meaning and impact of the cartoon? Even in its current form, in order to make sense of the cartoon, to get the joke, one must know at least a little bit about a lot of things—the high unemployment levels the United States has experienced since the Great Recession; the political controversy around extending government benefits for the jobless; the expectation that white American men should be able to find paid, secure employment; even the popularity of reality television programming. Without context, the punch line loses its punch. These sorts of "what if" exercises help us see and make sense of the unexamined assumptions embedded in the media representations we encounter every day. One of the major strengths of the anthropological approach to studying culture is precisely this exercise of situating the seemingly mundane and taken-for-granted in its wider context.

To understand what unemployment means, why it happens, and how it feels, we need to consider it within its appropriate context. And that, in short, is what this volume does. The anthropologists whose work is featured herein provide the context—historical, political, cultural, and economic—for analyzing unemployment from a variety of different angles across a variety of different settings.

One of the key contributions of this volume is the ethnographic portrayal of unemployment across multiple national contexts—in Argentina, Ethiopia, France, Mexico, Nicaragua, and South Korea as well as the United States—providing important vantage points for cultural critique (Marcus and Fischer 1986). These cross-cultural comparisons highlight the value of ethnographic inquiry for understanding broadly political-economic circumstances, disruptions, and transformations.

The diversity of these case studies extends beyond regional or national variations. The ethnographic subjects discussed herein are young and old, male and female, immigrant and native-born, of varying races and socioeconomic backgrounds. Some continue to look for paid employment; others face such structural and social obstacles that being unemployed has, in many respects, become their daily work. Yet all are unemployed or underemployed, and thus—despite the many differences between them—they share the experience of economic, cultural, and even bodily disenfranchisement. In all cases the consequences of unemployment are long-lasting, affecting social and familial relationships, personal wealth, self-identity, and mental and physical health well after re-employment. People do not simply recover; their worlds do not just return to normal. But the ways in which their worlds change, and the ways in which they remain the same, vary dramatically across contexts. Juxtaposing ethnographic accounts of unemployment across a variety of regions, professions, and populations also allows us to identify common themes and experiences without reducing the significance of the intersection of gender, class, age, race, and citizenship in specific cultural contexts.

The Great Global Recession

This volume was conceived after the Great Recession (2007–2009), a worldwide economic crisis that led to unprecedented levels of unemployment in developed and developing nations alike. The recession's official end in June 2009 did not quell anxieties in most affected countries, nor did it signal job recovery. The U.S. unemployment rate, for example, was 9.5 percent at the end of the recession. It peaked to 10 percent in October 2009, when over fifteen million people were still unemployed.[1] Among that number, 6.1 million were jobless for twenty-seven weeks or more, the highest proportion of long-term unemployment on record.[2] The average duration of unemployment was more than nine months. In December 2015, six years after the end of the recession, the unemployment rate returned to the pre-recession level of 5 percent in December 2007 (which is considered "full employment," a concept built around the idea that some people's joblessness is society's gain). At that point the number of long-term unemployed was still at three million.[3] In other words, even though the Great Recession is technically in the past, its impact is still being felt every day by millions of people in the United States and throughout the world.

The Great Recession affected the quality of employment as well as its quantity. A United Nations report found that "across the globe, many workers who did not lose their jobs were forced to accept reduced working hours as well as lower wages and benefits. In developing countries, a large number of workers lost their jobs in export sectors and were forced into informal and vulnerable employment elsewhere" (United Nations DESA 2011, 28). Even those fortunate enough to remain employed during this period experienced a profound unraveling of many of the benefits generally associated with formal employment.

In many nations rising unemployment and the declining quality of work life pushed into public view people and predicaments that had long been culturally marginal. In the United States, for instance, unemployed Americans have tended to become visible, if only temporarily, only in times of depression and recession, during which they are often perceived as threats to normative values and behaviors (Denning 2010, 79). The presumption has been that full-time, formal employment is the normal socioeconomic condition; conversely, unemployment is understood to be abnormal and temporary, despite economic evidence to the contrary, stretching as far back as the Great Depression in the 1930s. Yet in recent years stories of the long-term unemployed have been shared across popular media, from traditional news outlets to interactive news sites and popular blog networks.[4] They tell of personal feelings of grief, confusion, and indignation; broken marriages and families; social isolation and alienation; shattered identities and lost self-esteem; and deteriorating health and well-being. While there are exceptions (stories of strengthened marital and family bonds, of reprioritized social values, of recommitments to religious life, and of those who have not been affected at all), most narratives describe the social and personal costs of prolonged joblessness.

On a global level, chronic unemployment is hardly a novel phenomenon; conditions that are shockingly new to middle-class Americans, for instance, have been the norm for generations in other regions, especially among marginalized populations. As the chapters herein document, there is a tremendous amount of variability in how unemployment is framed and experienced across nations, regions, classes, races, genders, age groups, and sectors of the economy. In each region and for each population within that region there exist long and shifting narratives around both the presence and absence of employment.

Institutions, forms of knowledge and practice, social relationships, affective orientations—these are all critical contexts for making sense of unemployment. Our contributors develop complex linkages between intimate and macro-level structures of meaning and value. While appreciating the different ways people live and cope with economic insecurity and dispossession, all reveal that unemployment and employment are crucial cultural registers in shaping that experience. Local and national discourses around work and employment, for example, deeply inform notions of personhood, citizenship, and moral-economic value (see the chapters by Murphy and Perelman). These in turn affect how individuals receive and react to conditions of chronic unemployment. Unemployment is not simply understood and experienced as either in opposition to or as the loss of employment but in a complex relationship to its construction in particular contexts. Some of the subjects in the coming chapters, especially youth, have never had what might be called formal employment but continue to organize life course expectations and individual aspirations according to its promise (see the chapters by Mains and Murphy). Employment may not be normal worldwide, but it is normative; that is, it is part of a prescribed parcel of behaviors and attributes expected of "normal" and "valued" citizens.

In this volume we highlight unemployed people's individual and collective responses to conditions of economic insecurity and chronic unemployment, demonstrating their agency and cultural productivity in contexts of severe constraint. Our intent is not to romanticize these responses. Rather, the chapters demonstrate the complex and surprising ways people adjust to, resist, and accommodate circumstances of political and economic inequality and exclusion. Importantly, it is in their struggle to make meaningful lives under considerable duress that we see the emergence of new meanings and experiences of work and unemployment. By immersing the reader in how unemployment looks, feels, and smells, the chapters in this volume make their collective case that unemployment is more than simply the loss of a job.

Meanings of Work, Employment, and Unemployment

One of the challenges of this volume has been figuring out how to talk about work, employment, and unemployment in clear and consistent ways despite the terms' fluidity and the increasingly blurry boundaries dividing them. This challenge is in part semantic. In Western industrialized nations the terms *work* and *employment* are often used interchangeably to designate formal, regular, paid activity. To be unemployed is sometimes referred to as being "out of work." Yet work and formal employment are not always, or even often, the same thing. Cultural histories and ethnographic studies of the meaning of work reveal that work is the more expansive cultural concept while employment is narrower. Across time and culture, work has been central to how people understand social life both in and outside the domain of formal economic activity, including politics, leisure, social intercourse and organization, and gender (see Applebaum 1995; Budd 2011; Comaroff and Comaroff 1992). The Argentine trash pickers Perelman discusses in this volume, for instance, clearly work; they collect garbage in order to make money and retain their role as family providers in the absence of formal unemployment. Yet to highlight the ambiguity of pickers' employment status, Perelman refers to their labor as "non-work," as many of its practitioners, as well as many of their countrymen, see pickers as "unemployed" (*desempleado*). In this case, as in so many others, what counts as employment is a political issue with profound consequences. Distinctions based on categories of race, gender, and class have long delimited what may be regarded as legitimate employment and who may work particular jobs. Unwaged work—such as domestic work, child rearing, self-provisioning, the labor of peasants, and informal economies—has played an indispensable economic and social role in every single society, even the most industrialized ones (Smith, Wallerstein, and Evers 1984; Smith and Wallerstein 1992).

With the expansion of capitalism and wage labor across the globe, employment—in the sense of formal, steady, paid labor—has become the dominant, but not the exclusive, model for what work should look like (Williams 1983, 326). This privileging of employment has broad implications. In most modern capitalist economies, formal employment has come to structure how people think about and experience things like time, gender, life course trajectories, social networks, and domains of cultural authority. In much of the contemporary world employment has become a condition for doing other kinds of work, in the culturally expansive sense of the term, such as the work of building social relationships, attaining new social statuses, or gaining social respectability. For example, what it means to be an adult male in many societies is intimately linked with the securing of formal employment (see the chapters by Mains and Murphy). When such employment proves elusive, so does a man's ability to achieve adult status and the many potential benefits thereof (such as independent housing, marriage, children, and the respect of one's kin and peers). Those who lose their jobs, or cannot find jobs in the first place, stand to lose far more than just wages or a title.

Thinking about the many things jobs provide to workers requires a slight shift of perspective for many scholars. As Elaine Scarry (1994) has remarked, since the widespread penetration of industrial capitalism, we tend to associate work and employment with pain, self-denial, and loss of autonomy. It is of course politically and intellectually crucial to consider the ways in which workers suffer exploitation, alienation, discrimination, and stigmatization. Yet those same workers often associate their jobs with personal and national progress, freedom from patriarchal constraints, opportunities for leisure and consumption, and moral responsibility to family and kin.[5] Apparently oppressive forms of employment may also allow other kinds of culturally productive work—the making of selves, persons, and social relationships. Work is indeed exertion, sacrifice, and suffering, but it is also freedom, personal fulfillment, self-esteem, self-discipline, social maturity, and care for others. Work produces value—material, moral, symbolic, and social—and constitutes ways of life and forms of individual and collective identity as well as exclusion.[6]

Recognizing the complicated ways work is entangled with other cultural meanings, values, and statuses can help us appreciate the depth of personal and social suffering that accompany unemployment. Doing so also provides insight into the breadth of culturally creative responses to conditions of chronic economic insecurity and unemployment. The unemployed and those historically excluded from secure formal employment struggle but develop means to acquire and produce meaning and value, such as autonomy, respect, and sociality, often replicating the forms and practices, if not content, of formal employment.[7] People who may not be formally employed nevertheless find ways to feel employed, that is, to work. As described in Lane's chapter, unemployed U.S. technology workers dressed in business attire for weekly networking meetings and referred to job-seeking as "the hardest job I've ever had." The Ethiopian youth Mains writes about spent scarce funds on and obsessively checked their cell phones for urgent messages that rarely came. Members of the Nicaraguan workers cooperative Fisher studied attended meetings for more than five years to discuss a factory that had no working machinery and never produced a single item of clothing. For these groups, as for so many others, unemployment cannot be reduced to the absence of a job. It is instead a constituent component of contemporary life, a site for forging new ways of working, being, and thinking in these precarious neoliberal times. The ethnographic studies collected in this volume take that assumption as their jumping off point as they set out to document and make sense of this important and understudied cultural terrain.

Neoliberalism, Precarity, and Unemployment

This book is a product of recent heightened attention to unemployment and underemployment in anthropology.[8] The past several decades have seen considerable intellectual ferment about pervasive economic upheaval and dislocation across the globe. Ethnographic examinations of neoliberalism and, more recently, precarity, for example, have constructively complicated our understandings of the interconnections between cultures and capitalisms and the production of inequality, insecurity, and social-economic marginalization. Too seldom, however, has unemployment been the explicit focus of such investigations. Too commonly, unemployment has been understood more as symptom than a constituent component of the structure and experience of contemporary life.

We therefore see this volume as contributing to the vitality and relevance of contemporary anthropological projects about globalized inequality and insecurity but insist on the centrality of unemployment. Unemployment is culturally productive, not in the sense that it is a positive development but in the sense that it produces new cultural meanings, norms, and connections. As people adapt and make adjustments to their lives under circumstances of economic disenfranchisement and deprivation, they form new, even if tentative, identities, social relationships and, importantly, meanings of employment and unemployment. The experience and meaning of unemployment is integrally related to local constructions of work and employment, but unemployment is lived neither merely as their absence nor as a liminal state in between stable categories of employment. The chapters herein suggest that the distinction between employment and unemployment is increasingly blurred, if indeed it was ever as distinct as has been presumed, and this conflation has intensified with the normalization of unemployment in these precarious times. More and more, people work without employment. One cannot, we therefore argue, make sense of the precarious neoliberal world today without also making sense of unemployment.

For many scholars, the terms *neoliberalism* and *precarity* are familiar shorthand for a way of thinking about the political, economic, and cultural conditions under which most people in the world currently live. For students and others new to this subject matter, these terms may be less familiar, so we briefly explain them as well as how they relate to each other and to unemployment.

Neoliberalism

Neoliberalism is an unwieldy word, often underspecified and used as shorthand for contemporary capitalism and its ills (Ferguson 2009, 172). At its core, *neoliberalism* refers to a set of ideas about how the world works—or should work—when it comes to the relationship between people, governments, and the market. Neoliberal ideology privileges individual freedom, unfettered competition, and the self-regulating free market as the most effective means of achieving a healthy economy.[9] Under this model, the ideal state is non-interventionist, and its primary function is to assure competitive markets and protect individual liberties (rather than individual people), in particular the unassailability of private property.

Starting in the 1970s, neoliberal principles have been used to justify legislation and programs to privatize state-owned enterprises and public goods; to deregulate markets, repealing legal and policy encumbrances to their efficiency; and to liberalize trade, eliminating tariffs and other barriers to global commerce. Associated policies include the attenuation of environmental protections, the weakening of labor rights, the withdrawal of social services and welfare programs, the downsizing of government, and the removal of controls on financial activity (Steger and Roy 2010, 14). In addition to these we may add global development agendas and programs (that is, structural adjustment and austerity) enforced by powerful supranational institutions such as the International Monetary Fund (IMF) and the World Bank.

More abstractly, neoliberalism describes the increasingly blurred distinction between the realms of public government and private business. This blurring and its implications are the subject of Michel Foucault's studies of governmentality (Foucault 2009; Foucault and Burchell 2010), which expand the analysis of power and politics beyond the state to encompass the "rationalities" (the very way we think about problems and their solutions) embedded in the "technologies" (procedures and mechanisms) used to evaluate and manage conduct from the individual to the national level and beyond. Important in this conceptualization is Foucault's understanding that power results not merely in the subjugation of one group under another; rather, power produces identities and subjectivities. In other words, studies of neoliberalism encompass not just the enforcement of neoliberal ideals through specific political actions but also the ways in which individuals are encouraged and persuaded to manage their own conduct in order to become ideal individualistic and entrepreneurial neoliberal subjects (Brady 2014, 18).[10]

The relationship between neoliberalism and unemployment is at once obvious and more complicated than it seems. The spread of neoliberal ideas and implementation of neoliberal policies have made it easier and more culturally acceptable for companies to lay off workers, relocate jobs overseas, and privilege short-term stock prices over long-term investment in persons and places. All of this was accomplished in the name of freeing companies to compete on an increasingly global scale while "liberating" individual workers from the infantilizing shackles of secure employment. Proponents of these shifts cast high unemployment as an unavoidable, even beneficial, by-product of progress rather than the result of a long class struggle that, over the previous half-century, consolidated power and wealth in the hands of financial and political elites while fueling social and economic insecurity in countries around the world (Harvey 2005).

The lives of the unemployed men and women described in the ethnographic examples in this volume have been undeniably shaped by neoliberalism. And yet neoliberalism is not monolithic. It has not spread across the globe in an inexorable and identical manner. Despite our abbreviated overview above, neoliberalism is not an unvarying set of ideas and practices that is uniformly interpreted and experienced across contexts. One of the key contributions of anthropology to the examination of neoliberalism has been a varied collection of detailed ethnographic analyses of local productions, accommodations, and challenges to neoliberal ideologies, governance, and policies in settings typically imagined as outside liberal political histories and free markets (for instance, African nations and China). Ethnographically grounded research reveals that neoliberalism is a contingent, contested, and incomplete process, the dimensions of which take hold in uneven and unexpected ways, depending on local political histories (Ong 2006), policy regimes (Elyachar 2005), governmental cultures (Chalfin 2010), national identities (Rofel 2007), and cultural understandings of gender and moral respectability (Karim 2011; Lynch 2007) and life course statuses (Mains 2007). This volume offers a similarly grounded investigation of the connections between neoliberalism and unemployment specifically; the two are undoubtedly connected, but these chapters document the important ways in which the form and content of such connections vary by time and context.

Precarity

Adding a third variable to this already complicated relationship, one of the major impacts of the spread of neoliberalism has been the production of what scholars call precarity, or the increased experience of inequality and insecurity that has accompanied the destabilization of the institutions, expectations, and life trajectories around which people once built their lives (see Allison 2013; Berlant 2007). While neoliberalism is a set of ways to think and govern, precarity is an assemblage of ways to *feel*. Uncertainty and insecurity are not new phenomena, but in recent decades income and wealth polarization have grown not only between countries but also within them, as seven out of ten people live in countries where the gap between rich and poor is greater than it was thirty years ago (Seery and Arendar 2014, 8). Political corruption, public health crises, stalled development (personal and national), and crime and violent conflict are correlated with the stark rise in inequality and affective worlds of insecurity, suffering, and fear (see also Besteman 2009).

With regard to unemployment, precarity involves the dissolution of the opportunities and expectations around historical and culturally specific constructions of work and employment. It refers to the dismantling of stable structures of work and employment and the rise of labor that is irregular and contingent, that is, "precarious" labor (Millar 2014; Muehlebach and Shoshan 2012; Neilson and Rossiter 2008; Standing 2011).[11] Precariousness of livelihood and uncertainty of employment have always been a part of the lives of the working poor as well as many other people (Millar 2014, 34; Neilson and Rossiter 2005).[12] But precarious employment is now the norm; half of the world's workers are informally, casually, or irregularly employed (Allison 2012, 368n3). Thus "unstable work destabilizes daily living" (Allison 2012, 349). As certain forms of work are disappearing, so too are the institutional structures and relationships that shaped ways of thinking, feeling, and acting about one's place in social worlds. This has led to new configurations of the "normal"—new life cycle statuses and trajectories, new modes of belonging, and new moral evaluations that guide social-economic action and expectation. To be clear, these configurations are not simply new. As many of the contributors to this volume demonstrate, the social relationships, practices, and values about work and employment (in their specific regional and national contexts), even in their absence, continue to inform and shape the imaginaries and social-cultural adjustments of the unemployed (Muehlebach and Shoshan 2012). While precarity may be painful, as the stories herein attest, it is not simply uncertainty. Precarity is also longing and aspiration: longing for what should have been (stable employment and life) and aspirations for what should be (stable employment and life).

While Guy Standing has posited the precariat as a "class-in-the-making" (2011, vii), this prediction assumes a unity of experience and agenda that empirical research has yet to bear out. Millions of people around the world may be living increasingly uncertain lives, but the way they experience their precarious condition—how they explain it, where and when it pains them, whom they blame for it, and whether and how they seek to fix it—depends on factors more particular than universal. It is only through close ethnographic examinations of the on-the-ground, lived experiences of both employment and unemployment that we can come to understand the forms, meanings, and significance of the larger turn to neoliberalism and precarity.

Organization of the Book

We have organized the book's chapters around the volume's three central contributions to the anthropological study of unemployment. First, we call for a rethinking of the very concept of unemployment, particularly as it has been imagined in relationship to employment, economics, and human feeling. Second, we document how the lived experience of unemployment differs across national contexts and how unemployment itself is positioned within and in

opposition to existing national discourses such as those around solidarity, productivity, poverty, rurality, and reciprocity. Third, we consider the new identities, social relationships, and political movements produced by individual and
collective experiences of unemployment. Finally, we round out the volume with
an epilogue by Caitrin Lynch and Daniel Mains that explores the thematic connections between the chapters and points ahead to new directions for research
around unemployment.

Challenging Existing Understandings of Unemployment

Carrie Lane's chapter opens the volume with an important question: Is unemployment normal? For many men and women in these pages, unemployment
was and is a difficult and troubling experience, and yet, economic precarity was
neither a new nor intermittent condition but a persistent one, having envel-
oped much of their lives. Lane's subjects are American job seekers, in this case
in the high-technology industry (telecommunications, web design, programming, e-commerce). Despite the challenges of prolonged unemployment, these
white-collar, middle-class workers evince considerable resiliency and have not
only come to accept but to embrace dominant business ideologies of imperma-
nent employment. Layoffs did not necessarily dismantle their self-identification
as highly trained professionals; in fact, their identities were in some respects
buttressed by constant job-seeking and job change. Lane's findings refute
long-standing presumptions about the consequences of layoffs. Unemployment,
she uncovers, was not a liminal situation of untethered and displaced identities.
They did not expect or desire "reincorporation" into normative social-cultural
structures. Nonetheless, this does not mean that structures did not matter.
Rather, as she describes, job-seeking itself became work, constituting alternative
socialities, relationships, and sites of belonging. Interestingly, she states, in their
job searches they produce ways of feeling employed—recreating the rhythms,
roles, and rituals of employed life. What is new, though, is that the adjustments
that these high-tech workers have made have blurred the distinction between
employment and unemployment. Like many of the contributors to this volume,
Lane ethnographically tracks how chronic unemployment is transforming the
meanings, values, and practices of work.

In the next chapter, author David Karjanen offers a critique of economic
models of unemployment. He lays out a challenge to revisit the predominant
conceptions of unemployment and the unemployed, particularly with regard to
the experiences of African American job seekers in the United States. His careful
analysis of the premises of modern economic thought (including assumptions

and assertions about the social world, most pertinently that it is populated by rational, self-interested, individual actors) directs our attention to the blind spots that (mis)inform conventional economic understandings. By deploying ethnographic analysis, Karjanen demonstrates the potential of anthropological research to produce empirical and rigorous analyses of people's behaviors and motivations. Although it may seem prosaic to anthropologists, Karjanen offers a lesson well worth remembering as we evaluate our own methodologies, theoretical constructs, and descriptions of unemployment and the unemployed: People are complex social and historical beings, embedded in intricate, interacting structures.

Unemployment is often ambivalently portrayed in public culture, depicted as a temporary, if unfortunate, consequence of unleashing competition, entrepreneurial spirit, and individual freedoms. This ambivalence is sharpened when the fate of mass manufacturing in advanced industrial nations is the subject. The broad sweep of deindustrialization in the United States since the 1970s, for example, provoked fierce debate about blue-collar traditions and the obstacles to national and individual progress. Yet whether industrial labor's decline is being mourned or celebrated, the impact of blue-collar unemployment tends to be discussed in communal, regional, or national terms rather than at the level of embodied human experience. Jong Bum Kwon's research with male laid-off autoworkers in South Korea in the disastrous aftermath of the Asian financial crisis (1997–2001) offers a compelling analysis of the bodily cost of the loss of industrial work. Predominant imaginings of industrial labor in both the United States and Korea depict it as physically painful, mind-numbing repetition that constrains individual development. Focusing on the bodily experience of working on the assembly line, Kwon argues that industrial labor in this particular case was in fact a process of making *healthy* working bodies. After being laid off, workers felt severed not only from the factory but also from a vital part of their own bodies. They were not freed from painful physical labor; rather, they suffered a form of structural violence. His analysis also provokes a rethinking of employment and, consequently, unemployment. He suggests that we consider employment as a form of *occupation*, an affective and bodily process of habitation that mutually transforms worker and workplace in deeply felt and meaningful ways.

National Contexts and Discourses

Unemployment is a matter of the state because it provokes questions about moral order, about the composition and organization of social relationships, about the legitimacy of social-economic arrangements, and about national identity. Jack Murphy's contribution examines how unemployment in France in the mid-2000s resonated with long-held notions of *solidarité* (solidarity). With a deep intellectual and political history, solidarity functions as a symbol of a national social compact. Many French citizens deemed unemployment a threat to society itself, and the explosion of "riots" in the outer cities in the autumn of 2005 and mass street protests in January 2006 appeared to corroborate this fear. As unemployed youth in Limoges, a medium-sized peripheral city, Murphy's ethnographic subjects presumably embody the discontent and social exclusion that was widely thought to underlie the upheavals, but they belie simple characterizations. While they were clearly disenfranchised and living a life of *galère* (infantilizing dependence), Murphy's careful depiction of their everyday struggles challenges those national narratives, revealing the emergence of alternative forms of sociality and collective identity. While they may be denied normative adulthood, defined as social and economic autonomy achieved through stable employment, these youth improvised ways of belonging and asserting autonomous personhood. The question remains, however, whether the lives of these youth suggest the formation of new social classes.

The meaning and experience of unemployment are culturally and historically variable, informed by specific ideals of social dignity and moral-political belonging. Based on extended fieldwork with *cirujas* (pickers or scavengers of recyclable materials) in Buenos Aires, Mariano Perelman examines the contested imaginaries of work and employment in neoliberal Argentina. Since Juan Peron (president from 1946 to 1955), employment has been deeply linked to citizenship: rights and privileges of formal workers and obligations of the state to provide them basic welfare (housing, education, recreation). This arrangement laid the foundation for the ideals of dignified work and social identity (working man as provider of the family). In this context, not all work is considered employment. Thus, a scavenger who is occupied full time collecting waste matter considers himself *both* worker and unemployed, because picking does not secure "guarantees." With the entrenchment of neoliberal policies and ideologies withdrawing state employment opportunities and social services, however, the linkage is increasingly strained. Perelman shows that *cirujas* were forming new understandings of their work and work identity to adjust to conditions of chronic unemployment.

Karjanen's ethnographic case studies involve unemployed men and women in urban settings, the most common site of popular racialized preconceptions of economic disenfranchisement. Ann Kingsolver's contribution redirects our gaze toward the rural United States, which holds different but equally powerful spatialized imaginaries of racial poverty. Specifically examining the low country and the upcountry in South Carolina and parts of Appalachian Kentucky, Kingsolver argues that while those regions may be associated with long-standing poverty, they are rendered invisible in regards to unemployment. Poverty in fact has been naturalized to the region, as its residents have been depicted as culturally deprived (that is, steeped in a "culture of poverty") by politicians, scholars, and popular media alike. Placing the focus on un- and underemployment, Kingsolver renders visible the political economic structures that have impoverished the area and that enable the continued exploitation of its inhabitants. These are not isolated and backward places but sites of global capitalist extraction by multinational enterprises attracted to poor rural workers advertised as hospitable to low wages, anti-union policies, and inadequate working conditions. The urban and rural may stand apart in America's symbolic geography, but the poor and unemployed of those regions are entwined by global political-economic machinations.

Daniel Mains's ethnography investigates the struggles of disenfranchised youth: unemployed urban males in Jimma, Ethiopia, since the turn of the twenty-first century. The term *youth* is an ambiguous descriptor, describing not biological age but location in normative social trajectories. It is a category of persons burdened with ambivalence, a symbol of the future, signifying what should or should not come to pass. In other words, we imagine in youth both hope and fear for the future. As such, considerable anthropological attention has been placed on youth in contexts of neoliberal precarity. Mains cogently argues that among these men, unemployment was experienced as temporal and spatial problems to be solved. Rather than abstract philosophical concepts, time and space are lived and interpreted in and through social relationships. Employment is a social relationship, and particular kinds of employment index individual progress, namely the attainment of social respect and autonomy. Conversely, particular jobs bring about intense feelings of shame (*yiluññta*) because of their association with subservience. Expectations of progress at both national and individual levels have heightened in Ethiopia with modernization and greater access to education. With prolonged unemployment, young males are unable to insert themselves into narratives of national progress and self-development. These youth attempted to resolve the temporal problem with spatial fixes, migrating to other cities in Ethiopia (more commonly) or to the United States or elsewhere in Africa (less frequently) in order to avoid social scrutiny and reconfigure social relationships, thereby becoming different and ideally respected persons.

Renewed Selves and New Socialities

Economic relationships, as our authors demonstrate, are moral relationships deeply embedded in rich social-cultural contexts. Fran Rothstein takes this insight to shed light on labor migration patterns. Her study of migrants from San Cosme Mazatecochco, a rural community in central Mexico, residing in New Jersey ethnographically investigates a puzzling finding: During the long recession in the United States, more men were returning to Mexico than women. Migration is a strategy to deal with economic distress evident the world over. While an over-simplification, migratory movements tend to follow the vagaries of the relative economic circumstances between sending and receiving countries. Building on research that commenced in 2009 as well as on decades of previous fieldwork in San Cosme Mazatecochco, Rothstein shows that patterns of settlement and return are not, in fact, determined by naked economic calculus but are powerfully shaped by women and their capacity to enlarge and manage kin and social networks. San Cosmeros/as, she explains, participate in a flexible kinship and ritual system that can accommodate changing circumstances and incorporate varied individuals and groups. At the center of local and transnational networks are the women who do the work of kinship, maintaining kin contacts and organizing ritual celebrations to solidify social ties. These ties are crucial in obtaining and distributing information and resources and in anchoring members to particular locales. Kinship is a form of work, often done by women, and kinship is an important resource in responding to precarious forms of employment.

Migrants in Rothstein's study turn to their kin networks in difficult times. In contrast, amidst the hardship of prolonged unemployment in 2011–2012, Claudia Strauss's unemployed American workers looked to an ideology to sustain them, that of positive thinking. Positive thinking, of course, is not emblematic of an essential American character, but, as Strauss describes, it has a profound purchase on American society, both as a discourse and a technique of emotional self-management. Positive thinking appeals to unemployed workers as a way to keep up their spirits, remain optimistic, and present oneself as a "positive" individual. It has a long history, and Strauss identifies key sites of its production in contemporary American society, from popular positive psychology (for instance, Norman Vincent Peale's *The Power of Positive Thinking*) to Protestant and New Age religions. Some of the key purveyors are managers and professionals, which illuminates the long-standing connection between psychological and business discourses. Positive thinking resonates powerfully with neoliberal injunctions for individual, self-optimizing conduct. Not simply "thinking," positive thinking, as well as neoliberal ideologies, endorses affect management, defined as the constant monitoring of one's emotions and their physical manifestations. Cultural critics like Barbara Ehrenreich (2009a) have inveighed against positive thinking as an ideology that foreshortens social analysis and places the onus on the individual for her own success and failure. Strauss's respondents, however, did not blame themselves and did not misconstrue structures of inequality. Her interviews reveal that positive thinking may also be a form of self-care, a way of coping with the rejection and disappointment of repeated failed job searches. Positive thinking may enable one to imagine oneself in a future different from one's present situation of precarity.

Joshua Fisher's chapter interweaves Strauss's emphasis on the potentially trans-formative role of positivity with Rothstein's focus on the buoying power of human connection and community. His is an analysis of a small cotton-spinning coopera-tive called Génesis in Ciudad Sandino, Nicaragua. The cooperative is an example of transnational nongovernmental organization (NGO) projects to generate employ-ment and local communal responses to widespread unemployment. It is not a story of success in the usual sense. The purchased machinery never arrived, and the proj-ect was cancelled. Yet, it is instructive because, even without having produced a single thread, the co-op of forty-two women and men did not disband. Starting in 2007, they waited and worked without pay for five years. They continued to meet and collectively responded to their immediate social and financial needs. Those women and men demonstrated an important dimension of work: It is not simply about wages, profits, and efficiencies. Continuing to work, without pay, they pro-duced a sense of purpose, dignity, and hope for the future. Working collaboratively, they cleared a space for producing meaningful socialities and collective agencies.

Fisher's work closes the volume on a positive and provocative note, document-ing as it does the potential for meaningful if unpredictable responses to even the most entrenched structures of inequality and exploitation. He also brings us full circle, back to the question of how we conceptualize work and unemployment. As Fisher demonstrates, work is valued because it is productive in the manifold sense of making meaningful and dignified lives and communities. What is at stake in unemployment, as he and every other contributor to this volume can attest, is not simply a job. At stake are people's identities and relationships; their mental, physi-cal, and emotional health; their ability to fully participate in social, political, and economic life; and the futures they envision for themselves, their children, and their nations. What is at stake, in short, is everything.

THE LIMITS OF LIMINALITY

Anthropological Approaches to
Unemployment in the United States

Carrie M. Lane

For more than seventy years, the general consensus among scholars of work in the United States has been that the most crippling effect of job loss, especially for middle-class men, is the resulting loss of identity. Building on E. Wight Bakke's famous Depression-era studies, anthropologists, sociologists, and psychologists have amply documented unemployment's many negative effects for how men understand their own self-worth and social status (Bakke 1934, 1940; Newman 1988, 1993; Townsend 2002). Having pinned their sense of who they are to what they do for a living and their sense of what they do for a living to a single, stable job, laid-off white-collar workers are, according to Katherine Newman's seminal 1988 study *Falling from Grace*, "left hanging and socially isolated with no stable sense of who they are. Trained to see identity as a matter of occupation, yet unable to claim a place in the business culture they came from, they remain socially disabled and suspended in time" (Newman 1988, 93). Stuck in a liminal state[1] between the status of deservingly employed and that of undeserving unemployed, laid-off managers found themselves depressed, isolated, and adrift, a characterization of the unemployed that has proven remarkably resilient over time, in both academic scholarship and popular culture.[2]

And yet, that is not what I encountered during my own fieldwork among laid-off high-technology workers in the early 2000s. From 2001 to 2004, I immersed myself in what I refer to as the culture of job-seeking, attending dozens of different networking events, job fairs, and job search seminars in Dallas, Texas. I met hundreds of laid-off high-tech workers from fields as diverse as telecommunications, web site design, computer programming, dot-com consulting, and e-commerce. I ultimately interviewed more than seventy-five job seekers, some as many as five times, and in 2009 I conducted "where are they now" follow-up interviews with ten primary informants. Mirroring the white-collar high-tech labor force itself, a majority of the interviewees were white, middle- and upper-middle-class men, but the study also included white women and Asian Americans, Latinos, and African Americans of both sexes.[3] Most informants were between the ages of twenty-five and sixty-five. Nearly all were college-educated, and many had advanced degrees in business, engineering, and computer science. Their pre-layoff salaries ranged widely, but most made between $40,000 to $100,000 a year when steadily employed. As these demographic details indicate, these workers occupy a privileged niche in the American labor force, and their experiences cannot be taken as representative of American workers more broadly (see for example Karjanen and Kingsolver in this volume). Yet these are the very workers—educated, economically advantaged, and professionally connected—who are supposedly best positioned to withstand the vagaries of economic and industry shifts. And yet they, too, are increasingly subject—albeit in different ways and to varying degrees—to the same destabilizing forces and downward trajectories that plague other, less-advantaged corners of the American workforce.

Through my interviews and observations I learned that while tech workers were rarely thrilled to have been laid off, and while depression and isolation did rear their ugly heads now and then, the workers I met were neither shocked nor devastated by their layoffs. Their identities, their sense of themselves as valuable and skilled professionals, remained for the most part intact, proving exceptionally resilient even after, for some, years of unemployment. There were of course occasional departures from the optimistic individualism that characterized most job seekers' responses, but in the end job seekers tended to focus not on what or who had done them wrong but on what they themselves could do to advance and safeguard their professional futures.[4]

I asked myself why responses to job loss had changed so much in a relatively short time, just twenty years since Newman's study. Ultimately I concluded that just as the structure of white-collar work has changed over the previous decades, so too have cultural understandings of what it means to be employed, what it means to be unemployed, and how individual workers feel about both. Specifically, studies of white-collar unemployment to date have, nearly unanimously, presumed a norm—that of secure, long-term employment at a single company—and defined unemployment in opposition to that norm. Yet that "normal career"—in both its real and idealized forms—has changed, and thus our understanding of its alleged opposite, unemployment, must also change. The conceptualization of unemployment as a liminal state by definition requires a structure, and an accompanying set of stable social roles and statuses, into which groups or individuals will eventually be reintegrated once they progress through the liminal phase. Without the presumption of an eventual return to stability, the framing of unemployment as a liminal phase bookended by occupational and social stability ceases to make sense in the way it once did, and the clear distinction between unemployment and employment begins to unravel.

Drawing on my own research among white-collar workers facing unemployment in the first years of the twenty-first century, in this essay I describe four shifts that have contributed to the blurring, even breaking, of the boundary between employment and unemployment: increased frequency of job change; changing ideas of career success; the rise of cultural and social spaces for job seekers; and new discourses around work that rely less and less on paid employment. I then consider the implications of these changes for those who experience job loss as well as for those of us who study it.

The Normalization of Layoffs and Job Change

Perhaps the most important shift concerning white-collar unemployment today is that for the most part job loss is no longer unexpected, nor, for most workers, unprecedented. Nearly 60 percent of my interviewees had been laid off more than once.[5] White-collar layoffs, once rare, have become increasingly common since the 1970s; each of the last four recessions affected a higher percentage of white-collar workers than the last (Mishel, Bernstein, and Boushey 2003; Stettner and Wenger 2003; Shierholz and Mishel 2009). Even the most educated and highly skilled Americans are now regularly advised to keep an "emergency fund" on hand to cover their living expenses in case of an unforeseen layoff. The recommended amount of time such funds should cover has inched up over the last decade, from six to eight months to one to two years, according to some financial advisors, a telling indicator of increasing rates of prolonged unemployment, defined in the United States as being out of work for twenty-seven months or more (Mayer 2010).

Thus for most workers the sense of disbelief and betrayal that previous generations of managers experienced after layoffs seems downright antiquated. These workers either never had expected to spend their career at one company or had long ago surrendered such expectations. One job seeker in his late fifties had been laid off three times over the course of his professional life. "The first time," he said, "it was devastating. You know, 'Oh my gosh, what happened?' The second time it was easier."

Along with these changes has come a new perspective on what, exactly, employer and employee owe one another. In the words of one laid-off technology executive in his late fifties:

> The best way I like to look at it is that, you know, during the '80s, companies realized they don't have any loyalty to their employees anymore. During the '90s, employees realized they don't have any loyalty to their companies anymore. And now, I think, any employment is based on a need and a skill. You know, very much on a contractual basis. If a company has a need for my skills and I can supply that to them, they hire me. When that need is over with, when they don't need me anymore, sure, I'm terminated. [...] I don't know any company where it's in their charter, where it's in their goal as a company, to provide employment to people. You know, it's just not there. They're in business to provide a service or a product. They're not in business to hire people. And, you know, people are a resource. A very important resource. [...] But you're a resource, you know, so realize it.

For good or for bad, he and other job seekers say, the days in which hard work and loyalty were rewarded with secure employment are gone. Rather than opposing this shift, the unemployed high-tech workers I spoke with focused on being as "marketable" as possible (a form of self-commodification I discuss more fully later in this essay), positioning themselves in whatever way they believed would make them most valuable, not just to their next employer but to the employer after that, and, inevitably, the one after that.

Other job seekers shared personal experiences of coming to terms with this new reality and the demands it placed on individual workers. A job seeker in his late twenties explained, "When I first started out of school, yeah, I thought I was going to be the thirty-year [until] retirement person. When I started at [my first full-time job] I thought I would be with the company forever." When his one-year contract with that company was not renewed, he quickly found a new position, this time at an internet company; he again assumed he would be there for the long term. Following yet another layoff, news of which arrived on the day his wife delivered their twin sons, he has come to see things differently. "My vision has changed a lot now." Today, he regularly warns friends and colleagues not to assume that their current job will be a lasting one. "I tell everybody, whenever you find a job, you keep looking for your next job. Because three years from now, you're going to go through a downsize of some sort, and in ten years the market is going to fall again, like it has for centuries." His expectation of lifelong security in exchange for loyal hard work had been replaced by the expectation that no job is ever permanent, no amount of labor or loyalty enough to secure protection from the vagaries of corporate restructuring and economic volatility.

Whether voluntary or not, frequent job change has become the new normal. The average American worker now changes jobs at least ten times over a career and tends to stay in the same job for just under four and a half years. Younger workers in their twenties and thirties stay in jobs about half as long and are on track to hold between fifteen and twenty positions over the course of their work lives (BLS 2012; Meister 2012). Once pejoratively dismissed as "job hopping" and seen as a sign of frivolity or disloyalty, moving frequently from job to job has been reframed as a savvy career move, a way to earn promotions and raises more quickly while preventing one's skills and professional networks from growing stale.[6]

This perspective was enthusiastically endorsed by a team of career counselors I interviewed in Dallas. These counselors regularly advised their clients—most of whom were, or had been, corporate executives—to surrender the expectation of job security in favor of a more peripatetic model of employment:

> One thing they have to understand, and they haven't gotten this yet, is that we had a time where corporations took care of us for ten or twenty, thirty years. Really the HR [Human Resources] organizations of those companies managed our careers. What they have to understand when they come out [onto the labor market] is that they think it is just going to be hard to find a job, but when I get that job I'll be there for ten years. That's not going to happen. It is changing every three years. And so they have to accept that fact that you are going to be changing every three years. This is not a [situation where] you've been there for twenty years, you got laid off and now you're going to go find some other company and you're going to be there for the next twenty years. It's not going to happen. They're sorely mistaken if that's what they believe.

Despite this career counselor's conviction that job seekers need to alter their misguided mindsets and expectations (and indeed, charged clients for helping them do just that), most job seekers I interviewed actually already shared this perspective and were equally critical of those who did not.

One software engineer in his late twenties lamented his layoff from an aviation company but said that it was hardly unexpected and was in some ways even welcome. He had been with the company five and a half years at the time of his layoff. He believed he had already "overstayed" his time there and worried about being pigeonholed into a particular role or status. "Although I was doing more than what I was doing earlier, and definitely I had career progress and the career advancement and the salary increases, I knew I was branding myself as a particular [type of engineer]." He suspected he'd been promoted as high as he would ever go at that company and believed that he had already gained as much as he could from working there. "There's a certain amount of skill set that you can pick up from one place. After a while, you have learned all the tricks of the trade, unless you make a change within the company to move to other focus areas or other groups, which is an option if you're happy with the company. But otherwise the same old thing, it kind of gets boring after a while. It was time to move on." Being laid off, he concluded, had actually been good for his career, as he'd determined it was never in one's best interest to stay at a company for more than five years.

Another young worker, a married father of one who had lost his job in telecommunications a year earlier, echoed this sentiment:

> I think that if you stay in one place too long, you lose your edge. And I think that companies value their employees a lot less today maybe when they used to when my father was working. That, and I like the sense of adventure. I think if I stay in one place too long, there's a tendency to get bored, to get complacent. Now, all that said, if I were to come to the perfect company with the perfect culture, with management that I really liked working for, would I stay there for fifteen or twenty years? Sure. As long as there were a consistent challenge to the work, as long as there were opportunities to learn, to grow. But I don't think in this day and age that truly exists with any one particular company.

According to this perspective, frequent job change brings both personal and professional benefits. It keeps one's skills sharp and one's mind engaged. And although this job seeker holds out the possibility of an ideal company at which one might stay both content and inspired over the course of an entire career, he is clearly not holding his breath for that entity to appear.

Lest this perspective seem a young man's game, it is worth noting that older workers, both male and female, expressed similar beliefs. One job seeker in her late forties explained that most people today believe that their career is their own responsibility, not something that can be left in the hands of corporate employers:

> It's not [like] you get a job and then somebody watches out for you the rest of your life, or as long as you work hard you'll be paid appropriately and promoted appropriately and have a job for the rest of your life. Now I think it will take a more active role to evaluate the pros and cons of every situation and decide what you're going to put in and when you're going to get out, and that's the best way to move forward, and you probably do that every two years.

Placing the entire onus of managing one's career squarely on the shoulders of the individual worker, a topic to which I return in the next section, she names job change as the single most effective way to advance one's career. She even one-ups younger job seekers by advocating a switch every two years, rather than the three- or five-year timelines more commonly suggested.

As the experience of losing one's job has become more commonplace, the dramatic transition from employed to unemployed has been softened somewhat. People might not like being laid off—indeed, they might loathe it—but the experience is rarely unprecedented. Amid a sea of constant job change, being laid off can be reframed as a career move, albeit an involuntary one. For this shift to have occurred, it is not enough that layoffs and job change become increasingly common. It took another, equally significant shift to make that happen, one that has more to do with how people think about their jobs than how long they stay in them.

The Rise of the Protean Career

During the early years of the twentieth century, corporate employers fought doggedly, and shrewdly, to convince young, white, middle-class men to forego entrepreneurship for permanent employee status.[7] As part of their campaign to recruit and retain these prized employees, employers successfully reconceptualized the ideal career as a series of upward moves along a preset corporate ladder, usually at a single company. That model stuck, and through the 1960s secure cradle-to-grave employment was considered the just reward of loyal and hard-working organization men. In the latter part of the century an alternative model of career started to emerge, one that emphasized flexibility over predictability and, in its capaciousness, left decidedly more room for individual workers to chart their own unique paths to professional success. These "protean careers," a term coined by management expert Douglas T. Hall in the 1970s, were designed to be both self-directed and personally satisfying. Rather than allowing an employer to decide one's career trajectory it was left up to the individual to plan whether and how one might advance one's personal and professional interests (Hall 1976). This new model was allegedly designed to serve employers and employees alike, creating more fulfilled and productive workers. In this new imagining, stable employment was actually the enemy of individual freedom, a perspective that meshed beautifully with the neoliberal principles and policies gaining cultural traction at that same moment in American history.[8] As one executive put it, "To give my employees job security would be to disempower them and relieve them of the responsibility that they need to feel for their own success" (Ross 2003, 17).

Despite its lauded potential to empower workers, the consensus is that the shift to more flexible work has done the opposite. Coming as it did at the same time that American corporations eagerly embraced downsizing as a way to trim expenses and increase stock valuations, the protean career started to look less like an emancipatory tool for workers than a handy excuse for employers to divest themselves of responsibility for employees' well-being and professional futures. To be sure, some highly skilled workers have managed to benefit from the rise of contingent and contract work and have willingly traded full-time traditional employment for less secure but potentially more lucrative and exciting careers as independent contractors (Barley and Kunda 2004; Marschall 2012; Osnowitz 2010). In most cases, however, flexibility is just a euphemism for disposability, and the freedom to build one's own career has been transformed into the obligation to navigate increasingly uncertain professional waters with almost no guidance or support. The high costs of this transition for workers, their families, and American society have been well documented. Even Hall himself, the originator of the term *protean career* and one of the concept's most vocal advocates, later lamented the heavy pressure this type of career placed on individual workers, who found themselves overwhelmed by the demands of planning and preparing for professional futures that looked increasingly uncertain (Harrington 2001). The resulting losses are not just a matter of emotional hardship, financial adversity, or diminished professional opportunities; they also come in the form of squandered human capital, unrealized potential, and the erosion of certain values—loyalty, commitment, and upward mobility—that once served as the foundation of American ideas about work and its rewards.[9]

Yet the protean career, at least in its idealized form, has continued to gain cultural traction and now enjoys widespread popularity well beyond managerial circles. Today, the expectation that individuals take responsibility for managing their own careers is so ingrained as to seem hardly worthy of mention, and the attribute of flexibility is now prized far higher than the once-lauded traits of loyalty or perseverance. To be flexible, in this rendering, means being willing to be anything or do anything an employer might require. As one might imagine, this endeavor requires a complicated and continual process of impression management in order to continually reshape how one is perceived by potential employers. Consequently, the process of looking for work has become less about self-promotion and more about self-commodification, as job seekers are encouraged to see themselves as brands or commodities to be marketed and sold to potential employers. Although cultural critics have expressed dismay at the psychological and political implications of this commodification of the self, "the brand called you," like the protean career, has become such a commonplace that job seekers I interviewed regularly referred to their résumés as "marketing materials" and to themselves as "valuable commodities" to be "used" by employers without ever acknowledging that there might be other, less market-driven ways of conceptualizing the value of oneself and one's work.[10]

Along with this emphasis on flexibility and marketability has come a more capacious definition of what a good career actually looks like. Success is no longer defined by never having lost a job but by the ability to always find a new one, even if that means inventing one for yourself. According to this view, a career is something to be culled together from a series of different, sometimes overlapping stints of full-time employment, part-time employment, contract and consulting positions, and self-employment. It is understood that bouts of unemployment will occasionally be sandwiched between these various positions, and the loss of a single job, even multiple jobs, can be easily camouflaged, both on one's résumé and within one's more personal narrative of professional progress. Indeed, as we saw above, job loss can also be framed as the catalyst for moving on to different and better things, even if it hardly felt that way on the day the pink slip arrived.

Among job seekers, this reframing sometimes leads to an interesting reversal of the hierarchy between the employed and unemployed. Rather than seeing employed persons as the lucky, chosen few, job seekers sometimes dismiss those with secure positions as feminized dependents, describing them as "suckers," "children," and "willing victims."[11] One male job seeker in his forties, for instance, described his decision to start his own business as a way to escape being "a corporate whore," a decidedly gendered way to frame dependency on a single employer. Another younger job seeker, also male, chided his coworkers for expecting their employer to provide them with anything more than a paycheck for work completed. "You guys aren't children," he said. "You need to manage your own careers." Assuming the perspective of the company for which he worked, he continued, "We can help you, but if you don't take responsibility for your career growth, then you're hurting yourself. Why should a company have to do that for you?" Unemployed job seekers, in contrast, were positioned as independent free agents, the masters of their own protean destinies, however financially or professionally turbulent those destinies might turn out to be.

In addition to reversing at least some of the stigma traditionally associated with job loss and unemployment, this new model also undermines the dividing line between employment and its alleged foil, unemployment. After all, being unemployed and searching for one's next career are often accomplished simultaneously; starting one's own business can look a lot like unemployment until the first profits or investments roll in; and even the most popular contractor inevitably encounters periods during which her or his services are not engaged. Thus unemployment has morphed from representing the end of a career—or at least a serious detour therefrom—to an inevitable, even a natural part of the modern career progression.

Creating a Culture of Unemployment

As alluded to above, the experience of unemployment today looks very little like the stigmatized, liminal status Newman and others have described. Part of this has to do with the structural and attitudinal shifts outlined above, but this transformation is also the result of a third shift, this one involving the day-to-day lived experiences of unemployed persons.

Tech workers in my study often referred to job-seeking as "the hardest job you'll ever have," reconceptualizing the search for work as itself a valuable form of work. Although Barbara Ehrenreich (2009b) and others have criticized this framing of job-seeking as itself a job as an insidious form of social control designed to thwart political protest, many unemployed Americans continue to embrace it, priding themselves on being the very best job seekers they can be, regardless of whether their efforts result in re-employment. Job seekers went to great lengths to recreate the rhythms and trappings of employment in their unemployed days. They awoke early, dressed in business casual attire, and immediately got to work looking for work. One interviewee who conducted his job search in his home office had a sign on the office door that read "Daddy's at Home" on one side and "Daddy's at Work" on the other, which he flipped to indicate whether his wife and kids were free to interrupt him.

Job seekers found other ways of recreating the patterns of working life outside the home. Organized networking events, which most job seekers attended religiously, offered frequent opportunities to perform one's professional identity in a quasi-corporate setting, especially through the ritualized delivery of "commercials," weekly recitations of one's title and areas of expertise that allowed job seekers to perform their professional identities for a receptive audience. Other rituals included the exchange of business cards, which were printed with one's specialty—"database manager," "information architect," "website designer"—but of course lacked the name of a specific employer. Job seekers regularly swapped business cards with one another, assembling impressive databases of one another's cards and credentials, sometimes in old-school business card organizers, more often these days by scanning the cards into digital documents.

Whether unemployed people are well positioned to help one another land new jobs has been the subject of some debate. Many sociologists who study professional networks argue that unemployed people lack the professional clout to help others land new positions. In contrast, others contend that job seekers are in fact ideally positioned to assist other unemployed people because they are constantly attuned to what jobs are open and what companies and industries are hiring, have the time to reach out to their own networks on their associates' behalf, and are sympathetic to others' urgent desire for re-employment. Regardless of their success rate in terms of new jobs found, such groups clearly serve an important function for unemployed tech workers. In addition to providing comforting and self-affirming rituals, they offer a sense of community, camaraderie, and support during what is, even in the best of circumstances, a challenging and uncertain time. Many attendees confessed to me during interviews that they did not actually expect a specific group to help them find a new job but that they continued attending anyway because they so enjoyed the group and its members. One newly re-employed tech worker told me the only bad thing about his new job was that he no longer had time for the networking groups he had so assiduously attended during his time out of work. He hoped that he would one day find time to return to the groups (although not, he clarified, because of another job loss), both because it always paid to keep one's network up to date and because he missed the sense of community, so rare in modern life, that the group had provided.

Comfort and community aside, such groups had their negative aspects as well. Through formal and informal means, attendees were encouraged to focus explicitly on the positive and discouraged from talking about structural impediments to re-employment. Criticizing one's former employer was seen as crying over spilt milk, laments over the rising unemployment rate were met with cheery reassurances that someone, somewhere was getting a job despite the poor labor market, and dives into depression or discouragement led to warnings that a sad interviewee was rarely an impressive interviewee. In this way, the group reified an individualistic, optimistic approach to job-seeking while discouraging political discourse or collective action.[12]

Job seekers' attraction to these groups are clearly complex, as are the motives and functions of the groups themselves, yet their centrality to what I call the new culture of job-seeking is undeniable. Such groups exist in nearly every community across the country, hosted by schools, churches, nonprofit organizations, government agencies, and, occasionally, for-profit companies. On any given day, unemployed people have a variety of events, workshops, and get-togethers to choose from, all directed specifically at those who are looking for work. With approximately twelve million Americans currently unemployed (not counting those who are underemployed or are too discouraged to continue looking for work), the demand for such services is hardly surprising. Yet I would argue that the proliferation of such groups has other, more complicated roots.

Anthropologist Linda Layne (2000, 502) has argued that the stigma and isolation of unemployment experienced by previous generations might be lessened if we, as a culture, adopt rituals of job loss modeled after retirement parties that celebrate employees' contributions and mark their transition to a new stage of life.[13] Layne correctly identifies the potential benefit of rituals for the unemployed, but she misses the mark when she suggests retirement as a suitable parallel. As the structure and content of the networking meetings described above suggest, laid-off workers do not want to feel retired; they want to feel *employed*, and so they actively participate in a culture of job-seeking that resembles more than anything the structure and rhythm of working life. They dress like they're going to work, introduce themselves as if they're actually working, and, in their weekly networking meetings, deftly mimic the structure and tone of the endless corporate meetings most employed persons clamor to escape.

With the advent of this new job-seeking culture, complete with its own employment-inspired rhythms, roles, and rituals, the difference between unemployment and employment becomes increasingly unclear. This blurring is only intensified by recent reconfigurations of the structure and practices of paid employment itself. As more and more Americans telecommute, start their own home-based businesses, and work in jobs that are contract, short-term, or part-time, whether by choice or by necessity, the day-to-day experience of working starts to look suspiciously like the experience of looking for work. As I joked with my fellow panelists at the session that inspired this volume, it is not that hard to fake most white-collar work, and I include scholarly work in that category. We sit in front of computers, send emails and search websites, write and revise documents, and occasionally sit in meetings we find interminable. This is, in broad strokes, exactly what unemployed people spend their days doing. Thus white-collar unemployment has come to look remarkably like white-collar employment, but without the paycheck, a distinction to which I will now turn.

The Disassociation of Work and Pay

The fourth significant shift I see in the nature of the relationship between employment and unemployment concerns this last detail, the paycheck. Many, even most, of the people I referred to consistently in my research publications as "unemployed" or "job seekers" were in fact working for pay at one point or another during the time I spent among them. Some found short-term contract or consulting jobs, often for former employers, which allowed them to continue working in the high-tech sector, earn some money (although not benefits), and avoid unsightly gaps on their résumés. These gigs sometimes led to more permanent positions, and many were quite lucrative while they lasted.

Still other job seekers worked long hours volunteering for unfunded start-up companies with the hope that this unpaid labor would ultimately result in a full-time position once the company secured funding. Although I'm sure this tactic sometimes works, I did not hear of any such instances during my research. More often I heard tales of volunteers who felt underappreciated and overworked, who eventually decided that their time would be better spent focusing more directly on their job search. One woman, a Ph.D. in computer science, contributed weeks of unpaid time and expertise to a start-up specializing in streaming digital media before realizing that the "digital media" the founder planned to stream was pornography. She left immediately thereafter, saying that she had no interest in working for such a company and had begun to suspect it would not have led to a paid position anyway.

Others took what they described as "interim" positions to pay the bills while they continued searching for a job in their chosen field. They waited tables, unloaded trucks, delivered flowers, stocked shelves, sold jewelry at the mall or plants at a local nursery, taught Spanish at night, or tutored high school students by day. Although these jobs represented dramatic declines in both pay and status, job seekers tended to describe their decision to take such positions with pride, as evidence of their willingness to do whatever it takes to support themselves and, for some, their families. Drawing on long-standing American beliefs around the value of hard work, they transformed what might have been a narrative of downward mobility into one of moral resilience and the triumph of the human spirit.

Yet even these arguably employed individuals (for they were of course making money, although less than they used to) continued to think of themselves as unemployed and looking for work. During my fieldwork I met an experienced website designer and project manager who, after a layoff in his late forties, had returned to his college job of waiting tables. He continued to look for work in high-tech, but more than a year of unsuccessful searching and a number of financial setbacks had forced the decision for him. "We've reached a point financially," he said, referring to himself and his wife, whose teaching salary barely covered their basic living expenses, "where I just had to do something else to bring in some money. I decided to go back and start peddling steaks." The job was physically exhausting—"I'm finding out why a lot of middle-aged guys aren't waiting tables in restaurants"—and sometimes demeaning.

> You're also back in a situation where you're serving the public. [. . .] You get a lot of people who will come in and order you around in a way that you wouldn't do to anybody else, but they do it there simply because they can. It's the only place in the world where they can reasonably expect someone to do what they say. You do a lot of smiling and waving at people who desperately need the shit choked out of them. That gets tiresome, particularly when you're in an environment when you've taken an 85 percent cut in pay.

Despite its frustrations, the experience had actually given him a newfound clarity about his own identity. "I knew with absolute certainty," he explained, "that if somebody were to take a snapshot of this I could look at this and say, 'This is not my life.' Because I knew that while for a living I was waiting tables, I was not a waiter. I began to think of myself more in terms of a collection of skills and traits that could be applied to any number of things." For him, as it was for many others, his interim job was not "real," because it was not commensurate with his education, experience, and previous pay and status levels. Waiting tables did not line up with his sense of who he is and what he does, so he took comfort in embracing a flexible ideal in which he was not a single kind of worker but an ever-shifting bundle of marketable attributes.

For these workers, professional identity no longer depended on steady gainful employment in one's alleged profession. Their professional identities were buttressed by other means, such as through embracing the concept of the protean career and by participating in the identity-affirming networking events described above. If I carry a business card identifying me as a software developer, regularly attend networking events for software developers, recently received my certification in a new programming language, and donate my time developing software for my daughter's school, then by any but the very narrowest of definitions, I am in fact a software developer, regardless of my employment status. Together, the decline of secure employment, rise of the protean career, the growth of job-seeking culture, and changing notions of what counts as work have contributed to the erosion of what was once understood to be a clear delineation between employment and unemployment.

Conclusions

The profound implication of this unraveling of the employed/unemployed binary for scholarship around both work and unemployment was lost on me until well after I completed my research. Despite the obvious ways in which unemployed tech workers' activities and perspectives challenged the employed/unemployed boundary, when I wrote about this fieldwork I continually referred to my interviewees as "unemployed" and "jobless." In the introduction to my book *A Company of One*, I did briefly explain this decision. I wrote, in parentheses no less:

> (While I use the term "jobseeker" for all of my interviewees, as I explain more fully later, some individuals did have some form of employment at the time I interviewed them, including short-term or part-time positions in high tech, or generally low paid, low status jobs in entirely unrelated fields. Yet these workers characterized themselves as unemployed, and therefore so do I, because they continued to actively search

for work in, or related to, their former specialty at pay and status levels
closer to those of their former positions.) (Lane 2011, 8)

In other words, I skirted the hard intellectual work of investigating this apparent
contradiction by uncritically accepting job seekers' own language, even though
interpreting the meaning behind such discursive choices was exactly the task that
I, as an interpretive anthropologist, had set out for myself.

Only when collaborating with Jong Bum Kwon to design the conference panel
from which this volume grew did I begin thinking more carefully about how
anthropologists have traditionally approached the study of unemployment and
how they have, implicitly or explicitly, defined the state of being unemployed. It
was then that I realized I had missed, or more accurately dodged, an opportunity to address head-on the theoretical implications of the changes I was seeing.
Perhaps I was pulling my punches when I concluded simply that the structure
and meaning of unemployment have changed for today's workers. Perhaps the
bigger argument waiting to be made was that unemployment today isn't really
unemployment at all, at least not according to traditional definitions. Employment itself is increasingly insecure. Job loss has become more common and has
even been idealized under the mantle of flexibility. Structurally, as well as in its
rhythms and rituals, unemployment now looks—and feels—remarkably like
employment. Even paid labor does not necessarily count as employment anymore, not when individual workers define their professional identities through
other activities in addition to, or even entirely independent of, the labor they perform for pay. All of these realities combine to attest that labor, pay, and identity
became unlinked at some point in the previous decades, and in the years since
they have reassembled themselves in a more complicated configuration than the
dual categories or "employed" and "unemployed" can encompass. There is no
such thing as a liminal status when there are no longer two set statuses to be
caught betwixt and between. Thus the conceptualization of unemployment as
a liminal or inherently stigmatized state—however appropriate those characterizations may have been in describing previous eras—are ill suited to thinking
through the experience of work and unemployment today.

Shifts like this, in the nature of work and the meaning it holds for the people
who perform it (or wish they were given the opportunity to perform it), are by
no means unique to the high-tech industry, nor to white-collar work, nor to
the United States. As the chapters in this volume demonstrate, the concepts of
employment and unemployment, as well as the conceptual and methodological
tools we use to explore them, are ripe for dismantling and reimagining.

For my own research, that means unpacking the constructed divide between
people who work for pay and people who do not, as well as the cultural meanings and valuations ascribed to either side of that binary. For those of us who

set out to study unemployment, who, exactly, are our research subjects? Who counts as unemployed in the United States is a subject of long debate. It is widely acknowledged that official unemployment tallies dramatically undercount the actual number of people who would, using more commonsensical parameters, be considered unemployed. For example, the official rate includes only those unemployed persons who are able to work who have actively looked for employment in the preceding four weeks. This does not include "discouraged workers" who have given up looking for work, "marginally attached workers" who are unemployed and have looked for work in the last year but not the last month, or "persons employed part-time for economic reasons" who want full-time work but have settled for part-time employment. Had these categories of workers been included, the official U.S. unemployment rate would have more than doubled in recent years (BLS 2009; Plumer 2012).

Beyond such statistical debates looms the larger question of how remuneration, labor, and identity fit together. What does it mean when job loss and unemployment have become expected, even idealized, parts of the contemporary career? What is the appropriate way to describe individuals who conceptualize themselves as unemployed but are in fact employed in paid positions, albeit usually low-paid and low-status ones, while they continue to seek work in their preferred field? How should we categorize those who perform their professional specialty for no pay in the hopes of landing a future position or keeping their skills sharp and their minds busy? Adding another layer of complexity, what of the laid-off parent who assumes the role of primary caretaker for house and children while looking for paid employment? Is he or she unemployed, a homemaker, or both? In these and so many other cases, determining what exactly constitutes unemployment—and whether that term remains useful for thinking through connections between work, pay, and productivity—requires taking a longer, wider view of how the structure and experience of work have evolved over time and across regions, occupations, and populations. Only by adopting this broader perspective will scholars of unemployment be prepared to contribute new chapters to the ongoing story of what work means and what it means when work goes away, chapters that do justice to the rich, rigorous conversations started by the generations of scholars who preceded us.

THE LIMITS TO QUANTITATIVE THINKING

Engaging Economics on the Unemployed

David Karjanen

When unemployment is discussed in the public sphere, it is typically reduced to its most rudimentary characteristics: is it increasing or decreasing, the numbers are high, the numbers are low. Scholarly discussions of unemployment, primarily within the field of economics, also tend to flatten the issue, narrowly focusing on whether the unemployment rate is cyclical or due to structural or frictional forces, how to measure it, and so forth. Certainly these ways of thinking about and studying unemployment have value, as they help us understand certain aspects of unemployment. Yet they also miss out on other ways of thinking about unemployment. As I argue in this chapter, they fail to see unemployment as a social process shaped by asymmetrical power relations that operate simultaneously and intersect in complicated and important ways. Instead, they tend to examine unemployment largely as a set of aggregated individual behaviors (especially when looking at national-level statistics) and thus fail to consider how the processes of being unemployed and seeking work are shaped by existing social relationships and other factors that defy the model of job seekers as individual rational actors looking to maximize economic gain. To be certain, more nuanced analyses of unemployment do exist. Witness, for instance, the large volume of research on the complex, interactive relationships linking job loss and social capital, crime, and economic marginalization (Hagan 1993; Rose and Clear 1998; Gallie, Paugam, and Jacobs 2003). From a more theoretical perspective within anthropology, long-standing approaches within economic anthropology view economics not as the study of the economy. Rather, the economy, and those phenomena associated with it (unemployment, inflation, and so on) are constructs of western academic economics and not necessarily the empirically identifiable practices of production, distribution, consumption, and the like (Gregory 1989). Within economics and the history of modern social and economic thought exist substantive critiques (Hart and Lautzenheiser 2001; Mirowski 1989), but despite such criticisms there remains a clear need for more qualitative, historically informed and contextually and culturally elaborated approaches to understanding unemployment from different perspectives.

To demonstrate the value of such scholarship, in this chapter I draw on my own ethnography and surveys of economically marginalized residents of lower-income communities in San Diego, Detroit, and Minneapolis–Saint Paul. In San Diego, I draw on work on urban poverty over the past decade, including interviews with unemployed men and women seeking work through job training and ex-offender placement programs. More recently, this work has expanded to include unemployed individuals in Minneapolis–Saint Paul as well as fieldwork conducted in Detroit regarding the low-wage labor market. The qualitative case studies I draw on come from this broad, comparative ethnographic project.

The point here is that unemployment is theoretically a construct inextricably tied to an understanding of social context. Unemployment is not simply the absence of work for an individual or individuals; rather, it is an entire social process related to joblessness. Moreover, as I argue in this chapter, it is a relationship of social power and inequality operating on multiple dimensions within society. The implications of this perspective are central to how different fields approach the issue of unemployment. With debates on unemployment dominated largely by modeling and reductionist political arguments, little innovation in policy making or progress in understanding the complex issue of joblessness can occur. Pushing for different approaches allows us to unpack the complex set of social relations involved in hiring, firing, labor market dynamics, and so forth. As such, my aim here is to argue more specifically for considering the social relations of both employment and unemployment. In this sense, the view of joblessness as a social relation locates it within the complex social and power-laden relations that encompass hiring and firing processes.

Conventional economic frameworks—whether Keynesian, neoliberal, or even Marxian assertions of the jobless as a reserve army of labor—understand joblessness as a relationship between broader forces that can be measured in the economy: supply and demand, business cycles, changes in technology, and others. Models are developed and theories tested with quantitative data, and either there is evidence to support the model or not. Over time, the models evolve as more research is conducted, but with any complex social phenomena, the empirical verification of what is actually driving unemployment remains largely open to speculation. For instance, declines in labor force participation rates are seen as a product of workers becoming discouraged and no longer seeking work (hence they are no longer counted in unemployment statistics) or of demographic changes (workers retiring without enough younger ones to take their place). This set of assumptions tells us very little about unemployment and is impossible to verify empirically without actual survey data on why workers may or may not be leaving the workforce.

Qualitative and open-ended ethnographic or exploratory research takes a different epistemological tack. Generalizability is more difficult due to smaller sample sizes, but the depth and complexity of data are far greater. Also, rather than develop models and theories and test them against survey data, on-the-ground ethnographic research often collects the data first and then develops models or theories from them. One approach is more deductive, the other more inductive. Both are critical for understanding unemployment, so my argument is that anthropological research has a vital role to play not only in understanding unemployment as a social phenomenon but also in providing a more critical and insightful analysis of what drives, makes up, and ultimately constitutes unemployment as a social process.

In the following sections of this paper I examine several different approaches to the issue of unemployment used in conventional economics, including job search theory, human capital theory, and a focus on racial discrimination. For each I offer critiques based on my own and others' ethnographic and empirical research. My aim here is not solely to critique conventional economic modeling and theory but also to illustrate the utility of a more anthropological approach to unpacking unemployment as a dynamic social process.

Job Search Theory

Job search theory has been a central focus of labor economics. It aims to understand how individuals find work in the labor market. In the past four decades, labor economists have produced an extensive body of research related to job search theory (for instance, Lippman and McCall 1976; Devine and Kiefer 1991), emphasizing a bounded, rational-actor model of job-seeking behavior. In other words, this theoretical approach attempts to model how people choose a job. The prevailing approach is the basic sequential job search model. In this model, people look for a job and decide to take any offer that meets their wage needs, turning down lower-paying jobs until they find one that meets their reservation wage (the rate of pay they are willing to accept for a job). In order to model the movement of people into and out of the job market, other variables are included, like "search intensity." Search intensity is typically defined as a set of variables like "time spent in the previous week searching for work by hours." In this model, the worker must decide on the "intensity" of the job search. This decision depends on three factors: the marginal increase in the likelihood of obtaining a job in response to an increase in search intensity; the increase in the expected present value of income in response to obtaining a job; and the marginal cost of search effort. According to the standard models of job search theory, an increase in either of the first two factors or a decrease in the third raises the search intensity of unemployed workers. Job search theory is based on the idea that individuals maximize lifetime utility by moving through different job search strategies.

According to this modeling of job-seeking, a person's search for work becomes operationalized, that is, abstracted, into a specific set of characteristics devoid of context. This is a very narrow and specific construal of the behaviors surrounding seeking work. How, for instance, should we measure "maximizing lifetime util-ity"? This may be fine theoretically, to assume that people look for the best-paid job that they can get over the long term, but it may not be empirically true. Some job seekers face far more complex decisions than simply finding a job or not or whether or not a job meets a specific wage. Some job seekers can only think short term because of life circumstances that may change their employability, such as family changes or health issues. Or, as I observed in my fieldwork, work-ers in the inner city who face commuting costs to suburbs to find work may not be able to reach the best-paid job, something spatial mismatch theories, which are addressed in detail below, attempt to compensate for by including more and more variables into ever more complex models of commuting behavior. While much of this research may be very robust in findings, again, we are limited in what is observable based on the particular perspective. Additionally, by narrow-ing employment decisions into a very rigid cost-benefit type of analysis, only cer-tain costs and only certain benefits have been included. What about preferences such as racial discrimination or company politics? For instance, in my research on San Diego's inner-city labor market, I interviewed a woman in desperate need of a job because her unemployment compensation was about to run out. Her job counselor offered her a position working at Domino's Pizza, but she rejected it because of her opposition to the owners' practice of sending large sums of money toward campaigns to eliminate access to abortion. When I asked her if her personal politics were more important than a paycheck, she said that it was a matter of principle. Even more interesting, for her the reality of the job market for lower-wage workers means that she has a choice in the matter. As she put it, "I can get any old pizza job, burger job, they are always looking for help. I may as well work for one I don't find too revolting if I can help it." In other words, the overabundance of poor-quality, low-wage jobs in the inner city allows for a level of agency on the part of job seekers to make choices that are cultural, often highly personal, and completely outside of standardized job-seeking models.

Furthermore, in each city for which I have looked at the low-wage labor market, African Americans who are unemployed and seeking work raise the issue of employer discrimination. Some had experienced discrimination by specific employers or in specific industries in the past, so they no longer seek work in those companies or industries, even if there are plentiful jobs. For example, two men in Detroit who worked in the trucking industry for several years described persistent "hidden discrimination": never spoken about openly but put forward through employer actions. In their case, this consisted of always being given delivery routes that took the longest or that were the most difficult to complete and not being offered overtime despite continually making it known that they were interested if additional work was available. They also describe persistent racism against them by other employees. What this means for job-seeking models is that some industries may be entirely eliminated from someone's job search because of a poor work experience within that industry. Thus, the very industry or occupation in which someone has experience may be excluded from the job search process. This may appear irrational unless the full context of the unemployed person is established.

Job-seeking behavior is also influenced by very complex interaction effects among variables that may not be known or even considered in conventional thinking or scholarly research regarding how people find work. This is particularly true for ethnic minorities and the poor, who face far more complex barriers to employment than white or more affluent job seekers. For instance, two of the most widely held explanations regarding chronically high unemployment among inner-city residents are the spatial and skills mismatch hypotheses. The first refers to the movement (often described as related to suburban white flight) wherein employers moved out of inner cities, leaving poorer, inner-city residents with far fewer employment options and less ability to get to employers in the suburbs because of less access to adequate transportation. Skills mismatch refers to changes in industries or occupations that require new skills that some people may not have; it also covers the situation in which people's skills do not fit the jobs available in the areas in which they live. As a result of these factors, many inner-city residents, especially those who are less skilled, may remain jobless. The research in this regard is straightforward: There are cases in which both types of barriers to employment may be present, but in both models, important factors that emerge in ethnographic research are often overlooked.

To illustrate this point and to further show the complexity of job-seeking, and hence of unemployment as a complex social relationship, I turn to the many long-term unemployed men in Los Angeles and San Diego whom I have interviewed over the past several years. One of the immediate and unambiguous challenges for low-income, inner-city, African American and Latino men is financial insecurity, particularly the lack of credit. Without credit, it is very difficult to get an automobile, forcing job seekers to rely on public transportation, which in both cities is a massive investment of time as well as money. Even auto dealers who advertise loans for people with "zero credit/no money down" require employment and paycheck/bank account verification to provide the loan for a car. The problem, of course, is that it is difficult to get employment if one does not have a car in the first place—quite a conundrum. In some cases jobs are not easily accessible by public transportation, or the employer may require that the applicant has access to a vehicle—such as for delivery drivers, landscaping, and construction, for which in many cases employees have to provide their own transportation to a multitude of job sites. Additionally, without credit, many entry-level or cash-handling jobs are not available to prospective applicants. Some surveys find that nearly half or more of all employers use credit checks for job applicant screening (Rivlin 2013). This is especially true for industries like retail, where cashier positions that involve cash-handling often require a credit check and sometimes a minimum credit score to be employed. Of course, it is also difficult to build a credit history without a regular income. Thus, a significant portion of job seekers who are lower-income or from inner cities are already at a significant disadvantage in trying to find employment because of the all-important issue of one's credit history. The effects of this single barrier are multiple and interactive. We can add further layers of social relations that make it more difficult: Many Latinos in Southern California may have issues related to citizenship and therefore cannot rely on conventional banks for financing for fear of facing exposure as undocumented. As a result they have fewer options for financing regardless of their credit score. Similarly, African Americans also have much lower retail bank and financing usage.

These cases of individuals having employment preferences that do not fit job-seeking models well do not suggest modeling is not helpful, but they do suggest limitations. By having a very narrow, purely quantitative set of variables within an understanding of job-seeking behavior, we fail to understand the complexity lying behind those seeking work and foreclose a better understanding of why people may or may not be working or finding the work they want. In light of the clear complexity of job-seeking, as well as of the multiple, often interacting barriers that inner-city residents, particularly African Americans and Latinos, may face, it is highly reductionist and oversimplified to assume that job-seeking is a homogeneous process across different populations. Furthermore, if analyses of job-seeking remain focused on conventional variables, like spatial and skills mismatch, then some of the critically important mediating or, even more important, independent variables may be entirely overlooked. To date financial insecurity and predatory lending are not examined in any scholarship regarding unemployment, yet they clearly are important factors; for some people they are the most important factors.

The examples of financial insecurity and credit scores as barriers to employment not only demonstrates that the different factors related to job-seeking are complex, overlapping, and interactive but also suggests that they unfold in important temporal dimensions. An unplanned personal financial issue can lead to labor market disasters. These types of nonlinear, often complexly interrelated social processes may have more bearing on employment—including finding a job, keeping a job, and losing a job—than factors looked at in isolation by research on unemployment. Certainly they discredit simplistic public lamentations that "people just aren't working hard."

The example of Ellison, a Latino man who had a mechanical problem with his truck, illustrates the point. He worked two jobs: one in landscaping, the other as a handyman. His truck was essential for both jobs. As an independent contractor, he took odd jobs, typically by word of mouth, and had to get to the place where the work needed to be done. In Los Angeles, this meant traveling several miles through busy traffic. For his regular landscaping job, he required his truck to get him to the job sites. He worked with a crew of nearly a dozen other men, and they all provided their own transportation; there was no company truck to take them to each job site. Without warning, his transmission broke down, and the repair bill was estimated at nearly two thousand dollars. He could not afford to get it fixed, and without credit he could not get the repair done. Only after three weeks was he able to convince a repair shop to take the job on a payment plan, provided that he put down two hundred dollars and leave his truck at the shop. During this time he was unable to do any work as a handyman, with the exception of jobs that he could walk to and did not require carrying lots of building materials or heavy tools. He also lost his job with the landscaping company as business slowed down, and he was "the first to go." This was not, as some of the research might suggest, because he was an ethnic minority—the company is owned by a Latino, and most of the other workers were Latino as well—but because he did not have reliable transportation and it was not clear when he would have it again. Moreover, his sudden loss of income, combined with the need to make payments on his truck to get it back, forced him to borrow from family and eliminate all of his already limited savings; he fell behind on some bills, and his credit score was adversely impacted. As a result, due to the credit problem his labor market opportunities may in fact be even more limited than before.

Ellison's unemployment was caused by a combination of factors: unforeseen financial difficulties, transportation problems, and the mutually reinforcing problem of a loss of income that compounded the situation. This case illustrates how these factors are critical yet all too often not considered in research or debates on unemployment. (The role of credit scores as a barrier to employment has received some press coverage lately, but there is still no substantive scholarly research on this topic.) We could draw a clear conclusion from this single case that more research should be done to look at the extent of financial- and transportation-related barriers for employment for inner-city and lower-income residents. But these are of course only two among many equally complicated and understudied factors affecting real-world job searches. The vast and complex forces that influence job-seeking and ultimately employment for inner-city and poorer populations remain widely unstudied. Instead, inaccurate, often racially biased pronouncements about lazy ethnic minorities or a lack of work ethic often dominate public discourse on such topics. Clearly, the role of detailed, empirical, and well-documented qualitative and ethnographic research can do immeasurable good in furthering our understanding of these social processes.

Human Capital and Unemployment

According to human capital theory (Becker 1962), people invest in productivity-enhancing skills and strive to maximize the utility of this accumulated capital. Human capital is primarily defined as formal education and work experience. According to conventional labor economics, for unemployed people, there are no returns on previous investments in human capital (otherwise they would be employed). This occurs because the value of their human capital has not yet been realized in some form of employment. Accordingly, the unemployed should seek out more human capital—skills or training, which will allow them to get a position they would like in the economy.

Like job-seeking behavior more broadly, the process of finding a job must be seen within context. For instance, analysts, when they examine human capital and joblessness, seldom factor in racial or gender discrimination as variables. Overall, labor economics and macroeconomists tend to view the relationship to human capital in a very narrow way, asking questions such as "Do people with more human capital face less unemployment?" or "Is human capital holding back the long-term unemployed?" As a result, the debate about human capital and unemployment fails to address both a broader range of forces affecting unemployment and the nature of job-seeking behavior. For instance, are workers "discouraged" because they cannot find a job, or are they having a hard time finding a job because of persistent racial or other discrimination, which in turn makes it more difficult to find a job and further contributes to the multiply discouraging effects of being unemployed? This type of a question is only answerable through either a very in-depth survey or more ethnographically close research (participant observation, open-ended interviews, and so on).

This criticism is particularly true for the assumption that people can simply invest in human capital attainment as if it were a convenient, market-available good like ice cream or bread. Human capital takes far more time and effort than a consumer purchase. Training and education require a range of supporting factors—time, income, access to courses, knowledge of which skills and specialties are currently in demand, and so forth. The relative levels of human capital attainment fall across socioeconomic and racial/ethnic lines in the United States, meaning that for people of color and the poor, access to educational opportunities or even on-the-job training may be less available than it is for whites or upper-income members of society who are looking for work. Women who are single parents and are raising children may not have the time or resources for formal educational training. The poor, particularly the rural poor, may not have the high-speed connections and computer systems necessary to partake in online education (Mossberger, Tolbert, and Stansbury 2003; Warshauer and Knobel 2004).

Further complicating matters, many employers, particularly for lower-paid and entry-level positions in the service sector, are moving to web-based hiring and screening. McDonalds and many retail stores are just a few of the well-known areas where this is occurring in human resource practices. Yet it is not just private sector employers that have shifted toward internet-based hiring; nonprofit and government entities have also moved in this direction. A case from an applicant to the San Diego Community College District illustrates how the application process requires significant resources. I met Ronaldo by accident in the new Logan Heights library, an architecturally stunning fourteen-million-dollar building providing internet, computer classrooms, and nearly four thousand square feet of space. Ronaldo was in the middle of filling out online job applications for various positions. The most frustrating case, he explained, was the San Diego Community College District. The district had two jobs that were a good fit for his skills and background. He registered in the human resources system, created and uploaded his files, and created a username and password to manage his job applications. He prepared a scanned copy of his credentials and went through the lengthy application and online questionnaire. Twice the system froze, meaning that he had to return the next day to attempt to complete his application. After a third day of attempting to submit his application, it went through, and he waited for a reply.

After two weeks without receiving a phone call, Ronaldo checked the email account he had used when registering, but there was no message about the job (he did have several offers to refinance his house, an asset he does not actually have, and a message about getting rich while working from home). He assumed that he did not get the position, but he wanted to know that his information was in the system so that he could at least reapply for a different position in the future and not have to go through every part of the process again. After trying and failing to reach the human resources office on the phone, he sent them an email message. A few weeks later he received a reply that his information was in the system but that his first application had not been successful; he also learned that he could have checked his application status at the human resources website all along, which would have saved him a great deal of time and effort had he been advised of it from the outset.

All told, his unsuccessful application and follow-up took an estimated fourteen hours. He bemoaned the fact that he couldn't do this from home, but it didn't make sense to purchase a computer and pay for internet access when it was free at the library. However, for a single, unsuccessful job application he had to invest a tremendous amount of time. The broader problem this indicates is that the San Diego Community College District only accepts applications online. This limitation effectively screens out a large segment of the inner-city labor force. Staff are available to answer questions about the site but do not provide any assistance with completing any application. In other words, this type of employment application system already pre-screens out most people who do not have regular and reliable access to a computer and internet connection.

Research on job-seeking strategies by U.S. workers is limited by data sources, with recent research drawing on surveys conducted in the early 2000s (Suvankulov 2010). Overall in the United States, only 25 percent of unemployed job seekers regularly reported using the internet for job searches in 2004 (Hadass 2004). More recent research suggests that this figure has doubled to a majority of U.S. adults (54 percent), with nearly 45 percent applying for a job online, although far fewer ethnic minorities or those with lower rates of education appear to use the internet for job searches (Smith 2015). Moreover, the majority of employment advertisements online are aimed at those with some college or at least a high school degree or higher (Carnevale, Jayasundera, and Repnikov 2014). At the same time, many employers are moving entirely to online hiring or prefer online hiring to in-person or paper applications. One of the potential problems with online hiring systems is that the applicant pool can become skewed toward those with greater access to the internet and greater computer skills (as an example, updated browsers are needed for most websites, and a high-speed connection is essential for many applications). At Starbucks, for instance, relatively real-time openings can be searched by location and applied for fairly easily, but this tends to advantage those who are actively searching online; these job seekers can find out about positions quickly and apply instantly. Those with less frequent access to the internet are therefore left out of the hiring queue for many entry-level service positions in retail, food service, and even nonprofit and educational institutions.

Even vocational and technical programs that do not lead to a degree but still impart very marketable job skills—such as in the construction or technical service trades (medical assistants, dental hygienists, and so on)—can be very costly. While surveying low-wage workers in San Diego and Los Angeles, I found that many had considered such programs but then balked at program costs ranging as high as $40,000 for a potential wage of only $18,000 to $35,000 per year.

A case in point is Salvador, who when I interviewed him in 2005 had worked in construction for a decade and wanted to shift gears toward working in HVAC as an installer or even inspector. He planned to enroll in the program at San Diego City College for HVACR consultant certification. The HVAC program at the school is called the AIRE (Air Conditioning, Refrigeration, and Energy) Program and trains people for a range of career options that includes air conditioning or refrigeration contractor, service manager, dispatcher, HVAC or refrigeration service technician, manufacturer service representative, HVACR consultant, and control systems designer or commissioner. The AIRE Program also prepares students to enter into green careers that include solar energy technician or contractor, solar system design engineer, and HVAC and solar integration specialist, but these require an associate degree in Air Conditioning, Refrigeration and Environmental Control Technology, a program that focuses on high efficiency HVACR, advanced controls, and alternative energy systems. At that time, the program cost $46 per unit, totaling $2,760 for tuition overall, not including $3,000 in books and supplies, as well as other fees (the health service fee, the liability insurance fee, and parking permits totaled another hundred dollars). The total cost for the program, on average, ran around $6,000. This is far more affordable than some college programs, particularly the for-profit ones, which run as high as $40,000 but is still a significant investment. Salvador ultimately decided to hold off on attending the course indefinitely, not only for cost but also because he has two children and his wife, who had only recently returned to work, had unsteady employment at low wages. He qualified for some grants and financial aid but found the prospect of taking out loans unappealing.

Salvador also considered taking the courses one at a time over a few years, paying as he went, and attending only at night. Under that plan, even though class schedules are flexible, the inevitable result would be that he would spend some nights at class and the rest of the nights studying. At that rate the program would take three years, not just two. Yet as he noted, no one knows what the job market for HVAC would look like in three years, "maybe it will be another construction boom, or bust." After attending the first class, he wondered whether he was making a mistake or not: All of the other students were much younger. Why would a company hire him if they could hire someone half his age and pay them less? He had heard worrisome stories of friends and relatives who had earned associate degrees in different fields, only to find that there weren't any jobs, or they weren't actually paying what the recruiters said they would be paying. Thus, they could have saved all the time and money and just stuck to their old job. Eventually Salvador dropped the program—for now, he says—but he hopes to return if he feels confident that the investment will pay off.

When the economic crisis hit in 2008 and the construction industry collapsed in Southern California, Salvador was unemployed but somewhat relieved that he had chosen not to complete the HVAC course, because had he done so, he would have found himself in debt and without a job. Yet, without a more in-demand set of skills, he still remained at a disadvantage in the labor market.

The point here is that despite tremendous resources for education and seemingly very affordable prices, investing in human capital among the urban poor carries significant risks and unclear rewards. For those struggling to meet monthly bills, who are understandably somewhat risk-averse, obtaining potentially—but not certainly—useful labor market skills for several thousand dollars may not be the most attractive goal. Many jobs that offer higher pay and benefits, particularly those that are salary-based instead of paying an hourly wage, demand at least a two-year college degree, some a bachelor's degree. The problem again, however, is that there are clear barriers for working adults to obtain these credentials, particularly for parents, and income plays a major role in the decision-making process around skills upgrading. Qualitative data of this type complicate the assumptions of human capital theory. It is not possible to assume that human capital is attainable without taking cost and social/cultural understandings of risk and reward into account in skills upgrading.

In sum, human capital theory points out that those without the right skills do less favorably in the labor market, have higher unemployment rates, and so forth. The assumptions often following such observations are that people are too lazy or ill-informed to find or get new skills and training, conclusions that ignore the many critical qualitative challenges that people seeking jobs face.

Race, Discrimination, and Unemployment

Long-standing research in labor economics shows clear differences in employment and wages across different racial and ethnic groups (Heckman 1998; Moss and Tilly 2001; Darity and Mason 1998). The bulk of this work focuses on African Americans, showing that they have higher rates of unemployment, experience more discrimination in hiring, and, on average, secure lower wages than whites. Human capital theory has explained some, but not all, of these differences. Other research on racial discrimination and spatial mismatches (that African Americans are left behind in urban areas while jobs have moved out of cities to the suburbs) also explains part of the differences. In more recent analyses, more sophisticated models have been constructed to examine the relative importance of different factors related to higher unemployment among African Americans. For instance, perceived criminality and the use of background checks appear to remove African Americans from hiring pools unfairly (Holzer, Raphael, and Stoll 2006), and even purportedly objective and race-neutral standardized job tests appear to discriminate against ethnic minorities in the hiring process (Autor and Scarborough 2008). Recent attempts at a synthesis have failed to develop any clear explanation for the persistent gaps between blacks and whites and across different racial and ethnic groups (Lang and Lehman 2011). Some models account for wage differentials, and some provide evidence that changes in business cycles bring more difficult labor markets for ethnic minorities. On the latter, however, the evidence is still mixed. The "last hired, first fired," model suggests that minorities, especially African Americans, are, on average, the last to be hired in a good economy and the first to be let go during economic downturns (Couch and Fairlie 2010). What the precise social or cultural mechanisms are that contribute to the persistent gap in unemployment across racial and ethnic groups is clearly very difficult to assess with existing data, particularly with a dearth of surveys or quantitative data on racial discrimination and hiring practices. This is another area where qualitative research, ethnographic accounts, and the use of case studies can generate important insights. In the case of Devah Pager's research, both experimental and labor market statistics indicate racial discrimination in hiring and pay rates (Pager, Western, and Bonikowski 2009; Pager, Fryer, and Spenkuch 2011). In my own research, I have found similarly that employers have preferences based on race and gender and that these practices related to hiring are both inclusionary and exclusionary, often depending on the industry and occupation. For instance, Latinos may be viewed as preferable to hire in some cases, particularly in relation to African Americans, unless they are Latinas, in which case gender issues often complicate the hiring process and decision making (Karjanen 2008). On the other hand, African Americans are often viewed as the least desirable candidates for jobs on average, and they may lack the social networks that are critical to hiring that other ethnic groups may have (Royster 2003).

Existing research on this topic commendably includes issues such as racial discrimination and even spatial variables when analyzing black unemployment, but again, my concern is that it is also limited by variables that are not visible in survey data or other types of data. For instance, racial discrimination may be inherent in the very hiring process due to the requirements that have emerged over the past decade for many workers, such as the credit checks discussed in

the previous section. Thus, ethnographic research shows how it is often a combination of these factors that results in higher rates of unemployment among
some ethnic minorities. For instance, someone who has multiple, overlapping,
and often reinforcing barriers to employment faces not a specific set of factors
but the *interaction* of those factors as barriers to employment. Take someone
with transportation issues who also has a lack of credit. This person is reliant
on public transit or rides to work. Either of these modes of commuting can be
unreliable. Not having reliable transportation to and from work is often seen as
critical to hiring; employers cannot afford to have people show up late or not
know if they are going to show up at all. Retailers, for instance, often have a "three
strikes" policy on arriving late; if one has unreliable transportation, a car breaking down, a ride failing to show, or public transit not operating on schedule, three
late arrivals to work will result in dismissal. While every employee faces the same
demand of arriving at work on time, one's ability to meet that demand is often
shaped by one's economic circumstances and not one's willingness to work or
one's inherent punctuality. Indeed, public transit or shared rides to work are in
fact structurally imposed demands on workers over which they have no control.

The failure of economic models and most forms of quantitative data to see
these forces at work also leaves us with a distorted view of how racial discrimination operates for unemployed workers. Economics, race, discrimination, and
inner-city joblessness are clearly inextricably bound up in the immensely complex social relations of labor market dynamics and society more broadly. As
I discussed previously with the case of Ellison and his interwoven financial and
transportation issues, race was not the only issue. However, in other ways, race
and ethnicity can play important roles in shaping hiring and firing decisions.
What we find when looking at different challenges and the complexities of seeking employment, especially for those who are poor or who are ethnic minorities,
is that the labor market is not merely segmented but also highly complex, and
the barriers to gainful employment are often numerous and overlapping and
defy neat solutions. These may include both structural and institutional racism
but also the role of race and social networks in hiring systems. As Deidre Royster
(2003) has shown, white male networks for blue-collar jobs often exclude men
of color from hiring, further obstructing black men from obtaining blue-collar
jobs. I have found similar processes at work in hiring practice among businesses
in southern California. Some clearly state a preference for Latinos. Other managers indicate few preferences, but when assessed further, African Americans fall
at the bottom of the distribution of perceptions of preferred employee characteristics (Karjanen 2008). In some industries, there are clear hiring networks
that include or exclude along the lines of race, as hiring practices in some hotels
and restaurants have often been oriented along social networks, which are often

racially homogeneous. Thus, while overt racial discrimination may not be going on, people often refer friends or relatives for work, and if those people are all of the same racial or ethnic background, then the company or even industry sector may eventually be dominated by a single ethnic or racial group.

A More Heterodox View

Having just provided some critiques of the overly mechanistic and quantitative approach to unemployment by conventional economics in a number of areas, I turn here to a proposal for a more heterodox view, one buttressed by a more holistic approach based on more empirically grounded ethnographic perspectives, combined with some more radical approaches in labor economics. To briefly summarize a simplified position of conventional economics: Economic action is driven by interest and rationality. Self-interest and rationality are seen as the essential groundings of a "natural order" of market operations. This does not, however, provide room for addressing many of the thorny empirical issues that have emerged in the study of labor markets and the issue of unemployment more specifically. This also forces us to take the issue of embeddedness more seriously in our understanding of work and employment and of how labor is exchanged and commodified in contemporary capitalism. In this sense embeddedness refers to the ways that economic exchange (in the case under examination here, that of labor and wages between those seeking work and those who seek to hire labor) is articulated in a social and cultural context. It is within this context that social and cultural forces, as well as relations of power, can be integrated into our analysis of unemployment.

The simple point here is that employment or unemployment are not isolated, simple processes that can be encapsulated and modeled by conventional labor market theory in economics. As Karl Polanyi (1957) pointed out years ago, labor as a commodity is a misrepresentation of reality, and the labor market is a system of coarse fictions. More to the point, as radical Italian economist Ernesto Screpanti has put it:

> Workers do not sell a commodity. That is why their wage is not the price of a commodity. It is not the price of labor activities because these may be multifarious, heterogeneous, and variable and unknown at the time the wage is fixed; the wage in fact will not vary when labor activities vary. Nor is it the price of labor actions, because these are affected by the employer, not by the employee. Nor, finally is it the price of the labor services, because these are produced by labor actions and belong to the

employer ... wage is the compensation for loss of freedom, i.e. for obedience; and obedience is a social relation, not a commodity. (2001, 16)

Unemployment, then, is a social relation, and employment is, too; above all, we
are discussing relationships of social power, of force, of the very structure of differential access to resources and opportunities in a particular economic system.

We can add to the list of critiques here two conclusions regarding conventional labor economics approaches to unemployment: (1) a failure to understand
unemployment and job-seeking behavior as a function of broader institutional
arrangements within contemporary capitalism; and (2) an inability to understand how micro-level contextual factors influence the experience of unemployment and hence the potential effects of unemployment on displaced workers and
their resulting employability.

Let me conclude with some further case studies to illustrate my points. The
first issue is critical to how I would shift our analysis of unemployment from
modeling and convention to a more radical view. To illustrate how important
this is, to see joblessness as part of institutional structures and not simply supply and demand, we can look at the retail industry. For several years, some
colleagues and I have noted that the largest occupational growth appears to
be not just in the lower-wage service sector but specifically in the retail sector.
Yet despite massive job growth, two things have happened: (1) wages for retail
workers have not kept pace with inflation and in some markets have stagnated
or declined; and (2) despite high unemployment rates, even in the midst of the
recession, many retail jobs have gone unfilled. To put it in conventional economic terms, how can rising labor market demand result in stagnant or lower
wages and unfilled positions, particularly given the high employment supply,
otherwise known as high unemployment? Wages should instead be rising, and
more people should be taking these jobs, especially during a downturn such as
the Great Recession. When I raised this quandary to a number of colleagues, all
of whom are well-respected economists, there were no clear answers. The two
most common responses I received were: (1) there must be something wrong
with the data, because wages don't drop or stagnate when demand increases; or
(2) this must be some strange temporary phenomenon—wait and it will correct. The trend has continued, however, and I still have not heard a convincing
explanation.

My own explanation has typically been that the reason the wages and employment have fallen despite rising demand for workers in the industry is because
of restructuring; namely, the movement from department store and specialty
store retail to discount retail has eroded the wage rate for the industry, possibly through reducing union density in an already heavily non-union industry

(Basker 2007), thus potentially eroding both wage and benefit rates even further (Bernhardt 1999). In addition, the move toward discount retailing has eliminated many career ladders in the industry. For example, twenty years ago a person could get a job at a department store selling shoes, like Macy's and Nordstrom, and this was the primary model of retailing of the time, other than small specialty stores. A worker could move up in those companies through internal labor markets; they could earn a living, raise a family, even buy a home, working on commission as well as base salary, progressing through training programs, moving into management or buyer positions. This is not the same career ladder that Wal-Mart, Target, or other discount retailers have: there are no "shoe salesperson" positions at Wal-Mart or Target, just "sales associate," a term that people recognize as a fancy way of saying "entry level stock clerk or cashier with limited opportunity."

Workers know this. The unemployed know this. They have good labor market information about job quality in the retail sector. For the past decade, unemployed people, part-time workers, and people working low-wage temp jobs I have interviewed in San Diego, Minneapolis–Saint Paul, and Detroit have typically eschewed retail jobs when I raised the prospect of full-time employment in this sector. The reasons cited for their disdain of retail positions vary, but typically they point to low wages, limited benefits, poor working conditions, and no real room for occupational advancement. To quote a young woman from Minneapolis who is working part-time and has been looking for a full-time job for over a year, despite the strong demand for retail sector workers in the Twin Cities: "Retail! I worked in every store I could, for ten years. Ten years! Where did I get? Head cashier, stock clerk, and nowhere. I earn almost as much on temp jobs with fewer hours but have less bullshit." She also described what she felt was employer discrimination in the retail sector: "Some places you know are not going to promote you. You just know. You look around and do you see any people of color who are managers, assistants, even head cashiers? Nope. . . . So what kind of a message does that send?"

For this young woman and others with her perception of the industry, their reservation wage has not changed; they just do not want what they see as a crappy, dead-end job. To put it differently, job quality matters. There is no room for these preferences in conventional labor economics when looking at unemployment or reservation wages, however. My point here is that it is not worker characteristics but the institutional structures of capitalism that have shifted, encouraging more unemployment; de-unionization and the downgrading of retail has eroded that industry's earnings potential and career development, not a lack of available workers in the labor market. We have too many unemployed, and we also have too many poor-quality jobs for them.

Next, let me turn to conventional challenges in establishing how micro-level contextual factors influence the experience of unemployment, which has ramifications on the effects of unemployment on displaced workers. Mario is an African American man who is thirty years old. He has worked in a variety of jobs during his decade and a half in the labor force. He is a good example of how the general functioning of the employment/unemployment dichotomy simply does not obtain. In fact, the conventional models of labor economics which would aim at understanding Mario's job-seeking and employment status fail to capture any of the substantive factors that Mario faces in his employment decision making. He has faced racial discrimination, has limited hiring networks, lives in a segmented inner-city labor market where he has inadequate access to a lot of hiring information. He does not have the types of skills that are translatable to typical jobs, despite having the educational credentials of high school and some community college courses. In sum, he challenges many of the conventional assumptions of labor market theory regarding job-seeking and employment in that he faces barriers to employment based on his socioeconomic position, not the characteristics of himself as an individual (willingness to work, aptitude, and so on).

Conventional theory and modeling in labor economics, as we see in Mario's case, does not hold up well. As a result, Mario shows up as someone who is working part-time and should easily move into full-time employment instead of relying on unemployment insurance after he is fired from his job. As a result, little of conventional labor economics helps us understand Mario's persistent and seemingly chronic joblessness. Over a five-year period I have known Mario to have had more than two dozen "formal sector" jobs, but none lasted more than a year, and all were just part-time positions. He reflects the growing distortion of the U.S. economy as it attempts to adjust to a long, forty-year period of restructuring, downsizing, and offshoring.

What, then, does this all tell us? If the criticisms are accurate, how are we to understand unemployment? First, it is reasonable to say that we do need modeling, we do need labor economics, we do need macroeconomic statistics, and we do need ways of thinking about job-seeking and retention in a measurable, rigorous way. We also need, however, an understanding of unemployment as more than simply a model but instead as a social process. We need a sensitivity to and an understanding of how joblessness is in part a function not only of supply and demand and abstract forces but also of real agglomerations of power in a capitalist society. In short, existing premises are shallow, narrow, and miss the broader gestalt of labor market dynamics. We must admit that job loss is not a homogeneous experience. An immigrant from Latin America, working for low wages in the restaurant industry, supporting a large family outside of the United States, views job loss very differently than a white male lawyer for a large U.S. bank does. Race, class, and the vast differences in socioeconomic and cultural context make unemployment a very uneven and heterogeneous social force.

What is unemployment, then? It is a social and economic disruption of varying degrees and magnitude, depending on one's circumstances. What I am proposing here is a breaking open of economics, a push for a more social economics, and an invigorated political economy, all endeavors that can be furthered by anthropological explorations and insights.

OCCUPATION

Jong Bum Kwon

Unemployment hurts. Popular and academic accounts suggest subtle but disturbing connections between job loss and deteriorating physical health. The involuntarily unemployed (which is to say, laid off) commonly complain of back pain, stomach ailments, ear and nasal infections, and severe flu-like symptoms. Unemployment may even be fatal. Recent epidemiological research conducted in the United States indicates that increased risk of heart attack, stroke, diabetes, and arthritis are associated with unemployment. Life expectancy, according to some studies, is measurably shortened by unemployment, surprisingly even after re-employment (Kessler, Turner and House 1998; Strully 2009). And some unemployed people have described the experience itself as a sickness, not unlike cancer and chronic pain syndromes (Cottle 2003, 19).

While the unemployed may hurt, their bodies often are obscured or missing in social scientific accounts. Despite broad advances in the study of the body and increased attention to unemployment across a range of disciplines, their intimate connection has yet to be fully theorized. Exposing the tenacity of Cartesian dualism, unemployment's afflictions generally are relegated to psychosomatic affects: the psychological trauma of unemployment; the bodily reflex of chronic anxiety, depression, anger, and other kinds of mental distress (an approach dominant in social psychology and folk-popular representations); and psychological (and emotional) inability to adapt to changed circumstances or social-cultural disorientations and confusions, among others. Most anthropological research, for example, document the shattered coherence of the complex cultural scaffolding that had sustained identities and social locations. These have been invaluable in analyzing unemployment's intricate imbrication with gender (Dunk 2003; Pappas 1989); social status and class (Dudley 1994); and, most recently, life cycles and temporality (Jeffrey 2010; Mains 2007). The unemployed are interpreting subjects, adjusting to changed (as well as chronic) circumstances, and reworking (the pun is intended) forms of meaning and value. Notwithstanding the evident exchanges involving mind, body, and self, it is clear that ideational forms (discursive meaning) are privileged, and the body remains relatively mute and unintelligible.

This chapter focuses our attention to the embodied worker in order to understand the corporeal suffering of the unemployed. Employment is an embodied experience; people's experience and interpretation of their bodies are embedded in the structure and organization of formal work (Wolkowitz 2006, 1). While this may not be a profound insight, it is a necessary reminder that work is one of the primary sites where power (in terms of relations of authority, technologies, disciplinary regimes) insinuates into and conforms bodies. Power is registered in the normalization of bodily shape, conduct, comportment, and emotion management. It is felt in fatigue, cramped arms and legs, and aching backs, be it from sitting at desks in front of a computer to serving customers and enduring the mechanical march of the assembly line. Our bodies continue to be made and remade in and through specific forms of employment. My contention is that the bodily experience of unemployment is intimately related to particular constructions of workers' bodies during employment.

My analysis centers on the suffering bodies of male laid-off Daewoo Motor production workers in South Korea (hereafter Korea). During my two years of fieldwork (2000–2001) with the four hundred men who participated in the Daewoo Motor Union's struggle against mass redundancy (hereafter "Struggle"), I joined their ranks at labor demonstrations, standing against riot police and company security, and frequently shared shots of soju (a common clear spirit often compared to vodka) after union events. I listened to their often-brusque comments about familial strain, social alienation, worsening health, and diminishing prospects of returning to the factory. At a local Catholic Church, union yard, and protest tents (places of daily congregation for the laid-off men), I witnessed the deterioration of their bodies and attended to their remarks about their physical pains and dysfunctions—chronic back and hip pain, frequent debilitating headaches, sensations of vertigo, and constant stomach upset, among others.[1] Rather than the stunning experience of state violence, which they had regularly faced, or the progress of the labor movement, workers' everyday talk was punctuated by comments about their social isolation coupled with concern about their afflictions, which had come to stalk their very movements.

Daewoo workers described being laid off as being severed (*charŭta*). While the men used it idiomatically, much like "fired" in American vernacular, their evident pain indicated an emerging valence of physical violence. When combined with their telling of their experiences on the assembly line, the phrase registered as an embodied metaphor. Like many who work with their bodies to make a living, they spoke of a way of understanding and evaluating themselves and their place in the social world that came from years of physical labor on the assembly line, revealing a corporeal epistemology (Zandy 2004, 3–4; see also Scheper-Hughes 1992, 185). Their laboring bodies, which I distinguish as "Daewoo bodies," constituted a kind of bodily capital (Wacquant 1995). Their bodies were assembled and obtained value through their labors in the factory. They referred to the factory as *chŏngdŭn ilt'ŏ*, which may be roughly translated as "workplace of attachment." This phrase integrates Korean notions of affect and affective connection with labor and with the factory. The idiom suggests an understanding and experience of laboring on the assembly line as a mutual process of bodily incorporation. By their daily labor, they incorporated the factory into their bodily sense of self, even as the tools, machines, and car chassis absorbed their sweat and toil. Their being severed, therefore, was not simply severance, in the conventional sense, from their employment. Rather, as I argue, they were cut off from a vital part of their own bodies.

The factory was not simply a place of employment, an abstract, fungible space to earn a wage. Unemployment, therefore, was not simply a loss of a job. My ethnographic analysis suggests a necessary rethinking of our understanding of occupation as something beyond a person's job or form of employment. *Occupation* gestures toward that other dimension of meaning—to inhabit place. Here, I define *occupation* as embodied habitation but emphasize the mutual constitution of bodily self and place, whereby self and place are conjoined. *Occupation* is a product of articulating with, attaching to, and thereby inhabiting and being inhabited by particular places and practices. The factory, as *chŏngdŭn ilt'ŏ*, is as much a place of their assembly, of their bodily integrity—their sense of health and well-being—as it is of automobiles. In their *occupation* Daewoo workers' bodies became Daewoo bodies. To be laid off, then, was to be forcibly dislocated not simply from a space but, in their words, to be severed from *chŏngdŭn ilt'ŏ*, or from what I define as *occupation*. Their physical pains and dysfunctions indexed what may be understood as a process of bodily disassembly resulting in a state of disrepair.

In the following, I begin with the ascendance of neoliberalism and Korea's transition to a post-Fordist economy signaled by the Asian financial crisis (1997–2001). *Chŏngdŭn ilt'ŏ* and Daewoo bodies were produced under the developmental state model of industrial production and its dramatic dissolution saw the devaluation and disposability of industrial bodies. Thereafter, I examine the minor place of employment and working bodies in contemporary cultural research. Industrial bodies, in particular, have been ignored because of industrial labor's long-standing association with personal and bodily degradation. The connective tissue of my chapter is *chŏngdŭn ilt'ŏ*; in this section I analyze in detail Daewoo workers' experience of labor on the assembly line. Drawing on recent thinking about relational bodies and affect, I demonstrate how Daewoo bodies may best be understood as a kind of human and nonhuman assemblage. This investigation leads to understanding workers' experiences of being laid off as being severed.

Disposable Bodies in Neoliberal South Korea

The corporeal suffering of these laid-off Daewoo autoworkers cannot be fully understood without appreciating how working bodies were assembled (and then disassembled) under particular regimes of capitalist accumulation. The healthy bodies of these workers were assemblages of the developmental indus-trial economy—squarely in the authoritarian, nationalist, and Fordist mode of accumulation. The Korean economy had faced a crisis of profitability and global competitiveness since the 1980s, and the Asian financial crisis spectacularly dramatized the definitive failure of the developmental model. It affirmed the entrenchment of neoliberal labor policies, which dismantled the supposed rigid-ities of the Korean labor market; facilitated the execution of mass layoffs; and valorized the "flexible" ethos of finance capital. The materialization of Daewoo workers' specific symptoms in the aftermath of their being severed was deeply connected to the unprecedented disposability of their industrial bodies under the new neoliberal post-Fordist regime of accumulation in Korea.

While debate continues regarding the extent of Korea's adoption of neolib-eralism, there is general agreement over the profound political-economic and social-cultural transformations since the crisis. It has become increasingly clear that the crisis provided a political opportunity for reformist elites to restruc-ture key regulatory policies and institutional structures of accumulation along neoliberal principles (for instance, banking, monetary policy, controls on for-eign investment, autonomy of financial bodies) while complying with global free market "best practices" (Pirie 2008). Obtaining intellectual hegemony (at state agencies, corporate bodies, and nongovernmental organizations) during the cri-sis, neoliberal reformers accelerated the shift from mass production manufactur-ing to finance, information technology, and service-related employment. In the wake of the crisis, scholars of Korea have started ethnographic studies to identify the propagation of neoliberal rationalities and affects into a range of social fields, including social welfare (Song 2009); education (Abelmann and Park 2009; Choi 2005); and the burgeoning self-help industry (Seo 2011). They describe wide-spread adherence to, if not obsession with, "self-development" (*chagi kyebal*) and "self-management" (*chagi kwalli*). Distinguished from the normative person-hood of the developmental period, the individual self (subjectivity, affect, and body), rather than the company or nation, has emerged as both the means and object of improvement.

The pillars of Korea's phenomenal economic growth constructed during the developmental state period, in particular secure employment, were systematically dismantled. While much attention has deservedly been given to the unparalleled levels of unemployment during the crisis, the significance of the crisis lies in the restructured labor market, which facilitated an enduring redistribution of wealth from labor to capital (Pirie 2008).[2] The state managed to revise labor laws in 1998, at the height of the crisis, extracting hitherto unimaginable concessions from organized labor (institutionalization of mass layoffs, temporary contract labor, and extensive labor subcontracting), abrogating the core labor-capital compact established in the aftermath of the wave of strikes in the 1987–1989 period. Core workers, skilled male employees in permanent positions at large manufacturing companies, had obtained strong legal protections against dismissals, corporate welfare benefits (including health care, subsidized housing, and educational subsidies for children), and significant wage premiums relative to their counterparts in small companies in exchange for labor peace.[3] While state regulation of labor was indeed harsh and authoritarian, routinely employing tactics of violence, intimidation, and terror, extant labor laws had protected jobs, restricting employers' rights to dismiss and dispatch workers (Koo 2000). The Daewoo Struggle marked the last gasp of the developmental state regime of industrial capitalism. The massive job cuts at Daewoo Motors were the first and largest executed at a historically powerful union stronghold since the state's failed attempt at Hyundai Motors in 1998.[4]

Daewoo autoworkers were core workers of the developmental state. They had been employed at Korea's second-largest carmaker and one of the flagship companies of the Daewoo Group, a top-five conglomerate (*chaebŏl*). They had enjoyed relatively high wages, social prestige (for manual workers), benefits, and, most crucially, job security. Nearly all of the men had worked at least one decade at the factory, some nearly thirty years, and all had expected the factory to be their lifelong workplace (*pyŏngsaeng chikjang*). They had expected to "bury their bones" at the factory.

Despite this, Daewoo workers did show some ambivalence about their labor at the factory. They described working on the assembly line as eating "grease-rice" (*girŏmbap mŏkta*). It was not just grease that they consumed; it was also "rice." While the "grease-rice" may have been dirty and unappetizing, it was also sustenance, sustaining their bodies and their social worlds. They did complain of the assembly line's monotony; they acknowledged the stigma attached to manual labor, its perception as being for uneducated people lacking moral rectitude. While they preferred to be called *hoesawŏn* (company employee), which dissembled their actual labor, I heard them call themselves *kongdori* (factory boy), which pejoratively suggests servitude. Yet they were also "Daewoo men," employees of a major conglomerate, with the attendant material and cultural privileges. They had worn their Daewoo jackets as a symbol of distinction. They were different from other manual laborers, many stated. While they may have only a high school education, they were, they joked, "good catches," good marrying prospects. They were good providers and therefore good husbands and fathers.[5] The "good life," the "normal life" (*pyŏngbŏmhan saenghwal*), they understood, depended on the continued health and vitality of their bodies, which, they found, depended on their continued attachment to *chŏngdŭn ilt'ŏ*.

In making this particular argument, I am not suggesting that Daewoo bodies should be thought of simply as social bodies, with the body serving as a symbolic surface for social inscription for markers indicating masculinity, class, and status that are associated with core industrial workers. While it is clear that such meanings were referenced and claimed by the men, I shift attention to their lived, somatically felt bodies, as co-produced through prolonged physical labor inside the factory. Their embodied practices constituted a kind of bodily capital; their particular bodies were formed and obtained value by their sustained connection to their coworkers, tools, and objects of labor in the factory. Their Daewoo bodies enabled the accumulation of social-cultural capital outside the factory (Wolkowitz 2006, 62–64; Durand and Hatzfeld 2003; Wacquant 1995). It was in the particular context of the developmental regime that the factory could become *chŏngdŭn ilt'ŏ* and their particular bodies assembled.

Industrial Bodies

There is a long history of ambivalence about the meaning and value of work in Western thought (Applebaum 1995). The word *work* is applicable both to valuable and productive activity and to difficult and demeaning exertion. Work may be associated with self-fulfillment, moral standing, and social potency. Yet it may also be related to self-denial, moral degradation, and social submission. With the advent of post-Fordist modes of production and the increasing dominance of the service sector, work has been increasingly associated with suffering and alienation. Since the late twentieth century we have tended, as Scarry (1994, 52) noted, "to surround 'play' and 'desire' with connotations of inventiveness, innovation, spontaneity, sensuousness and to surround work with connotations of numbing routine, diminished consciousness (perhaps even false consciousness or unconsciousness)." This observation reflects what has come to be seen as a fundamental shift in the sites of value and identity production—from workplace and labor to expansive public cultures of consumption (Comaroff and Comaroff 2001, 4). The irony, of course, is that most people expend considerable time and energy in order to work, especially if we consider training for (including education), searching for, recovering from, and preparing for work (Weeks 2011, 2).

While there is long-standing ambivalence toward work in general, there is less so about industrial labor. Labor itself is more closely associated with pain and toil in part because it is identified with bodily exertion (Williams 1983, 334–335). Industrial labor epitomizes the corporeal suffering of work. It is linked not only to grueling physical effort but also to bodily subjection. The industrial body is perceived as an object of external control and manipulation that inevitably degrades the person. With industrialization, Adam Smith, for example, predicted that the division of labor into repetitive manual tasks would result in mental and moral degeneration (becoming a "stupid and ignorant . . . human creature"). Karl Marx graphically described bodily dismemberment ("appendage to the machine") as a metaphor for social-economic alienation. Such thinking continues to resonate. Harry Braverman's *Labor and Monopoly Capital* (1974) is the modern classic exposition. A critique of Taylor's scientific management, the volume excoriates the expropriation of workers' skill and control through the minute fragmentation of tasks, resulting in the diminishing of the human worker. Contemporary cultural analyses frequently draw from Foucauldian insights about the emergence of a modern "political anatomy." While Foucault shifted emphasis to the production of individuals, the disciplinary regimes under which norms of conduct and aptitudes are formed are conceived as breaking down, rearranging, and thereby producing "docile bodies" (Foucault 1979, 138).[6]

Furthermore, representations of industrial bodies tend to replicate Cartesian suspicions of the body. The mind is ultimately the seat of rationality and the source of the self. Industrial labor is deemed mindless work. Not only does the mechanical repetition of factory work deaden the mind, it requires no mind at all. The industrial worker is reduced to his body. There is in fact a frightening physicality in imaginations of the industrial laborer—irrational, uncivilized, filthy, carnal (Metcalfe 1990; Rancière et al. 2004). The disciplinary machinery of the factory did not simply create greater efficiencies but also, as labor historians have noted, were intended to subdue the dangerous nature of workers' fleshy bodies (Wolkowitz 2006, 58–59; Yanarella and Reid 1996).

Dominant imaginings of industrial labor tend to preclude the possibility of it as a source of workers' meaning-making, as a practice of self-making. In particular, Foucauldian analyses that emphasize the docile body curtail the possibility of meaningful agency and workers' identification with not only their labors but also their bodies. As Wolkowitz in her analytic summary of the sociology of labor argues, they may overstate the scope and uniformity of the effects of power (Wolkowitz 2006, 61). Industrial bodies, moreover, are not the "flexible bodies" valued in the contemporary imaginary of postindustrial societies (Martin 1995). Seen as imprisoned in machineries of power, industrial bodies are not only anachronistic but also anathema to the emancipatory ethos of neoliberalism—individual liberty, individual responsibility, and individual self-fashioning.

Alternative theories of the body suggest broader possibilities of embodiment and bodily valuation. One productive line of reasoning is bodily capital, a concept derived from Bourdieu's (1992) thinking on habitus, elaborated by Loïc Wacquant in his study of the "body-centered universe" of boxing (1995). Bodily capital signifies the practical incorporation (embodiment) of social values and structures. It indicates the participants' investments in the production and maintenance of their bodies within a given field of action; as for boxers, Wacquant describes their bodies as "at once the instrument and the object of their daily work, the medium, and the outcome of their occupational exertion" (Wacquant 1995, 66). Constituting the particular shape and form of bodies and bodily knowledge (not simply knowledge of the body), bodily capital may include the subtle accretions of skill, sensibility, coordinated gestures and movements, and styles of comportment. Ethnographies of the assembly line show similar acquisitions of bodily capital; for example, sensitivity to the quirks of particular car models and gestural refinements that preserve physical energy (Durand and Hatzfeld 2003; Wolkowitz 2006, 63–64). The analytic framework used by Bourdieu and Wacquant dissolves the mind-body dichotomy but maintains the distinction between human and nonhuman. My analysis proposes an intimate embodied connection between laborer and factory.

As I mentioned, Daewoo autoworkers considered the factory their chŏngdŭn ilt'ŏ. The idiom refers to their profound affective attachment to the factory. By "affect," I do not mean affection. Affect indicates one's bodily capacity to affect and be affected, indicating a kind of embodied connection between bodies (human and nonhuman) constituted through proximity and duration (Blackman 2008; Seigworth and Gregg 2010). According to relational and affective understandings of the body, bodies are not separate entities, distinguished from mind and passively shaped by exterior processes; bodies obtain their composition and particular capacities when conjoined with other bodies (human and nonhuman), with neither partner having primacy. Daewoo workers' bodies and workplace were conjoined, inseparable in their experience and in their specific actuality. Their bodies were assemblages, produced in their articulation with a range of material practices (or labors) on the assembly line and with the workplace (which includes the locker rooms, the tools, the machines, and the fellow workers) (Latour 2004).

Chŏngdŭn ilt'ŏ as Occupation

The phrase *chŏngdŭn ilt'ŏ* does not have an exact English correlate, but it may roughly be translated as the place of work or labor where an affective or bodily attachment is formed. The expression *chŏngdŭn ilt'ŏ* is made up of the compound noun *ilt'ŏ*, which combines *il*, meaning work or labor, with *t'ŏ*, meaning place or ground; the verb *dŭlta*, meaning to come or get into; and *chŏng*. The key term in the expression is *chŏng*; in terms of definition, an exact English equivalent is unavailable. It is typically translated as a term of emotion referring to affection and attachment (Kim 1981). In grammatical terms, the expression *chŏngdŭn ilt'ŏ* is a passive construction, which is significant. *Chŏngdŭn* is the past tense contraction of the expression *chŏng i tŭlta*, meaning *chŏng* is entering. In this form, the subject of the verb "*tŭlta*" (enter) is *chŏng*. "In other words," Kim writes, "*chŏng* occurs without any individual's active action or intention. This in turn implies its passive, gradual, and unconscious development on the part of [individuals] involved in *chŏng* relationships" (1981, 142). Its development may be understood as an effect of what Taussig calls the "sensateness of human interrelatedness": not "merely sensory impressions of light and sound and so forth, but also sensory impressions of social relations in all their moody ambiguity" (Taussig 1987, 463). *Chŏng* is embodied knowledge, or sense, of a social relationship sedimented through repeated and regular physical encounter, which may not occasion intention.

Although *chŏng* is most commonly used to describe interpersonal relationships, it may also express a relationship to an object or place. Most representative of a *chŏng*/place relationship is one's hometown or the place where one grew up. Just like many other Koreans, workers also often described their hometowns (*kohyang*) in terms of *chŏng*. In their discussions, there was a sense of the hometowns as being a part of them, not only in memory, but also in their bodies. Their hometowns formed their appetites, the shapes of their bodies, their gaits, their dictions, and their first intimate relationships.

To lay claim to the factory as *chŏngdŭn ilt'ŏ* is to claim that it is as formative as their hometowns, the places of their birth and original integration into an intimate social world. In an interview with two laborers, one of the men explained this understanding of *chŏngdŭn ilt'ŏ*:

> So I worked here for almost ten years, since my twenties, and raised my family, and now . . . we say *chŏng* is entering. How long did I live here, how long did I . . . to put it another way, I buried my youth here. Hometown, like the way we think of hometown—this was my first workplace, which is important. It was my first job, and the workplace that I went to for a long time. There is *chŏng* for the machines, for my co-workers.

In his statement, the sense of duration was critical to his understanding of *chŏngdŭn ilt'ŏ*. He was in his thirties; he had spent nearly ten years at the factory. As he says, it was the place where he buried his youth, where he became a man, a husband, and a father. Moreover, like his hometown, where he began his life, this factory was his first workplace, the start of his laboring life. In other interviews and conversations, workers made similar statements regarding the length of their laboring years at the factory. Making clear to impress the number of years upon the interviewer, many punctuated their narratives with statements such as "I gave my youth to the factory" or "I gave my life to the factory." Rather than merely melodramatic statements of personal sacrifice to the company, those comments indicated the depth of their attachment as the product of sustained occupation.

A provocative element in the above statement is the worker's *chŏng* relationship with the machines. Later in the interview, he remarked, "When we say our *chŏngdŭn ilt'ŏ*, for a long time we gave, put our bodies into our labor, our *chŏng*, into the machines, the products [*chaepum*; mostly cars], the people around us." There is an equation of his body with *chŏng* and of physical labor as a process that can yield *chŏng*. Labor is understood as a form of exchange, but rather than the formal, calculated exchange of abstract labor power for a wage, it is an exchange of *chŏng* with what must be considered an intimate and animate workplace of machines, cars on the assembly line and fellow workers.

Chŏng is not only given but also received. The reciprocation of *chŏng* is evident in the workers' descriptions of the labor process. They described it as "riding the line" (*t'ada*). The imagery suggests less an experience of their becoming an appendage to the machine and assembly line than an attunement. Rather than passive submission or constant wrestling with the pace and rigor of an alien force, it intimates an active entrainment with the line's movements. The notion of entrainment indicates a process of sensitization and synchronization. Ann Game, in her personal account of training her disabled horse to ride again, describes how the process entailed both her and her horse's becoming mutually receptive, or bodily in tune, with each other's rhythms (Game 2001). As a critique of the artificial separation of humans and nonhumans, Game demonstrates that what is important in learning a movement, a bodily skill, is a process of "inhabitation" embodying the cadence and flow of rhythms that connect human and nonhuman (2001, 8; cf. Blackman 2008, 9). "Riding the line" may be understood as a process of "occupation," one that emphasizes embodied connection, as well as interpenetration, rather than separation.

While learning is commonly considered a disembodied practice of knowledge acquisition, learning to ride the line entailed bodily incorporation and entrainment. Workers described the process with the verb *ikhida* and the idiom *mome baeda*. *Ikhida* means to accustom oneself or to get used to; it conveys a strong sense of bodily assimilation. The idiom *mome baeda* means to become habituated to, to become naturalized in bodies; it may be used to refer to particular mannerisms and dispositions. The verb *baeda* is also used to describe how things are permeated by or saturated with dyes, smoke, or other soluble materials. Applied to bodies, it also refers to immersion in immaterial but tangible sensations such as sound and scent. As employed by workers, the idiom equated experience on the line with a kind of bodily absorption rather than the product of mental apprehension. The feel of their tools, the movement of their backs and arms, the flow of automobile parts, over time, were felt rather than thought. The tasks and pace of the assembly line permeated their bodies directly.

Learning to ride entailed opening their bodies to the rhythms and sensations of the line. Succinctly and poetically, the other young worker, who had worked at the factory for fourteen years, elaborated upon the experience as leaving behind a scent and a rhythm:

> While you are working, the feeling of others around you . . . those people leave a scent. . . . The environment (*hwangyŏng*) has a flow, a rhythm . . . with the people, whatever the relationship, the labor itself.

The metaphors of scent and rhythm do not describe discrete phenomena that may be apprehended at a distance by reason or vision; rather, they refer to a kind of bodily immersion into a shared sensual world. The exchange of *chŏng* is significantly a felt connection that is absorbed and passed among people, things, and places. Workers' daily experiences in the factory, their embodied labor, transformed the factory and themselves into *chŏngdŭn ilt'ŏ*. The laborers did not simply work at the factory; they were, in fact, suffused by it, constituting the factory, by and through their bodies, as *occupation*. They, too, left a scent; they, too, were part of the *chŏngdŭn ilt'ŏ*.

The idiom *chŏngdŭn ilt'ŏ*, therefore, refers to their profound affective/bodily attachment to the factory. Daewoo workers' bodies and workplace were conjoined, inseparable in their experience and in their specific actuality. Their bodies were assemblages, produced in their articulation with a range of material practices (or labors) on the assembly line and with the workplace (Latour 2004). This articulation or connection may be understood as a kind of bodily attunement to the rhythms and rigors of work, from the physical exertion required of the line to the tempo of day-to-day working life. Being laid off, therefore, brought on a forceful, involuntary dis-articulation, or in their words, being "severed."

Disassembled Bodies

After being laid off, Daewoo assembly line workers complained of pain and a range of physical dysfunctions. They sought the counsel of doctors, but many reported that the diagnoses and treatments alleviated symptoms only partially. While their suffering may be attributed in part to the injuries sustained in clashes with riot police, as with most kinds of chronic pain their aches and maladies had little clinical certainty; according to conventional biomedical perspectives on the body, they were unspecified. Listening to their descriptions of specific symptoms and their narratives about laboring on the line, the cause of their suffering, however, became clear: It originated from being severed from *chŏngdŭn ilt'ŏ*. They were disjoined from a vital part of themselves and from the very processes by which their healthy bodies were assembled. "Severing" was not merely idiomatic phrasing but also embodied metaphor, not merely the linking of thought and image but also the disclosing of the mutual grounding of meaning, body, and lifeworld (Kirmayer 1992). It was not merely a manner of speaking.

One worker, smallish in stature and in his mid-thirties, for example, surmised that his chronic back and hip pain were the result of an injury incurred while on the line, but his narrative revealed a perplexing twist. He recounted,

> *Since* I don't have any desire [*ŭiyok*—will, motivation, purpose], my body's form has changed, become crooked. My back hurts, my body aches here and there. I go to a traditional Korean doctor, and the source of my pains [he said] is the work that I once did. My job was putting on car doors. I placed the doors and hammered them in. I crawled into the car, the upper half of my body inside and the lower half hanging outside. They X-rayed by body, and the origin of my problem is there, from the work. My health, it's not good, normal. You look at it this way; it's like being hurt on the job. *Now* I don't have any desire, and my condition, I don't know if I can work [anymore]. (emphasis added)

The key words are *since* and *now*, which mark the surfacing of pain *after* being laid off. Thus, what is salient in this narrative is not that he traced his current bodily condition to his past labors, accommodating his doctor's normative assessment of the bodily trauma of repetitive factory labor, but that his pain did not manifest until he was severed, until he was detached from the assembly line and deprived of his labor. While his back and hip may have been deformed during work, it was not experienced as pain until he was no longer able to labor.

Perhaps more provocatively, the loss of his labor affected his desire, his motivation, and the loss of desire was associated with the painful deformation of his body. While his affective state could be attributed to depression and other common psychological pathologies related to loss, I suggest another perspective. As proposed by recent theorizing of affect, desire is not autonomous, originating within an isolated individual, but is rather produced in connection with other bodies in an assemblage (Clough 2007). His desire emerged with his bodily articulation with the machines and cars. His desire expressed his immanent bodily capacity: to labor, to affect the cars on the assembly line (hammering in the doors) and in return to be affected by the labor process (his lower half hanging out of the chassis) shaping his posture and comportment (Latour 2004). Disarticulated from the line, his body came to be experienced as misshapen, and his lost bodily capacity felt as the loss of desire. When he stated that he doesn't know if he can work, he questioned not only his physical body but also his very desire to labor—that which had made him a Daewoo autoworker.

Other symptoms of workers' afflictions disclosed the bodily consequence of being severed from the rhythms and tempos of factory work. Two of the more common ailments were stomach and intestinal pain and bouts of vertigo. Both were powerful embodied metaphors for their sense of abrupt dislocation. For example, one worker reported, "Since I was laid off, when I get up after sitting for a while, my head flashes, as if struck by the sun. My head spins." Another stated, matter-of-factly, "I feel vertigo; I am dizzy." These symptoms were not merely expressions of a mental state but rather revealed the interdependence of mind, body, and space, capturing the felt experience of being severed from *chŏngdŭn ilt'ŏ* (Jackson 1996, 9). They did not think their dislocation but actually felt it, as if spinning, untethered from the factory.[7]

Gastrointestinal problems, similarly, indexed the felt disorientation of unemployment. During a lull at the union office after another unsatisfying lunch of instant noodles supplied by the union, I queried a small gathering of men about their physical conditions. One of the workers remarked, "Among those who participate in the Struggle, there probably isn't one person that doesn't have stomach problems." Another man, one of a small minority who had a history of union participation, speculated during an interview that only a few could claim health. Many did complain of searing sensations in their bellies, dull aches in their sides, troubling loss of appetite combined with weight gain. The diagnoses were readily apparent. They contrasted their current state as unemployed men with the stable rhythms afforded by factory labor, the recurring physical exertions on the line and resulting hunger and fatigue complemented by regular breaks and meals. Another man explained, "When I was going to work, I ate three square meals, and when I worked overtime, I ate another at the factory cafeteria, went home and ate one more. But now, I don't eat lunch or miss other meals. Living this way gives you stomach problems." The depletion and replenishment of their bodily energies had followed an expectant rhythm. Now severed, separated from physical work, their bodies felt confused, lacking appetite or desire.

In fact, their bodies lost their familiarity, taking on weight and losing particular faculties and facilities. In more lighthearted contexts, many joked about their expanding waistlines, commenting, as they rubbed their stomachs, "That's an unemployed man's gut." It was an indication of their lack of fitness for riding the line. In more serious moments, some of the men confided that they were plagued by anxious dreams in which they no longer "fit" into the factory. An older worker in his late forties described it as being unable to put on his work clothes. In his dream, he was in his locker room, preparing for his shift. No matter how he struggled to put on his uniform, the one he had worn for years, the one still stained with his sweat, it didn't fit. He was no longer able to embody his working self, fit into his working body. In casual conversations around the union offices, I often heard men question whether they could physically do their labor. They worried that their tools wouldn't fit their hands, that they weren't able to manipulate the tools like they once did, and that they could no longer endure the long hours and pace of the assembly line. They wondered if they could still ride the line.

Although many workers agreed with their doctors' diagnoses of having been hurt on the job, the emergence of their symptoms after being severed suggest a different interpretation. It was not the actual labors that caused them pain. As many of the workers stated in interviews and conversations, while their bodies may have been sore and fatigued from riding the line, they were nevertheless "happy." They had not experienced these kinds of pain. Their labors assembled their bodies. From their articulation with the line, their felt attachment with the machines, coworkers, and cars, emerged their bodily capacity to act, engage, and connect to their *chŏngdŭn ilt'ŏ*, in other words to feel alive, vital, healthy (Clough 2007, 2).

Crippled Bodies

Byŏngshin is a Korean term for cripple. It is derived from the two Sino-Korean characters for "sick" and "body." It is imbued with a sense of shame and social disgrace and is commonly used as a curse (Choi 2001, 435–436). In vernacular usage it has come to refer to people marked by disability and dysfunction. The laid-off men used *byŏngshin* to refer to themselves. For example, in the following, one of the oldest of the laid-off workers, who had spent his entire working life at this one factory, commented on the degradation that befalls the unemployed:

> The six-month unemployment compensation, that system makes a man into a *byŏngshin*. Why? Nowadays, wherever you go, no one will give one million *wŏn* for a month of work [approximately one thousand dollars at the time]. Then, rather than going somewhere else to get a job for seven, eight hundred thousand *wŏn*, it is better to just not work and receive unemployment. But after six months of not working, of getting used to that kind of life, you become a *byŏngshin*.

On the surface, this is a gruff commentary about the moral hazard of the social entitlement system. We had numerous exchanges over the years about how Korea had changed, usually centering on the failures of the government and the lackadaisical attitudes of the young. In this specific context, with the widespread experience of chronic pain among both the young and old, it spoke to the autoworkers' physical deterioration, which related to their being severed from *chŏngdŭn ilt'ŏ*, of having been left to a state of despair and dis-repair. I recalled the comment made by the young worker who experienced debilitating back and hip pain and a disturbing loss of desire. That man and many others had become, in the eyes of the older worker, *byŏngshin*.

While *byŏngshin* may not function as a common folk scheme or "master illness" describing the relations among individual and social bodies, it constituted an inchoate and emerging category indexing their social and moral status (Scheper-Hughes 1992). Elaborating upon the concept of "nervos," Scheper-Hughes wrote, "Rather than a torrent of indiscriminate sensations and symptoms, nervos is a somewhat inchoate, oblique, but nonetheless critical reflection by the poor on their bodies and on the work that has sapped their force and their vitality, leaving them dizzy, unbalanced, and, as it were, without a 'leg to stand'" (1992, 175). Likewise *byŏngshin* condensed in one symbol the experiences of their sickened bodies and their morally degraded state. *Byŏngshin* was a social illness, and it commented upon how unemployment had ruined their bodies and consequently their social-moral standing. When they called themselves "cripple," they always emphasized that they were hardworking men but had been made into *byŏngshin*. They were not born sick or felled by accident but were made useless and disposable by a social-political system that no longer valued industrial bodies.

The workers were highly cognizant of the (former) value of their bodies. At one of the daily noon meetings, "container demonstrations" at which the men congregated at the foot of the freight boxes barricading the factory grounds, for example, one of the union leaders reminded the gathering men, "you have to be healthy to work." From the head of the forming ranks, he held the microphone and pointed at several of the men to grab chairs for the workers whose backs and hips prevented them from sitting comfortably on the ground. They were but a handful of the many who complained of chronic pain. Their bodies were commonly public topics at demonstrations. I often heard union leaders proclaim, "Laborers [*nodongja*] have nothing but their bodies." In other instances, apart from the rallies and protests, I heard rank-and-file men often repeat that claim, also adding, "Our bodies are our fortune, our wealth [*chaesan*]."

Seeking clarification and elaboration, I inquired about the significance of those slogans with a department union leader. We sat on blue mats in a side room at the union offices on a slow uneventful day. His right leg, encased in a brace, was splayed out; the ligaments of his knee were torn by the sharpened edge of a riot police shield during a confrontation. I pointed to his knee, but he deflected my quiet query. He appeared to have more urgency for my initial question. He answered,

> You have watched us all the way through, right? "Laborers have nothing but their bodies." This is . . . as I said before . . . we don't have college degrees, we don't have high-level technical skills. In Korea, education level . . . we graduated from high school and learned our skills at the factory. That is our level, and at that level there is no "higher" or "lower." With that skill we eat and live. Also, we take care of our families. With our bodies, we labor and earn wages, to feed our families, live . . . really . . . to live; this is what it means to have nothing but our bodies.

In his statement, there is a tension between his understandings of industrial bodies: To say that they have nothing but their bodies is to acknowledge their low status in a society that increasingly valorizes intellectual and technical knowhow, signified by education and credentials, but, to say that they have nothing but their bodies is also to claim the worth of their bodies. Value resides in their productive capacities, bodily skill, and knowledge forged through labor. With their bodies they assembled cars and garnered wages, and with their bodies they fed and supported their families.

Workers understood, as only as their ailing bodies could communicate, "what [they] sold at the point of production is a pair of hands, a back, a set of muscles" (Donaldson 1991, 17). Their bodies were their wealth, the corporeal investments that produced their livelihood and social standing. As one of the union leaders stated, you have to be healthy to labor, but, the men's experience of being severed from *chŏngdŭn ilt'ŏ* also demonstrated that you have to labor in order to be healthy, to be "whole" in the figurative and actual sense. Now laid off, they had become *byŏngshin*. Dispossessed of the vital means to reproduce (assemble) their industrial bodies, they were, in fact, crippled. To be severed was not simply a turn of phrase but indexed actual and violent dislocation from the factory and from a part of themselves.

"Cripple" is a powerful social stigma. It is a marker of perceived social uselessness and dependency. In the 1980s and early 1990s, Korea's economic might and progress was symbolized by the giant smokestacks of heavy industry and its regimented industrial army, an apt metaphor for a labor force under authoritarian regimes. The Asian financial crisis spectacularly dramatized the hegemony of finance capital, announcing the ascendance of the information economy and the attendant speculative technologies and practices. Short-term commitments, short-term profits, and unprecedented job insecurity have replaced lifetime employment under highly disciplinary systems of Fordist production operating within a nationalist obsession with industrial development. Today, over 50 percent of the Korean workforce is engaged in nonstandard, irregular employment, and temporary work in the service industry is the fastest-growing economic sector. In this context, industrial workers are not simply unemployed; they are made redundant. Unemployment implies a temporary condition of serving in the industrial reserve army, to be potentially called back into service; to be redundant is to be disposable, unnecessary, wholly unproductive in the new economy (Bauman 2004, 12).

Conclusion

The purpose of this article is not to look back nostalgically at the Fordist factory but to think critically about the contemporary phase of capitalism in its neoliberal guise. Ideologically buttressing neoliberalism is the promise of "emancipation"—the setting free of individual initiative and talent, the entrepreneurial spirit, and the laboring body from the "iron cage" of industrial capitalism. Industrial labor, however, is deeply associated with mindless tedium, monotonous routine, and bodily degradation—a source of profound alienation and physical suffering. The Daewoo autoworkers would not completely disagree with this perspective. They, too, complained of the menial nature of automated manual labor; they also recognized that this kind of work was perceived as low-status and belittling. But recall the ambivalence of the wounded union leader who stated that factory workers did not have education, all they had were their bodies. And as their bodies attest, while factory labor may, on the one hand, degrade the worker, on the other, it may also enable their *occupation*.

Chŏngdŭn ilt'ŏ, I argue, was *occupation*. Their descriptions of their labors on the assembly line revealed that the factory was a sensual environment suffused with deep affects and meanings. There were distinct scents and rhythms—intimate compositions and movements of human and nonhuman bodies. These did not set the context, the spatial background of their labors. Through their prolonged daily labor, the men gave and received *chŏng*, becoming over time a part of them, constituting themselves as part of *chŏngdŭn ilt'ŏ*. Immersed in and forming a part of *chŏngdŭn ilt'ŏ*, they were formed as Daewoo bodies. In this sense, the factory was their *occupation*.

The Daewoo Struggle marked the last gasp of the developmental state regime of industrial capitalism. Neoliberalism did not free them from the factory but severed a part of themselves. Abandoned from the postindustrial economy, which values "immaterial" productivity (technological knowledge and affective labor), they were the relics of Korea's industrial past, cast as the new primitives of contemporary Korea. If there is any kind of freedom under a capitalist system of accumulation, it is to be free in that ironic sense described by Marx: compelled to freely sell one's labor power. Under neoliberalism, laid-off autoworkers were free to sell their labor in a market that devalues their industrial bodies. Workers' bodily pain and their understanding of themselves as *byŏngshin* were poignant testaments to their devaluation. Their crippled bodies had become, to borrow from Zygmunt Bauman, "industrial waste" (Bauman 2004).

The men fought to return to their *chŏngdŭn ilt'ŏ*. They were not militant unionists. In fact, an overwhelming majority adamantly denied any identification with the union, the union leaders, or the labor movement. They said that they were simply hardworking men hoping to return to their factories. What they had lost was not simply a means for their livelihood. It meant and felt much more. We tend to conceive of flexible labor, that constantly lauded form of contemporary employment, in terms of abstract, economic terms—replaceable labor power. By doing so, we ignore how "flexibility" requires the dismantling of the "habits of permanent, round-the-clock, steady and regular work" (Bauman 1998, 112). Derided as impediments of economic progress, these "habits" should not be dismissed as mere meaningless and mindless routines. They are deeply embodied and meaningful practices, constituting and constitutive of workers' *occupations*. As many of the contributors to this volume demonstrate, these "habits" or social-cultural structures (for instance, of personal relationships, the organization of time, national identity, ethical aspirations) are "sticky" and not easily undone. The unemployed may adjust and remake structures of meaning and belonging, but it is remarkable that the adjustments approximate those of what is conventionally thought of as employment. In fact, the experiences of the unemployed blur the line between employment and unemployment in contemporary global ecumene.

THE RISE OF THE PRECARIAT?

Unemployment and Social Identity in
a French Outer City

John P. Murphy

In fall 2005, as I began conducting ethnographic field research in the public housing projects circling the medium-sized, centrally located French city of Limoges,
rioting erupted nearly 250 miles away on the outskirts of Paris. A small group
of teenagers returning home from an afternoon playing soccer had been spotted
loitering at a construction site. As a squad car approached, the teenagers fled.
Although some were apprehended, three managed to evade the police by climb-
ing into a nearby electrical substation. This game of cat and mouse soon turned
deadly when these three youths were electrocuted. Two died instantly; the third,
badly burned, managed nonetheless to make his way back home, where word
of the electrocutions spread quickly. That night, young people descended into
the streets of their neighborhood, smashing bus stop shelters, torching cars, and
launching rocks and other readily available projectiles at the police called in to
quell the disturbance. Despite riot squad reinforcements, the unrest escalated in
the following nights, and by the time a return to "normalcy" was declared three
full weeks later, violence had engulfed over 270 French cities, including Limoges.[1]
The unprecedented scale of the conflict prompted President Jacques Chirac to
invoke a state of emergency—the first time a French official had done so since
the Algerian War more than fifty years earlier. Total monetary damages reached
well into the hundreds of millions of euros.

A great deal of ink has since been spilt trying to discern the causes of what
are now commonly known as the 2005 Riots. To be sure, the tragedy outside
of Paris ignited the fuse, but just what then enabled the violence to spread like
wildfire across France has remained a topic of heated debate. Pointing to the

immigrant origins (Mali, Tunisia, and Turkey) of the three electrocution victims, some scholars (e.g., Lagrange 2010; Mdembe 2009a; Mdembe 2009b) have broken with French republican tradition by arguing that the 2005 Riots, and life more generally in France's multiethnic outer cities, are best understood in cultural and racial terms.[2] Other researchers (e.g., Cesari 2005; Lapeyronnie 2009; Roy 2005) have insisted that a socioeconomic reading is more productive. Although they are careful not to discount the very real racial discrimination many outer-city youth endure, they point to the disintegration of the working class and the influx of neoliberal ideas and practices as key transformative processes and suggest that society is now best described as being sharply divided between those who are included (*les inclus*) and those who are excluded (*les exclus*). That outer-city youth in general—and not just those from immigrant backgrounds—face unemployment rates sometimes more than quadruple the national average provides evidence, these authors maintain, in support of their socioeconomic interpretation.

In a recent book, economist Guy Standing (2011) takes this latter analysis a step further. Linking the 2005 Riots to other recent examples of unrest, including the "Den Plirono" protests in Greece, the Arab Spring in much of the Middle East, and the international Occupy Movement, he argues that increasing employment insecurity in the global market system of the twenty-first century is yielding a troubling new category of people—a group he dubs the "precariat." This class-in-the-making, Standing suggests, is dangerous because it is, as yet, devoid of a collective consciousness and therefore of a voice. Both angry and anxious, its members, he insists, are liable to turn from "strugglers into deviants and loose cannons prone to listen to populist politicians and demagogues" (2011, 132). The only way to rein in the precariat, the only way to prevent it from becoming a "monster," Standing maintains, is to draw it into the political process by helping it to become a class for itself.

My aim in this essay is to interrogate this idea of a precariat, which, in France at least, has attracted a fair amount of popular and academic interest (e.g., Autain 2012; Castel 2011; Chabanet, Dufour, and Royall 2012). The story I tell here begins with the 2005 Riots, but it does not end there. Drawing on more than a year of ethnographic field research investigating the experiences and perspectives of a cohort of outer-city youth seeking work, I explore what anthropologists, sociologists, and other social science researchers commonly call social identity—meaning how people situate or place themselves in relation to perceived social groups. A few months after the 2005 Riots, in the spring of 2006, while I was still in the field, another social drama unfolded in France around a proposed employment bill, the Contrat Première Embauche (CPE). This "First Hire Contract," which promised to create more jobs for young people by slackening France's rigid labor laws, incited a great deal of anger among many French people, both the young and the not-so-young. *Précarité* (precarity), they insisted, would only worsen if the proposal became law. Curiously, most young people in the outer city of Limoges did not share this sentiment. In fact, many deliberately distanced themselves from the massive street protests the CPE generated in Limoges and other French cities. Why was this the case? Surely they, more than most people in France, had a stake in staving off economic insecurity. Answering this question, I argue, raises other questions about the rise of the so-called precariat. In what ways might this term obscure or conceal old and new structural inequalities? Moreover, how might it disqualify or invalidate alternative "socialities" and the creative adaptive strategies forged by those who face employment insecurity most acutely? These are pressing issues whose significance extends far beyond France's borders. Yet France offers a particularly compelling case study for examining them, precisely because in France the rhetoric of *solidarité* (solidarity) is especially well entrenched. Against this backdrop, claims made about precarity, the precariat, or an unraveling of the social fabric more generally in the face of spreading neoliberal ideologies and practices are apt to be thrust in bold relief.

Liberté, Égalité . . . Solidarité: Solidarity in French History and Thought

French conceptions of solidarity can be traced back to the revolutionary principle of fraternity (Borgetto 1993), which is itself rooted in Enlightenment thinking about poverty. In pre-Revolution France, poverty was customarily associated with an immutable station in life, and poor relief was considered the province of the Crown or the Church. But during the eighteenth century, Enlightenment thinkers began to link the lot of the poor to social and economic change. Economic progress, according to this new understanding, not only created wealth; it also produced poverty. Rather than shun its poor, society therefore had a "social obligation" toward its least fortunate members. To pay this debt, Revolution-era lawmakers proposed state-directed *bienfaisance*, including wage supplements and old-age pensions (Forrest 1981). Society as a whole, they maintained, would emerge stronger and more cohesive as a result of this assistance. A more fatalistic view of poverty resurfaced in France during the decades after the Revolution. However, in 1848, amid another political upheaval in Paris, insurrectionary workers rallied around the old revolutionary principles again, demanding not only the "right to assistance" but also the "right to work" (Sewell 1980). Ultimately unsuccessful, this uprising nonetheless firmly established what came to be known in nineteenth-century France as the "social question"—that is, how best to manage the social and economic problems stemming from industrialization and urbanization—at the center of French political life (Donzelot 1994 [1984]).

In the last decades of the nineteenth century, struggle over the social question gave rise to a prominent new social philosophy: solidarism (Hayward 1961). This theory took as its point of departure the newly developed idea that social life in advanced economies resembled biological life insofar as both involved diversity. Just as the different cells and organs of the body worked in tandem to ensure biological activity, difference in skill or occupation was, according to solidarists, essential to proper social function. Such a "division of labor," they maintained, produced "organic solidarity," by which individuals forged social ties to one another and to the collectivity of which they were a part (Durkheim 1984 [1893]). In his brief essay "Solidarité," Prime Minister Léon Bourgeois (1902 [1896]) proposed a new social contract based on this understanding of what binds members of industrial society together. Through social legislation, including free public education, social assistance for the poor, and support for voluntary mutualism, the state would lessen or ease—but by no means eradicate—inequalities arising from what Bourgeois and many of his contemporaries considered vital social difference.

Solidarity has remained an influential idea in France (Lamont 2000, 233–239), although as some scholars (e.g., Béland 2009) have noted, its meaning has shifted along with changing economic conditions. Whereas a century earlier, as France embarked upon a path of industrialization, solidarity referred to ideal social relations founded on "natural" or "essential" differences, in today's postindustrial economy it tends to be endowed with more humanistic qualities, most notably the ideas of "citizenship" and "participation." In other words, the kind of difference driving contemporary conceptions of solidarity has by and large been reduced to one fundamental sort: inclusion in the polity versus exclusion from it. And this distinction appears inextricably linked to employment and its absence.

If, as Serge Paugam (2000) has shown, the concept of social exclusion emerged in France in the late 1950s, when researchers and human rights groups began to attend to the "marginal" populations living in persistent poverty,[3] by the 1990s the notion had become nearly synonymous with unemployment, especially the sort of crushing difficulties youth were encountering in the job market in France's troubled outer cities (Wacquant 2008). It is closely linked to another term—*précarité*.[4] Although generally translated as "precariousness" but also sometimes "precarity" (Paugam and Russell 2000), this concept, as Chantal Nicole-Drancourt (1992, 57) has noted, can and does mean many things in France, from a subcategory of nonstandard employment (short-term contracts, temp work, internships, apprenticeships, and so on) to all forms of nonstandard employment to nonstandard employment and unemployment to the overall employment system. In the end, *précarité* for the French is not just about employment, underemployment, or unemployment. As the expression "*précarisation de la société*" (precarization of society), which has been in widespread circulation in the media and among politicians since the 1990s, suggests, it is perceived as a threat to *society in its entirety*. It embodies popular fears about "jungle" capitalism and "unchecked" globalization, fears I discovered to be on the tips of many tongues as I settled into Limoges to begin my fieldwork.

An Ethnography of Youth Unemployment

Best known for its fine china, Limoges may seem like an unlikely place to conduct a study on young people, outer cities, or unemployment. The Limousin, of which Limoges is the regional capital, is one of the most rural parts of France. It is also one of the least populated, with a disproportionate number of seniors. Furthermore, Limoges has never been the site of heavy industrial manufacture and, unlike larger urban centers, is not especially known for having troubled outer cities. Limoges was, however, a strategic choice. Despite the relative absence of heavy industry, this medium-sized city has a significant and well-documented working-class history grounded in a deeply rooted left-wing tradition that dates back to at least the Revolution and that has resulted in a robust labor movement (Corbin 1975; Merriman 1985).[5] This leftist tradition spurred the construction of a multitude of worker housing developments beginning as early as the first decade of the twentieth century (Limoges Municipal Council 2007). Today, a number of large-scale housing projects (some with close to two thousand units and one boasting nearly four thousand units) circle the city.[6] And because Limoges was never the site of heavy industrial manufacture, the effects of deindustrialization have been less significant there: A sizeable working population remains, with little out-migration of young people from what might be called "blue-collar"[7] backgrounds (Lavaud and Simonneau 2010). Limoges thus offered what I was looking for—a significant stock of public housing inhabited by a largely youthful population whose parents (or grandparents) had likely had at least some familiarity with the organized labor movement. That the city is relatively small was also advantageous: It did not take me long to map out my interlocutors' daily routines, which facilitated frequent encounters with them, and thanks to word of mouth, my presence and motives were quickly noted, which helped as I met new people.

Even if in terms of retaining jobs Limoges has done better than many French cities in recent decades, it has not been immune to unemployment or its consequences. Unemployment in the Limousin region has tended to follow national trends, with peaks ranging from just over 7 percent to just under 9 percent in the late 1980s, the late 1990s, and the mid-2000s (the period of my research). After dropping back to 6 percent in 2008, unemployment in the Limousin is on the rise again, surpassing 9 percent in 2012, compared to about 10 percent nationally (INSEE 2013). Figures relating to youth unemployment are higher and in Limoges vary widely between the city center and the periphery. In 1999, 18.1 percent of youth aged sixteen to twenty-five living in the city center declared they were looking for work, compared to more than double that number (39.2 percent) in the outer city (Duplouy 2003, 20).

By themselves, unemployment statistics do not provide a full picture of youth joblessness at the turn of the twenty-first century in Limoges. It is also necessary to consider the terms of the work arrangements of those young people who are employed. Whereas in 1990, 42 percent of young people twenty-five and under living in Limoges's outer city who had gained employment were employed on a contingent basis, by 1999 this figure had jumped to 52.7 percent (Duplouy 2003, 21).[8] This upward evolution of contingent employment corresponds to a mushrooming of temp agencies across the city. The slogan in the photograph below—"Temp work is a career, you'll love working with us . . ."—suggests that these new temporary forms of employment may well be considered a new employment paradigm rather than merely a stepping-stone to more permanent work arrangements.

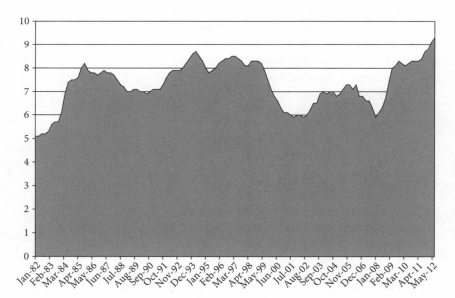

FIGURE 2.   Unemployment in the Limousin Region, 1982–2012. Chart created by author using data from INSEE (France's National Institute of Statistics and Economic Studies).

FIGURE 3. Temporary agency sign: "Temp work is a career, you'll love working with us . . ." Photo taken by the author.

Although my project focused on young people aged sixteen to twenty-four in the process of transitioning between school and the working world, my first interlocutors in Limoges were social workers and case managers, street educators (*éducateurs de rue*) and employment counselors, association leaders and program coordinators.[9] With the help of these social service providers, I identified entry points into three of the largest housing projects. These included a municipally funded "dry" bar (*bar sans alcool*) that also serves as a youth job information center, a "youth house" (*maison des jeunes*) that aids in the coordination of leisure activities for young people, and an after-school homework assistance center where I volunteered several days a week. I also became active in the local chapter of Jeunesse Ouvrière Chrétienne (JOC), an international faith-based organization for blue-collar youth. Through these associations and organizations, I was able to meet many local youth, and thanks to their social networks, I was eventually able to expand my base of informants to include young people who might not necessarily have frequented any of them.

In addition to ethnographic observation and informal discussion, I recorded life-history narratives. These taped, more formal interviews, carried out in two or three one-hour sessions over the course of several months, allowed me to probe the backgrounds and trajectories of thirty-three young people. Topics covered included family life and childhood, school, employment experiences, and plans for the future. The timing of these interviews was strategic. Because I undertook them during my last few months in Limoges, all of the respondents knew me well and thus tended to be more comfortable discussing personal information with me. Furthermore, I was able to ask them to reflect critically on the 2005 Riots and the CPE protests. What they had to say greatly enriched my analysis of the data I collected during the heat of those two conflicts.

France's urban peripheries tend to be ethnically diverse, including both immigrants and their descendants and "Franco-French" people. Limoges does not constitute an exception in this regard. Although never an important destination for immigrants, immigration patterns to Limoges have followed national trends. Drawn by the promise of economic opportunity (mostly in logging, mining, and, later, construction) successive waves of immigrants came first from neighboring European countries, then from North Africa, and more recently from Asia and Sub-Saharan Africa (Desbordes 2004; Marsac and Brousse 2005). According to 1999 census data, 5.3 percent of Limoges's population was foreign-born, compared to 7.4 percent on the national level (Boëldieu and Borrel 2000).[10] Within Limoges itself, most immigrants tend to live in the peripheral neighborhoods. In 1999, nearly 17 percent of the peripheral neighborhoods' residents were foreign-born, compared to only 3 percent in the city center (Duplouy 2003, 15). As for my interlocutors in Limoges's outer city, they included roughly as many young people with deep roots in France as children or grandchildren of immigrants. Unlike what might be the case in an American inner city, lines drawn in Limoges's outer-city housing projects did not center on race or ethnicity. Groups of friends, I found, frequently included individuals of diverse ethnic, racial, and national origin.

Space does not permit a detailed biographical account of the young people whose perspectives and experiences form the basis of my analysis. Below, I offer sketches of two individuals: Hanan and Jonathan.[11] To be sure, each story presents its own peculiarities. Yet, broadly speaking, they are representative of what other youths told me about themselves and their families, particularly the faith their parents placed in formal education and their own bitter realization that the credentials they earned in school offered little protection against unemployment.

I met Hanan at an outer-city homework assistance center, where she worked part-time and I contributed as a volunteer. Tall and slender with striking green eyes, Hanan was soft-spoken and reflective. Pursuing a degree in education at the University of Limoges, she had recently taken a course in sociology. Because of this, she expressed interest in my research. We often chatted about the progress of my work in between helping the junior high and high school students who visited the center; toward the end of my fieldwork period Hanan agreed to sit down with me for a taped, life-history interview.

Hanan's parents emigrated from Morocco. After marrying there, her father left his new bride behind to take advantage of the employment opportunities available in France. He first settled in eastern France, where he worked in the construction industry. This work was unstable, though, and during periods of inactivity, he returned to Morocco, where Hanan's oldest sister was born. Dissatisfied with his situation in eastern France, Hanan's father moved to a town, just south of Limoges, where a relative owned a butcher's shop. In 1975, following the closing of France's borders to new immigrants, his wife and daughter joined him, thanks to a law permitting the reunification of families. They settled in Limoges, where Hanan's father, along with many other immigrant men, found work in construction. Another daughter soon followed the first, and then in 1982 Hanan was born.

Hanan talked fondly about her childhood in her family's apartment, surrounded by her "attentive" parents and "protective" sisters. But she also recognized that she grew up in a sort of "cocoon." This revelation came to her when, at the age of fourteen, she took the public bus for the very first time in her life to attend high school in the city center. Kids from her neighborhood, she told me, usually did not go to that school; there was another high school, far closer to the housing project, but it had a bad reputation, at least according to her father. "He did everything in his power to make sure I went to the right high school," she explained. "For him, it was my ticket to university, and continuing my studies was extremely important. In his view, it was how I could get ahead, get a good job." Although a serious student, Hanan admitted that she did not want to attend that high school and described how out of place she felt in it, from the clothes she wore to the inflection of her voice, which, at first at least, invariably gave her away as being from the outer city. She told me, not without a touch of pride, that she had made a conscious effort to "lose that accent." Hanan ultimately earned her *baccalauréat* and headed off to university, but without a clear idea of what she wanted to study. She decided somewhat haphazardly on a two-year degree (Diplôme d'études universitaires générales, or DEUG) in Spanish, explaining that it brought her back toward "the south, to her roots." After a rocky first year, she ended up repeating the second year, ultimately unsuccessfully. Discouraged, she left school for a year to work part-time as an activities coordinator (*animatrice*) in a youth association located in her childhood neighborhood, where she still lived with her parents. Realizing that this was a dead-end job—the position was subsidized by the state and would likely vanish after the initial contract was concluded—and pressured by her father, she re-enrolled in university, this time with the objective to become a teacher. In hindsight, Hanan wishes that she had never pursued university study. "My parents didn't know anything about the school system. They pushed me to go as far as I could, but I would have been better off with a BTS [Brevet de technicien supérieur, an advanced vocational degree]." Confronted by several more years of school and then the all-important and in her words "very difficult" CAPES exam (the state-administered qualifying exam, required of all secondary school teachers), she was uncertain of her future.

Like Hanan, Jonathan worked at the homework assistance center, and it was in this context that I got to know him. "Full of energy" and "upbeat" are the best ways to describe his personality, which always seemed to me to be strangely at odds with his small, unassuming frame and pale countenance. Jonathan grew up in the same neighborhood as Hanan. The two knew each other as children but did not become friends until they worked together at the homework assistance center.

Jonathan is Franco-French, although his parents do not hail from Limoges. They were born and grew up in the surrounding Limousin hinterlands, where their parents (Jonathan's grandparents) worked in the agricultural sector. This lifestyle, Jonathan explained to me, was hard, not only because of the back-breaking nature of the work, but also due to its unreliability. The family's income depended a great deal on weather conditions: an overly dry or wet season could spell disaster for an already tight budget. After marrying in the early 1970s, Jonathan's parents made the move to Limoges in search of more stable, better-paying work. The first years were tough, Jonathan explained. Although in the countryside rumors of plentiful employment in "the City" circulated widely, by the time his parents arrived in Limoges the well of job opportunities seemed to be drying up. Jonathan's father ended up working odd jobs in construction, mostly in the housing projects, where he and his wife eventually settled. Meanwhile, Jonathan's mother worked as a housekeeper, mainly in the city center in the homes of "bourgeois" (his word) families. In the mid-1970s, Jonathan's father got a break: After working on the construction of Limoges's university hospital he was hired full-time in the new facility's maintenance department. Several years later, Jonathan's mother found full-time employment at City Hall, also in janitorial services. Both of Jonathan's parents still occupied these positions in 2005 and 2006. After a number of failed pregnancies, Jonathan was born in 1981; he is their only child.

Jonathan suspects that his status as an only child resulted in his parents focusing all of their hopes on him. And achieving these hopes, they made it clear to him, meant pursuing his studies as long as possible. "My parents have great respect for education. They wouldn't dare contradict a teacher," he recounted. Jonathan, by contrast, did not have the same depth of faith in the school system, as evidenced, for example, by his playful distortion of the French term for school guidance counselor (*conseiller d'orientation*): "They're all *disorientation* counselors, if your ask me!" Jonathan explained that after completing a vocational high school degree in electronics, he was ready to try his luck in the job market, but his mother would not have it. "She pushed really hard for me to continue. She even found a BTS program in Brive [a town to the south of Limoges] for me. She filled out all the paperwork and everything." To please his mother, Jonathan headed off to Brive, where he completed the two-year program and passed (the second time around) the final qualifying exam. Because the program included hands-on experience, Jonathan had in the meantime accrued enough hours to qualify for unemployment insurance. With this extra income, he returned to his parents' apartment, where, prodded yet again by his mother, he enrolled at the University of Limoges for a technical bachelor's degree in fiber optics. "I really wasn't interested in continuing school, but I had all this extra income. It was more than double what I'd get with a student stipend alone, so I figured, why not?" Aged twenty-five in 2005–2006, he still lived with his parents, despite having finished his bachelor's degree the previous year. He had since applied to (in his estimation) over one hundred positions but had yet to secure a stable job. His parents, he told me, struggled to understand.

Hanan's and Jonathan's reflections are strikingly similar, and this despite differences, notably race and gender, that researchers in France and elsewhere have long shown to play a significant role in determining employment outcomes. Tracking the effects of race on employment is complicated in France because the notion of race is widely deemed an illegitimate basis for human categorization; according to official French discourse, "race" describes divisions within the animal kingdom, not divisions among humans. This denunciation of the existence of human races can be traced to the universalist ideals of the French Revolution. However, it was not until after the atrocities of Nazi Germany and guilt over the complicity of France's Vichy regime in deporting Jews to concentration camps that the French government officially banned the collection and computerized storage of race-based data. Today, "color-blind" France collects no census or other data on the race or ethnicity of its citizens, and employers are forbidden from doing so as well. What data do exist suggest that racial discrimination during hiring is a widespread problem. In a number of well-publicized studies (Adida, Laitin, and Valfort 2010; Duguet et al. 2007), researchers responded to job ads in France with fictional applications bearing a single difference: the name of the candidate. In each study, candidates with "traditional" French names (for example, Nicolas) received far more callbacks than jobseekers whose names sounded "foreign," particularly those of North African origin.

Analyzing the significance of gender bias in hiring decisions is somewhat less problematic because the statistics on this question are more readily available. Until very recently, more young women than young men were out of work in

France. However, according to a new study commissioned by France's Center for Research on Qualifications (Barret, Ryk, and Volle 2014) this trend has reversed in the last several years, with on average 23 percent of young men now unemployed versus 20 percent of young women. The study's authors attribute this shift to an increase in educational attainment by young women, who now on the whole surpass their male counterparts in terms of the number and level of certificates and diplomas earned. Notwithstanding this development, the report concludes that in general women in France continue to earn less than men and are more likely to hold short-term and part-time work.

Of course, racial discrimination and gender discrimination in employment can overlap, but France's laws stipulating what kinds of statistics can and cannot be collected ensure that the combined effects are more difficult to discern. As we have seen, being of foreign ancestry appears to represent a major handicap in the job market, regardless of gender. Anecdotally, interlocutors in Limoges told me that young women of immigrant origin tended to fare better when seeking work than young men sharing the same roots. The reason, they suggested, was that potential employers in general perceive women as less "dangerous" or "aggressive."

Interlocutors in Limoges sometimes complained about racial and gender inequality. However, they never used these categories to present themselves as different from their neighborhood peers and thus deserving of special consideration in the job market. On the contrary, they denounced any and all forms of discrimination, including American-style affirmative action, which translates in French as *discrimination positive* (positive discrimination). They insisted that all job seekers should benefit from equal treatment, that physical differences such as race and gender should not matter. Two examples from my field notes, one concerning race and the other gender, help to illustrate this perspective.

In early spring 2006, I attended a round table on youth employment at City Hall. Organized by Jeunesse Ouvrière Chrétienne (JOC), it was meant to provide an opportunity for local youth (both members and nonmembers of JOC) and municipal officials to come together to discuss the results of a recent national survey on youth employment and employment practices. At the beginning of the evening, a narrative about a young Parisian named Mohamed was read aloud. Although of North-African descent, Mohamed, we learned, was born, raised, and educated in France, and he possessed French citizenship. He had earned a university diploma (*licence*), yet was still unable to find full-time, long-term work. To get by, Mohamed attempted to string together short-term contracts but complained that each time he entered a temp agency, he was asked to show his identity papers. Following the reading of Mohamed's story, Limoges's deputy mayor, an invited participant at the round table, expressed sympathy for the young man's plight but stated that she could not comprehend his objections to how he was treated in the temp agencies he visited. "It's only normal that candidates be asked to prove their eligibility to work in France," she argued. This assertion exasperated a number of young people in the audience. Véro, a young woman I knew from a JOC support group for unemployed youth, rose to her feet and vehemently countered the deputy mayor's claim, insisting that Mohamed was only asked to show his papers because he was not "white" (*blanc*). As someone of "Franco-French" origin (*d'origine franco-française*), she maintained, she had never been asked for identification when looking for work.

Following the round table, I joined a small group of young people I knew from the housing projects who had gathered in the parking lot outside of City Hall. As they smoked a quick cigarette before heading home, I asked them about the event, particularly the tension surrounding the deputy mayor's comment. Mouloud, whose parents had emigrated from Algeria, responded: "The thing is, the deputy mayor is right. Everyone should have to provide identification before being interviewed. The problem is that that's not how it works in real life. Racial discrimination is a serious concern." Mouloud went on to draw a connection with a recent proposal to establish "blind résumés" (résumés containing no information about a candidate's racial or ethnic identity). Following the 2005 Riots, some French politicians and others in France touted blind résumés as a solution to racial discrimination in the hiring process. "It's incredibly hypocritical!" Mouloud exclaimed. "What does that mean, a 'blind' résumé? I'll tell you what it means: It means you have to hide the fact that your parents or grandparents are immigrants just to get a job. What hypocrisy!" In the end, both the deputy mayor and Mouloud were committed to a color-blind ideal, where racial or ethnic difference should not matter in hiring decisions. It was not this ideal that frustrated Mouloud, but rather its uneven application in everyday life.

Among the youth I came to know in Limoges, gender bias tended to be viewed in a similar light to racial discrimination, as the following example suggests. During a December meeting of the JOC support group for unemployed youth, Véro reported that the previous day she had quit her new job. The group's members, who had closely followed Véro's job search during the previous months, were dismayed. Why on earth, they asked, would she give up a position she had worked so hard and for so long to obtain? Véro held a vocational certificate (Certificate d'Aptitude Professionelle, or CAP) in plumbing. Although jobs in this field were generally not as scarce as in some other areas, she still struggled to find work. During previous meetings of the support group, Véro hinted that this was because employers did not readily associate the plumbing trade with women's work. At this most recent meeting, she made an explicit accusation of gender discrimination: "I'm a trained plumber. I expected to put that training to use.

However, my macho boss, he had me cleaning out the foul-smelling office refrigerator all morning. Then he had the nerve to tell me to make coffee. I said no way!" Members of the group shared Véro's disgust, arguing that women were just as capable as men. One young woman referenced recent media coverage of the 2005 Riots: "According to all the journalists, it was a bunch of guys in the streets who were revolting, who were expressing their anger over the injustice they face, but I'll bet there were girls, too. How could the journalists be so sure? Everyone was wearing hoods. Who knows who were under those hoods?" Another young woman sympathized with Véro, explaining that she had been subjected to a similar experience at work. According to her, the only answer was to leave "backward" Limoges, even if she recognized that this would be hard to do with limited financial resources. "Go to Paris, go to Marseille, if you can," she recommended. "People are more educated in the big cities. They're not as sexist." For her, gender discrimination was not only unacceptable; it was also a relic of the past and a function of ignorance. Education appeared to be a solution.

In this sense, youth in Limoges's housing projects, both young men and young women, both those of immigrant ancestry and those who were "Franco-French," seemed to hold some measure of hope for the future. Racism and gender inequality, they told me, were not problems they encountered among their peers. Rather, these were social ills perpetuated by older generations, whose members either declined or did not have access to the same educational opportunities as they. These young people's frustration as they entered the job market stemmed from the brutal disjuncture they discovered between the universalist, egalitarian values proclaimed by France's public school system and the ugly reality of discrimination they encountered on the ground. To be sure, this disjuncture is nothing new, but the weight of its presence has undoubtedly been magnified in recent decades by the sharp contraction of the job market, which has in turn encouraged increasing numbers of young people to continue their studies. Considering race and gender is thus essential to evaluating claims made about the expansion of precarity and the rise of the so-called precariat, claims that inundated the airwaves and print media during the 2005 Riots and the CPE protests. As we shall see below, taking into account markers of social distinction historically associated with class position is just as critical, especially in this French context.

Riots, Protests, and the Perception of Dwindling Solidarity

That the 2005 Riots were symptomatic of a deep social malaise seemed obvious to many people in France. "This is a crisis," declared President of the Republic

Jacques Chirac when he addressed the nation, "a crisis of meaning, a crisis of values, a crisis of identity" (INA 2005). Even my interlocutors in Limoges's outer city, who tended in large part to identify with the rioters, or at least the plight of crushing unemployment they understood the rioters to face, unanimously condemned the violent approach taken, arguing that it wrongly disadvantaged already struggling people.[12] In particular, many young people told me they were baffled by all the torched cars in outer-city areas, recognizing that, given the inadequacy of public transportation in many peripheral neighborhoods, including Limoges's outer city, these vehicles most likely had been used by their owners to get to work or to seek employment.[13] "C'est chacun pour soi" (It's everyone for him- or herself), one young woman commented as we discussed what was happening in France's outer cities. Strikingly, I heard this same phrase—"C'est chacun pour soi"—repeated many times over the following spring, but in reference to the CPE protests.

The Contrat Première Embauche, announced by the administration of Dominique de Villepin in mid-January 2006 as part of a new "Law for Equal Opportunities" and retracted the following April in the face of massive protests, was both a continuation of past employment policy and a departure from it. It was a continuation insofar as it, like earlier initiatives, aimed at easing access to work for unemployed youth. It was a departure because the CPE was not a state-subsidized contract; unlike earlier programs, it did not promise the same measure of tax breaks or salary support to participating employers. Instead, in the hopes of spurring job growth, the CPE adjusted France's rigid labor law by stipulating a mandatory two-year "trial" period during which employers would have far greater leeway to dismiss new hires than under standard French practice. Seen by some as an attack on France's model of social protection, this last point proved highly contentious.

Opponents of the CPE vociferously contrasted what they saw as the CPE's most likely outcome—greater "social exclusion"—with the more desirable social arrangements grounded in "solidarity." News stories published at the time of the CPE conflict in Limoges's local press highlighted this contrast. Noting, for example, that many Limougeauds protesting the measure had nicknamed it "*contrat précarité exclusion,*" an article that appeared in one of the city's most widely read dailies bore the title "All generations stand up to the 'institutionalization of precarity.'" The following report, which focused on the first of the major anti-CPE demonstrations to take place in the city, stressed that high school and university students had not marched alone; there were also "hundreds of workers and union members . . . and hundreds of retirees, reaffirming their commitment to *intergenerational solidarity*" (Bourgnon 2006, emphasis added).[14] If this article insisted on the goodwill of older generations toward the younger one, other

FIGURE 4.   Anti-CPE protest by French youth. Photo taken by the author.

reports suggested that young people were equally concerned about their elders. Summarizing a demonstration organized by retirees toward the end of March to protest a different government initiative reforming the state pension system, an article titled "A Breath of Solidarity, Rue de la Préfecture" recounted, for example, how a procession of high school and university students had joined their voices to those of the protesting seniors. "This was," according to the author, "a moment of intergenerational convergence to challenge neoliberal policies" (Davoine 2006). Many other articles offered a similar interpretation of the anti-CPE movement, proliferating references to "convergence," "unity," "sharing," or "the will of the majority."

By highlighting "solidarity" in this way, this dominant discourse tended, however, to be reductionist, even essentializing. As the movement gained momentum, more precise language—high school students, university students—gave way to generalizations. Through liberal use of the catchall term *"jeunesse"* (youth), for example, the media suggested that the students who took to the streets against the CPE represented all French youth. One news headline published in Limoges trumpeted, "La Jeunesse replies: 'Resistance!'" (Catus 2006). Such homogenizing accounts proved troubling to many of my interlocutors in the outer city, who by and large drew lines between themselves and the student protestors. These lines, as we shall see, were based primarily on my interlocutors' understandings of who exactly is at risk of precarity. Its real victims, they maintained, could be identified by their familiarity with the crushing experience of what they called "*galère*."

Galère: Toward a Collective Consciousness?

Toward mid-March, when the anti-CPE movement was in full swing, I sat down with Thomas during his afternoon break in the atrium of the outer-city shopping center where he worked as a stock boy. A resident since birth of the surrounding neighborhood, composed mostly of low-income public housing, Thomas dropped out of school at the age of sixteen. For the next four years, he strung together odd jobs, mostly in construction, before finally landing a full-time position in his neighborhood's pharmacy. I met Thomas the previous fall through the social worker who had handled his case when he was looking for work. According to her, Thomas was a real "success story." Generally affable, on this sunny March afternoon he was contrariwise noticeably irritated. "I just don't get it," he complained, gesturing ambiguously toward the large glass entranceway of the shopping center, which looked out onto a road leading toward the city center. "Those students protesting," he pursued, "they don't work, they don't have any experience in the real world. So why are they so concerned about the CPE?" Thomas explained that earlier that morning, while running errands in the city center, he got stuck for over an hour at a protestor-mounted roadblock and as a result was late for his afternoon shift. Fariba, who also lived in Limoges's outer city but who, unlike Thomas, continued to struggle to find work since dropping out of high school three years earlier, echoed Thomas's resentment of the protestors: "Those high school kids and university students, they have it so easy. What do they know about work or precarity? Let them walk a day in my shoes!"

In general, most of my interlocutors in the outer city were ambivalent about the CPE. In fact, only a few self-proclaimed "activists" participated in the protests that took place in Limoges, which began in February and stretched into April. For the majority of the young people I came to know, the CPE was not all that different from previous government initiatives meant to aid underemployed youth, such as themselves, who lived in France's disadvantaged outer cities. Longtime participants in these successive programs, which tended to function on the basis of generating short-term employment contracts, they had become accustomed to, if not exactly comfortable with, a lack of employment security and, as a result, saw the CPE as a continuation rather than a shift in familiar government policy. "The CPE . . . it's for youth like us, the youth in trouble of the outer cities [*jeunes en difficulté des banlieues*], the youth who galèrent," summarized Véro, who, despite holding a vocational certificate in plumbing, had mostly only been able to find low-paying odd jobs that had little to do with her training.

Mentioned in Véro's pronouncement, the verb *galérer* and the corresponding noun *galère* were words I heard over and over again in Limoges's housing projects.[15] "Outer-city youth do not live, they galèrent," one interlocutor explained to me early during my fieldwork. *Galérer*, in this sense, was understood as meaning to be the victim of a chronic lack of employment. It involved living hand-to-mouth. But even worse, it entailed confronting the infantilizing experience of having to rely on social service or family support. In the end, *galérer* meant putting adult life—what my interlocutors called "real life"—on hold without any foreseeable improvement. Examining something as seemingly simple as their everyday uses of cell phones aids, I think, in understanding their experience of *galère*.

Cell phones are fairly ubiquitous in Limoges's outer city, where, I discovered, they hold far more value than their simple functionality. For my interlocutors, they were both a reminder of the problems they faced and a means of deflecting or deferring them. Cell phones first appeared in France in the early 1990s and were already widespread by the turn of the twenty-first century. However, even as the technology developed and the market opened to competition, owning and operating a cell phone have remained fairly expensive propositions. Cell phone costs depend primarily on the type of service plan chosen by the customer when service is initiated. Most cell phone plans fall under one of two categories: pay-as-you-go accounts (*sans abonnement*) and long-term contracts (*forfaits*). While the pay-as-you-go option requires no commitment from the customer (he or she simply refills a drained account by purchasing a prepaid card), contracts oblige users to sign on for twelve or twenty-four months (the longer the commitment, the less costly the plan). Generally speaking, prepaid service is much more expensive than a contract, running on average €0.50 per minute (compared to between €0.20 and €0.30 with a contract). Additionally, whereas contract customers typically benefit from substantial subsidies when purchasing cell phone hardware (most service providers offer their contract customers entry-level phones free of charge or for a token euro, when a new contract is initiated), prepaid customers usually have to shell out full or close-to-full price for their phones, the least expensive of which in 2005–2006 ran around forty euros.[16]

Nearly all of my interlocutors in Limoges's housing projects carried cell phones with them wherever they went, and early during my fieldwork initial contacts seemed genuinely surprised that I did not have a cell phone, requiring me to explain repeatedly that I had to wait for my residency card to be issued before I could obtain one.[17] Oddly though, or so it seemed to me at first, I rarely observed my interlocutors talking on their cell phones, and when they did, it was usually only for short amounts of time, each call lasting no more than a minute or two. Why did these young Limougeauds place so much emphasis on having a cell phone if they used it only occasionally? The answer to this question had everything to do with their experience of *galère*—specifically, the limits they found placed on the independence that, in their estimation, they, as young adults, should enjoy.

For these youth, having a cell phone, I came to understand, is about much more than easy access to untethered communication. Owning a first cell phone is seen as a sort of rite of passage, a step closer to adulthood and the achievement of greater autonomy. With a cell phone, in theory they can talk wherever, whenever, and to whomever they want, without having to rely on the family phone. "Having a cell phone is essential," Rachid asserted. "I'm able to stay in touch with friends, and I can keep my conversations private. That's not always easy in the neighborhood's cramped apartments." Yasmine agreed: "I couldn't live without my cell phone. It makes me feel so much more independent." Although both legally adults, neither Rachid nor Yasmine had yet to move out of their parents' apartments, and their situation was by no means exceptional. Most of the young people I came to know still lived with their parents and often complained about the constraints this arrangement placed on their personal freedom, citing for example the imposition of curfews or the close supervision of their comings and goings. They used cell phones as a Band-Aid fix. Even if they could not afford to live on their own, they explained, cell phones gave them some measure of autonomy.

As symbols of this autonomy, then, cell phones were frequently displayed to the public eye. If they were not worn in a visible manner, like in a belt cradle, for example, they were regularly pulled out of pockets and bags, even when no messages were registered on them and their owners had no intention of making a call. During one day of observations at a youth association in one of the housing projects, I witnessed a young man remove his cell phone from his pants' pocket no fewer than ten times in about as many minutes. When asked if he was expecting an important call, he shot me a look that could have been interpreted as menacing or embarrassed—I could not decide which—but then replied that he was not. Although today this behavior would hardly seem surprising given the popularity of Facebook, Instagram, Twitter, or Tumblr, recall that my fieldwork took place in 2005 and 2006, before the advent of such smartphone apps. For nearly all of my interlocutors, cell phones also replaced wristwatches, thanks to the digital clocks built into most models. "You still wear a watch?" questioned Karim, the sharp-tongued fourteen-year-old I tutored in one of the housing projects. "That's *so* passé," he sniggered. All consideration of current fashion trends aside, using cell phones as timepieces offered youth one more excuse to display these prized possessions, boosting in the process their status among peers.

Because of their limited financial resources, it made sense for youth such as Rachid, Yasmine, and Karim to opt for the less expensive contract when choosing a service plan; however, few had done so. Instead, they mostly chose the more costly prepaid account. This decision was usually not the result of ignorance about the cost difference, nor was it a function of a "capricious" or "hard-to-pin-down" nature, as some human service providers in Limoges attributed to outer-city youth. On the contrary, most young people recognized that a contract would have saved them money and told me that they readily would have chosen this option. They simply did not have the requisite steady income. In fact, although in the long run contracts are less costly than accounts, even the least expensive among them requires monthly payments of about forty euros. By contrast, prepaid cards may be had for as little as five euros. With a contract, customers also run the risk of accruing additional charges if the plan's set monthly minutes are surpassed. Opting for a prepaid account is a way to avert this undesirable outcome. Instead of accumulating extra charges when the available minutes are expended, the line is put "on hold," and the phone stops working until the account is refilled with funds. In other words, the prepaid accounts afforded these young people added flexibility.

Many young people in the housing projects did, in fact, frequently run out of minutes. More than once, interlocutors who promised to call me never did so. Later, when I would run into them, they almost always explained that they were out of minutes. Of course, this may have only been a pretext, their way of letting me know politely that they were not interested in talking to a foreign anthropologist. However, those I reached by phone generally seemed happy to talk, often for longer periods than during the calls I observed them make among themselves. A more likely interpretation, then, is that they were resistant to using their own minutes, if they had any minutes left to use. Unlike the United States, where both outgoing and incoming calls are billed as used minutes, in France only outgoing calls deplete minute stores, both for prepaid and contract customers. So when I was the party who initiated a call, my interlocutor would not consume any of his or her prepaid minutes.

Youth on Limoges's periphery also kept track of one another's minutes. I frequently overheard or took part in conversations during which young people explained that a friend was momentarily unreachable by phone because his or her minutes were depleted. In order to avoid this undesirable outcome, they tended to send text messages rather than making calls. Text messages, costing on average €0.10 each, are much less expensive than calls (which, recall, average €0.50 per minute for prepaid accounts). On some occasions, adults perceived this behavior as a sign of unwelcome individualism. "You've seen all those kids typing away furiously on their cell phones," the director of Limoges's youth unemployment office (*mission locale*) remarked with exasperation during an interview with me. "They don't even take the time to have a normal conversation anymore. What's our society coming to?" Rather than an indication that these young people are not interested in keeping in touch with one another—or in collective life within their neighborhoods more generally—it seems to me that my interlocutors' calculated use of text messages as a way to stretch out limited financial resources suggests their rootedness in local communities.

This rootedness was reflected and reinforced by frequent exchange. Here, the type of objects exchanged seems significant. These included for the most part nonessentials, especially cigarettes, but also videos and music (generally downloaded from the internet). By contrast, I rarely observed or heard of exchanges involving money or food staples. It seems to me that the explanation for this is twofold. First, my interlocutors categorically refused to be considered part of the socially excluded (*les exclus*), with whom they associated the truly destitute, such as vagabonds or street people. "We're not poor," they insisted. "We're not like the bums who roam the streets, who don't have anywhere to sleep at night." Entering into exchange centered on life essentials would have meant to them that they were little better off than this category of people. That is not to say, however, that my interlocutors did not recognize that they would likely never have the same access to certain goods as other groups. Such goods might not be required for maintaining life, but in the culture of consumption that characterizes France, as in most other contemporary western societies, they (like cell phones, some might argue) are associated with dominant understandings of what it means to be fully a person. In their eyes, it is precisely a lack of access to things like music, videos, and cigarettes—things that conspicuously give pleasure in social settings—that marks them, as a group, as different, as undeniably deficient.[18] Exchange of nonessentials helps to compensate for this deficiency, erasing, albeit superficially, their difference. More broadly, it may be seen as part of a group strategy for coping collectively with an experience they share: *galère*.

Returning then for a moment to their interpretations of the anti-CPE movement, if the CPE was in fact geared toward outer-city youth and their *galère*, why, they asked, were middle-class students, who would likely secure good jobs anyway thanks to their academic credentials and social connections, so up in arms over it? Was not the explicit goal of the CPE to get outer-city youth working, at least temporarily? Framed this way, the anti-CPE movement might have little to do with "solidarity," or at least that is what my interlocutors argued. "When you see all those high school kids on strike, even some of the university students, I really don't agree," Lionel, another perennially unemployed outer-city youth said to me. He went on to explain that during the strikes that sometimes took place when he was in high school, he and his classmates did not always know (or care) what they were striking for: "We just wanted to skip class, have a good time." He suspected similar motives among the CPE protestors: "The thing is, it was nice in April. You don't want to work when you're in high school, so the CPE was a good excuse for them to go on strike." Rachid, another outer-city youth who had a job as an aide in what was widely considered a prestigious city-center high school, confirmed Lionel's suspicions, explaining that he had asked students in that high school point-blank why they were protesting. Their response was that they had gone on strike "because they were looking for an excuse to be outside, to skip classes." For Lionel and Rachid and many other young people in Limoges's outer city, the middle-class youth who participated in the CPE protests were motivated far less by a commitment to social solidarity than the pursuit of individual pleasure. "C'est chacun pour soi," they insisted.

Even those few youth I knew who were active in the movement tended to disassociate themselves from the student protestors. Yanis, who was eighteen and living in a residence hall for young workers (*foyer de jeunes travailleurs*) while completing an internship in hotel services, was involved in the movement, even traveling once to Lyon (a distance of nearly 250 miles) to attend a regional organizational meeting. He spoke to me about the movement's leadership:

> You know, that guy, I can't remember his name, he's the head of the National Student Union (UNEF), he was on TV all the time. Well, he's just like the politicians. He was there to be seen, to advance his career, end of story. He doesn't give a damn about precarity, he doesn't give a damn about young people like me. When they retracted the CPE, he was there, all smiles in front of the cameras, patting himself on the back. But precarity still exists! That guy, he doesn't care about our problems. It really disgusts me.

As the anti-CPE movement gained traction, Bruno Julliard, president of UNEF at the time, became the student opposition's most visible spokesperson. Yanis's comments suggest that he did not believe that the student protestors, whose interests Julliard was supposed to represent, really understand the difficulties he and his peers face, still less France's political elite. Rather, in his estimation both groups were acting in calculated self-interest.

Why, if in their conversations with me the young people I came to know in Limoges's outer city argued so vigorously against the CPE protestors' claims to precarity, did they not speak up publicly? Why did they not demand recognition of what they saw as their particular plight? What, in the final analysis, prevented their collective experience of *galère* from translating into a collective voice? One last example from my field notes, this one involving the production of an amateur film, helps sort through this puzzle.

In the early spring of 2006, I was invited by several young people to attend the shoot of a film they were working on. With a cast of eleven (all unemployed, outer-city youth), this police thriller was the initiative of a close-knit group of three friends, who, along with others recruited from their social networks, were "looking for a way to occupy their time." Recorded with a handheld camcorder over the course of several months, the film became more than just a leisure activity. Its participants treated it as if it were a *job*. Filming often spanned full days, and because the youth involved in the project hoped to screen their film at the neighborhood festival that took place every June, production became frenzied as this event approached. On one particularly "busy" day, customary cigarette breaks were even foregone. "We've got a job to do," one member of the cast told me, "and we're going to get it done!"

Around this time, one member of the cast abruptly stopped attending shoots. A new job (a six-month contract), I learned, prevented her from doing so. In order to avoid falling behind schedule, the rest of the cast rewrote the script, explaining the young woman's absence by a kidnapping. They hoped that she would return to film a final scene in which she would be liberated from her captor by the story's two unlikely heroes. The young woman never did return to the project, however, and this plunged the group into a panic. They hastily recast the role and reshot all of the footage featuring her. Although members of the cast denied harboring any ill feelings toward the young woman, she was noticeably absent during the film's screening, and afterward I only saw her once with this group of friends, even though before the film she had been a regular presence whenever they gathered.

The commotion surrounding the film helps us gain perspective on the contrasting results of precarity in Limoges's housing projects. On the one hand, the project serves to temper claims made by Standing (2011) but also others working specifically in France (e.g., Dubet 1987), according to which precarity unavoidably leads to social deviance and ultimately anomie. I label the film project, along with the forms of exchange described above, "outer-city sociality." Rather than attempts to undo society, they were *collective efforts*. Born out of the condition of *galère*, they aimed at recreating, albeit with limited means, various norms of the social mainstream, including conspicuous consumption and steady employment. On the other, the film project, however anecdotal, demonstrates the tenuousness of this outer-city sociality. It suggests that differences among individuals—even temporary ones—may prevent the development of any sort of overarching consciousness, much less one capable of generating political action. Even if all of my interlocutors lived in similar material conditions (the housing projects) and complained loudly about *galère*, their educational backgrounds and experiences in the job market were far from identical. Some had a high school diploma; others did not. Some had undertaken or were undertaking professional training; others not. Some had completed a year or two of university coursework and then abandoned their studies; others were still pursuing university degrees. Some had been out of work for months; others shifted between temporary jobs (full-time or part-time); and still others (a very small minority) had secured long-term, full-time employment. Groups of friends, I noted, were often constituted along these lines, and sometimes changes in status provoked momentary or longer-term rifts within them.

Moreover, dominant and culturally driven conceptions of solidarity seemed to stand in the way. Solidarity, recall, first gained currency in France at the turn of the twentieth century. At that time, it was thought to be forged through "natural" or "essential" forms of diversity. Today, understandings of what makes for solidarity seem to have shifted, at least in Limoges's outer city, where the idea tends to be equated with the notion of inclusion, which itself is viewed as a function of employment. Despite their participation in outer-city sociality, my interlocutors complained frequently about what they viewed as a lack of solidarity in their neighborhoods. In fact, "C'est chacun pour soi" was a phrase they used as much to describe one another as to talk about outsiders. This expression did not carry the sort of dog-eat-dog mentality, the idea that only the strongest or smartest succeed, that one might encounter in the United States. Rather, it was used to criticize what was seen as a general disaffection or disinterest vis-à-vis others, manifest, according to my interlocutors, in myriad quotidian ways, from urinating or spitting in public stairwells to throwing trash from windows or "tagging" exterior walls, to "mooching"—that is, taking without ever giving back. "What's solidarity?" one young man, who had been out of work for three months, asked me. He continued:

> Sitting on the corner and smoking cigarettes all day, is that what you call solidarity? Or are you going to knock on my door and tell me to come look for work with you? That's real solidarity, but you don't see that today. Today, it's just a bunch of kids who are letting each other fall apart. If you want to make it, if you want to get out of here, you've got to fend for yourself [*tu dois te débrouiller tout seul*]. C'est chacun pour soi.

As this commentary suggests, for my interlocutors solidarity was above all about *social inclusion*, which they envisioned as possible only through *employment*. Without good, stable work, French men and women, they insisted, have little chance of achieving full participation in the social and economic life of the nation. Although they did not necessarily discount the emotional support interactions with others in their neighborhoods provided, they viewed these connections as offering little chance of leading to long-term employment.

In the end, this conception of solidarity is perhaps not unique to the French case. Even if my interlocutors viewed *galère* as being a defining feature of their existence and thus a part of their social identity, none wanted this to be the case. Writing on the concept of the precariat, Loïc Wacquant argues:

> The precariat is a sort of *stillborn group*, whose gestation is necessarily unfinished since one can work to consolidate it only to help its members flee from it, either by finding a haven in stable wage labor or by escaping from the world of work altogether (through social redistribution and state protection). Contrary to the proletariat in the Marxist vision of history, which is called upon to abolish itself in the long term by uniting and universalizing itself, the precariat can only make itself to immediately unmake itself. (2008, 247, emphasis in original)

As Wacquant suggests, these youth would flee their condition at the first opportunity. It is thus hard to imagine how *galère* could be a source of solidarity for them. To struggle to eliminate it would mean to disband the group it constitutes. Likewise, it seems unlikely that the precariat could ever form a class for itself in the Marxist sense—that is, a particular social stratum organized to promote its own interests. That is not to say that the concept of the precariat could not be mobilized as a *popular political strategy*—as a way of organizing those heterogeneous individuals who are more or less affected by employment insecurity to demand improvement of their similar—but not identical—conditions. But as this French case study suggests, to do so would require somehow bridging the various fault lines separating them.

Conclusion: A Problem of Naming

In this essay, I have been concerned with what is happening to people's sense of social identity in the face of rising unemployment and employment insecurity. Social identity in France appears in the past to have been closely tied to class identity, which was itself based on an organicist conception of solidarity wherein the existence of different social classes was viewed as essential to proper social functioning. In today's global economy, as unemployment and employment insecurity spread, many in France insist that society is becoming dangerously fragmented. Individuals, they argue, are losing sight of shared values and interests. Scholarship on the collapse of the working class in particular tends to reflect this perspective. By and large, this literature focuses on how old forms of working-class organization and politics, centered on relationships developed on the shop floor, have been replaced, especially among the generation coming of age today, by corrosive individualism (e.g., Beaud and Pialoux 1999; Renahy 2005; Schwartz 1990; Terrail 1990). I wonder, though, to what extent the problem raised is a function of the frame of analysis used. In other words, by adopting "working class" as the most meaningful category of analysis—and this despite acknowledging its disintegration—how might this work fail to recognize the value of the everyday collective strategies deployed by such people as my inter-locutors in Limoges, as they grapple with their situation? The result is, in effect, the imposition of negative identities. That is, these youth are constantly being described—in scholarship, in the news, and by politicians—in terms of what they are not. Small wonder that they internalize this perspective themselves.

More recent studies (e.g., Castel 2007; Lagrange 2010; Ndiaye 2008) have sug-gested that at least some youth in France's outer cities have at last managed to forge positive identities. The catch: These identities are based on these youth's immigrant backgrounds.[19] In France, where the horrors of Second World War but-tressed popular belief that the French republican contract should protect people from the abuses of arbitrary racial or ethnic classification, such a development is far more likely to generate concern than celebration. Whether or not young people in France's outer cities are using racial or ethnic markers to situate themselves or others, I am concerned about how this cultural reading might obfuscate some of the sources or consequences of social inequality today.[20] To illustrate this point, consider how Gérard Larcher, the French employment minister at the time of the 2005 Riots, blamed the unrest on the polygamous practices of some immigrants from North and Sub-Saharan Africa: "Since part of our society displays this anti-social behavior [polygamy], it is not surprising that [outer-city youth] have diffi-culty finding work. . . . If people are not employable, they will not be employed" (*Le Monde* 2005). Whether or not my interlocutors came from polygamous families, I doubt very much that they would point to polygamy as a cause for their being out of work. Rather, they saw themselves as the victims of structural inequalities arising from a new employment paradigm in which employers value flexibility over stabil-ity, and workers, especially the least qualified among them, are entirely disposable.

All this is to say that today, as a result of a trend toward a more flexible labor market, we are confronted by a problem of naming. People can no longer be tidily arranged into different social classes.[21] At the same time, broader categories, like that of the precariat, seem incapable of capturing people's lived experience, frac-tured as it is along multiple fault lines, some old, others emergent. Faced by this messiness, anthropologists, it seems to me, have an especially important role to play as we strive to understand the problems people face in order to aid in proposing solutions. With its intense focus on people's everyday perspectives and practices in particular settings, ethnographic research is especially well poised to offer impor-tant insights into the shifting landscape of employment in the twenty-first century.

CONTESTING UNEMPLOYMENT

The Case of the *Cirujas* in Buenos Aires

Mariano D. Perelman

Since he was young, Osvaldo had worked in plumbing, first as a plumber's helper and then as a plumber. But in 2001, for him as for thousands of Argentines, jobs started to disappear. Argentina entered into an unprecedented political, social, and economic crisis.[1] Osvaldo and his wife, who also could not find a job, had four children to take care of. As time passed and no other job opportunities materialized, Osvaldo turned to the stigmatized activity of collecting garbage (known as *cirujeo*). When I first met Osvaldo in June 2003, he was thirty-eight years old and had been picking junk (waste materials for use or sale) for about two years. It was men in his own neighborhood, themselves *cirujeando*, who first encouraged him to begin collecting: "They told me, 'Buddy, make a cart for collecting. You and your family should not have to go through hardships.' So I started." As Osvaldo explained to me, "There is no *laburo* [work], businesses and industries are dead, and construction is also dead. There are many people who worked in construction or in factories, people that have worked all of their lives in a factory and now, unfortunately, have to collect cardboard."

After two years of *cirujear*, he had come to refer to the activity as a form of *laburo* (work). However, he never stopped considering himself as an unoccupied person, as unemployed. One afternoon, I asked him, "If someone asks you in a survey whether you are an occupied person or unemployed, what would you say?" His answer was emphatic: "Idle, unoccupied." "Unoccupied?" I asked again. "Yes, because this activity does not guarantee me anything. This means I'm an unemployed. This means I'm an unemployed, unemployed-occupied person!"

Cirujeo is the activity of informal waste collecting. *Ciruja*—as the people that perform *cirujeo* are known—is a transformation of *cirujano* (surgeon) and can be translated as "scavenger" or "picker."[2] Although the social transformations during the 1990s (products of the neoliberalization of the economy and of the society) and the national currency devaluation of early 2002 (which caused the prices of recyclable materials to increase exponentially) were processes that contributed to the mass presence of pickers in the streets of Buenos Aires, what can be recognized as informal waste collection has a long history. Despite the different forms it has taken and the different names by which people dedicated to informal waste collecting have been known, it and its practitioners have always been stigmatized, and it has always been linked to both poverty and marginalization.

Cirujas collect in the streets of the city, especially in the richest neighborhoods, where the amount and quality of the waste are both high. The vast numbers of people collecting in the center of a city constructed for the elites of the nation contributed to the construction of the stigma of collectors as unwanted foreigners. Collection is a mostly nocturnal activity: According to the formal collecting system, the waste must be taken out to the street between 8:00 and 9:00 p.m. Then the garbage truck picks up the bags, compacts them, and takes them out of town to bury on sanitary landfills.

Cirujeo does not only involve looking into the garbage for materials that can be reused or recycled. In addition to collection, the activity consists of many other actions, such as the separation and classification of some collected materials, the cleaning of others, the preparation of the tools for collecting (such as the carts and the canvas where the *cirujas* put everything they collect). Much of the waste, such as cardboard, paper, glass, metal, plastic, and polystyrene, is transformed into commodities to be sold to warehouses (also called "deposits") that then sell these materials to other, larger establishments. Generally, the activity involves the whole family. Sometimes the whole group collects together; other times, only some of the members come out to *cirujear*. However at some point in the process of these multiples activities (separation, cleaning, selling) the entire family is generally involved.

Osvaldo points out that he considers himself an unemployed person, as he is unemployed.[3] Like many men in Argentina, he also considers himself a worker. Being a worker means that to earn a living there are some activities that can or must be done.[4] Not all activities from which it is possible to get money are considered work, nor are all men that earn money considered workers. When Osvaldo told me that he was an "unemployed-occupied" person in 2003, he was comparing his actual situation with a historically constructed idea of what it means to be a worker and, of course, with his own experience. For him, being employed (that is to say "to work") remains dependent on certain activities that he had performed and that, as he said, gives some "guarantees" (such as social security, a regular salary, and status). He emphasizes a series of social recognitions that being a worker brings and the social imaginary of the figure of the worker as the actor with the means to access a dignified life. In 2003 the *cirujeo*, for him as for most Argentines (Perelman 2012), was not seen as "work" or as a legitimate way of earning money (Perelman 2011b). A few years later, *cirujeo* had different meanings for Osvaldo and others, as many *cirujas* during these years contested the hegemonic ideals of work and nonwork as they related to *cirujeo*.

Unemployment is a social category that transforms the meanings of different social situations and individual trajectories. This category expresses complex processes that involve more than just the quantitative imbalance between supply and demand of employment. The social construction of unemployment is, for instance, highly gendered as well as class-specific (Fernández Álvarez and Manzano 2007, 145–146). There are normative and statistical visions of unemployment: Some exchange relationships are considered to be under the sphere of employment, while others are not. This, however, does not mean that people who are unemployed do not work. Also intimately connected with the social meaning of unemployment are the subjective processes that construct both the ideal worker and the "unemployed worker" within specific historical contexts.

For the case of the *cirujeo*, then, in this chapter I am interested in the experience of surviving by activities that are considered nonwork. I explore the social construction of "being unemployed" as a way in which normative ideas of unemployment and employment and subjective perceptions of these ideas are rooted. In the Argentine case, I argue, people who recently started to *cirujear* are considered unemployed because they have a history tied to hegemonic forms of work. In contrast, *cirujeos* who have never been normatively employed have a very different experience of *cirujeo*, one not located within the framework of unemployment. For those who come to the occupation after having worked in other, higher-status occupations, resorting to *cirujeo* appears as a legitimate mode of survival among many other possible options but requires a process of adaptation.

Argentine social scientists have tended to see the *cirujeo* as a "novelty" and have focused mainly on trying to understand the new structure of the activity. This series of investigations advanced fundamentally upon two axes. One group focused on the relation between *cirujeo* and the environment (Suárez 1998; Suárez 2001; Schamber 2008; Paiva 2006, 2007, 2008). A second group addressed the *cirujeo* as a survival activity. This group may be divided among those who see the *cirujeo* as a (positive) response to poverty (Reynals 2002; Koehs 2005, 2007) and those who analyze the activity in the context of the consequences of neoliberal policies of disarticulation in the labor market (Busso and Gorbán 2004; Gorbán 2004, 2006; Dimarco 2005; Gutiérrez 2005; Perelman 2007a). To distinguish between those who have recently resorted to the activity ("fallen into poverty") and those with a trajectory linked to the task, investigations differentiated between *nuevos cirujas* (new *cirujas*) and *viejos cirujas* or *cirujas estructurales* (old or structural *cirujas*) (Paiva 2008; Perelman 2007a; Suárez 2001; Schamber and Suárez 2007; Schamber 2008). In a previous article (Perelman 2007a) I established a difference between new *cirujas* (the ones that began recently to *cirujear* and had a trajectory as formal workers) and structural *cirujas* (those who had "always" been *cirujas*). I argued that for this second group, scavenging is seen as a "normal" way of living. By contrast, for the former, who have just begun to develop the activity, it was experienced as a sharp break in their labor career.

In this chapter, then, I deepen my investigation of those differences by looking at the everyday lived experiences of a specific group of workers at a specific moment in time. I argue that discourses and ideologies of unemployment are produced and reproduced in these historical experiences. Centering on how people of flesh and blood experience labor processes, I demonstrate that the relationship between employment and unemployment is not fixed. Instead, as I show, one activity can be seen as work while at the same time, those who perform it are seen as unemployed.

This chapter is based on ethnographic fieldwork I conducted between 2002 and 2009. Over the course of eight years I followed, observed, and interviewed (individually and collectively) different *cirujas*. Some of them had been doing the activity for several decades; others had started doing it only a few years before; still others began doing it during my fieldwork. Although all of them worked in the city of Buenos Aires, some of them were living in the city and others in the suburbs. The research focused on men and women who because of their age might have had a pre-*cirujeo* career path. As in any ethnographic approach, the fieldwork combined different methodologies and was based on my extended presence in the field, observations, and formal and informal interviews. Over the long fieldwork process I could watch how things changed. I saw how the new *cirujas* built the activity into a legitimate way of living (Perelman 2011b) and how those with experience in the activity were reconfiguring its past and its trajectory in the present (Perelman 2010).

Argentina from Full Employment to Unemployment

As I have developed elsewhere (Perelman 2007b), work has become one of the most powerful disciplinary forces of modernity. Work as an institution implies a particular "art of governance" (Foucault 1969) that seeks to construct a certain type of subject. As part of this process, only some types of activities are conceptualized as "work." Different influential traditions active in the last century, such as humanism, Marxism, and Christianity, have contributed to the construction of the assessment of work as constitutive of the human condition (cf. Meda 1995) and to particular subjectivities. Grassi (2003a) points out that this conception of work modeled the identity (more precisely, the multiple identities) of the collective subject and of individuals. Work constituted a mode of national integration when the emergence of "the social question" made nationalist sentiment insufficient. For Grassi, the formation of welfare states expresses the institutionalization of a social integration mode that has work as a core value. This mode of integration was not univocal. Schematically it is possible to establish two directions: One was the extension of citizenship to include social rights (including those of the working classes); the other direction was the constitution of the category of worker as the recipient of certain condition-specific rights (labor rights). The latter was the case in Argentina.

Since Peronism, work has been intertwined with the idea of citizenship in Argentina (Grassi, Hintze, and Neufeld 1994; Svampa 2005). Rights emanate from employment and, in many respects, begin with how work was shaped under the first administration of Juan D. Perón (1946–1955). *Peronismo* sought to forge a series of work imaginaries that fostered models of man, woman, family, and a lasting notion of citizenship and social inclusion that persisted in the imaginary of workers after the military deposed Perón in 1955 (James 2006). The idea of citizenship merged with the democratization of well-being (Torre and Pastoriza 2002), especially for the lower strata of the society.

Between 1946 and 1955, with improved income distribution and the expansion of consumption, prosperity flowed along an urban social pyramid. The city represented access to a greater variety of goods and a democratization of benefits and social policies. For workers newly incorporated into the labor market in particular, there was a tangible growth of social expectations beyond subsistence (Torre and Pastoriza 2002, 283). That decade was characterized by upward mobility. Obtaining a job in the formal or informal market was taken for granted. The welfare of working families as a function of the welfare state guaranteed basic needs, including housing, education, access to culture, and recreation. In this model, the working man was the provider of material resources while the place of the woman was at home, as a mother and shaper of future generations. The formation of a social welfare state under Perón gave a new cultural centrality to work, consumption, and social rights. By the early 1970s, Argentina differed from other countries in the region in that there were more salaried positions, the size of the underutilized workforce was lower, and those seeking work were fewer. So-called low-productivity occupations had no major presence, salary purchasing power was high, and wage differences from sector to sector were small (Beccaria 2001, 19–20).

The state of the mid-twentieth century instituted itself as an active player in economic policy, aligning its actions with the establishment of an order that put work and the category of worker in the center of the scene, in relation to both the legal and identity construction of the subject (Grassi, Hintze, and Neufeld 1994; Grassi 2003b). Social rights, including, for example, paid vacations and medical care, stressed the importance of union membership, thus withholding access to many rights from those involved in the informal labor market. Job unavailability was not taken into account, nor was the possibility that a base salary might not satisfy the needs of a worker, let alone his or her family.

On the eve of the March 1976 coup d'état that ushered in seven years of violent military rule, many considered Argentina an almost full-employment society. Argentines understood their participation in the formal workplace—often by way of the Peronist state and its successors—as a legitimate way to consume and to reproduce life models (Beccaria and López 1997; Grassi 2003b). If the 1960s was a period of high employment growth and of socioeconomic improvements for many (Lindenboim 2008), the reverse was the case after the military coup in 1976, and conditions worsened at an accelerated pace during the long neoliberal decade (1989–2002). Throughout this entire period, unemployment grew apace, impacting sectors previously less vulnerable to economic shifts. From 1975 to 2001, the Permanent Household Survey run by the National Institute of Statistics and Census shows an unemployment rise in greater Buenos Aires from 2.4 percent in April 1975 to 17.4 percent in 2001, with a peak in May 1995 of 20.2 percent. Underemployment went from 4.7 percent in 1975 to 15.6 percent in 2001 (see the statistical almanac of the National Institute of Statistics and Census of Argentina). Neoliberal policy prompted the sharp rise in unemployment after 1990. The process was based on a number of policies enacted by the state as part of the privatization of public services and the corresponding shrinking of state social programs. Openness to speculative financial capital and the dominance of the speculative capital model produced a contraction of the labor market, generating a wave of unemployment.[5]

Predominant political discourses suggested that matters of policy were somehow necessary for modernization and reform—neoliberalism was framed as a cultural-political project with inherent and pervasive values and moralities. While the economic and cultural foundations of Argentina's neoliberal order were laid during the last military dictatorship, they were consolidated during the administrations of President Carlos Menem (1989–1999). After the economic turmoil at the end of President Raúl Alfonsín's government (1983–1989), Menem's government generated the idea that the neoliberal model was the only solution to the social crisis. That model linked policies favorable to foreign investors and commerce with the assertion that forty years of Peronist-driven models for

TABLE 1.   Argentina: Evolution of unemployment and underemployment rates, 1974–2003

ANNUAL AVERAGE	UNEMPLOYMENT	UNDEREMPLOYMENT
1974–1980	3.5%	4.7%
1981–1990	5.8%	7.2%
1991	6.5%	8.3%
1992	7.0%	8.2%
1993	9.6%	9.1%
1994	11.4%	10.3%
1995	17.5%	11.9%
1996	17.2%	13.1%
1997	14.9%	13.2%
1998	12.9%	13.5%
1999	14.3%	14.3%
2000	15.1%	15.1%
2001	17.4%	15.6%
2002	19.7%	19.3%
2003	16.0%	17.7%

Source: Table created by author using statistics from INDEC (National Institute of Statistics and Census of Argentina).

state-directed economic growth and social welfare had produced the current crisis. Under Menem, the roles of the state and of trade unions in society were reduced radically. State companies and providers of basic services, including those for gas, water, telephone, railway transport, airlines, and oil, were privatized in giveaways to foreign and domestic investors. Thousands lost their jobs in the deindustrialization of the economy that ensued.

Along with the dollarization of the economy, undertaken to increase convertibility, which established a one-to-one parity between the Argentine peso and the U.S. dollar, labor legislation and social policy discarded the Peronist-era notion of heightened expectations for workers in favor of bare minima for survival (Basualdo 2001). Economic growth (measured in foreign investment rates, inflation levels, and the buying power of the Argentine peso abroad) was shaky and came at the expense of working Argentines (Barbeito and Lo Vuolo 1992). As the government enacted the neoliberal precepts of structural adjustment and dismantled the state, finance capital took its place. As a result, what Maristela Svampa (2005) has called an exclusive society was created. Thousands became poor. However, while authorities and many in society continued to address poverty as a social problem, related problems in the grey zone of work (illegal hiring, unemployment, the bankruptcy of welfare systems, and rapidly shrinking salaries) were treated strictly as a market-driven economic problem—growing pains of the new neoliberal order (Grassi 2000). In that context, the state and private capital worked to reduce labor costs as a priority. Under neoliberal doctrine, formal work became unreasonably expensive and a devalued asset. The moral discourse that regarded work as an essential factor of humanization and the means for realizing the "potentialities of individuals" gave way to a more purely economic discourse focused on jobs and market distortions (Grassi 2000, 63). These neoliberal transformations have had an undeniable effect on the ways Argentines imagine what constitutes legitimate work. In conjunction with growing unemployment, the dispute over what work is and what it is not expanded and crossed new borders.

The Experience of Being Unemployed

Unlike the subjects of other studies on unemployed people, who once considered themselves "stable" workers or who used to have stable jobs (such as working in the same company for several years) (cf. Lane 2011), many *cirujas* never knew stability in this way. For many pickers, instability was the norm, and they learned to live with it. However, this instability became more and more pressing after the mid-1990s, when unemployment rose to historic levels. In a context where employment was scarce and the people of entire neighborhoods were forced to do anything to survive, in times when social assistance was not enough, "looking for a job" was useless. Therefore, thousands of people began to look for alternative ways of living. As I have developed elsewhere, the *cirujeo* cannot be understood only by the growth of unemployment. Due to the (lack of) recycling policies, an increase in the prices of certain materials that could be found in the trash, the devaluation of the currency, and the increasing demand for recyclable materials by factories, informal waste collection became a possible survival strategy for many families of the suburban areas of Buenos Aires.

For those *cirujas* who once held stable positions (or had spouses who did), the experience of being without work and needing to perform a survival activity was experienced differently by men and women according to their previous experiences and according to the way in which they remembered these experiences and their pasts. Nevertheless, in this new experience it is possible to see some common processes, ways of acting and feeling regarding the (lack) of work. Even many *cirujas* who never had a formal job compared their situation with such jobs or with a time when stability was the rule. Many *cirujas* wanted to look for other forms of work, but they did not do it. Many *cirujas* felt shame because of collecting, but in other respects they were also proud of it. To use Osvaldo's formulation, they felt they were "unemployed-occupied persons." The experience of seeing themselves as workers but at the same time as unemployed provided the backdrop to these feelings and transformations and to the way in which the activity of picking was itself performed.

Cirujeo and Shame

For most of those who started collecting, *cirujeo* was not their first choice after losing their jobs. Not everyone is able to rapidly resort to an activity as stigmatized as picking. Starting the activity did not come naturally. One of the biggest obstacles for "taking the plunge" ("*dar el paso*") was shame. Lutz (1986) has argued that feelings (such as shame) are socially constructed and express personal values that, as singular emotional experiences felt and lived by a specific social actor, are the result of a relationship among individuals, culture, and society. The individual experience of feeling shame at being a *ciruja* is not simply a natural reaction that emerges from working with garbage but is instead a response that must be contextualized within historical and cultural frameworks as well as personal trajectories. This can be seen in the following accounts of *cirujas* who expressed shame at their involvement with the activity as well as those, described later, for whom *cirujando* evoked no shame at all.

Prior to becoming *cirujas*, Noemí was a housekeeper and Daniel worked as a public transport driver. Due to the economic crisis and personnel reduction, he was laid off. He then worked in a minor local bus line until 1999, when the company went broke. Daniel then started to perform "odd jobs" (*changas*) in construction as well as freight delivery services and transportation until all these options also disappeared. When they could no longer afford their home, Daniel and Noemí went to live in a settlement located in a suburban area of Buenos Aires. They had no income and three daughters to support. Noemí and her neighbor started begging for food in restaurants, bakeries, and stores, first in the area near their homes and later in the city of Buenos Aires. From there, they gradually turned to *cirujeo*: They accepted not only food but also clothes, cardboard, and other waste materials that they could then sell or repair for personal use. For Daniel, who used to have a job, it was hard to make the decision to start collecting: He was afraid his neighbors could see him; he was ashamed that he, the breadwinner, had to be scavenging in garbage bags for food, medicine, and materials to sell. He was especially ashamed of being supported by his wife. The big city of Buenos Aires seemed to give him the anonymity that he needed, and thus, once she started collecting there rather than near their home, Noemí was able to convince him to *cirujear*.

Estela, who at the time of my fieldwork with her (between 2003 and 2006) was about fifty years old, had previously been employed in a shoe factory. She had been "a qualified worker of the shoe industry," she said wistfully. One of the main differences she noticed between her current situation and her past job was that at that time she got a regular salary every fifteen days, so she was able to make plans. By the late 1980s, she was laid off as part of a personnel reduction. After being unemployed for a couple of years, she got a job cleaning for a telecommunications company. She worked there for two years, and in 1992 she became unemployed. A couple of years later her husband, who had worked for twenty-two years in a paper factory (and died in 2001), was laid off too. They had nine children, and the family's networks were not enough to support them. As was the case in many of the families I interviewed (including Daniel and Noemí), it was the woman who decided to go to *cirujear*. According to Estela, "He [her husband] did not like the idea, but there was no other choice. You have no idea how hard it was for our families to accept that we were *cirujeando*!" She told me that the decision was not easy. "I was ashamed. As I was [once] working in a factory, I felt ashamed to do that. But then I overcame these feelings and went with a cart to *cirujear*." She went to a warehouse and rented a cart and started to travel to the city of Buenos Aires to collect.

As in these cases, in many interviews the idea of the *cirujeo* as an unworthy activity, as something that they would not want to do, was central. During my fieldwork I noticed how pickers tried to hide themselves; I observed the way that neighbors see collectors with contempt and fear. *Cirujeo* implies a visibility of poverty. This public visibility enables the construction and (re)production of the stigma. *Cirujas* cannot hide their activity for two reasons. One is objective: With a cart full of collected things, the way they look is impossible to disguise. This visibility occurs in the neighborhoods where they live and in the ones where they collect and has different subjective implications in each. As in the case of Daniel and Noemí, he did not want to collect near where they lived because he was ashamed to be seen collecting by his neighbors.

At the same time, however, the neighborhoods *cirujas* lived in were central to the process by which they started collecting. Information about *cirujeo* circulated inside the neighborhoods: how to perform it, what to collect, how to access loans and rent a cart, and with whom to go. But above all, legitimating discourses and collective appraisal of the *cirujeo* as a worthy activity circulated in the nearby space of the shantytowns. The neighbors with some experience doing *cirujeo* taught others the craft. Local materials buyers' provided carts (as in the case of Estela) to those who were entering in the activity. The increasing number of people dedicated to the *cirujeo* transformed the former vision of the activity from something unusual, abnormal, and stigmatized to a "common" way of living.[6]

As the above cases show, perceptions and conceptions of the new collectors are gendered. Historically, Argentine men have been the providers of household incomes. Adequate provision, however, was not achieved by any means that would earn money but was reserved for certain labor forms socially recognized as work. In this sense, for the new pickers, shame appears, as in Daniel's case, because he is unemployed and unable to support his family and also because he has to be supported by a woman. Shame also appears because he has resorted to an activity historically not seen as work.

While before the 2001 crisis there were few women collecting, in recent years there has been a feminization of the *cirujeo*. As in the cases of Estela and Noemí, many women were the first to start collecting to support their families. This shift not only altered the place of women but also of men. As Cross and Ullivarri (2013, 16) wrote: "It is possible to think of crises as disruptive of assigned roles. Crises are circumstances where gaps are somehow opened. Between despair and necessity women find spaces to break or disarm their obligations and to extend their scopes to an outside that although it does not extend to the classical production spaces, constitute extra-domestic scenarios."[7] It would be reductive to say, however, that it was easier for women to start *cirujeando* than for men. While men's and women's work experiences and expectations of legitimate access to social reproduction have been different, for women to *cirujear* involved claiming a role beyond taking care of the house: It was they who had to "burden their backs."[8] Starting *cirujeando* was experienced by these women as an obligation but it was also re-signified, in many cases, as a way of leaving the neighborhood space (Gorbán 2009).

In many cases, women were the ones who started supporting their families by collecting, and the men followed later. This produced new forms of gendered bodily scars (Sutton 2008) because to their domestic activities women added collecting. For women, the initial shame was quickly surpassed by the need to take care of their families. They were proud of this and also of succeeding in places—the street and the night—and roles—carrying heavy loads—that were seen as masculine and dangerous. This process transformed the women's subjectivities and mitigated or even eradicated any shame they felt about collecting.

The complicated and varying relationship between *cirujeo* and shame is further demonstrated in my conversations with structural *cirujas*—those who always have been collectors and live the performance of the activity as the "natural" way of living. For them, not only was there no shame attached to the activity, they were in fact proud of their work as collectors. For the structural *cirujas*, being a *ciruja* cannot be considered as—in the case of the new ones who still hope to be formal workers—a broken life career (or a moral career, to use the frame of Goffman 2009). The pride of being a *ciruja* refers to the idea that they were doing something worthy, that they always lived from the garbage and that this activity was as natural as any other. And even more, there is a vindication of their trajectory. As Juan Carlos once told me, "To be in *La Quema* [the city where he works] was like being at home, with that I tell you everything." The same idea was expressed by José, who still proudly says, "I am *Quemero*," referring to an identity belonging to those who have lived and worked in the Quema. The proudness is also expressed in constant acts of differentiation with the new *cirujas*. Those who always have been *cirujas* (the Spanish translation is *ser ciruja* and not *estar cirujeando*, distinguishing between collecting as a permanent identity versus something you are currently doing) considered themselves the "real" *cirujas*, the ones that worked in the Quema, where the labor conditions were dreadful and where collecting was much more socially stigmatized than today.

As de Gaulejac (1996) has written, shame arises when the subject faces an extreme confusion between what one is for others and what one is for oneself. Shame occurs when the subject has a stigmatized, fixed, and petrified image of oneself in the eyes of others, a humiliating and disabling image that cannot be broken or modified. In many *cirujas*, shame arose when they stopped being formal workers or when they could not continue doing remunerative tasks that they considered worthy. This complicated their identity process as workers. And this shame can be understood, as I pointed out, as not individual but as cultural and social.

For the new collectors, being a *ciruja* meant doing something that for others was not considered work. In these feelings and practices it is possible to appreciate the way the construction of "man" is rooted in the notion of working, the way work is gendered. In Daniel, as in many men, the experience of being a man and being a worker (again here it is possible to say that he *es un trabajador*—is a worker—but he *está desempleado*—is unemployed) was operating as a segmented experience. As I have indicated, usually it was the women who decided to go to *cirujear*. In the cases of Estela and Noemí, their shame stemmed from the idea that they were doing something that was not worthy. And this feeling can only be understood as part of their social expectations. As Estela told me, "We are all people who have worked and we want to work, and be well looked [upon] by the others." But for men, the experience of being unemployed and the fear of becoming *ciruja* were different. For those who had been formal workers or who had oscillated between formal and informal activities, not having a job (even more, being a *ciruja*) became a permanent shameful stigma. This stigma is based on a deeply discrediting attribute: There are some attributes (such as being a *ciruja*) that stigmatize, confirming the normality of those who do not have the attribute. For pickers, this is an "attribute" that is impossible to conceal: Once on the street, they cannot hide who they are, even though many would like to.

Although when I did fieldwork social relations related to work were not the same as they were in previous decades, actors continued feeling that dignity is defined through formal employment. This notion was constructed by the nationalist narratives, but it was also presented in a moral way and in social interventions (policies) that even in the neoliberal era, provide benefits to formal workers over informal workers or the unemployed. Being a *ciruja*, then, was not part of this moral discourse about work, nor did it provide social benefits.

In this context, the question that arises is why, despite the lingering stigma, lack of social benefits, and strong increase in employment rates since 2003, many of these individuals continue collecting.[9] I believe two processes can give us some tools for understanding the stabilization of *cirujeo*. One of them is the naturalizing of the activity that takes place when the *cirujeo* is transformed into work, a process that, as the examples above and below demonstrate, is never fully complete or uncontested. The other process, related to the first, is the way in which the activity is structured.

Cirujeo as Work

The *cirujeo* "is not a spontaneous and natural form [of] work," not "a desirable activity, and in some sectors of society is a criminal activity."

—City general prosecutor arguing that *cirujeo* does not count as work and is therefore not covered by a constitutional guarantee of the freedom of labor. Field notes, November 6, 2002.

Poor people, collecting the cardboard all filthy, rotten. . . . Luckily I have a job, poor people.

—Middle-class woman watching *cirujas* work. Field notes, September 2002

The activity of recovering materials manifests the internalization of a culture of work and not [of] crime [. . .] the *cartoneros* [cardboard collectors] invent work where there is not [any]. . . . Moreover, many pickers, while taking the cart to retrieve waste, they understand they have made a choice for working, [as] distinct [from] criminal options.

—Transcript of a statement made by a researcher in the public audience to declare unconstitutional the prohibition of the *cirujeo* to the court. Material provided by the researcher.

Through ethnographic analysis, we can understand that *cirujas'* self-presentation as workers is not only based on the historical process of the construction of gender as a particular kind of worker; it is also a performative act that functions as a discourse to gain legitimacy from others, who might otherwise consider them to be lazy or thieves. Nevertheless, Osvaldo calls himself an unemployed worker and, at the same time, an unemployed-occupied person.

The idea of working as a *ciruja* or, to be more precise, of being a *ciruja* was not seen by many collectors as a desirable lifestyle but as an option that was preferable to other possibilities. As noted above, one of the obstacles to *cirujear* that I have perceived in people who had a history tied to employment was the feeling of shame that they were doing something that they do not consider worthy and decent. These feelings were related not only to the notions of work I have referred to above but also to the construction of *cirujeo* as a "nonwork" and as an activity linked to poverty, vagrancy, marginality, and illegality (see Perelman 2012). Their choice to nevertheless become a *ciruja* depended on their ability to reconceptualize *cirujeo* as a legitimate way of life. One of the main components of that transformation was the relationship collectors developed between *cirujeo*-work and dignity.

Cirujas seek legitimacy by conceptualizing their occupation as decent work in order to try to return, at least in their own view, to the world of those who earn a living legitimately (by working) and, by doing so, to make their existence more comfortable. As part of society, however, pickers have to deal daily with conflictive situations and with moral discourses other than their own.[10] Those who consider *cirujeo* a legitimate way of making a living continuously have to negotiate both their own and others' beliefs regarding the activity and its moral implications. Thus, *cirujas* construct dignity not only in relation to work but also in regard to the expectations of others.

As I have mentioned, overcoming the feeling of shame and breaking the fear of "taking the plunge" ("*dar el paso*") is a first step toward coming to terms with one's identity as a *ciruja* or at least one's current status as someone who collects. As Estela told me, even today she feels "the stare," but she does not care anymore: "You feel shame of being watched the first time and many other times. You turn around and you realize that people are watching that you open a bag and you're looking at what they left inside." Once they take that first step, however, there are still other obstacles to connecting this new condition to the idea of working. As the quotations with which I began this section show, there is a lack of articulation between working and *cirujear*.

Felipe is a forty-year-old *ciruja*. In an interview, he recollected his previous work experience and expressed a desire to recover the good times:

> I used to have a remunerative job. My children were part of the social security system, and we had economic security. I was not in an outstanding financial situation, but at least I could say, "Next month I'm going to get X amount of money. I'm going to buy my son a pair of shoes, a coat." Or as I did when I worked at a restaurant, that one day I took them [his relatives] on my free day to the Rural Expo.[11] I had the opportunity to go to the Expo, to take them to watch a movie, to buy a good TV, a good videocassette recorder and even rent a video and watch it, to do those kinds of things.

For Felipe, being a *ciruja* is opposed to his notion of work, as it is not a "remunerative job," even though it of course does provide an income, albeit a small and irregular one. At first, he referred to the notion of work as employment in which he earned a salary. There are different kinds of jobs than salaried ones, as entrepreneurs or freelancers well know. Nevertheless, his idea of a job is based on his experience as a salary-earner. For him, being a worker comes down to having economic security and purchasing capacity. He said that he was ashamed to do an unwanted activity in contrast to other activities he had previously performed to make a living (such as kitchen helper at a restaurant). However, he still describes his current activity as work, saying, "This is work. I am not stealing, I am not begging."

For Felipe, dignity attached to work is about formal employment but is about more as well. Felipe mentioned his job loss as a material problem, resulting in the loss of his purchasing capacity. His story referred not only to a lack of money but to a specific way of acquiring it. *Cirujeo* may be a form of work in opposition to other activities, but it is not "work" as he performed it in the restaurant. By comparing *cirujeo* to other activities such as stealing, he distinguished *cirujeo* from "real" work while also distancing himself from the discourses and visions that equate *cirujas* with criminal activities.

Collectors like Felipe try to incorporate *cirujas* into the category of workers by juxtaposing the activity to stealing or begging, even as they mark its distance from other, more respectable positions they have held. This is another step to transform it into a worthy activity. The intention of including the task within the imaginary of work and, from there, giving dignity to their lives is a conflictive process that comprises a symbolic struggle around the moralities and social discourses about work. For many interviewees, collection is an activity integrated into the system of legitimate ways to make a living within the notion of work but valued differently from their past labor (formal) activities.

In the above testimony, Estela clearly expressed the division between being a worker and engaging in *cirujeo*. Although when young she was familiar with the activity, as she had lived near a garbage dump and her husband had experience dealing with the activity, she differentiated it from other activities that she considered more valuable. As has been mentioned by several informants, she rapidly noticed that it was not the same to have some kind of knowledge about and contact with the activity and to actually perform it.[12] Estela recalled that her husband "did not like" the idea of going out to collect. The opinion of their families was also central—"You have no idea the problem for our families to accept that we were *cirujeando*!"

The narrative of Daniel and Noemí is similar. Once, Daniel articulated the opinion he had of people who collected back when he was a driver: "I swear I saw them pass and I felt like screaming, 'Go to work, lazy shit.' Now I have a different vision. They are not *cirujas* by choice but because they have no choice. Besides, doing this is not wrong, I earn my money *laburando* [working]. It's work where you have to go out every day, rain or shine, if you're healthy or sick, because if you don't go out, you do not get money."

Some similarities can be observed in the cases I have described. They all are families that used to sell their labor in the formal market (some of them through unregistered employments in the informal economy, some in precarious formal jobs, and others in secure formal jobs). They were used to being part of the social security system and to having purchasing capacity. Then, when they became unemployed, they resorted to *cirujeo*. All of them mentioned they were ashamed and went through a process of adjustment about the activity. This reframing was not an entirely individual experience. Daniel recalled thinking *cirujas* were "fucking lazy," but then he "became aware" that picking was a job like any other. But for Daniel as for Felipe and Estela, adjustment was also possible because they were not alone. As Estela told me, "I saw many people starting to come out, it was not an odd thing."[13]

An important insight that can be drawn from these and many other stories is the way in which the relationship of *cirujeo* to dignity is built. As I said, the most fundamental task is to establish the idea that the activity is work. Here, the notion of work appears fetishized, as it seems that it confers dignity in and of itself. The idea of work is often accompanied by the idea that it is a dignified job (*trabajo digno*). There is, therefore, the need not only to establish one's work as "a job like any other" but also to distance it from activities that appear to be socially "unworthy," such as stealing.

Unlike other cases that emerged with the crisis, such as worker-controlled factories in which workers linked the notion of decent work to the notion of genuine work—their reason for recuperating the plant was to keep their employees in the factory (Fernández Álvarez 2007)—in the case of these new *cirujas*, as their work is not widely considered to be work, the idea of dignity can only emerge from a purely abstract notion of work. Many times, *cirujas* themselves mention this activity as nonwork (Perelman 2011b). This viewpoint underlies responses like Felipe's ("If I could get a job in a restaurant, I would gladly take it") or, as was usual during my fieldwork, when *cirujas* introduced themselves as unemployed despite earning money through their collecting. Nevertheless, their position as picker-workers is an attempt to stay within the frame of normality and thus to become worthy subjects in their own eyes as well as in the eyes of others. This is why the effort "to get money" and "to create work" even while unemployed is at the center of their descriptions of who they are and what they do.

Dignity, for the *ciruja*, is related to pride in creating work and the effort of "going out every day" even if they are sick or feel pain, regardless of weather conditions, hot or cold, if it rains or it is sunny. This focus on pride and effort is necessary to overcome the feeling of shame and the stares of others. In order to construct themselves as people who perform a dignified activity, *cirujas* question the hegemonic imaginaries about workers, but at the same time, they appeal to the hegemonic discourse of work in order to describe *cirujeo*. There is a process of moral adjustment in which feelings that are apparently contradictory, pride and shame, emerge.

Generating Predictability and Stability in Unemployment

Cirujas not only actively try to establish their income situation as work, they are also constantly producing predictability.[14] To them, the activity of collecting becomes work only through the creation of the sort of predictable and stable social and economic relationships they recollect from previous work experiences. Through the creation of these stable relationships, *cirujas* constitute themselves as workers.

There is an economic aspect to such processes as well: *Cirujas* depend on what they can daily find. They therefore need to transform the prohibited recovery of waste found in streets into a legitimate, predictable form of work. To do this, *cirujas* interact with neighbors of the city of Buenos Aires and with the buyers of these materials. Pickers usually build stable route-based *clients*: people or establishments that keep recycling materials for them. The generation and maintenance of these personal relations make up a practice that enhances their ability to obtain materials, generating a sense of security and gaining access to other "benefits," such as clothing, food, or furniture that neighbors no longer want.

Collectors spend a great amount of time every day generating and maintaining these relations. One of the most important things they do is to behave well: Leave everything clean after rummaging through the bags; do not obstruct traffic with their carts; do not shout; do not be drunk; have friendly talks with the clients, and so on. Such "good behavior" was for many doormen and neighbors the explanation of why they kept the garbage bags for some *cirujas*. A building doorman who liked to help Daniel once told me, "he is unemployed, but he is a good guy." The idea that Daniel is a "good guy" referred to a personal knowledge that was created with the passage of time and through daily talks and greetings, and from the doorman observing Daniel's actions while he collected. Daniel tried to be cordial and respectful to the neighbors. Once he told me, "When I search in bags, I have to take care not to break them, because if I did this, people won't give me any more. I must leave everything clean. I must make myself presentable; I must be kind. Those who break bags are those without fixed routes." All this made him a "good guy."

Personal knowledge also has another stabilizing effect. Among *cirujas* and clients, not only material elements circulate. Another useful way to maintain loyalties and good behavior is the expectation created of upward mobility and the possibility of leaving the activity of collecting behind. *Cirujas* see neighbors as people who can employ them for other tasks to help them move beyond *cirujeo*. During my fieldwork, I heard from collectors stories about other collectors who, by talking with people, showed themselves and others that they had a craft and that they were employed. One of the collectors told me that "in order to make it happen, you must show others what you are, that you are good, hardworking, a decent man."

In two different (and apparently contradictory) ways, this imaginary regarding a kind of "good" behavior was making some *cirujas* better *cirujas*. On the one hand, to be a good *ciruja* that picks garbage implies daily work contributing to the stabilization of the task. On the other hand, the imaginary of the possibility of leaving behind that situation also contributes to being a better *ciruja*.

The intention to create a network in order to obtain some degree of stability is not only achieved by the outline of collection routes but also in the process of sales. As in the neighbor-*ciruja* relationship, the relations collectors establish with the middlemen (*depositeros*) of the warehouses where they sell their materials are not only economic. These relationships include different types of exchanges as well as varied forms and levels of personal acquaintance.

Cirujas are not employees of the warehouses. Nevertheless, in a mutual effort to ensure stability, interdependence is generated as if they were employees. One way of establishing reciprocal obligations is by renting a cart. To get one, the *depositeros* require that *cirujas* sell them their goods. This situation implies that *cirujas* are dependent on them but at the same time are released from having to invest time and money in the acquisition of the cart. The warehouses located in the neighborhoods where the *cirujas* live enable them to perform the activity with relatively little investment of their own capital.

During my fieldwork, I noticed that pickers often resorted to a *depositero* in order to solve any difficulties that arose. The most typical cases were related to the cart loan or lease, cash advances, requests for food supplies, the need to keep the carts in the warehouse, and even help with some domestic problems. Carlos, for instance, once needed money to give his daughter a birthday party, so he asked for a cash advance from the *depositero* where he used to sell. The answer was positive, but the owner of the place reminded him that he was giving him this money because Carlos had always been loyal to him. Many *cirujas* request state social assistance plans from the *depositeros*.[15] Many *depositeros* used to have political connections with the local governments, so they can provide discretionary plans to whomever they want. *Cirujas* know of these relationships and appeal to them when they need help. In 2003 María had a problem in the local government with her social plan. She went to the warehouse where she used to sell, and Ramón, the owner, took care of her claim and helped her to solve the issue.

As I said, many *cirujas* started collecting by renting a cart. Estela remembered that "they loaned the cart, but I must sell everything to them." The use of a cart owned by the *depositero* implies a certain subjugation, but renting a cart also allows *cirujas* to not park the cart at their own door, evading the stigmatizing gaze of the neighbors referred to earlier.

To get access to these benefits, the relationship between *ciruja* and *depositero* should be personal and should extend in time, beyond the relationship of buying and selling.[16] The needs of the *cirujas* create the conditions for the opening of a cycle of exchange relationships between them and the *depositeros*. *Depositeros* and *cirujas* know that if the "gift" is not returned, it will become a debt, a sustainable obligation that can even lead to the end of the relationship; at the same time, such debts and their repayment are also vital to the creation and maintenance of that relationship.[17] Loyalty and personal prestige are central components of the maintenance of the relationship. Therefore, buying and selling cannot be seen only as individual acts but should be understood within a wider frame of social relations.

The idea of social mobility is also a factor that contributes to the making of better and more stable *cirujas*. Loyalty to a certain *depositero* opens the way to be seen as workers. Many current employees used to be sellers. To be eligible, they have to be loyal: Sell regularly and offer up all of their merchandise—not keeping the good stuff for those who pay better prices. This conception of a social imaginary of mobility, linked to the idea of being a more stable worker, is exploited by *depositeros* who have a workforce ready to be faithful to them; in exchange, pickers have the chance to work and obtain a "higher social status."

In the interaction between clients and *cirujas*, it is necessary to get predictability through daily relations, which produces a stabilizing effect on the activity. As time goes by, the *cirujas* were more and more tied to the activity, becoming more stable in their unemployment, thus becoming, in Osvaldo's words, unemployed-occupied people.

Stabilization and predictability emerge as part of the search for a labor relationship. The "guarantees" and ideas that Osvaldo, Felipe, and Estela talked about are related to the search for stability. Stability and predictability are central not only as an economic vector but also as part of the way social relations are constructed. They are a form of relations and social ties, but they are also moral ideas, values in which actors believe. All of this is not always transparent for the actors themselves. In many cases they are not conscious that stabilization is being produced. Even more, as in many cases I saw during my fieldwork, actors' actions contribute to an unwanted stabilization, as there was a huge gap between what they said they wanted for their futures and the way they related with other actors. Thus, actors' actions contributed to their stabilization in a still-stigmatized activity they did not necessarily want to continue.

Some Final Words

Although it seems obvious, it is worth remembering that the effects of unemployment are social. My approach to *cirujeo* as work and as part of the experience of people living with unemployment makes sense in the context of Argentine history and labor processes. The feeling of shame, for instance, and the idea that unemployed people are marginal can only be understood within a social and personal idea of what work is and what being unemployed means, both socially and personally.

Centering on the experience of people of flesh and blood enables me to approach not only what unemployment means and how it is felt but also why some people remain involved in that world. In the case of *cirujeo*, it is interesting to notice how some activities, even those seen as nonwork, require constant work to be able to survive and even to try to leave behind the world of unemployment (in this case, the world of *cirujeo*). As a paradox, the intention to get out of that situation may actually cause actors to remain in unemployment longer. The logic and the relations among actors in *cirujeo* reinforce their unemployment work or, as Osvaldo said, the notion of being unemployed-occupied, in two ways. One way refers to the process of stabilization. The construction of predictability is based on daily practices, in debts (both moral and financial) that must be constantly reinforced and respected. To do so, actors must behave in certain ways, must be "there" at all times to contribute to the stabilization. As Sigaud (1996) has pointed out with regard to the relations between unions and workers in a sugar mill in Pernambuco, Brazil, participants become prisoners of the dynamics of these relationships. The second way, related to the first, is that labor conditions, and social relations based on labor relations set the framework for the possibility of getting a job. In the case of the *cirujeo*, the stabilization of the work and the passage of time also contribute to the eventual framing of *cirujeo* as work and then to a level of comfort with the task.

To study unemployment is to study employment, that is, to tackle modes of exploitation and social forms of production. From the analysis of an activity performed by people expelled from the formal market, one ultimately comes back to the market, specifically to the historical experience of a group of people making a living outside the formal labor market. The experience of "being unemployed" or being an "unemployed-occupied person" gives evidence that markets are constructed and also affirms the continued importance of the idea of the worker in Argentina, an idea that not only determines access to social distribution and security but also plays an important role in the notion of the self.

ZONES OF IN/VISIBILITY

Commodification of Rural Unemployment in South Carolina

Ann E. Kingsolver

This chapter is about the commodification of unemployment in an economic development discourse in the United States informed by neoliberal capitalist logic, of which Milton Friedman was a major architect. The status of unemployment in the economy—as feeding the market or as starving the worker—has long figured in a debate between U.S. policymakers. One side follows John Maynard Keynes (1936), who claimed that full employment was necessary for a healthy economy, since that would give workers the basis to participate in all aspects of economic life. The other side aligns with Friedman, who stated in his Nobel lecture on economics that "a dynamic, highly progressive economy, which offers ever-changing opportunities and fosters flexibility, may have a high natural rate of unemployment" (1977, 459). The latter position prevails in both U.S. and South Carolina economic policy; this chapter takes up the question of how rural unemployment is not passively tolerated but is actively commodified and marketed in state economic development discourse as official representatives of South Carolina work to attract capital investment.

Over the past century, the contingency and precarity of Southern workers has been used as a marketing tool to recruit industrial employers from northern states and from other nations in advertisements that tout the advantages to employers of a Southern workforce eager to work for low wages, a workforce with low mobility due to indebtedness and the suppression of labor unions—in other words, an ideal climate for investors who have historically argued that their profit margins were shrinking due to the demands of labor for security and of states for shared revenues. South Carolina has particularly exemplified extreme economic inequality between those controlling the means of production and those providing labor for the state's economy, from the institutionalized racialized inequalities of the colonial plantation economy to the post-Reconstruction institutionalized debt-based economy of the mill towns as textile production moved from the North to the South in the United States and other industries followed. The story is not this simple, of course, since capitalists have always been difficult to "locate" as either Northern or Southern, given elite investors' numerous transregional and transnational addresses, but the state policies of South Carolina have consistently and unsubtly been shaped (except during the brief period of African American legislative control during Reconstruction) by the promotion of the well-being of capitalist investors rather than the well-being of the residents of the state. The economic marginalization of rural, Native American, and African American residents has been especially notable, underscored, in one vivid example, by disinvestment in rural education so stark that it was the topic of a powerful documentary called *Corridor of Shame* (Ferillo 2005).

The state's strategy to invest in attracting out-of-state capital rather than in investing in human capital within South Carolina is very much in keeping with the neoliberal logic that has dominated U.S. governance for the past half-century, and those forging that strategy and the many voters who support them appear to believe strongly that reducing the power of labor unions and getting the state out of the way of the market is good for South Carolinians, as some of the quotations in this chapter show. The commodification of rural unemployment is part of a larger marketing strategy featuring low-wage, non-unionized, and contingent labor; as competition with other regional and transnational potential industrial sites has increased, the precarity of workers being advertised in this strategy has also increased. Examples of the commodification of precarious workers in South Carolina in this chapter include the normalization of hiring through temporary staffing agencies—insulating employers from traditional commitments to workers—and the increasing use within South Carolina of "foreign trade zones" and labor by those imprisoned and detained under threat of deportation from the United States. By focusing on the commodification of unemployment (and using both political economic and interpretive theoretical lenses as well as ethnographic methods to do so), it is possible to follow the paradoxical logic of the escalating promotion of precarity in state economic development discourse ostensibly intended to protect the public from precarity. Rural unemployment has been both largely invisible in the public sphere as a social issue in South Carolina (as it is nationally) and hypervisible when it is commodified as part of an incentives package to attract transnational corporate employers like Adidas and Boeing, both of which have major assembly plants in the state. The next section provides background on unemployment and social and economic marginalization in South Carolina, disproportionately experienced as racialized economic precarity, as well as on the history of South Carolina's status as a right-to-work state (a strong selling point in the current industrial recruitment market). Following that are a section describing the way foreign trade zones and staffing agencies have been combined with the commodification of rural unemployment in state strategies to attract assembly plant construction by large corporations like Boeing and Adidas and the conclusion, which points to further state strategies to market rural unemployment and institutionalized labor.

Differential Experiences of Economic Precarity in South Carolina

South Carolina has a population of just over 4.75 million residents living on around thirty thousand square miles of land ranging from the oceanfront "low country" through the "midlands" to the "upcountry" in the northwestern part of the state, which includes a few counties in the service area of the thirteen-state Appalachian Regional Commission. Three quarters of a million of those South Carolinians are considered rural by the U.S. Census; around two-thirds of those residents identify as white (or European American), 28 percent as African American, and over 5 percent as Latino/a. Residents who identify as Latino/a, Asian American, Native American, and in other ways are often not represented strongly in state discourses because of the entrenched black-white binary in racializing processes (Omi and Winant 1994) organizing the distribution of symbolic, economic, and political power in the state (see Kingsolver 2006). According to the U.S. Census, the rural unemployment rate in 2012 was over 12 percent while the urban unemployment rate was under 9 percent. Even before the 2008 national economic crisis, South Carolinians were already stressed economically; many of the state's residents had been charging groceries and utility bills to credit cards for several years, which made it very difficult to handle the credit crisis and the changes in U.S. bankruptcy regulations that made addressing debt more difficult for individuals and less difficult for corporations (see Kingsolver 2008). Many households had difficulty meeting basic needs, including health insurance. Between 2000 and 2007, a period in which the number of uninsured children nationally fell by 2.8 percent, the number of uninsured children in South Carolina *rose* by 76 percent (U.S. Census Bureau annual figures, compared in AFL-CIO 2009). In 2007, over 20 percent of children under 18 were living in poverty (Food Research and Action Center 2008). Between 2007 and 2009, unemployment and food insecurity increased dramatically in the state. By the beginning of 2009, South Carolina's unemployment rate was second only to Michigan's in the United States, and the number of families seeking food assistance from South Carolina's Harvest Hope Food Bank rose by 142 percent between January 2008 and January 2009 (The Harvest 2009).

These figures on unemployment and economic insecurity do not necessarily render visible the sometimes extreme racialization of economic inequalities, which needs further illustration. The rural I-95 north-south corridor that lies just west of the coastal low country—documented in *Corridor of Shame*—is made up of counties with rural, majority–African American populations who have in part been displaced by coastal development (controlled mostly by European American, or white, investors) and who often provide the service work for those (often gated) coastal communities. Even before the 2008 economic crisis there was food insecurity and high unemployment in Allendale, South Carolina, one of those communities. Allendale residents were experiencing over 25 percent unemployment, and many workers were riding on buses for over four hours a day to work low-paying service jobs for majority-white consumers in coastal sites like Hilton Head. In Beaufort County, just outside the gated communities of Hilton Head, Farrigan and Glasmeier (n.d., 3) calculated that in 2000, the nonwhite unemployment rate was 247 percent higher than the white unemployment rate, a racialized disparity that did not show up in the county's publicized employment figures. Rural unemployment is paradoxically invisible—or "hidden in plain view" (Orenstein 2011, 38) like the foreign trade zones increasingly placed in rural areas—when it comes to discussions of rural unemployment as a social issue, but hypervisible when it is commodified and marketed to potential employers. The commodification of rural unemployment indexes assumptions about the desirability to potential corporate consumers of a fairly captive (in part due to access to transportation), low-wage, non-unionized labor force.

When I moved to South Carolina in 1996 to teach at the University of South Carolina and was working on the book *NAFTA Stories: Hopes and Dreams in Mexico and the United States* (Kingsolver 2001), I became very interested in the foreign trade zones that had been established to market the availability of low taxes and low wages in South Carolina to international manufacturers and how little most residents of the state seemed to be aware of the existence of these zones. Foreign trade zones were established in the United States through the Foreign Trade Zone Act of 1934, and are intended "to help encourage domestic warehousing, manufacturing and processing activity. States and local communities use foreign-trade zones as part of their overall economic growth efforts to improve their international business service structure. In this way, FTZs contribute to the enhancement of their investment climate for commerce and industry" (Catalog of Federal Domestic Assistance 2015). Foreign trade zones, or FTZs, are administered through U.S. Customs and Border Protection. FTZs must be in proximity to ports of entry, either by sea or by air. South Carolina has had an aggressive strategy of establishing FTZs and marketing those zones for industrial recruitment, as will be described later in this chapter.

The commodification of rural unemployment must be understood within a strategy of commodifying rurality itself in the marketing of potential sites for industrial development. The commodification of rurality (Kingsolver 2011, 94–99) is a strategy for economic development utilized in state discourse—for instance, by departments of commerce—and also by rural residents (not that these are mutually exclusive). Some market rural land to urban residents as a bucolic getaway, invoking the stereotypes of authenticity, simplicity, neighborliness, "slow" living, historical landscapes—in short, the possibility of reaping the advantages of small-town life without having put in the long-term social capital investments. Attracting cash investments in rural economies that are hard pressed to keep school, water, and health care systems going with small-scale municipal or county revenue streams can be a popular argument in a public forum. Another way in which rurality is commodified is in terms of a rural workforce. In South Carolina, that rural workforce has been aggressively marketed without much of a voice in its representation. In the next section, there are examples of such commodification aimed at transnational corporations shopping for a low-wage, non-unionized workforce.

Between 2000 and 2013, I did ethnographic research on the construction and interpretation of social and economic marginalization in South Carolina, sometimes with students. Those projects focused on the conflict over the Confederate battle flag flying over the state house (Kingsolver 2006); the looming mortgage crisis and the increase in predatory payday lending (Kingsolver 2008); food insecurity (Kingsolver et al. 2010); the possibility of implementing a living wage in a right-to-work state (Kingsolver 2010a); anti-immigrant legislation (Kingsolver 2010b); the move to render homelessness invisible in the business district of the state capital (Kingsolver 2012); and the project described in this chapter on the in/visibility of rural unemployment and the commodification of rural workforces. In 2012, Micah Sorum, working as my research assistant, and I interviewed individuals placed in a range of positions relative to rural unemployment: service providers for the homeless and the food-insecure, legal aid workers, government representatives, business promoters, unemployed residents, employment services providers, labor union representatives, and others. Interviews were done in the low country, midlands, and upcountry regions of the state in rural and urban areas. Particular attention was paid in the research design to rural areas in which there are transnational corporate employers utilizing foreign trade zones, since rural unemployment has been used as a specific strategy to recruit such employers to the state of South Carolina. The research design underwent ethical review and approval through the Institutional Review Board of the University of South

Carolina. The names of individuals and some organizations have been changed or withheld in this publication at their request.

South Carolina's economy was built in the colonial era through the combined investments of often-absentee capital and low-wage and non-wage labor—especially enslaved African labor in indigo, rice, and cotton production. During Reconstruction, the "slavocracy," as Cook and Watson (1985) call the landed elite from the pre–Civil War era in the southern United States, diminished in power as industrial capitalization increased, with a need to mobilize debt-bonded or low-wage labor for textile and other mills. South Carolina's transportation network—railroads and then highways—was organized largely around the milltown form of production. The milltowns were total institutions, and when they closed in the mid- to late twentieth century, they left many communities that had had low unemployment with extremely high unemployment rates. Textile manufacturing was maintained into the twentieth century through the Multi-Fibre Arrangement (MFA), which protected the garment sector in the United States by imposing quotas on imports from nations in which the same companies could pay lower wages. After the MFA expired in 2005, the last plants closed, but the bulk of the milltowns had shut down much earlier. Those available (and often skilled) milltown workforces were marketed to transnational manufacturing employers in the late twentieth and early twenty-first centuries by state and local chambers of commerce and other industrial recruiters with the additional advertisement that the rural unemployed labor force was not likely to be unionized because of South Carolina's status as a right-to-work state.

Nearly half of the states in the United States have, like South Carolina, implemented right-to-work legislation. In the 1950s, states began passing differential legislation in relation to a loophole in the federal Taft-Hartley Act, which regulates how union membership is established in workplaces; it was possible for states to pass more restrictive rules on union membership but more permissive rules would be overridden by the federal legislation. "Right-to-work" state laws created more barriers to workers joining unions by, for example, making it illegal for workers to have the opportunity to check a box indicating a desire to join a union at the time of employment. In South Carolina's right-to-work legislation, passed in 1954, there are provisions preventing employers from requiring workers to join a union and workers from picketing. The latter was invoked in 2000 to justify South Carolina's new counterterrorist police unit's firing on unarmed longshoremen picketing in the road by the Charleston harbor (see Erem and Durrenberger 2008). As with so many ideological conflicts, proponents of different positions have different labels for the opposite position; "right-to-work state" supporters distinguish themselves from those they call "forced union state" supporters, and their opponents refer to "anti-union" instead of "right-to-work" states. There are no simple assertions to be made about this political division in the United States. For example, labor union membership is increasing in South Carolina although it is a right-to-work state in which state development spokes-people are busy commodifying the state's population as non-unionized to attract employers. Union membership rose by 19 percent (11,000 workers) between 2012 and 2013 as national union membership remained flat (Hananel 2014).

Foreign Trade Zones, Staffing Agencies, and Industrial Recruitment

One example of the marketing of right-to-work status and rural unemployment for the purpose of economic development could be seen in 2014 on the promotional website of the Greer Development Corporation. Greer, South Carolina, is the international headquarters for the Michelin tire company. BMW located its U.S. assembly plant between Greer and Spartanburg in an otherwise largely rural region. This is considered, in state development rhetoric, to be a gem in the crown of international industries in South Carolina. In the twenty-first century, the state strategy to increase and maintain employment has been very focused on attracting international investment in manufacturing and shipping. According to the South Carolina Department of Commerce (2013), the state ranked "2nd in the nation in the percent of its workforce employed by United States affiliates of foreign companies." Those employers, from over forty countries, had operations in nearly every South Carolina county. The state has marketed its rural workforce heavily to attract over $41 billion dollars of investment in the last fifty years. Recently, Chinese-owned factories, such as the Haier appliance plant, have been built in very rural regions of South Carolina; they have received less regional and national press coverage than employers in the state like BMW and Boeing. One state strategy for job creation in rural areas has been to try to attract call centers as employers in rural areas.

Rural workers are commodified as a waiting family for what Collins (2003) would describe as patron management in state recruitment discourse. Explaining how South Carolina's workforce figured in Boeing's decision to build Dreamliner aircraft in what had previously been a low country swamp, Commerce Secretary Bobby Hitt stated:

> We have the physical infrastructure of the port and the rail system, the roads, but the most important, our secret sauce, our secret ingredient in South Carolina is actually our folks. . . . Employees are very loyal. The relationship is what's key. We are relationship people here in South Carolina. . . . We want to trust and work with our companies and stay

with them, and even do it through generations. That's just who we are, and that's just how we are wired. (South Carolina Educational TV 2012)

The assumption that workers are spoken for, rather than speaking for themselves, is common in industrial recruitment literature, and rural labor is characterized as not very mobile, wage-competitive, or organized. On the Greer Development Corporation website (www.greerdevelopment.com), unemployment and underemployment in the area are cited as a real plus for prospective businesses:

> The quality of an area's workforce is vitally important when considering relocation or expansion of a business. The Greer area is one of the fastest growing areas in South Carolina that offers a population that is young, diverse, educated and upwardly mobile. The metropolitan area of Upstate South Carolina has over 1 million residents and a laborforce of over 900,000. Unemployment and underemployment in the area offer new and existing businesses an available supply of workers to choose from as they grow their business. . . .
>
> South Carolina is a right-to-work state, which prohibits the existence of closed union shops, maintenance of membership clauses, preferential hiring and any other stipulations mandating union membership. The Greer area is home to several of the nation's leading labor law firms and a united community effort is made to minimize the need for unions.

The Greer Development Corporation in 2012 marketed the underemployed in this way:

> In a 30-mile radius of Greer 21.4 percent of the resident labor force had individual gross annual income earnings of $12,000 or less per annum in tax year 2001. This is equal to approximately $5.77 per hour based on a 2,080-hour work year common to business and industry. This percentage represents 94,376 residents. Workers from this relatively low earnings group are among the first to respond to more rewarding job opportunities and are a valuable source of experienced, recruitable workers to new and expanding businesses.

Sealing the deal with prospective employers, offering available non-unionized workers, deferred or lowered tax rates, and often free or subsidized industrial sites, is a highly competitive activity that involves a lot of secrecy.

One upcountry resident, Paula, said that when BMW was being recruited, very few residents of the area knew about it. "They always used code names," she said, referring to the government officials recruiting BMW. "We don't know all that goes on when they promise all these things to companies to get here." Two new plants were about to open in her rural area, but she said that no one knew what companies were going to be the employers. Paula said that most of the big companies, like BMW and Adidas, used temporary staffing agencies to find their labor force, which mean that "people have to work part-time, with no benefits, and no job security." One of the big manufacturers using this labor model, she said, will send workers home on a scheduled work day if there is nothing to do because a truck has not arrived. Since they are not paid for their time or their gas money, "you could end up losing more money than you make" with that company, Paula said. A lack of public transportation in rural areas intensifies this problem, since one may have had to make a significant investment in trying to get to work that day. "When we are low, they stomp us lower. Big industries come in and more or less kill you," she said. Many people will take the risk of contingent employment, she explained, because of the stigma of being called lazy or receiving unemployment benefits. She said that in Columbia, the state capital, a law had been proposed that would force people to volunteer their labor in order to receive unemployment benefits, but it did not pass. "It makes you wonder how in touch the Columbia people are with the working class," Paula commented. "If people are volunteering, how are they able to apply for jobs or take care of their children?"

Another resident, Laura, said that many people she knew would not take the temporary work assignments at the plant Paula mentioned, because they required workers to work twelve-hour shifts standing on their feet the whole time. "This is too long. Also, what do moms do with their children for this amount of time?" Child care was mentioned as a complicating factor in taking temporary low-wage employment, since there would be a net loss after factoring in travel time, gas costs, and the expense of child care. Another assumption about rural workers used to justify lower wages or irregular hours is that they have the social capital to cover child care through extended family networks. When asked about the large new employers in rural foreign trade zones in the upcountry, Laura said that they never provide "transportation to the plants or benefits" and that people are considered interchangeable through the temporary agencies. "They don't want to invest in one person," she said. They also, because of the screening they take on for the transnational corporations, do not hire felons or workers without citizenship so there is an increasing pattern, one Christian minister in the upcountry described, of workforces that are divided by racialization and citizenship, with Latino workers concentrated in "agricultural, lawn care, construction, and roofing" work rather than manufacturing.

The upcountry has a very distinct demographic pattern in cities fairly close to each other within a larger rural region, and this is important to consider in relation to how workforces are marketed. Among those who responded to the 2000 U.S. Census in Greer, over 70 percent of residents identified as white, 19.5 percent as

African American, and 8 percent as Latino (or "Hispanic"); in Greenville, 62 percent of residents identified as white, 31 percent as African American, and 3.4 percent as Latino; and in Spartanburg, 50 percent of residents identified as African American, 47 percent as white, 1.8 percent as Latino, and 1.3 percent as Asian, with those identifying as Native American also comprising under 2 percent in each community. So Greer, where BMW is headquartered, is majority-white, and Spartanburg is majority-African American. Greer has a much higher number of Latino residents than Greenville or Spartanburg. Spartanburg has twice as many families living under the poverty line as Greer and Greenville. This is to illustrate that it is impossible to understand unemployment through a unified lens of urban/rural identity or upcountry/midlands/low country identity in South Carolina.

There are micropolitics of racialized and classed marginalization from, or claims to, economic, social, and political resources, then, but there are also patterns of disparity shared by rural areas across the state. In 2013, for example, Governor Nikki Haley proposed to shut down all rural unemployment offices: "The S.C. Department of Employment and Workforce announced it would end face-to-face unemployment assistance at 17 rural offices, forcing residents in those areas to drive to another office for personalized help" (Largen 2013). Because of the lack of access to public (and private, in many cases) transportation and other challenges of making arrangements to travel to urban unemployment offices, this would have been a disproportionate hardship on the rural unemployed. Lack of access to the internet to be able to use unemployment services remotely was also a problem that was articulated by opponents of this proposed economic savings measure to the state. The South Carolina Employment Security Commission, which had been an independent commission with largely African American leadership, was restructured after the economic crisis of 2008 and 2009 to report directly to the South Carolina governor as part of the cabinet, and it was renamed the Department of Employment and Workforce. I argue that this reflects a shift in emphasis from the economic security of South Carolinians to the needs of potential corporate employers the state was trying to attract, with unemployment itself being commodified in that project to attract new employers to the state. In a parallel neoliberal move, there has been a shift from holding employers accountable for the well-being of workers to protecting employers from accountability to workers in the general move toward hiring through temporary staffing agencies.

The role of temporary staffing agencies has strongly increased in South Carolina since the economic crisis of 2008. An employment services professional told me in an interview:

> Since 2008, when we went through that really bad recession and everything came to a standstill, as people are beginning to hire, they're going

into full-time employment, but they're actually temps, because they're going through staffing agencies. Two things: a safety for the company because I get to really try you out before I hire you, and they're saving money because they don't have to pay benefits. So you go in through those staffing agencies, and that's how a lot of companies are pulling them in. We've seen an increase in staffing agencies using our services over the last year because so many companies, that's how you have to get into the company. You have to get in through that staffing agency. We've seen some new ones. I'd never heard of them before. And they're continuously changing their names. They're being bought by other companies. There are staffing companies everywhere. That's what you tend to see. And some of them don't even put staffing on there. We have definitely seen an increase in staffing agencies since 2008. Bosch, even Boeing they hire through staffing companies and then they will pull you from there. The staffing agency is responsible for everything. . . . The staffing companies have grown so much.

The temporary agencies that provide staffing for the large manufacturing plants in the upcountry of South Carolina and for all employment in foreign trade zones (because of U.S. Customs security regulations) screen workers' criminal records and citizenship status, which has a magnifying effect in the segmentation of the labor force. Jordan Segall (2011) argues that discrimination against ex-felons, increasing in number because of an emphasis in the judicial system on plea-bargaining, "exaggerates the preexisting structural disadvantage of minority overrepresentation in prisons by making employers more likely to make racially biased hiring decisions," citing a study in which African Americans seeking employment were almost twice as likely to be asked about felon status than white jobseekers. In South Carolina, another professional in the employment services sector told me that it is nearly impossible for employment seekers with felonies on their record or without citizenship to get internships or jobs in the medical sector or in the foreign trade zones. She said, "The mom and pops are willing to give them some kind of a chance. You may have to take a job for less money. We tell them not to give up." She said that most of the jobs advertised in the South Carolina labor market require some kind of clearance.

Returning to what Paula said about secrecy in the recruitment of employers in rural areas and all across South Carolina, such surreptitiousness was mentioned in other interviews, and government officials have even discussed recruitment and the arrangements made with companies for staffing and training as though it were a stealth operation. Commerce Secretary Hitt said:

Part of it is our philosophy that if you will come to South Carolina to invest in us we will invest in our people. This has been probably the most important ingredient that we have. It's sort of below the surface with the public. They don't really know it's there. It's not just the technical schools, although those are the theaters where this is acted out. But it's a special group. It's almost like our own special forces in education that goes and helps companies have the specialized candidate group that can walk in and do the job. (South Carolina ETV 2012)

Recruitment packages often include training programs, especially partnerships with community and technical colleges. In the low country, an economic development professional explained the Ready South Carolina program that secured training for Boeing employees through Trident Technical College in this way:

They have down here a simulated Boeing plant. So what they'll do, is they'll recruit. The state pays. They'll pay for the recruitment, the initial screening, the aptitude testing, and then once they've passed these hurdles, then Boeing hires them as trainees. So our technical college system sets up a curriculum that's totally specialized to that company. So they say you screw this screw in like this. And they have a mini Boeing plant at Trident Tech I just toured a couple of weeks ago. Where they have a fuselage, you know, and these people have to go through these certain modules of training. And if they can get through all the different modules . . . they're also trained, at that point, in the mentality of working. Their core ethics, or whatever you want to call it. Like they'll get a set of tools when they come in in the morning. And when they leave, if there's one bolt missing, nobody goes anywhere. Because if you put an extra bolt in an airplane . . . so they train them not only into the physical work, but into the company. . . . Once it reaches a certain point, they're on the Boeing payroll.

An AFL-CIO representative told me that the trainees are told in the technical college programs not to join unions. One student/worker had reported this to her but did not want to file a formal complaint for fear of retaliation. A business recruiter told me that the state Ready SC program, which recruited workers to be trained through the technical college program for Boeing, got so many online applications on its first day that the website crashed. The state's rhetoric throughout the courting of Boeing had, after all, been focused on creating jobs.

Mark Sanford, governor of the state from 2003 to 2011, directly attributed the cementing of the deal with Boeing to build a manufacturing plant for the 787 Dreamliner plant to South Carolina's being a right-to-work state:

Boeing's decision to expand their presence in our state with an infusion of jobs and capital investment—the largest announcement in South Carolina history—represents not only enormously good news for our

state's economy, but also a telling dividend from our state's continued efforts to better our business climate. For us, that means lowering
taxes, easing regulatory burdens in our state's tort and workers' compensation systems, and keeping South Carolina a right-to-work state.
(Sanford 2009)

Boeing's decision to build this aircraft assembly plant in South Carolina represented a shift of more of its production to southeastern right-to-work states from
its assembly plant in Evergreen, Washington, where the workforce was strongly
unionized. A leader in the AFL-CIO in South Carolina told me that while unionized
workers had been involved in the construction of the plant and transportation
of supplies to the site, most of the new jobs were through staffing agencies, and
many skilled workers from the national aircraft industry were taking lower-paid
jobs in South Carolina. A worker in the employment services sector told me that
many of the Charleston-area workers registering for unemployment benefits
were skilled workers who had moved to the area with hopes of acquiring a job
with Boeing.

The Boeing 787 Dreamliner exemplifies leveraged use of a global supply chain
to create one product with the lowest expenses, at least the expenses that are
on the ledger (which may not include, for example, environmental impacts or
the human capital costs of pursuing the lowest wages, laying off experienced
workers and replacing them with inexperienced workers). A single Boeing 787
aircraft is composed of parts made by fifty-three companies in eleven countries
(Turner 2010). A special airplane was created just to fly large sections of assembled fuselage to other plants for final assembly, usually in a foreign trade zone
like the plant in South Carolina. FTZ status, granted by the U.S. Department of
Commerce since World War I in seaport and airport zones, where it is possible
to have high international traffic in imports and exports, defers tariffs on parts
being moved in and out of this country (and others, through their equivalent
foreign trade or export processing zones) to facilitate multi-national assembly.
Only the final product is taxed, and according to the World Trade Organization
regulations negotiated through many rounds of the General Agreement on Tariffs and Trade—along with separate free trade agreements—it is possible to label
a product "Made in the U.S.A." with only the final assembly rather than the entire
manufacture having taken place within the national borders. Boeing has made
strong use of foreign trade zones, copying Toyota's international just-in-time and
"lean" manufacturing techniques and moving from a "family-like" corporate culture with a geographical home in the Puget Sound in the mid-twentieth century
to a transnational labor force that expands and contracts with the needs of the
market (Greenberg et al. 2010). The company has been through a merger with

rival aeronautic company McDonnell Douglas, major downsizing after 9/11, uncertainty in planning for U.S. defense contracts because of the economic crisis, pressure on the machinists' union in Washington state to weaken their contract or lose jobs to plants in right-to-work states like South Carolina, and recent mishaps with lithium batteries in the 787 Dreamliner.

The state of South Carolina invested a great deal in becoming one of the sites in Boeing's tapestry of transnational assembly: $450 million in incentives in 2009, with another $120 million offered to the company in 2013 (Wise 2013). As states were in competition for Boeing's 777X aircraft production, Governor Nikki Haley asserted that the edge South Carolina had over Washington state was its right-to-work status:

> "I feel bad for the governor of Washington. It is a terrible thing when you see great industry in your state trying to work and you have the union go in and try to kill it," Haley said. "I don't want them in this state. We don't need them in this state. Our companies take care of those who take care of them, but when a union enters your state, they completely take over the business climate and they kill jobs," she said. "We are not going to have that in the state of South Carolina." (Wise 2013)

A leader of the AFL-CIO in South Carolina said that workers at the Boeing plant in South Carolina were getting approximately $10 less per hour in wages for equivalent work in Washington; she felt that there was a fear factor in talking about work at the plant, as with other jobs in the foreign trade zones in South Carolina: "It's like when they walk in, they're no longer in South Carolina, they're in a different environment. They don't talk much about that." I am engaged in a larger project on how workers interpret the jurisdictions that pertain to foreign trade zones, since it can seem like a foreign space set down in a rural field governed by U.S. Customs, and that can lead to questions about whether local, state, or national laws are suspended in that zone.

A state business promoter told me that there was increasing activity in foreign trade zones in rural areas, because unemployed workers were not commuting as much. "They are putting these distribution centers, to me, in the middle of nowhere. The land is cheap, and the workforce is cheap." Starbucks, for example, has a major distribution center in a foreign trade zone in rural South Carolina. The U.S. Commerce rules allow inland FTZs as long as they are within 60 miles or 90 minutes by car from the edge of a county that has a port of entry, like a harbor or an international airport. The recruiter described visiting one of the FTZs in the upcountry: "It's this old farm land, and three million square feet. When I found it, I don't know if I went the wrong way, but I had to go through goat farms to get to it. It's literally in the middle of nowhere." She described another FTZ site that is hidden behind old warehouses in another rural area: "You don't even see this two-million-square-foot building until you turn and go down the road. And then it's like, 'Oh, my God.'" This global engagement and marginalization is a paradoxically in/visible rural experience in South Carolina.

Increasing Commodification of Rural Unemployment and Institutionalized Labor

Just as there is concentration of ownership of capital as a result of mergers like that of Boeing and McDonnell Douglas, in other economic sectors there is also a growing concentration of control over the commodification and control of unemployment itself. Not only has rural unemployment been used as a selling point in attracting new employers, but the growth in contingent (insecurely employed or unemployed) labor itself also represents a new transnational industry. The temporary staffing industry is, as illustrated in this chapter, is "increasingly playing a systemic, macroregulatory role in the U.S. labour market" (Peck and Theodore 2007).

Another growing transnational industry is the private prison sector. The GEO Group, a transnational detention corporation, purchased and took over Just Care in South Carolina in 2009, expanding to manage health, mental health, and disability services in South Carolina prisons. In my ethnographic research on rural unemployment in South Carolina, I learned of a large proposed detention facility to be constructed in or near a foreign trade zone. Under Section 287(g) of the Immigration and Nationality Act, U.S. Immigration and Customs Enforcement (ICE) can delegate the authority for immigration enforcement to state and local law enforcement. In South Carolina, that means that those without citizenship can be put in detention facilities in the state, often without full access to interpretation and legal services and without clearly set terms of detention. Detention is, itself, a growing industry. A lawyer in South Carolina told us that, currently, those who are detained pending deportation are housed outside of Atlanta, Georgia, and that there are no nonprofit legal services offering removal or detention defense services in South Carolina. Those in prison have long been the most disenfranchised workforce in South Carolina. The Prison Industry Enterprise (PIE) program enables prisons to ask that those imprisoned work voluntarily, with room, board, and other expenses deducted from their pay. It is possible that those detained by ICE in South Carolina could be envisioned as low-wage labor through the PIE program. This is an indication of where the logic of state protection of industries rather than residents could lead. There is significant lobbying by GEO Group and Corrections Corporation of America (CCA) for the contracts to house those without U.S. citizenship detained through ICE; together, they "netted $296.9 million in revenues from ICE contracts" in 2012 (Fang 2013).

Another trend toward concentration is in the unemployment services industry. Rural counties often have difficulty maintaining individual services on the capital reinvested in the locality, and state governments in competition to lower tax rates to potential out-of-state employers and to offer a low-wage workforce are in the same situation. South Carolina, Georgia, and North Carolina are pooling their unemployment benefit systems:

> The unemployment insurance system, dubbed Southern Consortium Unemployment Insurance Benefits Initiative, is a nearly $60 million project that combines the systems of S.C. Department of Employment and Workforce, N.C. Division of Employment Security and Georgia Department of Labor.
>
> The project tapped Capgemini Government Solutions LLC, a subsidiary of Paris-based Capgemini Group, to design both technical and business processes for the system. (Richardson 2014)

This may make the online process of applying for unemployment benefits go more smoothly, but it also centralizes a database of unemployed residents in the Southeast to facilitate the marketing of that relatively low-wage labor force while South Carolina is simultaneously laying off workers in the unemployment services sector and eliminating or reducing staff in rural unemployment offices and, along with it, the potential to voice individual experiences of rural unemployment.

Conclusion

This chapter has described rural unemployment as being increasingly commodified as a factor in selling regions—like the low country and the upcountry of South Carolina—as competitively disempowered labor sites within transnational production, distribution, and consumption. As consumers demand lower prices, this pressure continues. It is a paradoxical strategy in that the rhetoric of economic development is used to promote the well-being of those whose precarity fuels it. But this is by no means the end of the story. South Carolinians are not only managers or workers but also consumers and voters and as such participate in many complex, cross-cutting discourses in relation to identity, employment, and views of the future. There is rural agency in constructing sustainable and collaborative livelihoods across various divisions; *rural* does not mean "isolated," although that is symbolically invoked (rural workers have long been involved in many labor circuits); further, there are state workers who do not reproduce state discourse. Everyone with whom we talked in this project believed that they were contributing somehow to the well-being of South Carolinians through their actions. How might it be possible to contest selective visibility and attend more to, and counter, the naturalization and commodification of precarity? Rural, marginalized, and unemployed workers often have excellent analyses of this process, as we heard in this ethnographic project in South Carolina, and transregional discussions like those facilitated between factory workers in Chihuahua and Guanajuato, Mexico, and eastern Tennessee through the Tennessee Industrial Renewal Network (Ansley and Lewis 2011) are an excellent way to demonstrate that a flexible labor force can mean an agentive one, not only the one imagined as passively commodified.

YOUTH UNEMPLOYMENT, PROGRESS, AND SHAME IN URBAN ETHIOPIA

Daniel Mains

Idle groups of young men rocking on the heels of their thick-soled leather shoes, hands in pockets, wearing clean button-down shirts untucked over loose-fitting jeans—such scenes were common in Ethiopian cities during the late 1990s and early 2000s. In urban Ethiopia, the unemployment rate for young people between the ages of eighteen and thirty was estimated to be higher than 50 percent, and most of the unemployed were first-time job seekers who remained without work for three to four years (Serneels 2004).[1] Unemployed young men in Jimma, an ethnically and religiously diverse city of approximately 120,000 inhabitants located in the southwest of the country, often joked that the only change in their lives involved following the contours of the shade from one side of the street to the other with the passing of the sun. These young men spoke about time as an overabundant and potentially dangerous quantity. They passed their days chewing *chat*, a locally grown stimulant; watching the latest videos from Hollywood, Bollywood, or, much more infrequently, Ethiopia; and, above all, engaging with one another in *chewata*, the playful conversation that is a favorite pastime of many Ethiopians.

When I asked young men about unemployment, they stated that there simply was no work to be had, but when I pushed, pointing to other youth who were working, they claimed that it was impossible to work in Ethiopia because of *yiluññta*. To have *yiluññta* is to experience an intense shame based on what others think and say about one and one's family (Poluha 2004, 147; Heinonen 2011). *Yiluññta* is like a mosquito faintly whining in the ear, a reminder that others are watching and judging. During a group discussion, one young unemployed man explained, "We would never work as a porter here. There is *yiluññta* here and that kind of work is not respected. People will shout orders at you and you are expected to obey. If we go abroad we can work without being insulted. We don't care about seeing other countries, but we want to be free to work and help our families."

In this chapter I examine *yiluññta* and occupational status to draw attention to the importance of social relationships for understanding unemployment as well as the related problem of experiencing progress through time. In Ethiopia, employment is often conceived not only in terms of labor and wages but also in relation to the social interactions associated with particular occupations. Similar to the way they view work, young men in urban Ethiopia evaluate progress in terms of social relationships, and they conceive of spatial movement as the solution to their inability to experience changes in their social position with the passage of time.

I describe the development of a large, young, urban unemployed population in Ethiopia as a three-part process that includes the expansion of education, a reduction in employment opportunity in the public sector, and the operation of cultural values that cause available forms of work to be considered undesirable. Whereas the first two aspects of this process are common to many world areas, the third is specific to the Ethiopian case. The second half of the chapter examines young men's discourses surrounding progress and migration. Young men in Jimma often made comments like, "We live like chickens, we are just eating and sleeping" to express their frustrations with their inability to progress over time.[2] A life of "eating and sleeping" or "simply sitting" was contrasted with one that involved change or improvement. Living like chickens implied that life lacked meaning, that one simply moved here and there without any purpose besides filling one's stomach. Ideally, for young men, life would proceed along a series of incremental improvements, but most saw themselves in ten years still living with their parents and unable to marry or start families of their own.

The "solution" to this temporal problem of achieving progress, both imaginatively and in terms of actual social strategies, involved a kind of "spatial fix," but one that was quite different from that made famous by David Harvey (1991). Young men sought to move across space—both within Ethiopia and outside it to South Africa, to Europe, and, most commonly, to the United States—to escape *yiluññta* and to take on work that they would never have performed at home. Within this discourse, a progressive view of time was restored as the successful migrant was imagined to return to Jimma to carry out projects like building four-story hotels and founding NGOs. The desire to migrate is common to youth living in many impoverished countries, but *yiluññta* and notions of occupational status highlight the manner in which both space and time are often conceptualized in terms of social relationships.

My analysis is based on fieldwork conducted between 2003 and 2005 as well as brief visits to Jimma in 2008, 2009, and 2012. I worked primarily with young men between the ages of eighteen and thirty. The young men in my study represented a variety of backgrounds in terms of class, ethnicity, and religion. Nearly all unemployed young men lived with their families and were dependent on them for financial support. My sample was representative of urban Ethiopia in that most of the unemployed young men in it had completed secondary school and all had at least completed the eighth grade. I carried out interviews and engaged in casual conversation and group discussions in the spaces in the city where young men congregated—cafes, video houses, barbershops, and street corners.

Yiluññta, Occupational Status, and Social Relationships

Young men frequently claimed that high rates of unemployment were partly a result of *yiluññta*. They often said that Ethiopians do not appreciate work (*sira yinaqel*) and that, although one could earn money shining shoes or performing other small jobs, this type of work was not respected. To engage in low-status employment was to adopt a particular position in one's relations with others. It was the undesirability of that position that often caused youth to choose to remain unemployed. Contrary to analyses of late capitalism that claim consumption has taken the place of work in the construction of identity (Baudrillard 1981), issues of occupational status indicate that the relationship between identity and production continues to be highly relevant.

Stigmatized occupations were often those that involved menial labor or were associated with traditional craftworkers. Among most Ethiopian ethnic groups and in East Africa, generally, craftworkers involved in carpentry, blacksmithing, weaving, and pottery have been highly stigmatized.[3] Although important ideological differences underlie the two cases, the treatment of craftworkers was similar to that of lower castes within the Hindu caste system (Levine 1974; Pankhurst 2003, 12–17). Alula Pankhurst (2003) explains that in Ethiopia craftworkers were marginalized in terms of space, economics, politics, and social life. Marriage with non-craftworkers was prohibited, and craftworkers frequently lacked locally defined rights to land. In most cases, they worked as tenant farmers on the land of others and were required to give the products of their work to their patrons, receiving only token amounts of grain in return. Craftworkers did not observe the same religion-based food taboos as Muslims and Orthodox Christians. For example, craftworkers are said to have eaten certain forbidden wild game like monkey or hippopotamus.

Although sharing food and eating from the same dish constitute an important part of most Ethiopian cultures, craftworkers were not permitted to share the same utensils or dishes with others. If craftworkers were guests in the home of a non-craftworker, they would eat from banana leaves or other items that could be disposed of after the meal. Craftworkers frequently were thought to possess an evil eye, which also contributed to the general discrimination they faced throughout their day-to-day lives.

Pankhurst and Dena Freeman (2003) explain that notions of personhood are important for maintaining the marginalized status of artisans in rural areas. The farmers in their study asserted that artisans were not fully human. Despite documenting a discourse centered on factors like cleanliness and eating habits, Pankhurst and Freeman argue that the continued low status of artisans was based on their lack of access to land and the social relationships that come with land rights. Even when artisans were able to increase their wealth, this did not translate into status and full personhood unless they were able to obtain land rights. As was the case for marginalized rural artisans, in Jimma money alone was not enough to improve the social position of lower occupations.[4]

After the 1974 revolution, discrimination against craftworkers was banned by the Marxist Derg regime, but at the time of my research youth informants claimed that a powerful stigma was still present. This stigma was broadly applied to all forms of work that resembled traditional crafts. For example, youth claimed that, because they work with metal, welders are often subject to some of the same stigmas as blacksmiths and are referred to by the same pejorative terms. Other non-craftworker occupations, like porter, waiter, or shoeshine, were also grouped together within the general category of "lower work" (ziqitteña sira). Workers in these occupations did not have rigid constraints placed on their behavior, but young men generally considered these types of employment to be undesirable and potentially shameful.

These professions were undesirable not because workers received low payment for demanding work (even shining shoes could sometimes bring a relatively high income) but because of yiluññta, specifically the fear of what others might think or say about one or one's family if one were seen performing this type of work. As one young man explained, "In Ethiopia there is work, but most people don't do it. Young people would rather depend on their parents than take lower work. If they can't get government work they would rather just sit and wait. They are afraid of what people will say about them if they work."

Although low-status work did not have the established, culturally prescribed restrictions on social interactions associated with artisan professions in the past, performing this type of work still placed one into a distinctive social category—a type of person who is treated differently from others.[5] As one young man put it in regard to lower work, "If someone says 'come,' you've got to come." Working in lower occupations meant placing oneself at the bottom of relations of authority, and one had to be prepared to accept this transformation. During my research, I spent long periods of time conducting participant-observation among young men working as streetside bicycle repairmen, watch vendors, barbers, and other occupations that were stigmatized in a contemporary urban context. In interactions with others, they were consistently spoken to in the imperative and were rarely able to engage in equitable conversation. Working young men complained of being the objects of insults, for instance being called "thief." Lower workers would generally not be invited to weddings or other important social events. If they arrived on their own, they would not be turned away, but their presence would most likely be ignored, and no one would greet them or encourage them to eat.

Hierarchical relations are pervasive in Ethiopia, but there is a difference between subordinating oneself on the basis of age or gender and doing so in exchange for money. For a woman to submit to a man or a young person to submit to an elder is seen as model behavior that one should strive to emulate (Poluha 2004). In these cases, showing respect or deference is thought to be chosen freely and to be a sign of good character. The individual who is deferred to is expected to provide some level of protection or guidance for his or her subordinates. The parent-child and teacher-student relationships are good examples of this dynamic. In contrast, showing deference in the context of work does not involve a personal relationship. The worker is simply following orders to access money, and there is no expectation of a deeper relationship. The worker exists at the bottom of a power hierarchy without a corresponding personal relationship of protection and obedience.

In some cases, a positive form of relationship does exist between the worker and his customers. In Amharic, both the vendor and customer are referred to as *demibeña* if a relationship exists between them. To have a *demibeña* relationship implies a degree of loyalty. The customer should not buy elsewhere, and the vendor should give a favorable price. Although the *demibeña* relationship is important, it only exists at the moment of the transaction. The vendor and seller are on equal terms for a moment, each helping the other to obtain his or her needs, and then that relationship ends until another purchase is made. It does not generally encompass other aspects of social life. One's *demibeña* would not be expected to attend one's wedding. The form is a means of establishing civility in an otherwise tense interaction, but it does not imply the existence of a relationship that resembles the patron-client model and extends beyond the moment of exchange.

The *demibeña* relationship may be contrasted with the prestigious nature of the government employment that played a key role in youth aspirations. When asked about the type of work that they wanted, the majority of youth simply responded "government work" (*mengist sira*). Government work encompasses a wide range of professions from janitor to clerk to administrator, and youth expressed a general desire for public employment rather than for a particular occupation. The desire for status has limits. Beginning around 2008 Ethiopia has experienced rapid inflation, and government salaries have not kept up with the cost of living. Although it is increasingly rare for youth to aspire to government employment, this was quite common in Jimma during the early 2000s.

The prestige of the government worker derives from the fact that work-related subordination and exchange take place on the basis of relationships that extend into all aspects of life and are not limited to the moment of the transaction. As they are for the low-status worker, giving, receiving, and subordination are present. But there is little sense that one is directly exchanging one's labor for what one receives. Unlike that of lower workers, the salary of government employees does not directly correspond to production. It is common for government workers to spend long periods of time away from work attending funerals and other social events, which implies that their salary is not directly based on time spent at work. Furthermore, relationships between government workers extend beyond the workplace. For example, an administrator will usually attend the funeral of a janitor if the two are employees in the same government compound. Many of the material benefits controlled by government workers are connected to access to powerful individuals and the chance to distribute better housing, education, and employment. Giving and receiving in this context take place because a relationship exists, not just at the moment of the transaction but in all aspects of life.

This contrast should not be conceived of as exchange for profit versus a relationship-based form of exchange, with exchange for profit representing the intrusion of a market economy (Taussig 1980). Urban Ethiopians did not necessarily evaluate accumulation through exchange negatively. Successful business owners depended on impersonal exchange to accumulate wealth, and they possessed high levels of prestige. Unlike working youth, however, business owners were never in a position to sell their labor to a customer directly. This meant that their interactions with others did not entail subordinating themselves with the intention of accessing wealth. Business owners did directly engage in relationships with their employees, but they were in a position of power and frequently sought to imbue these relationships with personal qualities that went beyond a simple exchange. Low status was associated not so much with the intent to accumulate profits as with the subordination of oneself without the presence of a relationship that extended to other aspects of life beyond the moment of exchange.

In this sense, youth evaluated an occupation not only on the basis of its utility in accumulating wealth but also in terms of its association with a particular quality of social relations. The government employment that most youth desired provided a secure form of income, and it also placed one within a hierarchy of power that was accompanied by close personal relationships. As I detail in the following section, because of local and international economic shifts, government work was not available, and most youth chose unemployment. Nevertheless, it is not quite accurate to conceive of youth as choosing between unemployment and employment. Youth were faced with a choice between contrasting ways of positioning themselves socially, and the shame of *yiluññta* prevented them from engaging in socially undesirable work. This was true not only of relatively well-off young men but also of those who came from families with very few economic resources.[6] To work or not to work was a social decision.

Education and Expectations

The role of *yiluññta* and values surrounding occupational status in creating a large population of unemployed youth is a historically specific phenomenon. That working in particular occupations should be considered shameful is a result of expectations surrounding education and the urban opportunity structure. These dynamics are also partly responsible for the recent emergence of youth as a distinct social category.

It was with the growth of permanent cities that notions of occupational status began to develop beyond the traditional stigmas applied to artisans. The expansion of northern settlers into southern Ethiopia and the consequent appropriation of land during the late nineteenth and early twentieth centuries, described by Bahru Zewde (2002) and Donald Donham (1986), also occurred in Jimma. In Jimma, however, the process was delayed by a peace treaty between King Abba Jifar II of Jimma and Menelik II, emperor of Ethiopia. Most of the movement of northerners, especially Orthodox Christian Amhara and Oromo from the Shoa region, into the Jimma area took place under the reign of Haile Selassie, beginning after the brief Italian occupation ended in 1941. Individuals who received land after the Italian occupation quickly expanded their wealth through farming and trade. The pattern was to have a large piece of land in the countryside and also a home in the city. Money from the sale of coffee, which is grown extensively in the area surrounding Jimma, funded the building of a house in the city and engagement in trade.

The creation of a wealthy landowning class in Jimma attracted others to the city. In particular, large numbers of people from the Dawro, Kambata, Yem, and Kafa ethnic groups living in the area surrounding Jimma moved to the city in search of wage labor. Some came only to earn money during the coffee harvest, but others stayed and found work as servants or manual laborers for landowners. With little education or knowledge of Amharic, the language of commerce in most of urban Ethiopia, these new migrants had difficulty finding anything but the most menial of jobs. After 1941, the prestige and desirability of government employment as an urban occupation developed in Jimma. The prestige of government work was partly based on the traditional hierarchical relationship between nobility and farmers. As Hoben (1970, 222) notes in describing Addis Ababa under the reign of Haile Selassie, the government administrator replaced the authority of the lord to demand tribute and labor, and education took the place of military activity as a means for accessing social mobility. Landowner- ship and longer residence in the city increased one's chances of obtaining an education. A secondary school degree virtually guaranteed one a position as an administrator or a teacher. An occupational hierarchy between those with and those without government work began to develop. Government workers had both political and economic power, whereas others generally performed the ser- vice work and manual labor necessary to maintain life in the city. To some extent, a patron-client relationship existed between these two strata. In much the same manner that a rural lord could provide access to land, government administra- tors and landowners could give their clients urban employment, better housing, and other opportunities. The revolutionary Derg regime (1974–1991) eliminated most opportunities to accumulate wealth through private enterprise, causing the value of government work to increase.

For the parents of the youth in my study, who came of age under Haile Selassie and early in the Derg regime, education was the key to accessing status through government employment. Class sizes were smaller than today, the quality of edu- cation was higher, and secondary graduates could rely on receiving good gov- ernment jobs. Although the particularities differ, similar relationships linking government employment, education, and class have been described for other parts of Africa (Berry 1985; Covell 1987; Sharp 2002).

It has become increasingly common for urban youth to complete secondary school. In general, these youth have aspired to use their education to access gov- ernment employment, but for most this has not been possible. Tekeste Negash (1996, 79) argues that the expansion of education under the Derg regime defied "rationality," creating a population of young people unable to find employ- ment. Under the Derg, the public sector also expanded, and although it may not have been able to absorb all secondary school graduates, its expansion cer- tainly prevented extremely high levels of unemployment, like those that began in the 1990s. The total urban unemployment rate for individuals between the ages of ten and sixty-five rose from 7.9 percent in 1984 to 22 percent in 1994 to

26.4 percent in 1999, with young people forming the bulk of the unemployed (Genene et al. 2001). The students in government schools during the early 2000s were very different from the elite group of the past. With the increase in the number of students, the quality of education has declined. Today a typical government secondary school classroom contains about eighty-five students, sharing books and learning in English, a language that many students do not understand well. In 1994, only around 10 percent of young people between the ages of twenty and twenty-nine had advanced to postsecondary education (Central Statistical Authority 1999). Although the few youth who do obtain a postsecondary degree are generally able to access desirable government employment, the vast majority leave school with few practical skills and little hope of securing employment.[7]

The decrease in the value of education created a gap between young people's probable life trajectories and their aspirations and led to widespread "diploma disease" (Dore 1976; Gould 1993) or "diploma inflation" (Bourdieu 1984, 142–143).[8] This dynamic is common in many parts of the world, but where a decrease in the value of education and access to government work led youth to create opportunities in the informal sector elsewhere (Cole 2004), they did not do so in Ethiopia. In the absence of jobs that young people believed accorded with their education status, urban Ethiopian youth of all class backgrounds frequently were forced to accept extended periods of unemployment.

Global political and economic shifts also prevented youth from attaining their aspirations. An inability to compete with the nations of East and South Asia in the manufacture of low-cost commodities, the burden of servicing interest on debt, and the economic policies associated with structural adjustment have all contributed to economic decline in Africa (Arrighi 2002). In Ethiopia, an IMF-imposed reduction in the size of the public sector has been particularly significant, as it has eliminated desirable opportunities for government employment. If *yiluññta* and local values concerning occupation have combined with the expansion of education to lead urban youth to seek government employment, then structural adjustment policies acted as a vise that closed off any opportunity for a growing population of educated urban youth to achieve their aspirations.

In this context, the manner in which young people move through time has shifted and has caused the meaning of *youth* to change. Although the Amharic term for *youth, wettat,* is not new, a distinct phase of life that could be referred to as "youth" had not existed in Amhara culture (Levine 1965, 96–98). Young men and women gradually took on adult responsibilities until, in terms of work, their day-to-day lives more or less resembled those of their parents. Once this point was reached, the next step was marriage. With the introduction of formal education in the mid-twentieth century, this dynamic gradually began to change. Rather than taking on the roles of their parents, educated youth expected to become government workers. The expansion of education and the contraction of the public sector have created an environment in which individuals experience a prolonged period of time between childhood and adulthood. Many of the young men in my study were in their early thirties and still had not found viable employment. Some young men with family connections were eventually able to find work that was not stigmatized. For this small population of middle-class young men, it seems that extended unemployment may have been a successful economic strategy. Avoiding the stigma associated with available forms of work allowed them to maintain social networks that could eventually provide acceptable, if not high-status, employment (Mains 2012). However, for many young men it was unclear if their dependence on their parents would ever end. In discussing youth in Madagascar, Jennifer Cole (2005) has suggested that youth no longer be conceptualized as a transitional phase leading up to adulthood, as it now appears to be quite common to remain in the category of youth indefinitely. In an environment of economic decline, individuals occupying this expanding category of youth experience a changed relationship to their future.

The ability to remain unemployed for a long period of time is a reflection of the relatively privileged social and economic position occupied by most urban young men. The unemployed young men in my study represented a variety of class backgrounds, but all of them were born and raised in the city, and this provided them with a distinct advantage in relation to Ethiopia's predominantly rural population. Even youth from poor families had extended social networks that provided them with the support necessary to remain unemployed for a period of years. Some came from households headed by single mothers with monthly incomes of less than 200 birr (approximately twenty-five dollars in 2004) earned from brewing and selling beer, and others came from households in which both parents were government administrators and the monthly income was around 2,000 birr. I collected budgets from twenty unemployed young men who were more or less evenly distributed in terms of class background and documented their income from nonwork-related sources for an entire month. These journals revealed that, although all young men had adequate support to survive on a day-to-day basis, total income varied dramatically on the basis of class and neighborhood of residence. Middle-class young men's incomes from gifts were often nearly equal to the amounts earned by working young men. This may explain why, in my study, no young men who worked in stigmatized occupations were from middle-class backgrounds. The vast majority of unemployed young men, however, received gift incomes only large enough to cover the basic costs of living; they were foregoing economic gain by avoiding low-status work.

Progress and Social Relationships

Reinhart Koselleck (1985 [1979]) explains that notions of "progress" appear at points in history when the relationship between experience and expectations shifts. Expectations for the future are generally based on what one has experienced in the past, but with the development of a belief in the inevitability of progress, this changes. In discussing the advent of "progress" in relation to increased technological innovation in Europe, Koselleck explains, "What was new was that the expectations that reached out for the future became detached from all that previous experience had to offer" (1985, 279). In other words, progress is the expectation that the future will not be like one's past and that, instead, it will be qualitatively better.

Not only has education created expectations among urban youth that they will be able to access high-status government employment; it has also conditioned them to expect to lead lives that involve progress. Education is a progressive process in that it involves gradual linear improvements. As one advances from grade to grade, it is assumed that this movement creates a change within oneself. The educated individual expects to be transformed so that his or her future will be better than the present. Contrasts between unemployment and life as a student are revealing. For unemployed young men, school was the last structured activity they were involved in. One way school differs from unemployment is that it simply makes a person very busy and therefore eliminates the problem of how to pass large swaths of time. Possibly a more significant difference is how the two contexts affect one's relationship to his future. As one young man who had been unemployed for two years after completing the twelfth grade put it, "When I was a student I had no thoughts. I learned, I studied, and I didn't worry about the future. Now I always think about the future. I don't know how long this condition will last. Maybe it will be the same year after year." In contrast to student life, unemployment is the absence of change. Days pass, but one's material and social positions remain the same. Long-term unemployment prevents youth from imagining a desirable future and placing their day-to-day lives within a narrative of progress. The social category of youth, as it exists for urban young men, emerges not just through an extended period of uncertainty regarding one's future but with the development of expectations of progress.

Because of the expansion of education and urbanization, the young men I studied were far more embedded in an ideology of progress through education than previous generations. Most urban youth were the sons and daughters of parents who did not advance beyond primary education. Although the parents had lived through a Marxist revolution that was associated with particular notions of modernity (Donham 1999), their lack of education meant that they often did not internalize an ideology of progress as it pertained to their own lives. The mother of an unemployed young man explained that "today's generation is different. They are educated and they have knowledge about the world. Today they want so many things." In describing their life histories, most parents spoke of the movement from a rural area to Jimma as a major shift in their lives. After arriving in Jimma, they generally accepted whatever work was available and were not as concerned with issues of status as their children. Parents often argued that their children's lives should be different from their own specifically because of their higher level of education, and they were disappointed when this did not prove the case.

Young men's narratives of aspiration typically began with education, followed by work, and then helping younger siblings before moving out of their parents' home to marry and start families. Finally, young men believed that a man should support his parents and, if possible, create a project or business that would benefit the community. Most urban youth were able to attain the first step in this narrative and pursue their educations to the secondary level, but they were unable to find employment, which created a dead end in their pursuit of other aspirations.

Many young men believed that nearly insurmountable financial barriers prevented them from dating, marrying, and having children. They claimed that they would not marry before the age of thirty or thirty-five and then only if they became wealthy. Children were seen as a natural and desirable result of marriage—the next step in youth narratives of aspiration—and the financial burden of raising children was an additional factor preventing young men from achieving their aspirations. To simply raise children did not involve any great costs, but most young men desired a future for their children that would be better than their own. The following quotation comes from an unemployed young man who first explained to me that he would not accept available forms of work like carpentry or waiting tables because they would not allow him and his family to experience progress:

> Without something big [a source of money] I won't even think about marriage or children. Even if I am rich, I will never have more than two children. With two kids I can educate them properly so that they can reach the university. If they don't reach the university, I will send them to America. Of course I could get a job and have children now. Even if I was only making 100 birr a month I could feed them *shuro* [a spicy chick pea paste], but that kind of life is not good for children. They will not learn properly, and they will end up shining shoes or something like that. You want your children to have a better life than yourself. You want them to improve and have a good life.

A similar perspective comes from a young man who earned money by selling sandals he made out of tires but who continued to live with his parents:

> I don't want to marry unless I have a different type work. I need something different before I try to start a family, but once I arrange my own life I definitely want a family. I only want two children. In the past people have just been having kids without saving money or thinking about the future. In my neighborhood, kids are everywhere. This is fine if you have a big compound, but in my neighborhood there are no compounds; all of the houses are packed in together. People sleep three or four to a bed. At my house we all sleep in one room. We all come home at night and watch television, and then when the programming ends at 10:00 or 11:00, we turn it off and go to sleep. If you want to stay up and study you can't, because there is only one light for one room, and you can't keep everyone else awake. Then in the morning we all wake up at the same time. Everyone in my neighborhood is like this.

The emphasis on raising one's children in a different manner than one was raised so that they could have a better life was common among young men. These statements contrast education and small families with symbols of lower-class urban life like *shuro* and sharing rooms to construct different future trajectories. *Shuro* and sharing rooms represent the mistakes of one's parents, whereas having fewer children is thought to allow a heavy investment in education and open up more opportunities for higher learning and desirable employment. Each of these narratives expresses a desire to move from a position of dependence on one's parents to supporting one's own children. Young men conceived of progress not only in terms of repositioning oneself within social relationships but also in ensuring that one's children enjoy this status as well.

The underlying problem in achieving such progress was that the smooth transition between education and government employment had been ruptured. Many young men could have found work in low-status professions, but this would not have allowed them to develop the social relationships associated with their particularly urban Ethiopian notions of success or to access an adequate income for raising children in the manner they desired. Young men sought both to preserve the quality of their social relationships with others by avoiding low-status work and to raise a family in which their children would lead modern progressive lives that involve more than "eating and sleeping." As achieving this goal was felt to be impossible, many young men chose to remain unemployed. They could not access the economic resources necessary to become an adult in a normative sense, and, therefore, they could not move through time in the manner they desired. Young men were in the ambiguous position of continuing to aspire to become adults and reposition themselves within social relations but lacking any faith that this process could be accomplished locally.

James Ferguson (2006) argues that economic shifts associated with neoliberalism have derailed Africans from participating in progressive narratives of development, creating a situation in which improving one's standard of living through linear progress is no longer possible. In other words, the separation between experience and expectations that Koselleck associates with progress is never actualized in the form of a new experience. Narratives of progress are still imagined, and expectations of a life that is different and better than previous experience still exist, but they do not become reality. The derailment from progressive narratives that Ferguson identifies is particularly acute among youth. The peculiar position of youth, existing as "not yet adults" for an indefinite period of time, means that their condition is, to a large degree, defined through their relationship to the future.

Using Space to Achieve Progress in Relationships

Many young men believed that their interrelated temporal problems could be addressed with the spatial solution of migration, preferably to the United States or Europe. In the narratives of young men, people experienced time differently outside of Ethiopia. As one unemployed young man put it during a heated conversation at a *chat* house, "I can do more in six months in America than I can in five years in Ethiopia. In America there is progress." This quotation implies that linear change through time is possible only in certain spaces and supports Ferguson's (2006) suggestion that, as Africa has been separated from temporal narratives of development, qualities of space have become fixed in relation to modernity.

The rise of the U.S. Diversity Visa (DV) Lottery as a means of experiencing change or progress represents the transition from temporal to spatial strategies for attaining one's aspirations. Although few American-born U.S. citizens are aware of the annual DV Lottery, it is eagerly anticipated in much of the rest of the world. Every year, fifty thousand winners from countries around the world are selected to receive a U.S. visa. In 2006 nearly seven thousand Ethiopians were finalists in the DV Lottery, and of these approximately two-thirds eventually received visas. To be a DV applicant, one had to be a secondary school graduate, have a sponsor in the United States (someone who will provide initial support) and a job skill, and not be infected with HIV. Many Ethiopians who have entered the United States in the early 2000s had family members with Diversity Visas or had won a lottery themselves. Although Ethiopia receives a relatively high number of Diversity Visas, the roughly four thousand winners who migrate to the United States every year via the lottery are a small fraction of those who enter the lottery. For most, the lottery is a dream that takes the place of working locally and participating in a temporal narrative of becoming.

Within young men's discussions, winning the DV Lottery did not fit into a larger narrative of progress. Unlike education, one does not win the DV Lottery by following a set of rules for development or passing through a series of stages. In practice, social networks are extremely important for accessing a sponsor abroad and funds for travel and for negotiating a complicated bureaucratic process that involves extensive paperwork in English and an interview at the U.S. embassy (Piot 2010). Most youth, however, do not acknowledge these realities and speak of the lottery primarily in terms of chance. One simply wins or does not win. Access to technology, wealth, and the prestige of living in the United States is acquired not through disciplining oneself to advance from education to employment but through good luck. In the absence of a temporal process of becoming, the DV Lottery is a spatial strategy that instantly allows one to be modern.

Fitting with the lottery, youth narratives often constructed migration as facilitating a transformation of identity. The notion that migration and the appropriation of stylistic practices (particularly fashion) may allow a re-creation of one's identity has been effectively explored in other studies of urban youth in Africa (De Boeck 1999; Friedman 1994; Gondola 1999; Hansen 2000; MacGaffey and Bazenguissa-Ganga 2000; Newell 2005). For example, in relation to the Congolese subculture of La Sape, Didier Gondola writes that "popular culture allows African urban youth to build a dreamlike order, otherwise unreachable" (1999, 24) and that "the sapeur does not dress like a CEO to imitate the CEO. He is a CEO" (1999, 32). Sasha Newell (2005) extends this analysis of popular culture and argues that migration is also a form of consumption. Migration is in part a symbolic process that allows the traveler to accumulate cultural capital through an association with "modern" or "developed" world areas. Within this construct of migration as a symbolic act, one's identity is transformed through association with place without one personally undergoing a temporal process of becoming.

During an afternoon that I spent with a group of young men as they chewed *chat* and talked, one of them told me about a dream he had had the night before: "I was in New York City at an amazing club. We were dancing and drinking and it was wonderful. Jennifer [Lopez] was singing. You were there too. I didn't want to wake up." Young men also frequently "dreamed" about life in the United States during the day as they chewed *chat* and socialized (Mains 2012). They spent hours speculating about life in different cities and the possibility of meeting celebrities. From Ethiopia, this lifestyle can only be dreamed of, but if one wins the DV Lottery, this dream becomes a reality.

Actually moving to the United States, a world that was usually accessed only through dreams, was believed to cause an internal transformation in oneself. That same afternoon, one of the young *chat* chewers showed me "before and after" photographs of his brother—one before his departure for the United States and one after. The difference was not immediately apparent to me, but he explained: "Of course he has become fat, but the really beautiful thing is his skin. His skin glows. Before he was old and starving, but now in America he is young and healthy." According to these young men, the United States is a land where there are no beggars, everyone is fat, and people pay the equivalent of half a month's salary for a low-level Ethiopian government worker to have their dogs washed. In response to my attempts to provide a more complete picture of life in the United States, one of the young men shouted, "Listen Danny, the life of a dog in America is better than a human in Ethiopia!"

In discussions that reference Western pop culture and compare Ethiopia to the United States, young men were defining their own lives in terms of absence—the absence of entertainment, the absence of health, the absence of modernity. These narratives are similar to Charles Piot's (2005) notion of "living in exile" within one's own country—isolated from the modern life that one desires. To migrate was to transform oneself completely. The statement "We live like chickens" and the negative comparison of an Ethiopian's life with that of a dog in the United States imply that there is something not quite human about life in Ethiopia. There is a sense that one cannot really be a full person without leaving the country.

Although they may conceive of Ethiopia as inherently "backward," through movement young men quickly shift from "living like a chicken" to the sort of healthy and meaningful life assumed to exist elsewhere. Within youth discourse, it is spaces and not people that are fixed in time, thus allowing individuals to experience progress through spatial movement. Change occurs not just with movement but also by referencing symbolic qualities associated with other spaces. In this sense, one can experience progress through the manipulation of spatial qualities despite the inability to participate in temporal narratives of progress.

The use of space to overcome problems of time within a context of economic decline is a strategy widely employed within Africa and other parts of the world. In urban Ethiopia, spatial movement was not only a tool for circumventing the problem of becoming, it also allowed young men to escape the confines of local relationships. In general, the West—the United States in particular—was conceived as a space in which social freedom was possible. One young man with a particularly strong interest in travel abroad explained, "In Ethiopia there is *yiluññta*. We are not free here. In America I would do so many things. I like to play sports, but in Ethiopia I cannot wear shorts. People will talk and insult me. In America I could wear shorts. I would be free to do whatever I wanted." Although wearing shorts may seem trivial, it represents a general sense that one could escape local cultural norms through migration.

The following quotations from young people illustrate the relationship between occupational status and a desire to migrate. From a group of vocational students:

> Everyone wants to go to leave Ethiopia. This is because work is not appreciated here. A person who does street work like shining shoes and washing cars will be insulted, especially if they are educated. They won't be accepted by society. My father has a friend who works in South Africa selling socks on the street. He is an adult with a good education. Someone like him would never do this in Ethiopia. Of course he can make more money in South Africa, but also there is no *yiluññta* there. An educated person like my father's friend will be insulted here, and he may have to fight.

From a different group of vocational students:

> STUDENT 1: The best reason for leaving Ethiopia is to work and make money, but *yiluññta* is also important. A shoeshine can make fifteen or twenty birr a day [$2–$2.50]. This is good money, but they will be insulted. If I have to do this kind of work, I would have to go to a new city first.
>
> STUDENT 2: I want to work part-time while I am a student, but there is *yiluññta*. Even if they don't insult you, they won't respect you, they will order you around, and no one wants to be known as a shoeshine.
>
> STUDENT 3: I've seen in movies that comedians make money telling jokes on the street in America, but you can't do this in Ethiopia.

In practice, women were much more likely to travel abroad for work, usually to the Middle East to work as domestic servants. *Yiluññta* and a restructuring of social relations were also relevant for this type of occupational migration, but the dynamics were significantly different than those I have described here for young men. Young women generally worked on a contractual basis and stayed abroad for only a few years. Although they usually sent remittances to their families, they were unable to accumulate the large sums of wealth accessed by migrants in Europe or the United States. I knew of many cases in which unemployed young men were supported largely by remittances sent by their sisters working in the Middle East. Perhaps as a result of spatial distance, this subversion of gendered norms concerning reciprocity and power created little tension among women migrants and their male kin.

Migration abroad was a narrative that was rarely put into practice by young men, but migration within Ethiopia was more common. Choosing to live without the support of family or friends was, of course, no small sacrifice to make. One young man from the Wollo region left his rural home and worked as a waiter in Jimma. He explained that he had moved so far away (two to three days from his home by bus) in order to avoid shaming himself in front of family and friends. He lacked even minimal social support in Jimma. When the room he rented was robbed, he lost all of his possessions, and he had no one to turn to for aid. Despite these hardships, he felt that he had made the right decision by leaving his home. This man's story was typical of restaurant workers; nearly all of the waiters that I interviewed had migrated from elsewhere. This example also indicates that spatial movement did not necessarily require one to leave the country to escape *yiluññta*. Avoiding the shame of stigma could be accomplished by moving locally, but this did not provide the symbolic association with modernity and the opportunity to earn high incomes that caused young men to perceive international migration as being so effective in facilitating a change in one's status.

The shame of working in a low-status occupation was entirely social. If one was surrounded by strangers, then the stress of *yiluññta* was forgotten. Spatial movement as a solution to problems of time was embedded in local values concerning occupation. Cultural norms were experienced as barriers to one's aspirations for progress, and it was only by temporarily escaping those norms that a young man could return to and reenter his community with a different and more desirable social position. An extensive literature describes the importance of migration in Africa, usually in relation to accessing urban wage labor, for accumulating the resources necessary to take on the role of an adult. For example, in her study of the Nuer, Sharon Hutchinson (1996) describes young men performing wage labor in the city to accumulate the cash necessary to return home, expand their cattle herds, and start families. Others have argued that accessing the modern qualities of space is as important in motivating migration as differences in economic opportunity (Newell 2005). The Ethiopian case is distinct because it is more than just differences in access to material goods or qualities associated with modernity that motivated migration. Rather, young men sought to leave Ethiopia partly because of differences in the way individuals were thought to interact in different spaces.

The fundamental quality that allows spatial movement to solve the problem of experiencing progress in social relationships is a shift in the manner that productive activity is evaluated. Within Ethiopia, young men evaluated work primarily in terms of how it situated one in relation to others. They conceived of work outside of Ethiopia as essentially the exchange of one's labor power and time for wages. For unemployed young men, progress in terms of one's position within relationships at home was achieved by moving to a space in which work is not assessed in terms of relationships. The choice to work as a taxi driver in the United States was based not on the position of that occupation within a hierarchy of power but on the possibility of earning money. This is not to say that working outside of Ethiopia was divorced from *yiluññta* and social relationships. Money earned elsewhere was usually invested in Ethiopia, and work and time in Ethiopia continued to be evaluated in terms of relationships. The government employment that previously allowed one simultaneously to work and to engage in positive relations, however, was no longer a realistic possibility. This led young men to conceive of the construction of desirable relationships as possible only by moving to a space where work and time functioned differently.

In practice, accessing these spaces was accomplished primarily through social networks. As noted above, even in the case of a seemingly random process like the DV Lottery, networks were very important. Often, young men who managed to migrate had family living abroad who could provide assistance. To move without these connections was virtually impossible. In this sense, networks of people facilitated the movement that allowed one to escape temporarily from social relationships and, ideally, to reposition oneself within those same relationships eventually. At each step in the process, the meanings of different spaces were determined largely by their implications for social relationships.

Conclusion

Many of the dynamics that I have described in this article are common to youth living in a variety of different areas in the world. To varying degrees, a decrease in the value of education, constriction in opportunity within the public sector, difficulty in taking on the responsibilities associated with adulthood, and an increased interest in migration are all themes in recent studies of youth. The specific argument I have developed, however, is based on rethinking these processes through a close analysis of *yiluññta* and values concerning occupational status. I have argued that urban youth in Ethiopia evaluated employment not so much on the basis of income and labor time but rather in terms of the manner in which work situated one within social relationships. By extending this argument to discourses and practices concerning progress and international migration, I have demonstrated that both time and space are inextricable from social relationships.

The case of young men in urban Ethiopia demonstrates the problem of a strict dichotomy between unemployment and employment. Categorizing urban young men as employed or unemployed overlooks the more salient issue of their position within social relationships. The young men I studied were primarily concerned with how they interacted with others in day-to-day life and their abil-ity to reposition themselves within relations of reciprocity. Young men wished to move to the United States not simply to find work but also to use spatial distance to separate themselves from relationships. This is not to say that employment is not important. However, an overreliance on (un)employment as an analytical category masks the struggles with social relationships that are fundamental to young men's lives. Rather than categorizing young people based on their employ-ment status, it is often more useful to examine how they are situated within social relationships, both in the present and in relation to an imagined future.

8

LABOR ON THE MOVE

Kinship, Social Networks, and Precarious Work among Mexican Migrants

Frances Abrahamer Rothstein

Residents of San Cosme Mazatecochco, a rural community in central Mexico, have a long history of dealing with changing economic circumstances and fluctuating demands for their labor. Despite many ups and downs, until recently few people from Mazatecochco migrated to the United States. Since the mid-1990s, however, hundreds of men and women from Mazatecochco have come to the United States, especially to New Jersey and Connecticut. This chapter describes how San Cosmeros/as have dealt with neoliberal policies, especially free trade, which led to the loss of their factory jobs in national textile factories and then the decline in their small-scale local garment manufacturing, by migrating to the United States. Then, as the U.S. economy deteriorated with the Great Recession, many returned to Mexico. Men without wives have been more likely to return, whereas men and women who have families and social networks in the United States have been able to use those networks to cushion the effects of the under- and unemployment brought about by the Recession and are more likely to remain in the United States.

This chapter examines who has returned and why. In doing so it demonstrates the relationship between un- and underemployment and migration flows; it also documents the critical roles kinship and community play in sustaining populations in and out of employment and throughout the migration process. Particular attention is paid to how gender, kinship, and economic conditions in the United States, Mazatecochco, and the state of Tlaxcala, where the community is located, influenced their decision to return. My research and Mexican census information show that men more than women are returning to Mexico. As the

U.S. economy deteriorated in the Great Recession, many (especially men) lost their jobs completely or had the number of days they could be employed reduced. Many of these men, especially those who did not have family in the United States who could help them through difficult times, returned home.

The chapter is divided into four sections. In the first part, "Contemporary Capitalism," I discuss the theoretical methods used in this analysis to understand migration. Following Stephen Castles, migration (including return migration) is viewed as an integral part of the broader transformation process of globalization (2010, 2011). Most of the research on globalization and migration has focused on why migrants migrate. In section two, "Precarious Work and Mexican Return Migration," I discuss the differential pattern of return migration for Mexican men and women in general and for Tlaxcala and Mazatecochco in particular, and·I describe the precarious nature of migrants' employment in the United States, especially for men during the Recession, and improvements in the local and regional economies in Mexico. I suggest here that return migration is related to the broader process of globalization and economic conditions in the United States and in Mexico. But, social factors, especially kinship and family networks, can cushion the effects of a deteriorating economy. In the third section, "Who Returns and Why?" I discuss how family and kin networks can become a deciding factor. This, I argue, means also that return varies with the nature of those networks. The conclusion discusses the implications of the findings for further research that takes a broader approach to migration and un- and underemployment. For San Cosmeros/as, in both Mexico and the United States, the problem is less one of unemployment than underemployment and flexible and precarious labor. Increasingly, both in the United States and Mexico (as elsewhere in the world), employers have little or no commitment to workers. Although migrants did sometimes lose their jobs completely, given that their work is usually not secure, the problem they faced, especially during the Great Recession, was that it became even more likely to be temporary, part-time, and insecure. Kin networks (which require the presence of women) mitigated the effects of precarious work.

This discussion is based on four decades of ethnographic research in Mazatecochco (1971–2014) and five years of research (2009–present) on migrants from Mazatecochco in a medium-sized city in New Jersey that I call "Riverview."[1] Research in Mazatecochco included over five years of fieldwork in the community. Research on migrants in the United States involved visiting migrants primarily in New Jersey for stays ranging from one day to three weeks and visits from migrants in New York City at my home and on outings such as visits with friends to the Statue of Liberty, the American Museum of Natural History, and Jones Beach. During these stays and visits in Mexico and in the United States I conducted in-depth, semi-structured personal interviews with fifty return migrants (thirty-five men and fifteen women) and fifty migrants (thirty women and twenty men) in New Jersey and had numerous informal conversations with them, members of their families, and other members of their communities, including local and regional leaders, in a variety of contexts including fiestas such as the celebration of Carnival, Christmas, weddings, baptisms, and birthdays as well as visits to their homes or in mine.[2]

Contemporary Capitalism: Flexible Accumulation, Globalization, Social Networks, and Migration

Stephen Castles has suggested that to understand global migration we need to use a social transformation perspective (2010, 2011). Castles sees social transformation as fundamental changes that are more than "the continual processes of incremental social change that are always at work." Rather, they are "closely linked to major shifts in dominant economic, political and strategic relationships" (2010, 1576). Furthermore, Castles sees international migration as tied to the global labor market associated with neoliberal globalization (2011, 313).

The approach used in this paper also sees migration as part of a broader transformation as suggested by Castles, but whereas Castles stresses political changes at the end of the Cold War, I see the transformation as emerging in the 1970s and suggest that contemporary globalization and the transformation with which it is associated can best be understood in terms of capitalist accumulation.[3] As Eric Wolf (1997, 298) suggests, following Marx, capital accumulation occurs and capitalism emerges when wealth is used to buy labor to produce more wealth. Over time and space, capitalist accumulation has taken different forms, and the relation between capital and labor has changed. The analysis used here begins with the current form of capital accumulation, what Harvey (1990) calls "flexible accumulation." Flexible accumulation refers particularly to the flexible commitment of capital to particular places and workers. More specifically, "It rests on flexibility with respect to labour processes, labour markets, products and patterns of consumption" (Harvey 1990, 147).

Although Castles does not use the term *flexible accumulation*, much of his discussion of migration discusses the contemporary pattern of capital's flexible commitment to labor and place. More specifically, he describes a phase of global class relations initiated by the economic recession in the 1970s that is characterized (like Harvey's pattern of flexible accumulation) by the movement of capital investment and a change to a flexible workforce (Castles 2011).

Although flexible labor figures prominently in many discussions of migration since the 1980s,[4] what distinguishes Castles's approach is his insistence on seeing migration more holistically than many analysts. Not only does he recognize the importance of global restructuring and labor-market dimensions of migration, but he stresses "the many non-economic factors that make migration such an all-embracing experience" and "connectivity between localities and mediations between levels" (2010, 1582). Thus, Castles provides a framework to describe and analyze the movement of people, particularly for employment, which encompasses the struggle for survival over time and place through, but not confined to, selling one's labor. Elsewhere, Castles writes:

> The social transformation processes crucial to the reordering of labor relations are mediated through local historical and cultural patterns, which allow people to develop specific types of adaptation and resistance. These can take the form of religious or nationalist movements, but also of individual- or familial-level strategies as well as collective action against exploitation. (2011, 319)

Similarly, although Harvey does not specifically discuss migration, more generally he suggests:

> It is also at such times of fragmentation and economic insecurity that the desire for stable values leads to a heightened emphasis upon the authority of basic institutions—the family, religion, the state. . . . Such connections are, at least plausible, and they ought, therefore, to be given more careful scrutiny. (1990, 171–172 citing Simmel 1978)

How are the fragmentation, insecurity, and reordering of social relations, adaptation, and resistance mentioned by Harvey and Castles tied to social and cultural patterns of Mazatecochco's migrants at home and away?

When I went to Mazatecochco in 2012 to conduct exploratory research on return migration, I found that more men had returned than women. Additionally, when asked why they had returned, although economic conditions in the United States were important, return migrants all stressed family as a key reason for their return. A father was dying; a mother was ill; a wife had left Mazatecochco to live with another man. I knew from my research in New Jersey that migrants from Mazatecochco were using kinship and ritual practices similar to those at home to expand their social networks and to build social capital that facilitated their adaption to their new circumstances (see Rothstein 2015). I knew also that these practices depended on the presence of women. Among migrants from Mazatecochco, the increased presence of women has enabled a system of flexible kinship, similar to that found in Mazatecochco, to function also in the United States.

Several studies have shown the importance of women in the kinship and ritual systems of Mexican communities such as Mazatecochco (Rothstein 1982; Stephen

2005a). What has less often been noted is that the increased presence of women among migrants facilitates the continued importance of kinship and ritual systems in the United States. Although men have significant roles in the rituals and family gatherings that take place, women are, as di Leonardo (1992) has noted for Italian American women in the United States, the organizers of home celebrations and play the major role in creating and maintaining kin relations. Women perform what di Leonardo calls "the work of kinship." Such kin work involves "the conception, maintenance, and ritual celebration of cross-household kin ties," including "the organization of holiday gatherings; the creation and maintenance of quasi-kin relations; the decision to neglect or to intensify particular ties; [and] the mental work of reflection about all these activities" (1987, 442–443).

The kinship practices of San Cosmeros/as have always been flexible. As Rothstein has pointed out, this means that kinship is stressed in ideology and practice, but three characteristics enable the system to change and adapt to different circumstances: (1) "bilateral recognition of relatives through men and women along with relations through marriage and *compadrazgo* (ritual kinship)," (2) "the recognition of kin despite physical, genealogical, and social distance," and (3) "the fact that beyond some minimal obligations, particular kin relations are not attached to particular obligations" (1999, 583). This flexibility allowed them to adapt to changing circumstances throughout the twentieth century. For migrants in the United States, women's presence facilitates the creation, maintenance, and adaptation of former practices and values of kinship and ritual that help migrants survive and challenge constraints of class, gender, and legality.[5] The presence of women and the kin networks they facilitate have always been important for San Cosmeros/as. They have been even more important in cushioning the effects of the Great Recession when employment, especially of men, became even more precarious than it was before the Recession.

Precarious Work and Mexican Return Migration

In what a Pew Hispanic Center report on Mexican migration called a "notable reversal of the historic pattern," more Mexicans left the United States between 2005 and 2010 than arrived (Passel, Cohn, and Gonzalez-Barrera 2012). Other recent discussions of Mexican migration to the United States also indicate that the migration rate has declined significantly and the number of Mexicans arriving in the United States has fallen sharply (Preston 2012). Despite an enormous amount of data on migration rates to the United States, however, there is much less information on the extent of Mexican return migration or on who returns.

Recently, several studies have suggested differences between those who return and those who stay. Rendall, Brownell, and Kups (2009), Masferrer and Roberts (2012), and Van Hook and Zhang (2011) found that men had higher rates of return than women. Some studies of settlement have also found that women are more likely to stay in the United States than men. Reyes found that the length of stay was longer for women than men. Whereas 45 percent of the adult Mexican women in her study stayed longer than ten years, only 26 percent of the adult men stayed longer than ten years (1997, 48). If, as suggested by these studies, women are returning less often than men, we need to understand why.

Numerous economic factors are assumed to be associated with return. Disappointing work experiences in the host county are thought to hasten return (Van Hook and Zhang 2011), and migrants' expectations of the home economy play a significant role (Cassarino 2004). Lindstrom (1996) found that economic opportunities, especially investment opportunities, in the home community or region are important. Recent research by Masferrer and Roberts (2012) which found that migrants are returning more to new sending areas (that is, those that have only recently been involved in migration), prosperous communities, and growing metropolitan areas lends support to this perspective. Other studies have also stressed economic conditions at home and in the receiving county along with immigration policy in the receiving country (e.g., Cobo, Giorguli, and Alba 2010). A study that examined a combination of factors also found that although economic factors, as measured by human capital and economic integration in the United States, influenced return, social capital, as measured by marital status, household size, and the presence of children in the United States, was more closely related to return (Van Hook and Zhang 2011). Unfortunately, these studies do not look at gender.

Preliminary research in Mazatecochco in 2012 indicated that women seemed to be returning less than men. Research in 2014 confirmed this pattern. Recent Mexican analyses support the suggestion that the incidence of returns among men is greater. An analysis by INEGI (Instituto Nacional de Estadística y Geografía, or the National Institute of Statistics and Geography), focusing on the period between 2005 and 2010, found that a lower proportion of women returned to Mexico than men (28.8% versus 32.5%). In the state of Tlaxcala, the difference was even greater: 26.1 percent of the women who migrated returned, compared to 34.2 percent of the male migrants. In a discussion of types of migrants, Alba suggests that "circular migrants tend to be younger and predominantly male, while settled migrants are more evenly split between men and women" (2010, 5). Other studies also indicate that the ratio of women to men among settled Mexican migrants is higher (Reyes 1997).

Given the general neglect of both return migration and, until recently, gender and migration,[6] it is not surprising that little is known about variations by gender,

class, marital status, education, age, work experience, occupational opportunities, and likelihood of men and women returning. My research in Mazatecochco
and among migrants in New Jersey as well as hints from studies of migrants in
the United States suggest also that, along with gender, we must include a discussion of family and kinship.

Although studies of migration always note the importance of family and
broader social networks in the decision to migrate, the research on the role of
social networks in settlement versus return has been less systematic. There is a
great deal of research on the relation between social networks and employment.
Most of this research relies, however, on problematic measures of networks and
focuses only on men's social networks.[7] Especially when economic conditions
are precarious, the absence of family and kin networks, particularly among male
migrants, may contribute to higher rates of return migration. Before discussing
how the presence of women, family, and kin networks may lessen the impact of
male under- and unemployment, it is necessary to consider economic conditions
for migrants at home and in the United States in recent years.

Precarious Work at Home and in the United States

Although the Great Recession in the United States was officially over in June 2009
and unemployment of immigrant Mexicans decreased 1 percent between 2009
and 2010, unemployment of Mexicans in the United States remained high
(12% in 2010 compared to 5.5% in 2007) (CONAPO 2011, 252). Furthermore,
underemployment also grew. Between 2008 and 2010 the proportion of Mexican immigrants working less than forty hours a week almost doubled, from
9.8 percent to 19 percent (CONAPO 2011, 256).[8] Not surprisingly, this decline in
hours worked was associated with a decline in wages. Between 2007 and 2010 the
average annual salary of Mexican immigrants declined from $22,579 to $21,224
(CONAPO 2011, 257). Not only did wages decline and unemployment increase,
but given that most Mexican migrants, including the vast majority of those from
Mazatecochco, are undocumented, they are concentrated in informal work, especially landscaping and construction for men and domestic work for women. As
Munck, Schierup, and Delgado Wise have pointed out, informality is "at the root
of the precarious work which is now the norm" in the global north as well as the
global south (2011, 253).

As the conditions for Mexican migrants in the United States failed to improve,
since 2010 the Tlaxcalan economy has been showing signs of recovery. According
to newspaper accounts, the economy of Tlaxcala has been growing more than the

national economy (5.1% compared to 3.9%) (Jiménez Guillén 2012, 3; Avendaño 2014, 5). Conversations with return migrants in August 2012 and later in 2014 indicated that they were all currently working. This coincided with my impression that the local small-scale garment industry and commercial activity in the community had grown. When I was there in 2009, the garment industry was suffering (Rothstein 2010; Montiel Torres 2014). In fact, it was the decline in the local small-scale garment industry in the late 1990s and early 2000s that had originally contributed to the growth in migration from Mazatecochco beginning in the 1990s.

People in Mazatecochco have experienced changing economic conditions and fluctuating demands for their labor for years. In the 1940s a growing population on a limited land base led to the migration of men from the community to Mexico City (sixty miles away) or Puebla (ten miles away) to work in the national textile industry. In the 1980s, as free trade grew, textile workers from Mazatecochco, along with hundreds of thousands of other textile workers, lost their factory jobs. In the late 1980s, a few families who had been clothing vendors and were buying clothing that they sold at regional markets began producing garments in small family *talleres* (workshops). By the mid-1990s there were hundreds of workshops in Mazatecochco producing garments. Although some of the workers and worker/owners of the smaller workshops sew the pieces designed and cut by the owners of the larger workshops, it should be noted that neither the smaller nor the larger workshops are tied to transnational garment manufacturing. As competition within the community and from garments produced elsewhere increased, many of the small workshops closed, and the larger workshops looked to more distant communities for cheaper labor. Many of the migrants in New Jersey had either owned small workshops, usually in what people in Mazatecochco call *maquilas* because they sewed the cut pieces that larger owners produced, or had been workers in the larger workshops, which were now having the sewing done in other places where workers were cheaper. A few of the larger workshop owners have also migrated, but some who were able to innovate and diversify have survived.[9]

Recent national and regional growth (Gould 2011; Jiménez Guillén 2012; *El Sol de Tlaxcala* 2012, 2014) seems to have led to a revival of the local garment industry. Many of the return migrants are working in garment workshops, either their own or belonging to others. With the revival of the garment industry, other commercial activities seem to have prospered as well. The streets are lined with a wide variety of commercial establishments and services offering clothing stores, electronic games, cell phones, music lessons, English classes, and the like, as well as small restaurants and a sophisticated café with espresso, cappuccino, hamburgers, apple pie, and other foods not traditionally eaten in the community.

Women also make and sell prepared traditional foods, such as *chileatole* (a corn soup) and *chiles en nogada*,[10] which they deliver on weekends. In this respect Mazatecochco is similar in occupational distribution to the state of Tlaxcala. Between 2000 and 2010 participation in the agricultural, industrial, and construction sectors decreased, while the commercial and service sectors increased significantly (INEGI 2010, 55).

Who Returns and Why?

Who returns depends obviously on who goes. Until recently, Mexican women migrated much less frequently than men, and if they did migrate, they often went with or following husbands (Donato 2010). Mazatecochco, located in central Mexico, is a new sending community in a region that did not traditionally have high migration to the United States. By the time people from Mazatecochco began to migrate, most women were employed or generating income through informal activities, including as family workers in garment workshops. When people from Mazatecochco began to migrate, the gender pattern was not that of the traditional sending communities. Both men and women migrate, and many of the women migrants from Mazatecochco have migrated, like many of the men, autonomously, that is, they were not following spouses or parents (Rothstein 2010). Like the men, as the regional and local economy deteriorated, women migrated for jobs.

Although the local and regional economies have improved recently, most of the employment in Mazatecochco and in the region is, like migrants' work in the United States, informal, part-time, and precarious. The proportion, for example, of the economically active population in the state of Tlaxcala that has access to health benefits has declined, as has the proportion of the economically active population earning two or more times the minimum daily salary, which is considered what a family needs to live (INEGI 2010, table 4).[11] Thus, despite economic growth in the state and the appearance of prosperity in the community, most of the available work is still poorly paid and insecure.

One of the main sources of employment for women and men in Mazatecochco for the last two decades has been in small-scale garment production. As indicated above, many merchants (the term used for the owners of the larger workshops that produce and sell their production) began subcontracting to workers in other communities where labor was cheaper. They still, however, rely on local workers for some tasks, such as designing, cutting, distributing, and collecting the cut pieces and marketing the completed garment, as well as for sewing when the demand for sewing is high. In 2014, as demand for their garments increased, merchants also began relying more on local workers to sew the garments. At peak times, for example, before the school year begins, merchants sometimes have a hard time finding people to whom they can subcontract sewing projects. Although about twenty of the larger owners of the workshops appear to be doing well, the workers and smaller producers have a more difficult time. Even when times are relatively good, the garment market fluctuates greatly, not only with competition and the overall economy but also seasonally. When there are orders, they have work. When there are no orders, there is no work. Even when there is work, the pay is low and there are no benefits. Underneath what appears to be growing productive and commercial activity, there is insecure precarious work.

Why, then, have some San Cosermos/as returned? And who is more likely to return? When I went to Mazatecochco in August 2012 I had expected that people returned because of the decline in the U.S. economy and the apparent improvements in the local and regional economies, as much of the research on return migration suggested (Lindstrom 1996; Rogers 2009; Boccagni and Lagomarsino 2011). The Mexican economy has been improving. Indeed, according to one report, "Mexico's gross domestic product expanded last year [2010] at the fastest pace in a decade as Latin America's second-biggest economy recovered from a 2009 recession provoked by the global financial crisis" (Gould 2011; cf. Cave 2011, Malkin and Romero 2012). In a 2012 address, the governor of the state of Tlaxcala pointed out that although the state had lost 13.5 percent (71,111) of its jobs between 2000 and 2010, unemployment had recently dropped from 13.5 percent in October 2011 to 11 percent and foreign investment had grown by 337 percent (*El Sol de Tlaxcala* 2012). Foreign investment in the state has continued to grow, and unemployment in Mexico has continued to decline (*El Sol de Tlaxcala* 2014). This economic growth has coincided also with a change in Mexico's demographic structure that benefits job seekers. Births per woman and population growth since the 1970s have declined. Consequently, as fewer young people are now entering the labor force, competition for jobs is less and the possibilities for finding a job are better.

As indicated above, some research, including data from the state of Tlaxcala, has suggested that men are more likely to return than women. But although there are many suggestions as to why men more than women return, the question has not been systematically explored. Surprisingly, despite the enormous amount of attention that social networks have received for their influence on who migrates, there has been less interest in the role of social networks in settlement and even less on return. Although some research has looked at the presence of the immediate family or the relation between social networks and employment,[12] broader social networks have received less attention. There are hints, however, that such networks may be important. Reyes (1997), for example, has suggested that the presence of family and social networks may decrease the likelihood of return.

Although I had expected economic opportunities to be the main reason for return, everyone I talked to cited some family reason rather than economic factors for their return—a daughter got married, a mother was lonely, a father was sick, a wife was waiting, or a wife had not waited. In response to my questions about their dislikes regarding life in the United States, especially those who had no family members there, most said that they missed their families. They also stressed the need to work and to have money to survive. As one woman said, "You have to work, *mucho* bills." Another man commented that if you had no money, you had no food or anything else. This is very different than in Mazatecochco, where everyone has family, food, and a roof over one's head even if they are un- or underemployed. Thus unemployment in the context of life in the United States was experienced very differently, both emotionally and financially, than unemployment in Mazatecochco.

In New Jersey, most of the men I talked to lived in a rented house or apartment with a number of other men and sometimes women. Usually, several people sleep in narrow beds in a single room. In most cases, a person prepares their own food or buys ready-made food just for themselves. Although some of the women I know in the United States are living in or have lived in similar conditions, they are much more likely to be living with kin, either because they came with or joined husbands or parents or, more commonly, because they have formed families here. While men also form families here, the ratio of Mexican migrant men to Mexican migrant women is to women's advantage because of the greater availability of men.[13] Although couples and families have returned to Mazatecochco, my research suggests that women and families are more likely to remain in the United States than men who live alone or with other men, even if the others are sons or brothers.

Having kin in the United States has numerous advantages. Living with kin, especially one or more women, offers additional security and a safety net. Not only do most women work for pay, but most of the men I met in New Jersey also work in construction or landscaping. The women work in domestic work. Although men earn more ($15 per hour compared to $8 or $10 per hour for women), their work is seasonal. Even when times are good, men who work in construction or landscaping often find themselves unemployed in the winter. During the Recession, men in landscaping and construction often found themselves working fewer hours during other seasons as well. While women's pay is lower, their work is year-round. Women's domestic work also seemed to be less affected by the decline in the U.S. economy.

Women's presence is also crucial in the maintenance of broader kin and social networks through the celebration of ritual and life cycle events such as Carnival, the community's saints day, Christmas, and birthdays.

In Mazatecochco, despite precarious work and economic insecurity, there is always family and a flexible kinship system, which is an integral part of life there. This kinship system, which incorporates real, ritual, and affinal kin, has helped San Cosmeros/as deal with adversity as well as opportunity at home and in the United States.[14] But in the United States, many do not have that system or the safety net it can provide. Thus, when times are particularly bad, as in the Recession, for those without kin, especially female kin, return migration may seem like an attractive alternative, especially if the local and regional economies in Mexico appear to be improving.

Kinship in Mazatecochco and New Jersey

The system of flexible kinship in Mazatecochco has helped San Cosmeros/as secure many changes, such as potable water and electricity in the 1960s. In 1971, San Cosmeros/as used kin connections to replace their one school, which had only six rooms and four grades, with two larger primary schools with six grades each. Also in 1971, again with the help of kin connections, they were able to establish a kindergarten. In the late 1970s, 1980s, and 1990s, their ties enabled them to add a tele-secondary school (with most classes taught via television) and then a regular secondary school and a high school. Before Mazatecochco had secondary and high schools, kinship connections with people elsewhere enabled the sons and daughters of Mazatecochco to live with those kin and attend schools in other communities. Kin in Mazatecochco and elsewhere also helped San Cosmeros/as get jobs in textile factories in Mexico City or Puebla throughout the 1950s, 1960s, and 1970s (Rothstein 1982).

Migrants to the United States also rely on kin, *compadrazgo* (ritual kinship involving godparenthood in which the ties between the co-parents, the child's parents and the godparents, are stressed), and marriage and friendship ties to come to the United States and find housing and jobs. Several studies of migrants have suggested that migrants are frequently disappointed because the social networks that they expect to rely upon in the United States often let them down (e.g., Menjívar 2000). D'Aubeterre Buznego (2002), however, suggests that kin ties may have new vigor in social reproductive support of migrant social life. For example, migrant kin often provide housing, childcare, and other assistance to newcomers when they arrive. Although migrants from Mazatecochco do experience disappointments when kin cannot or do not help them, many San Cosmeros/as seem to have avoided such disappointments because, as they have always done, they are flexible with regard to their expectations of kin (Rothstein 2016).

In the United States, as in Mexico, San Cosmeros/as incorporate new contacts through marriage or co-residence, *compadrazgo*, and cooperation at work and play. Thus, they integrate new friends and acquaintances with new resources into their social networks. That they can do so is due to the flexibility of the kinship/ritual system they experienced in Mexico.

But the system needs women. Women maintain the kin contacts; through their work organizing fiestas, to which kin and friends are invited, kin ties are reinforced and expanded. For example, at a recent celebration in New Jersey on Christmas Eve, about seventy-five people gathered in the home of several families who live in a large house. Included were their biological, affinal, and ritual kin who lived in the area as well as friends and coworkers. The five women (two of whom were married, one single mother, and two of their teenaged daughters) who lived in the house and two of their friends prepared traditional dishes including *barbacoa* (a slow-cooked lamb dish) and *ponche* (fruit punch) for all the guests, many of whom had not known one another before.

As indicated above, the increased presence of women has enabled a system of flexible kinship, similar to that in Mazatecochco, to function in the United States as well. For migrants in the United States, women's presence facilitates the creation, maintenance, and adaptation of former practices and values of kinship and ritual that help migrants survive and challenge constraints of class, gender, and legality.[15]

Many migrants are here, however, without kin. This appears to be more common for men. Some may be "target earners" whose wives are in Mexico. Van Hook and Zhang found not only that more Mexican men return home but also that unmarried men and married men whose wives were in Mexico were more likely to return (2011, 17). Single men or men whose wives are in Mexico spend most of their time working, spend little money in the United States, and send most of their earnings home. When I asked one man in the United States whose wife and children were in Mexico why he worked very long hours seven days a week, he said that having little leisure time meant that he did not have much time to spend money and therefore had more money to send home to his family.[16] Even those who do not have wives at home often spend most of their time working so that they can save their money for when they do return home. Migrants also avoid socializing in public because doing so may attract the attention of the authorities.

Once one family member is married (officially or consensually) in New Jersey, other family members, other kin, and ritual kin and friends can all begin to participate in a variety of activities in homes or rented spaces in which they could not previously participate (as, for example, in the religious cargo system). At another Christmas Eve celebration, for example, the extended family of a man who had recently gotten married (including his parents, sisters, sisters' spouses and children, and their *compadres*) were invited to the house of the newly married couple along with the extended family of the wife (including three married sisters and their families and friends). About fifty people were present at the celebration. By incorporating new contacts through marriage or co-residence, *compadrazgo*, and friends made through work and play, they integrate new friends and acquaintances with new resources into their social networks. These networks help migrants find jobs and information about daily life. A woman at one of these Christmas celebrations who needed child care for her two children met a woman who provided such care. Don Miguel, an unemployed man, met a man, Don José, a roofer who takes his crew from New Jersey to roofing jobs in various parts of New York City. They discussed the possibility of Don Miguel becoming part of Don José's crew. Subsequently, Miguel did join José's crew.[17] A woman with documents who became the partner of an undocumented man who worked with her brother met her partner's family at one of their fiestas. Although she was no longer living with her partner, she was the owner on paper of a car purchased by her former partner and several of his undocumented brothers. The brothers use the car to run an informal taxi service. In return for her functioning as the official owner of the car and carrying the insurance, the brothers help her out financially and in a variety of other ways, including by providing transportation for her, her mother with whom she lives, and her children.

Although not every family has access to the money and labor necessary for such celebrations, those that do have an advantage. These celebrations allow migrants to create and reinforce social ties and to bring people together so that they and all the members of their network keep up to date on the various resources to which different people have access. Information about jobs, housing, public services, acquisition of a driver's license and car insurance, *la migra* (immigration police), and information about what other migrants are doing and where are shared. For example, a young woman who attended a Carnival celebration at the home of her brother's wife's sister found a job through someone she met at that celebration.

As Kibria has suggested, "Immigrant household and family are valuable dimensions to examine not only migration movements, but also processes by which immigrants economically adapt to the 'host' society" (1994, 82). She goes on to suggest that heterogeneous households consisting of members of various generations and sexes allow their members a wider structure of opportunities. Households of married San Cosmeros/as in the United States often include collateral relatives and friends as well as an extended family. This greater diversity further increases the household's access to the contacts of the various members as well as providing more paid and unpaid labor. Heterogeneity thus brings together "diverse resources into the household economy, a strategy that helps to mitigate the instability and scarcity of available resources" (Kibria 1994, 82). The networks that San Cosmeros/as bring together periodically for various life cycle and ritual celebrations embed them in broader networks beyond the household and give them access to even more diverse resources. As Hellman points out, it is helpful if one's network includes also people who "really know how to get around" and who can suggest, for example, how to get a "real fake" driver's license (2007, 200). Although such networks are important when times are good, they are even more important during economic crises, when under- and unemployment increase. Don Jaime who lived in the United States with his two sons and several other men returned in 2010 after being in the United States for eight years. He said that during his last year there, his employment in construction declined from full time to one or two days a week. During his last four months in the United States, he worked even less, only twelve days. His sons who were also working in construction similarly experienced reduced hours of work and returned. Don Jaime said he had wanted his wife to come to the United States, but she did not want to join them because in the United States one has to buy everything. In Mexico she had a house and corn and could work in the family's tortilla business. Another man who was there without any family who also returned in 2010 said that he managed to get by during the winter when there was heavy snow by shoveling snow but in the spring he decided to go home.

Conclusion: Work and Lack of Work in a Broader Context

I do not want to suggest that the only migrants who return are male migrants who are in the United States without kin or that many men do not find partners and increase their participation in social networks. As Hellman (2007) suggests, those who have no network of their own often "latch on to networks" of others. Delaunay and Lestage (1998) have similarly noted that in comparison to households in Mexico, households of Mexican migrants in the United States often include collateral relatives and friends. I am suggesting, however, that we need to examine more thoroughly the relationship that connects gender, kinship, social networks, employment (including under- and unemployment), and return migration. Anthropologists have a long history of studying kinship and noting its relation to all aspects of life. For some reason, however, kinship and work (or lack of work) has not been studied extensively. In their abstract for the panel on which this volume is based, Carrie Lane and Jong Bum Kwon noted that "the panel seeks to . . . explore how unemployment and underemployment may not be peripheral anthropological concerns but critical to the vitality and relevance of contemporary anthropological projects" (2012).

I conclude by stressing this point. Un- and underemployment are closely linked to many of anthropology's most enduring and central concerns: kinship and identity. The ways that kinship, family, identity, and work interrelate demands our attention. As cited by Lane, Katherine Newman's study of white-collar unemployment in the 1980s points out that unemployed managers "are left hanging and socially isolated with no stable sense of who they are" (1988, 93). Similarly, the laid-off Korean workers Kwon discusses in this volume saw themselves as "severed." On the other hand, for the high-tech workers that Lane writes about in this volume, loss of work did not lead to a loss of identity. Nor did it do so for the Nicaraguan members of the Génesis cooperative described by Fisher in this volume, or many of the Mexican migrants I know in New Jersey, especially those who are or become part of families.

Many years ago, research on kinship among poor and working-class families, such as that by Carol Stack (1975), showed the embeddedness of workers in complex family relations and networks. More recently, Stack (1996) followed the same families who had migrated to the North as they returned decades later to their natal communities in the rural South. She found that although economic problems were important, the "call to home" was very much about family. As noted earlier, as Castles suggests the social transformation processes tied to the reordering of labor relations (which include migrant labor) can be mediated through family-level strategies or, as Harvey points out, "fragmentation and economic insecurity" can lead to "a heightened emphasis upon the authority of basic institutions" such as the family. "Such connections" he goes on to say, "are, at least plausible, and they ought to be given more careful scrutiny" (1990, 171–172). In that way, we may not only get a better grasp of what people in precarious work do, but also what they do not do and why.

POSITIVE THINKING ABOUT BEING OUT OF WORK IN SOUTHERN CALIFORNIA AFTER THE GREAT RECESSION

Claudia Strauss

When I began my research with southern Californians who were looking for work in 2011 and 2012, I had no premonition of my finding that many of them had been coping with the stress of long-term unemployment by drawing on a spiritually based positive thinking ideology.

I first noticed positive thinking when I studied my interview with Carl Mathews, an unemployed security guard. He had been out of work for a year, and we were talking about his problems finding a job and paying his mortgage when he said that there were no programs to help people in his situation, and all he could do was submit applications and "pray about it." When I followed up on that comment, he launched into the following remarks:

> See, it's not the problem you have, it's how you deal with it. I don't have to like my situation, but I can be content enough to know that hey, every day's a new day, every day you've got a chance to start it over again, every "no" you get, you get closer to a "yes." Stay positive. . . . Ain't no bad days, just bad situations. Because if you wake up—it's a good day. A lot of people didn't wake up. A lot of people with jobs today are dead. Just because I'm unemployed don't mean it's the end of the world. It just means I've got to try harder to make things happen.

Near the end of the interview, when I asked about his hopes for the future, he said, "I believe in being positive. It's the only thing to look forward to in the hope for a better tomorrow always."

Carl Mathews's comments are a prime example of positive thinking. Positive thinking enjoins people to see the bright side to negative circumstances such as illness and financial setbacks, to maintain optimism that things are going to get better, and to try harder. One is supposed to cultivate this affirmative view even when circumstances do not seem to warrant it, because positive thinking, according to this ideology, is a force that helps to create the circumstances one hopes for.

Positive thinking, in this sense, is not the same as mere hope; it is more active.[1] Crapanzano (2003) writes of "the inaction, the resignation, and the passivity that hope can promote" through "offering us unlikely possibilities" (19). He contrasts passive hope with more agentive "philosophies of optimism, which stress 'the power of positive thinking,'" which, according to motivational speakers, "can be taught and learned" (2003, 18).

Exemplars of positive thinking abound in contemporary American society. Pamela Druckerman remarks that unlike French children's stories in which characters do not succeed in resolving problems, "in the English-speaking [fiction] world, every problem seems to have a solution, and prosperity is just around the corner" (Druckerman 2012, 162). The narrative psychologist Dan McAdams found that in the life stories of Americans trying to make a positive difference there is often a redemption plot: "Negative emotional scenes will often lead directly to positive outcomes. Suffering will consistently be redeemed" (McAdams 2006, 5, 9).[2] McAdams traces the roots of American redemption stories to Judeo-Christian sources (the Israelites' deliverance from bondage in Egypt, salvation from sin in Christian conversion tales) and "such quintessentially American ideas as *manifest destiny*, [and] *the chosen people*" (McAdams 2006, 11, emphasis in original), highlighting the way redemption can be both a personal and a national narrative.

Still, positive thinking is not a timeless American outlook; its cultural authority and manifestations have changed. In *Bright-Sided: How Positive Thinking Is Undermining America*, Barbara Ehrenreich (2009a) traces the beginnings of modern positive thinking ideology in the United States to the New Thought movement in the mid-nineteenth century. Adherents of New Thought, such as Mary Baker Eddy, the founder of Christian Science, rejected the gloomy emphasis on guilt and sin of strict Protestantism, stressing instead the power of positive thoughts to bring about good fortune. Ehrenreich explains that these themes were promulgated in such influential twentieth-century books as Napoleon Hill's *Think and Grow Rich* (1937), Norman Vincent Peale's bestseller *The Power of Positive Thinking* (1952), and Rhonda Byrne's film and book *The Secret* (2006), and further developed in contemporary positive psychology in the academy and in the "prosperity gospel" (God wants you to be rich) preached in some evangelical megachurches.

Despite the supposed entrenchment of positive thinking in American culture for more than a century, it has not been much discussed in studies of Americans who are out of work. Such studies have generally focused on displaced workers' loss of self-esteem and identity (Pappas 1989) and their self-blame due to the dominant ideology of meritocratic individualism (Newman 1988). Newman commented that the baby boomers she interviewed were abandoning typically American optimism (1993, 4–5). It is not until the end of the twentieth century and the beginning of the twenty-first that reports begin discussing positive thinking as a recommended outlook of American job seekers (Ehrenreich 2005, 2009b; Lane 2011, 2016; Sharone 2014).[3] The current prominence of positive thinking for job seekers probably stems from the nature of employment as well as the qualities of unemployment at the present time. There are also influences from cultural trends not directly related to work.

Earlier versions of positive thinking may be reshaped to emphasize the attributes that are necessary given the new regimes of flexible accumulation and the consequent insecurity of employment in neoliberal economies. Some scholars have described the way white-collar workers take on a salesperson's pumped-up buoyancy both to sell themselves within their companies while they are working (Kunda and Van Maanen 1999) and to find a new job when they are out of work (Lane 2011). Others have noted that this trend extends to former blue-collar workers as well, as they are displaced from steady jobs and turn to ones paid on commission. Walkerdine (2006) describes a former manual worker in Australia who complained that society no longer valued people who were quiet and loyal like him; instead one was supposed to be outgoing and sell oneself. The global neoliberal demand to construct an "enterprising self" (Heelas and Morris 1992) may be one factor that feeds and shapes the kind of positive attitude that is recommended for job seekers at all economic levels in the United States.

By contrast, Sharone (2014) argues that global neoliberalism does not explain the pressure to display a positive mental attitude. Although neoliberal attacks on job security and the welfare state operate in Israel as well as the United States, he found that it was the U.S. white-collar job seekers, not the Israeli ones, who felt the need to maintain an upbeat attitude. Sharone traces the need to project an upbeat personality in the United States to the importance of creating good "chemistry" with a potential employer.[4] In Israel, having the right skills is more important because initial screenings of job seekers are conducted by third-party staffing agencies.

For the unemployed in the United States, what is new is the need to keep up their spirits and remain optimistic during very long periods of being out of work. As of this writing in 2014 the long-term unemployment rate in the United States is the highest the Bureau of Labor Statistics has ever recorded since it began tracking these statistics in 1948 (Mayer 2010, 3; Lee 2014). You might not need to keep reminding yourself to stay positive if you are out of work for only a few months. Such reminders become much more insistent when the months stretch into years, when being out of work for a long time becomes one more strike against an applicant in employers' minds (Rampell 2011; Lowrey 2013), and when one's financial resources dwindle and the options look bleak, especially given the insecurity of social welfare provision in the United States.

What may also be new is the widespread acceptance of the importance of "wellness" and a good "quality of life" as well as the stress on optimism in the field of positive psychology (e.g., Seligman 1990). Popular magazines, television talk shows, and career counselors transmit these views.

As we will see, there has also been an important shift in many Christian churches from messages that God punishes the lazy and sinful to ones that stress His unconditional love. Many New Age spiritual movements differ from Christianity in their theology but likewise promote optimism, because anything one wants is available through the power of one's mind. Faith is often one strand of positive thinking.

Positive thinking is imbibed not just from these intellectual sources; it is also spread through everyday habits of talking about one's situation. The ways of talking and thinking that are typical of positive thinking are an example of what I have termed *conventional discourses*. A conventional discourse is a simple schema that is frequently expressed in an opinion community (Strauss 2012). Over time, opinion communities develop set views along with formulaic ways of expressing those views. Positive thinking as a set of practices includes such standard ways of interpreting and talking about negative circumstances. However, positive thinking is not just a conventional discourse; it is also emotional management to keep fear and despair at bay. Thus, I am treating positive thinking neither as a natural human response to setbacks, on the one hand, nor as an indelible cultural theme, on the other, but as a self-project, a deliberate effort to think and feel a certain way that is disseminated through a variety of channels but that reaches and appeals to some people more than others.[5]

Positive thinking discourse and practice have surprising effects, ones that are not exactly what some commentators have expected. Ehrenreich (2009a) contends that positive thinking ideology is a new way of blaming the victim: If you are still out of work—or your cancer is getting worse—maybe you have not been trying hard enough to discipline your emotions to maintain a positive attitude. Furthermore, telling people to work on their attitudes turns their attention away from the structural causes of unemployment. Thus, although positive thinking seems less punitive than classic versions of the Protestant work ethic, she concludes that it has the same effect of self-blame (Ehrenreich 2005, 2009a; see also Sharone 2014).

Yet, while Ehrenreich has mordant observations about the propagandists on behalf of positive thinking, she does not provide much information about the ways American job seekers react to, interpret, and use that ideology. For the men and women I talked to, positive thinking is undoubtedly a form of emotional labor, but it has another side of self-care in the face of repeated rejection and financial insecurity. While it places attention on management of self, rather than organizing for change, the self-affirmation it promotes is consistent with blaming outside forces rather than oneself. Thus, while individualistic, it is an individualism that is also compatible with social critique.

Other social critics have described the psychological effects of "precarity," the loss of stable careers and lives in neoliberal economies (Sennett 1998; Ross 2009). Lauren Berlant insightfully conceives of the present moment as an "impasse," which she defines as "a holding station that doesn't hold securely but opens out into anxiety . . . dogpaddling around a space whose contours remain obscure." It is a spot-on description of the uncertain lives of those I interviewed, but I disagree with her claim that "the impasse is a space of time lived without a narrative genre" (Berlant 2011, 199). It is when lives are insecure that discourses and practices for managing that insecurity, like positive thinking, are most likely to proliferate. Positive thinking is, as Jong Bum Kwon puts it, "about projecting oneself, actively, towards a future, a future without guarantees" (personal communication, June 28, 2013).

Finding the Unemployed

Between September 2011 and June 2012, I interviewed fifty-two unemployed or underemployed southern Californian men and women.[6] In addition, an assistant interviewed eleven Spanish-speaking unemployed workers. To meet them, I attended career counseling sessions and networking groups or stood outside job fairs passing out flyers describing my project. I also asked everyone I knew for contacts and in that way found some people who were out of work but too discouraged to go to job fairs or career counseling sessions. I deliberately chose people from a variety of former occupations, socioeconomic levels, and ethnic groups. Twelve had never had a household income above $40,000. They included an auto parts salesman, a bank clerical assistant, a former Hare Krishna devotee, a roofer, and a man who was recently released from prison. Fifteen had formerly had household incomes of more than $150,000 earned from their own and/or their spouse's job in fields such as finance, construction, entertainment, leisure, management, and sales. The remaining thirty-six had former household incomes between those low- and high-income ends, from a variety of occupations in the public and private sectors. Twenty-five self-identify as white/Euro American, twelve as black/African American, twenty-one as Latino/a, and five as Asian American. I met with all but one of them for two lengthy recorded interviews. In addition, I took notes on the career counseling sessions and networking events I attended.

According to the National Bureau of Economic Research (2010), the Great Recession in the United States began December 2007. By the time I met my interviewees, in 2011 and 2012, the recession had ended officially, but employers were still not hiring in large numbers in southern California. In fall of 2011 the Los Angeles and Riverside metro areas were the second- and third-worst in the United States in the ratio of job seekers for every opening (Adams 2011).[7] Almost all of my interviewees were among the long-term unemployed, defined as those out of work for more than six months. Three-quarters had been out of work for more than a year, and about half of that group had not had a full-time job in more than two years, despite (in most cases) scouring job websites and submitting innumerable applications.[8] Many were behind on their mortgage or rent payments. Some had already lost their homes and had had to move in with a parent or sibling, downsize to less expensive lodgings, or depend on a friend or acquaintance to extend them a place to live rent-free. One was living in a homeless shelter. A frightening number had dipped into their retirement accounts, and a few had depleted all of their savings. An overall sense of my interviewees' precarious finances can be seen in their answers to a questionnaire I administered after the second interview. In response to the question, "What do you think of your personal financial situation these days?" where 1 was "very good" and 5 was "very bad," the mean was 3.6 (between the midpoint and "bad").

Despite their financial insecurity, their average response to the next question on the survey ("What do you think of your situation in general? How would you say you are feeling?"), was 2.5 (between the midpoint and "good")—not great, but a full point better than their self-reported financial situation. Unlike the unemployed in countries with a robust welfare system, where reports highlight psychological and social problems more than financial difficulties (e.g., Letkemann 2005; Roberman 2013), my southern Californian interviewees' self-reported state can be summed up as, "My finances are not good, but I'm feeling okay."

An overall quantitative summary hides a great deal, however,[9] because it averages different situations. Some interviewees portrayed supportive family and friends; others described friends who no longer invited them out because they could not pay their way, partners who were upset with them, and parents or children whom they felt they had failed. Some felt no threat to their basic identities; others anguished about whether to continue to hold out for the kind of work they loved and the status they had previously held or to abandon those expectations.

Putting a number on how they were feeling also hides the fact that the same person would say different things at different times. Several of those who responded they were feeling "Good" in response to the questionnaire were under treatment for depression, and a few mentioned suicidal thoughts during the interviews. Unlike the unemployed high-tech workers in Texas interviewed by Lane (2011) from 2001 to 2004, almost none of my interviewees were taking unemployment in stride as what one should expect in this day and age. Many of them worked at feeling positive against the prevailing winds that had been blowing them toward negative thoughts and feelings.

Since my project examines conventional ways of framing one's opinion or telling one's story, it is particularly relevant to consider what expectations affected the way my interviewees presented themselves to me. The interviews began with my request, "Please tell me about your life, leading up to your situation now." Some responded in ways I coded as positive thinking, describing the beneficial side of losing their job, the importance of maintaining a positive attitude, and their optimism for the future. However, with interviews that typically stretched for more than two hours over coffee or lunch and continued for at least two and in some cases more meetings, other narratives and feelings would eventually emerge, ones less consistent with positive thinking ideology. Many said that there were not many opportunities, normally, to talk about their feelings about being out of work; they seemed to approach the interview not in the mode of the self-promoting job seeker but as a kind of therapy, an occasion to reveal less socially acceptable feelings of anger and depression. Still others used the interviews as an opportunity to voice their experiences for documentary purposes, so that others would know what they had gone through, a frame that also did not sugarcoat suffering. Even those who treated the interviews as one more networking meeting that might eventually help them land a job did not consistently maintain a self-promoting stance. No matter how they started, in most cases they presented a mix of thoughts and feelings that was not confined to a single frame of interpretation.

What makes me wince on reading the interview transcripts are the times I revealed my own positive thinking bias. For example, after Carl Mathews made the comments quoted at the beginning of this paper ("every day's a new day, every day you've got a chance to start it over again, every 'no' you get, you get closer to a 'yes'"), I responded, "I like that. I like that. I mean that's what I thought when I first met you, that it seemed like you were an upbeat, positive person." Fortunately, my feedback did not prevent Carl from later revealing much darker thoughts. If nothing else, this analysis of positive thinking has given me greater awareness of the extent to which positive thinking suffuses my own automatic responses.

Working at a Positive Attitude: Positive Thinking as Emotional Discipline

First I will present positive thinking as a disciplining of one's attitudes, then positive thinking as a form of self-care. Ultimately, however, that is a false dichotomy, because those who accepted the discipline of maintaining a positive attitude did so because they wanted the outcomes it was supposed to provide: not only a job but also greater peace of mind during the job search.

Positive thinking in the contemporary United States is in part about keeping oneself in an upbeat frame of mind to ward off the moroseness that will prevent constructive action. Unlike the rural college students in India described in Craig Jeffrey's *Timepass* (2010), the focus of positive thinking among American job seekers was on maintaining a go-getting attitude, not learning to pass time pleasurably while waiting for a job.[10]

The importance of maintaining a positive attitude during the job search was stressed by a career counselor, Heather Wieshlow, who was the featured speaker at a weekly gathering of job seekers I attended in December 2011 that was organized by the San Bernardino County unemployment office. Heather wore a red Santa cap and distributed a Christmas-themed handout, entitled "Top 10 Tips from Santa for Individuals in Career Transition." The first tip on the sheet (ahead of practicalities like "Preparation" and "Time Management") was "Attitude." Her handout explained, "During the job search process it is extremely important to keep a positive attitude about the future and your abilities. Stay away from people who tell you how 'horrible' it is out there, they won't help you get your job any faster."

Why is it important for job seekers to maintain a positive attitude? Career counselors say that one reason is that employers are more likely to hire someone who is confident and positive, someone who can sell themselves (Walkerdine 2006) and can perform the emotional labor required in a service economy (Hochschild 2003 [1983]). Anastasia Tang, a laid-off Human Resources administrator, recalled the advice she received from a recruiter about how to comport herself. "He said, 'Just be yourself, be honest, be happy, be positive. You know, be positive.'" Anastasia could see the wisdom of that advice: "Because when you work in the job too, when you come in they want to see you're a happy person. They don't want to hire people who are depressed, who seem to have, 'Oh woe be me' for everything."

However, it is not enough to put on a cheerful face in encounters with potential employers. To find a job when few are available, job seekers are advised to network to learn about openings that have not yet been posted and to obtain recommendations from insiders. Networking takes different forms. It can mean meeting with other job seekers in regular networking groups. It can mean contacting everyone one knows to remind them that one is looking and ask if they know of any opportunities. It can mean mentioning the kind of opening you are looking for in the midst of casual conversations with acquaintances. In all of those situations, one should exude self-confidence. That extends the situations in which one needs a positive self-presentation to any new social encounter.

This can be tiring. When I met Lisa Rose, a nonprofit administrator, for a follow-up interview in 2013, I asked her about the positive thinking that was so evident in her earlier interview. She said, "I do think there's a burdensome aspect to it, which is the idea of maintaining a veneer or maintaining—even just trying to maintain the positivity that you want." Elizabeth Montgomery, a high-end office furniture saleswoman who had been out of work for two and half years despite a sterling career and unrelenting networking, articulated the exhausting side of constantly putting on a positive face. As a saleswoman, she knew how to switch on a confident self-presentation. However, she confessed to weariness:

> I know something will happen. It's just, it's kind of like sales. We gotta throw so much up there and something'll land. But I'll be honest, I did how many events this week? Four. And I'm tired. [. . .] It's like keeping your face and smiling. The one [*speaker*] last night was saying, you know, "You gotta be positive." But there's moments, you know.[11]

She does not complete the last thought, but the implication is that there are moments when it is hard to maintain a positive outlook, understandably.

Maintaining a positive attitude about the future also wards off hopelessness during a protracted job search. It is difficult to summon the energy to look for work if you are disheartened, so you need to keep your spirits up. And it is natural to feel down if you have been searching unsuccessfully for over a year. My interviewee Phoenix Rises (her chosen pseudonym, reflective of her redemption hopes) had been trying for more than two years to secure another job as a special education teacher following an injury she suffered on the job. With an edge of desperation and determination, she stated, "The only way I lose is if I *stop*. If I stop *believing* in myself, if I stop *believing* in the fact that there *is* something out there for me somewhere, then I lose. And I will lose if I don't stay in control of my mind. I have to master my mind every single day." Mastering her mind was necessary because she admitted to being depressed, having come close to a nervous breakdown, and even to feeling suicidal on occasion. She could not give up, because her husband was disabled, they had sold their home, their savings were nearly gone, her adult daughter was calling her a "loser," and she needed to bring in an income.

Whatever the reason, many of the unemployed I met believe, as a laid-off teacher, Della Jones, put it, "if I'm negative, that's all I'm ever going to get and

I'm gonna stay there." When Ann Lopez finally obtained a job, she wrote me that it showed, "THINK POSITIVE AND POSITIVE THINGS WILL HAPPEN TO YOU."

According to this ideology, positive thinking leads to positive outcomes, negative thinking to negative outcomes, so it is necessary to stay positive during the job search.

Protecting the Product: Positive Thinking as Self-Care

Elizabeth Montgomery's comment about "keeping your face and smiling" shows that maintaining a positive self-presentation can be draining. Yet there is another side to positive thinking. The injunction to maintain a positive outlook is not just a matter of emotional disciplining, as social critics emphasize. It also implies self-care to mitigate the stress created by being out of work.[12]

The laid-off nonprofit administrator, Lisa Rose, talked about her various strategies for emotion management: "There's this constant of managing your emotions around security, money, all of that. I mean, you're just constantly managing that. And so for me it's been meditation, exercise, talking with friends, listening to upbeat music." There is a subtle difference between Lisa Rose's talk of "managing your emotions" and Phoenix Rises's comment about the need to "master my mind." Phoenix Rises masters her mind in order to continue looking for work. Lisa Rose's emphasis instead is on feeling better as a goal in itself. As Carl Mathews, the unemployed security guard, put it, "Stay positive, that way you don't feel bad, you don't go through mood swings, you don't lose weight and attention, you don't miss meals, you don't go through the depression thing."

Indeed, there is a rationale for self-care in neoliberal logic, for if you are selling yourself (Kunda and Van Maanen 1999; Lane 2011), you have to protect the product you are selling. Heather Wieshlow, the career counselor quoted earlier, made this point as well. On her handout for job seekers, tip number 8 was "Renew": "The job search process is an emotional and strategic process. If you haven't taken time to renew yourself mentally, physically and emotionally a future employer will sense it. Take time to renew and 'sharpen your saw' so that you are more effective at the search and in the interviews." In her comments about this tip, she said, "You are the product; if you burn your product out, you will have nothing to sell." I saw several job seekers in the audience nod their heads in agreement.

How did my interviewees care for themselves to maintain their positive emotions? Like Lisa Rose, many of them exercised. Only a few could afford a gym membership, but a large number took advantage of the southern California climate to bike, walk, and run several times a week if not daily.[13] Several talked about the emotional support provided by their ongoing small networking or accountability groups. These are the small groups of fellow job seekers with whom they meet on a regular basis. Unlike events with strangers, members of these small groups become friends, and one does not have to put on an act with them. Some of my interviewees, like Lisa Rose, meditated, and as I will discuss later, spirituality was important for several: a faith in God or in the power of visualization. A speaker I heard at an evangelical church's career counseling ministry recommended avoiding the news because it highlights negativity.[14] Elizabeth Montgomery, the saleswoman quoted above, agreed: "Our media, you can't listen to it every day. It just will bring you down. It's gonna bring you down. It's all about the negative and none about the positive." This is a conventional discourse of motivational speakers and career counselors; other researchers report hearing the same advice (Ehrenreich 2009a, 57ff.; Sharone 2014, 39).

Maintaining positive emotions also means reframing one's situation to highlight the positive side of losing a job or being out of work, for example, by using what we could call a "blessing in disguise" conventional discourse. The "blessing in disguise" discourse might take the form that they had been unhappy in their last job, so when they were fired, it was actually a good thing. Callie, Phoenix Rises's friend who joined us for part of an interview, commented that when she lost her job as a payroll worker, "Part of it was I was happy I was gone. It was such a caustic environment." Lisa Rose offered an extended example of the "blessing in disguise" narrative about her last job. Interestingly, she criticized her former employers for creating a workplace where one could not maintain a positive outlook: "Every day was painful. [. . .] I'd really try every day to be positive, but I was having to work really hard to be positive there. [*Laughs*] So I'll end this chapter by saying, being laid off was the best thing that ever happened to me."[15]

Not only could losing one's job be narrated as a blessing in disguise, so could remaining unemployed—at least for a while. Lisa Rose continued her comments above:

> LR: So I'll end this chapter by saying, being laid off was the best thing that ever happened to me.
> CS: Really?
> LR: Yes. Because it gave me a chance to take a look at what was the role of work in my life. It was too strong, too big a dimension. I'd let work become too big a part of who I saw myself to be. And in the absence of having a job, you see this much more starkly than when you're working.

Lisa Rose also mentioned that while she was out of work, her mother-in-law got sick and she was able to help her: "I'm not sure how I would've been able to do it if I had been working full-time. So I'm grateful that in that moment I was free to do that."

Closely related to the "blessing in disguise" narrative about losing their last job, there was also the conventional discourse about their current insecure circumstances I termed "count my blessings." The point of the "count my blessings" discourse is that no matter how bad one's own situation seems, there are others who are worse off, so one should be grateful. For example, Anastasia Tang, an immigrant from Asia, compared herself with someone else she read about in her field of Human Resources who had been laid off:

> He said he didn't have a car last month. I'm just imagining how does he go for interviews and all that? And here—I've got a roof over my head, I'm able to eat, at least enjoy my life in that sense. I'm able to do some gardening because I want to sort of have something to look forward to, I'm able to spend time with my children, cook and all those things. So in that sense I think I'm very blessed. I'm lucky. [. . .] Because I look at other people who are down and out, sometimes they say they're down to their last loaf, can't pay this bill, cannot pay that bill. Maybe not even a dollar in savings. I mean, then I think I should be thankful, right? I should be thankful. [. . .] I have to keep reminding myself even though I know it sounds so corny, or it should be common sense that you should be thankful. But I just try to tell myself, "Look, there's the bad days and good days" but you try to keep your spirits up. [. . .] I've got to *think* that way. If not, what do you look forward to if you're depressed every day . . .?

When Anastasia Tang says "I should be thankful," there seems to be both a moral and pragmatic side of that "should." Morally she should turn her pity to others who are worse off rather than feel sorry for herself. This returns us to the sense of positive thinking as what is socially expected. At the same time, Anastasia keeps reminding herself to be grateful for what she has just so she feels better. Both elements are present. It is not that Anastasia is an ideal subject of positive thinking ideology, working on her attitude and not complaining about her situation. That there is a more complex story is hinted in her wording, "then I think I should be thankful, right? I should be thankful," which suggests she knows that this is how she *ought* to think, not how she *does* tend to think. Indeed, Anastasia's "count my blessings" comments emerged over an hour into the interview, and they were preceded by lengthy complaints about her last position, where they seemed to turn against her after she took maternity leave and prioritized her children over company events. Now she was supposed to ask her "asshole" former boss for a reference so she could get another job. Meanwhile, her husband had burned out and quit his job shortly after she was laid off, and she did not feel she could ask her parents in Asia for help because they had sacrificed so much to send her to the United States for her education. It was in the midst of this tale of her troubles that she paused to say that she knows she should be grateful for what she has. She seemed to be trying to convince herself in order to keep her spirits up.

The "count my blessings" discourse was also voiced when someone had given up hope of a better future. If it is used to adjust one's expectations and learn to be content with one's situation, it is not positive thinking. "Count my blessings" becomes a positive thinking technique when it is used to shake off discouragement and initiate active efforts to bring about change, as Anastasia did.

Christian and New Age Positive Thinking: A Loving God and an Abundant Universe

When my interviewees say they are "blessed" they may also mean it in its Judeo-Christian sense, as having received a gift from God. For the devout, to fail to count one's blessings is to lack proper gratitude for all the good things that God has provided. Spiritual practices and beliefs, especially Christian and New Age ones, were a significant influence on my interviewees' positive thinking. *New Age* was not a term my interviewees used, but it usefully encompasses a range of metaphysical beliefs and spiritual practices that are outside the mainstream of Western religions and emphasize the power of visualization and other mind-over-matter techniques.[16]

In some ways, Christian and New Age belief systems are opposites. God, a separate, transcendent being with a will of His own, is at the center of Christian beliefs. By contrast, although New Age beliefs encompass a wide range of sources, from mystical elements of Eastern and Western religious doctrines to indigenous beliefs and practices from every part of the world, they share an understanding of spirituality as both part of the whole universe and also in each person. In most New Age philosophies, "Everyone is God," as the actress Shirley MacLaine put it (quoted by Heelas 1996, 2).

These differing conceptions of divinity lead to different notions of individual agency. Christians are not supposed to feel in charge of their life, as I heard at the Career Coaching and Counseling Ministry at the evangelical Saddleback Church. The introductory lecture for new attendees had a secular first half and a religious second half entitled "God's Will & Direction For Your Life." One of the Power-Point slides explained, "Whatever happens, He is in charge, He is in control."

In this conception your being out of work is all part of God's plan. As the slide explained, "God may have you in transition precisely so you can help others," perhaps by bringing them to Christ, as the founder of that ministry had when he was unemployed. For those who adhere to one or another of various New Age philosophies, by contrast, since there is no transcendent being with a plan for you, it is up to you to master the secrets of the universe to attract what you want.

In other respects, however, there are important similarities between the influences of Christian and New Age beliefs on contemporary positive thinking. Both can explain why one should believe that one's life will get better.

For Christians, optimism rests on a contemporary conception of God as loving and benign. The old Protestant work ethic was hardly cheery: to be virtuous, one had to be committed to unremitting work. Happiness was not important. The Protestant work ethic provided no comfort for those who were unable to work and were not prospering. Nowadays, while some preachers continue to portray a judgmental God who punishes the sinful, it is instead more common to depict a kindly, forgiving God who wants us to prosper (Ehrenreich 2009a; Luhrmann 2012). The first slide in the "God's Will & Direction For Your Life" lecture at the Saddleback Church quoted Jeremiah 29:11 ("'For I know the plan I have for you,' declares the Lord, 'plans to prosper you and not to harm you, plans to give you hope and a future'"). Some of my interviewees took comfort in this. Fred Hernandez, who could not find a job because of his prior convictions, said he would be in despair if he did not believe he was in "the hand of a loving, caring, forgiving God." Della Jones stated, "The one that has the power to create the world knew me ahead of time and has a plan for me."

There is a basis for optimism in New Age philosophies as well. If all is Spirit or Mind, reality can be changed simply through focused mental attention and visualization. Furthermore, "'The Universe is a masterpiece of abundance,'" according to Rhonda Byrne's bestseller, *The Secret* (2006). "When you open yourself to feel the abundance of the Universe, you'll experience the wonder, joy, bliss, and all the great things the Universe has for you—good health, good wealth, good nature" (Lisa Nichols, quoted in Byrne 2006, 126–127). At the time I met my interviewee Gabriella Gomez, a part-time yoga instructor and massage therapist, she was in danger of losing her free lodgings, but when worries arise, she repeats, "I live, move, and breathe, and have my being in a field of abundance. All good things are happening."

Both spiritual systems provide techniques believers can use to try to obtain their goals, such as prayer for the Christians (Carl Mathews said that he prayed about his situation) and visualization, chanting, and related techniques in various New Age practices. Gabriella Gomez uses vision boards; Phoenix Rises and her friend Callie, who were Buddhists in the Soka Gakkai sect of Nichiren

Buddhism, chanted for what they wanted.[17] Both devout Christians and follow-ers of New Age practices used their spiritual practices as a supplement to, not a substitute for, the mundane job-seeking activities of scanning websites, sending in applications, networking, and so on.

If prayer and visualization do not yield the desired outcomes, both Christian and some New Age believers have ways of explaining those anomalies. For Chris-tians, God answers prayers, but "in His own way and in His own time," so His answer may not come immediately or in the form you thought you wanted.[18] In some New Age systems of belief, you do not get to say *how* you obtain the goal you focused on—that is up to the universe. The results may be unanticipated. Callie, the Soka Gakkai Buddhist, had disliked her previous job and then was fired from it. She joked that the universe was saying, "Your prayer was answered. Next time, you need to be a little bit more specific!'"

Finally, both Christians and New Age practitioners hold beliefs that elevate spiritual over material goals, so if their prayers for material things are not answered, they can adjust their attitude and be grateful for the suffering that has made them a better person. In this spiritual framework, that is still a sort of redemption.

All Is Not Positive

Not everyone I talked to espoused positive thinking, stressing the good side of being out of work and expressing optimism for the future. For example, Amber Washington was angry: "I understand people going in and shooting up places where they used to work that they've been fired. I understand that anger and that mentality of wanting to kill, wanting to destroy something because of their own stuff that's going on inside of me and people not treating you with respect." While Amber was an outlier in her frank anger, some others told their stories without any positive thinking discourses. Pepper Hill cited the country song, "It sounds like life to me," by Darryl Worley, the point of which is that tough times are to be expected ("sounds like life to me, it ain't no fantasy"). This alternative perspective is well represented in American country music, but making the best of a subpar situation as one's lot in life is at odds with the positive thinking ideology. Positive thinking is instead the mindset that one can have a better future. Of the fifty-one people whose interviews I have coded so far, thirty-four definitely exhibited posi-tive thinking, three displayed some traces of it, but fourteen did not.

Nor did even the most enthusiastic proponents of positive thinking always manage to maintain that outlook. For example, there was a striking difference between my first and second interviews with Carl Mathews. In the first, he was a poster boy for positive thinking. At the time I was interviewing him, about a year into his period of unemployment, he was behind on his mortgage and had declared bankruptcy. Formerly he had made over $120,000 a year by working a lot of overtime, but now his circumstances were growing very difficult. Still, he recounted in proper "count my blessings" fashion how he admonished his wife when she complained that his being out of work left them with no spending money: "So I say, so, 'What is there to complain about? You should be happy.' [. . .] We're not living like the Rockefellers, but we're far away from living on the streets too."

In the second interview, his tone was different. He had been talking about what he could not afford and his expectation that his wife would leave him, when the following story emerged:

> You know your whole situation changes. For a person that worked all the time to come to this, you never notice it 'til it happens to *you*. You know. Things disturb me more now than it used to disturb me before. I was going on a job interview one time, I was right down the street at the Jack in the Box. And I seen this white guy, he was—it's the daytime, he's in the trash can in the daytime pulling out food and eating it. And he don't care who's looking at him he just pulling it out eating it and eating it. And all the food he couldn't eat he's putting it in his pocket. And I almost didn't want to buy anything [to] eat at that point, not because he disgusted me but because I saw myself in his shoes. He didn't disgust me because I've seen people do that before. I just figured God bless them. I hate that he had to do like that. Ordinarily I'd be the kind of guy to go out and buy him something to eat. But I looked at him and it shook me up so bad because I said, "I'm one step from that. That could be me eating out of that same trash can having those same people look at me." It made me almost not want to eat. [. . .] You know, I'm clean, I'm looking good now, I'm going on interviews, but how long is it going to last? How long would it be before I'm going be [*out of*] my home? How long it going to be before I probably get divorced or whatever, won't have no benefits and won't have nowhere to go, nowhere to hide?

I asked Mathews if he could move into his parents' house if it were necessary. He said maybe, but he refused to be derailed by what might have been an unconscious attempt on my part to turn the conversation in a more positive direction:

> The thing is, though, I know this . . . it's sad but I used to always say how could somebody kill theyself but I can understand why. Sometimes it's better to die than go through all that. You know, and I don't wish death

on nobody, but everybody knows what they can take. You know, it's like this, if this is what it is. . . . You know, I ain't gonna be eating out of garbage cans. Dead people don't have to worry about eating. Dead people don't have to worry about nothing no more.

These comments were unsettling. However upbeat Carl tends to be, however much he prays, tries to count his blessings and stay positive, he is confronted with the realities of living in a country that can leave you alone on the streets with "nowhere to go, nowhere to hide."

Positive thinking is not completely penetrating. Those discourses do not reach or persuade everyone, and even those who embrace it can also entertain bleaker visions of the future.

Who Is to Blame?

According to Barbara Ehrenreich, "Positive thinking has made itself useful as an apology for the crueler aspects of the market economy":

> If optimism is the key to material success, and if you can achieve an optimistic outlook through the discipline of positive thinking, then there is no excuse for failure. The flip side of positivity is thus a harsh insistence on personal responsibility: if your business fails or your job is eliminated, it must [be] because you didn't try hard enough, didn't believe firmly enough in the inevitability of your success. (2009a, 8)

Similarly, Sharone (2014) argues that the need for white-collar American job seekers to create and project upbeat personalities and good chemistry with potential employers leads them toward self-blame rather than system blame.

My interviewees did blame themselves a little. Overall, however, I was struck by how rarely they articulated self-blame. Instead, the majority recounted that they had never before had so much trouble finding a job and quite reasonably focused on what was different now: too few jobs and too many job seekers in their area of southern California. Interviewees also explained that there is discrimination both against the middle-aged and against the long-term unemployed, categories most of them fell into.

For example, Charles Toppes had been a regional director of operations for a furniture manufacturing company. He explained that his work always met or exceeded goals, but the companies were mismanaged at higher levels. He was in his late fifties and had been looking for work for about a year and a half "because there's such a glut of talent in the industry right now." He also commented, "It's been difficult for me to get a job because I'm so-called 'over-qualified.' But I know that in some cases the 'over-qualified' meant that I was just a little bit too old." Furthermore, the weak economy had reduced demand: "And you've heard I'm sure of all the cash and money that all these companies are sitting on; it's because the demand is not there for their product and as long as the demand is not there for the product [. . .], they don't have to acquire the talent that's necessary." He had some regrets about having pursued a career in the manufacture of durable household goods because that work was moving overseas. However, he did not blame himself because how could he have been expected to predict this change in economic trends thirty years earlier, when he began his career? He commented, "As technologies arise [. . .] it puts limitations on people."

In a written questionnaire I distributed at the end of the interviews, I asked, "In your opinion, which is more often to blame if a person is poor, a lack of effort on their own part, or circumstances beyond their control?" Almost two-thirds of my interviewees (65%) replied "both," and another 22 percent chose "circumstances beyond their control." Only 12 percent put the blame solely on the individual's lack of effort.

There was variation in the extent to which people thought they could overcome the odds if they made a greater effort to believe in the inevitability of their success. Those who embraced New Age philosophies carried a heavier burden of trying, as Phoenix Rises put it, to "master my mind" because of the causal power they attributed to thought. Still, that did not stop Phoenix Rises and others from criticizing the market economy. In response to another written question, Phoenix Rises was one of fourteen interviewees who agreed with the statement "Left to itself the free market economy creates more problems than opportunities because it creates too much inequality and leaves too many people in poverty." Twelve more agreed both with that statement and with its reverse, "The free market creates more opportunities than problems." In other words, almost half of my interviewees entertained doubts about the market forces that created the hardships they were experiencing.

The expectation that positive thinking ideology will force the unemployed to blame themselves overlooks the fact that job seekers are supposed to be self-confident (Lane 2011).[19] They are told to practice telling "power stories": challenges they faced on the job and how they succeeded, backed up with hard facts and figures. I think it goes deeper than that, not just to how the unemployed narrate their situation but also to how they think about it. Stephen Smith's comments brought this home to me. Stephen, formerly a high-level executive for a large corporation, had been out of work for almost three years when we met.[20] Stephen commented that his wife, a retired former executive herself, says it is his fault he was not working. I asked if he agreed with her. He said he did "a little bit," but he added, "I can't go there. I'd give up the fight." This makes sense. To sell yourself, you have to believe in the product. And if you start believing something is really wrong with you, that it truly is your fault you are not working, it will make the job search much harder.

Embracing positive thinking did not mystify my interviewees' awareness of the forces that crashed the economy. Some were very angry about the role of big banks. For example, Carl Mathews had this militant comment when I asked what he thought of the Occupy Wall Street movement, which arose at the same time I began my interviews in the fall of 2011:

> CS: What do you think about the Occupy Movement?
> CARL MATHEWS: Wonderful. About time. How long can you beat some-
> body down? How long can you take advantage of people? I like what
> they did with the banks on November 22nd, everybody was going to
> credit unions. Credit unions were getting people by the hundreds of
> thousands. You know what? I loved it. Get out of them banks, show
> them that they can't do what they want to do. [. . .] The corporations
> now got to understand: you've got to help us. You got helped by Bush,
> but you still don't want to help us. Get rid of them. I love it. They
> gonna keep on doing it, and pretty soon it's people who will prevail.
> CS: You think so?
> CM: It's just going to take a while. You know why? It's peaceful now,
> but it won't be so for long. And this is something, it's not a racially
> motivated thing, it ain't black, it ain't Mexican, it ain't Jews, ain't
> homosexuals, it's everybody, holding hands, fighting for the same
> thing, the 99 percent. That's what's going on. Pretty soon—you can
> only tear gas and mace people so long, but let's face it, we got more
> people out here with guns than police officers.

Most of my interviewees were not ready to take up arms, but I heard quite a bit of anger about big banks and corporate greed. Some interviewees instead took a neoliberal approach, blaming "overregulation" and other factors creating a bad business climate in California or in the United States. Nonetheless, whether they blamed greedy businesses or excessive government control, the majority placed their economic problems in a larger economic and political framework.

Lisa Rose, another frequent expositor of positive thinking, wrote me after she saw an earlier draft of this paper:

> I become concerned that people become passive or accepting of things
> that could be addressed differently or for which outrage is a natural and
> normal reaction.[21] I'm not one of those people who says "that it's all

good"—it isn't, and we have the right to name what is really happening despite our desire to maintain a positive outlook.

As I have found in my prior research (e.g., Strauss 2002, 2012), people are capable of combining ideas that analysts would think are incompatible, such as positive thinking and active social and political critique.

The Implications of Positive Thinking

What are the implications if positive thinking is as widespread among the jobless in America as I found among my interviewees?

Unlike Ehrenreich and Sharone, I did not find that positive thinking ideology necessarily led my interviewees to blame themselves for their struggles. They are correct, however, that the focus of positive thinking is mostly individualistic. (I say "mostly" because in Christian variants, the individual is subordinate to God.) One should be grateful for what one has and confident about one's abilities and the future. Unlike the South Korean and Nicaraguan cases examined by Jong Bum Kwon and Josh Fisher in this volume, the focus of positive thinking is working on the self, not organizing for social change.

However, organizing for social change is not precluded if one embraces positive thinking, as Carl Mathews' fervent support for the Occupy Wall Street movement shows. Political activism too relies on a kind of positive thinking that present circumstances do not have to be endured, the hopeful view that ordinary people can make change. While the kind of positive thinking preached to job seekers does not especially encourage political action, it does not discourage it either.

Above all, positive thinking, with its clear vision of a future in which suffering is redeemed with a happy ending, provides a narrative to those whom Lauren Berlant (2011) describes as at an impasse, without a narrative. It is a narrative that may give false hope and lead to even greater disappointment. But having some way of imagining the future may be preferable to having none.

THE UNEMPLOYED COOPERATIVE

Community Responses to Joblessness in Nicaragua

Josh Fisher

Nicaraguan political leaders were cautiously optimistic when the Central Bank of Nicaragua released its national employment numbers for 2012. Annual unemployment rates had dropped for the second year in a row, down to 7.3 percent—about the same rate as the United States at the time—from a peak of over 10 percent during the global financial crisis. In newspapers, on the radio, and on television, the trend was touted as a political victory for President Daniel Ortega and for the political revival of the socialist Sandinista Party in 2006, sixteen years after it had been ousted from power. As political opponents were quick to retort, however, the numbers still had a long way to go to return to the levels seen during the pro-business policies of Enrique Bolaños in the mid-2000s, when they hovered around 4 percent. Despite the Sandinistas' many efforts to improve health care, bolster the labor code, and curb hunger and malnourishment, such as through the "Zero Hunger" campaign, net job creation dipped significantly during the Ortega presidency, and that meant that they were failing.

As elsewhere, unemployment numbers in Nicaragua are highly politicized spectacles of the overall "health" of an economy. Increases of even a fraction of a point are wielded as political weapons, while slight decreases are celebrated as validations of existing power arrangements (e.g., Didier 2007). At the same time, for most poor and working-class Nicaraguans who may enjoy but rare glimpses of those halls of political power, these same statistics are an absurd rendition of economic life. At the same time that unemployment was under 5 percent during the Bolaños years, it is worth noting that approximately 70 percent of Nicaraguans were living in poverty, struggling to make ends meet on less than two dollars per day for an equivalent income of $700 per year. And because meager work like hawking gum on the street corner or selling bags of drinking water at stoplights was technically counted as "employment," rates of *underemployment*—defined as a wage that is insufficient to meet basic needs—was between 60 and 65 percent nationally, a figure that spiked to upwards of 80 percent in the poorest communities (USAID 2006, 124). Nevertheless, it is the widespread experience of unemployment in daily life, rather than a part of some political numbers game, that continually propels unemployment to the top of Nicaraguans' long list of concerns (Castillo 2012).

Whatever the political utility of the issue, one realization that many social scientists have come to is that statistics are far from transparent indicators of any economy, at least insofar as they reflect people's lived experiences. Instead, they are symptomatic of a larger trend, common in modern economics but very much at odds with disciplines like cultural anthropology: the transformation of real people, and all of the important ethical questions about what a person minimally needs and deserves in life, into inhuman statistical blocs (e.g., Ferguson 1990; Thompson 1963). What emerges from this dismal conversion is a highly sanitized, highly specialized, and highly inhuman rendition of that "delicate tissue" (Thompson 1963) of economic life.

Of course, in the process of converting the reality of unemployment to state-recognized statistics, the idea of work undergoes a transformation as well. Only certain kinds of work "count," namely wage labor for capitalist production. Meanwhile, the wide range of other social and economic activities rarely enters into any such calculus (Gibson-Graham 1996; Mitchell 1998). Yet much of this work continues to be of tremendous social value. This is the work done by caregivers and domestic laborers, by those who self-provision or work in unremunerated jobs, by those who make ends meet through informal or illicit economies, or even by the "reserve army" of the unemployed billions—all of whom collectively sustain the global economic system.

For anthropologists, I argue, the task at hand is not simply to expand the definition of what counts as "work" or, for that matter, as "an economy." Rather, more ambitiously, the task is to push beyond the binary style of thinking that has framed important issues like unemployment all too narrowly as the *absence of work*, the marginalization from some productive "core" economy. Unemployment is no simple absence. It is work of a different kind. Sometimes it is the solitary burden of an individual coming to terms with the great damage of being excluded from what society values, productively and otherwise. Other times it is the burden of a community trying to support one another in their mutual hardship, to challenge economic policy, or even to blaze new trails and to create viable economic alternatives. There are plenty of examples of each, from economies of artisans relying on their creative energies to make ends meet (Chibnik 2010; Grimes and

Milgram 2000; Nash 1993), to "job clubs" helping people navigate the byzantine paths of welfare policies and job searches (Brodkin and Marston 2013), to community "meet-ups" where people who may or may not previously know one another gather to network, to share resources, or just to commiserate.[1] In some cases, what starts as mundane meet-ups eventually emerges with a significantly more political edge. In Argentina after the economic crisis of 2001, for example, the Movement for Unemployed Workers (MTD) organized the barrios of Buenos Aires into autonomous zones, each with its own community economy consisting of subsistence food projects, schools, and community centers. Residents even took over abandoned factories that had been vacated by the crash (Chatterton 2004; Dinerstein 2001; Petras 2002). In Brazil, similarly, the well-known Landless Workers Movement (Movimento dos Trabalhadores Rurais Sem Terra, MST) has created an autonomous space for the unemployed by coordinating land seizures and launching semiautonomous community economies (Wolford 2010; Wright and Wolford 2003). Mounting evidence suggests that, even though systematic change may well be beyond the reach of regular people who are not well situated within those systems, communities can carve out for themselves pockets of hope, possibility, and change (Cameron and Gibson 2005).

In this chapter, I illustrate the potential for cooperative responses to unemployment. Over the last decade in Ciudad Sandino, Nicaragua, with the assistance of a U.S.-based nongovernmental organization called the Center for Sustainable Development (CSD), a group of unemployed men and women has been working to find a solution to the great damage widespread unemployment has caused in their community. They have built what promised to be the world's first worker-owned, organic, and fair trade–certified garment production chain in the world. In 2007, the third and final stage of this project commenced with the construction of a small cotton-spinning cooperative called Génesis. Unfortunately, their story is not one of success. Months quickly turned into years, and eventually plans for the plant sputtered and came to a halt. Génesis and CSD allege that a U.S.-based machinery trading company defrauded them of hundreds of thousands of dollars meant to supply the project's machinery. Then in 2012, five years after they first broke ground—still having never spun a single bit of thread or received a single paycheck for their work—the forty-two women and men of Génesis voted almost unanimously to give up on the cotton-spinning project. What is perhaps most remarkable in the story of Génesis is that after all those years, still unemployed, members continued to show up, to hold formal meetings, to debate and strategize, to share in the community space, and to support one another materially, financially, socially, and emotionally—as a cooperative. Indeed, as of this writing, even though the cotton-spinning project has been put on hold indefinitely, Génesis persists. They meet on the grounds of a local primary school, where they continue to pool resources, debate, strategize, and generally share in that community space.

My research draws on ethnographic fieldwork between 2007 and 2012, including approximately fifty individual and group interviews and more than a year of continuous participant observation between 2007 and 2008 (funded by the National Science Foundation). The research also draws on my professional experience as the technical director of an employment creation workshop called the Organization Workshop (OW), which occurred during the early phases of the construction of Génesis (Fisher 2010). Thus, to speak reflexively, my own efforts here come from a broader drive to understand and situate work as a social practice, rather than mere subsistence, and to allow the ethical and political commitment of those whom I consider friends, colleagues, teachers to emerge as such. I argue, in that respect, that a case study of the Génesis cooperative is much more than another piece of evidence suggesting that people are creative in "dealing with" unemployment to marginalization more generally. We need to consider the efforts involved in being unemployed—as much as the efforts of any working person—as social practice. They do not merely attempt to make ends meet. They do not respond passively to unemployment. Rather, Génesis demonstrates the potential of cooperative responses to unemployment on another level entirely. In the face of systematic unemployment, they demonstrate the capacity for thinking through those individualist economic ideologies, which may push them toward conflict and competition with one another, in order to construct inchoate forms of what J. K. Gibson-Graham (2006) calls "community economies." In this chapter, I argue that what is at stake in unemployment is not only life itself—"bare life," as Agamben (1998) calls it—for community economies are not simply about productivity, profit, or mere subsistence. Rather, entangled with that complex quantitative question about *what one deserves*—philosophers call this "distributive justice"—is a rather more qualitative question about *who one is*—"the qualified life," to use Agamben's less publicized term. In his survey of unemployment in the United States, the philosopher Paul Gomberg (2007) makes a very similar point. What is at stake in economic justice is not only having work, but having "good work"—what he calls "contributive justice." Contributive justice refers not to what people deserve but to what they should be expected or allowed to contribute to various spheres of social, cultural, and economic life. While the distribution of wealth and work opportunities in the United States is most certainly unjust, he argues, what is still missing from the conversation about unemployment and underemployment is that many people are condemned to spend their lives idle or doing mechanical and repetitive tasks that are not worth their time and effort. (David Graeber [2013], in another stream of thinking, has called this phenomenon "bullshit jobs.")

So I argue in this chapter that what is at stake in the "community economies" of employment and unemployment alike, for Génesis, is the hope of *meaningful work*: the elusive possibility of a space for sociality, solidarity, and autonomy. I also argue that, in the case of Génesis in particular, arriving at such a perspective on work does not come easily. It requires substantial personal transformation—new daily habits, new practices of the self, and new and unfamiliar forms of social relation in everyday life—which means redefining not only the very meaning of *work* but also what it means to be unemployed with a purpose. In both cases, the measure is not what one receives in exchange but how these new and creative social practices might emerge as meaningful communal activities—a good in, of, and for itself.

Help Wanted: Development, Cooperativism, and the Problem of Unemployment

Directly to the west of Nicaragua's capital city of Managua, and nearly contiguous with it, lies the smaller city of Ciudad Sandino. As elsewhere in Nicaragua, unemployment is a major concern. Yet Ciudad Sandino, perhaps more than most other Nicaraguan cities, illustrates the spatial distribution of poverty so often obscured by statistical representations. Unemployment rates, here, are formally between 10 and 15 percent, though the mayor's office estimates that underemployment is closer to 80 percent.[2] In fact, according to recent calculations, only 35 percent of the working-age population in Ciudad Sandino, a city of more than two hundred thousand, has any form of stable employment. In fact, upwards of 70 percent of that population survives on household incomes below the poverty line (INIDE 2008).

The reasons are historical as much as they are the product of the contemporary global economy. Ciudad Sandino is the result of more than forty years of natural and human-made disasters.[3] In 1968, a flood displaced thousands from their homes along the shoreline of Lake Managua, many of whom were relocated to some fallow cotton fields to the west of Managua, where they became its first inhabitants. A few years later in 1972, a major earthquake leveled nine hundred square blocks in Managua and left hundreds of thousands more homeless. Many of the displaced were relocated to the same encampment, now labeled "Permanent National Emergency Operation 3" (OPEN-3), more than doubling its size in a matter of weeks. In the bloody years leading up to the 1979 revolution that overthrew the brutal forty-two-year dictatorship of the Somoza family, OPEN-3 became a haven for the urban poor, the marginalized, and the oppressed, including political refugees fleeing Somoza's military forces—a fact memorialized after the victorious revolution with the city's new name, Ciudad Sandino (after Augusto César Sandino, the folk hero and namesake of the Sandinista political party). Then again in 1998, Hurricane Mitch displaced tens of thousands more from their homes along the same shoreline of Lake Managua. The majority were relocated, once again, to the muddy cow pastures on the outer edges of Ciudad Sandino. For that reason, while Ciudad Sandino does not have a strong identity of its own—or, for that matter, a common term to refer to its inhabitants (Arellano 2009)—it has long been a place for the displaced in Nicaragua.

Today's Ciudad Sandino is the material product of these many structural forces. Each of its *etapas* (stages) references one such disaster or another. High unemployment rates and the highest population density in the country (around 4,500 people per square mile) is closely linked to a wide range of other social and economic problems, including poverty, food insecurity, deforestation, crime, and disease (INIDE 2008). Basic infrastructure like roads, drainage, and waste management is deficient because the city enjoys a meager tax base of only $2.30 annually per person for all city services, thus also leaving very little in the coffers for any kind of employment initiative. Twelve free trade zones (also known as *zonas francas, maquiladoras*, or sweatshops) dot the perimeter of the city and produce all manner of popular clothing brands sold all over the world, but these facilities are also tax-free havens. They drain local resources and contribute almost nothing to local economic development and offer employees sub-subsistence wages of around 70 cents per day (e.g., Méndez 2005). As a result, while its own residents do not identify strongly with the place, many Managua residents, despite the meager geographic distance, perceive a strong spatial inequality. Some are even hesitant to travel to "Ciudad *Siniestra*," a nickname that carries a triple meaning: leftist, sinister (*siniestra*), as well as an accident or disaster (*un siniestro*).

For the many NGOs working in Ciudad Sandino in areas of local economic development, job creation is of paramount importance. Even though macroeconomic indicators have stabilized in the era of structural adjustment, austerity, and attempts to attract foreign direct investment through low-cost labor—most iconically in the free trade zones—unemployment and especially underemployment levels have remained consistently high. This situation has had resounding effects on local community health, security, and well-being. Hence, NGOs have often found the need to effect change on a smaller scale. A small, North Carolina–based NGO called the Center for Sustainable Development (CSD) was seeking to address precisely this problem when in 2007 it set out to build a cotton-spinning plant called Génesis. According to Roger, a spokesperson for CSD's project in Nicaragua, while government efforts to create jobs in the free trade zones have succeeded in lowering the overall unemployment numbers, they have also fallen well short of successfully encouraging real, local economic development.[4] Hence the need for an alternative that focuses on generating employment, not for the sake of the economy *per se* but rather for the community. Roger explains:

> The only thing that the maquilas have successfully done is give politicians something to talk about when they need to show they've created jobs. . . . The truth is that it's nearly impossible to get anything sustainable going in a community where basic incomes are still lacking because there's no work. As an organization that focuses on community development, which is to say one that puts the well-being of community above and beyond the economy, we simply can't afford to wait for the job fairies of free market capitalism, to magically create employment and somehow hoist this community out of poverty. Our goal with these cooperatives is to create a viable and just alternative to the maquiladoras. One that will compete with them and, perhaps in an ideal world, run them out of business one day.

For CSD, cooperatives are the preferred model for "keeping dollars local," as they frequently frame their efforts. By contrast with conventional enterprises, cooperative workers, who form a collective, are the owners of the business and manage it democratically. Moreover, because those worker-owners are normally members of the local community, rather than foreign financiers, the economic benefits of cooperatives also tend to have a more direct line of influence on local economic development.

Of course, Génesis was not CSD's only attempt at local economic development. Génesis was the missing link in a much larger project: the world's first vertically-integrated garment production chain, located entirely within Nicaragua, to be certified organic and fair trade, all the way from cotton seed to end product. This much bigger project took root in 2000 when, in the wake of the widespread devastation wrought by Hurricane Mitch, the NGO organized a women's sewing cooperative called the Fair Trade Zone (a cooperative, notably, that has since gained the status of the world's first worker-owned free trade zone in 2004; see Fisher 2013). As that project grew and experienced notable successes, CSD also reached an agreement with a large agricultural cooperative in Nicaragua called COPROEXNIC in 2005 to rotate cotton into their organic sesame and peanut fields. In that larger commodity chain, Génesis was the missing link and yet another attempt to provide well-paying jobs, quite unlike the *maquiladoras*.

Job-Creators and Employment Futures

The Génesis cooperative was founded in early 2007 by forty-two members in total—thirty-four women and eight men. The motley group spanned a range of ages from eighteen to eighty. They were former manual laborers, domestic workers, bus drivers, office workers, public workers, and even accountants and lawyers. And they came to the project with a wide variety of political orientations, experiences, and socioeconomic situations. Despite all of those differences, however, they were united by several factors. First of all, the group represented a wide range of the chronically unemployed in Ciudad Sandino, men and women who had some job skills but who, for one reason or another, had sought work without success for years at a time. Second, despite their unemployment, their goal was not to find work of any kind but rather work that dignified and promised financial stability. Third, these were not the poorest of the poor in Ciudad Sandino but were relatively well off compared to many in Ciudad Sandino: Some had professional degrees and maybe even some savings. Others had family or other networks of social support willing to finance an individual's participation in the fledgling project by lending money for food and other household necessities. Ximena, for example, was reciprocally supported by her husband (whom she often helps out in his small carpentry shop), her sister (whom she helps out in her *pulpería* or small, neighborhood shop), and her two working children. Even though the project carried no guarantee of success, nor a wage in the immediate term, she could afford the risk. At the same time, she recognizes, there are many in Ciudad Sandino who could nary afford to divert their attention from the daily task of simply making ends meet. For her, the payoff was more than worth the risk. Ximena explains: "You know what it means to be part of a cooperative? It means that you can never, *never* be laid off. You can never be replaced by a machine. It means that you *are* the business, and it cannot exist without you."

It is also worth noting the sharp gender differential between those who ultimately became members of Génesis and those who did not. Adilia, a middle-aged mother of three who is a worker-owner in the Fair Trade Zone, Génesis' partner cooperative, argues that a major factor is the different attitudes of men and women toward being unemployed:

> Men sit around all day, watching television, feeling bad. They drink whatever money they have. They say "I'm a painter and there's no work painting," so they stay out of work . . . because their pride is hurt. Then they get depressed and angry because they are not contributing, they feel worthless, and they take it out on the rest of us. We women are more entrepreneurial [*empresarial*]. We say, "Oh, there's work doing something else, I'll do that." Even if we're not accustomed to the work, we

always find a way to contribute. We stay strong as women because we have to, because our children depend on us, and we can't give up.

In other words, according to Adilia, the identities of men are closely tied to formal employment, conceptualized as economic activity in the *calle* (street or public sphere), as well as to the role of provisioning the household (Babb 2001; Gutmann 2006, 158–159). Consequently, lack of work implies both financial consequence and a toll on one's dignity and self-worth. And yet, the unwillingness to fill in around the house, to perform those tasks most closely associated with "women's work," or even to pursue alternatives forms of income generation might be perceived as a threatening reversal of gender roles and potentially escalates to domestic violence (Olavarría 2003; Vigoya 2001; Welsh 2002). For many Nicaraguan women and mothers, on the other hand, what is at stake in employment is less a matter of status *per se* than one's ability to provision the household and maintaining a minimum, culturally-defined level of subsistence (Mulinari 1995; Schmalzbauer, Verghese, and Vadera 2007). According to Adilia, in times of scarcity, a mother's work, in particular, might require a wide range of entrepreneurial survival strategies, including vending food and drink on the street, earning extra income by taking in laundry from neighbors, and participating in direct selling programs (Casanova 2011), in addition to a plethora of strategies for self-denial and "individual belt-tightening" (Stephen 2005b). Adilia continues:

> You have to do anything for your children [*Uno hace cualquier cosa por los hijos*]. . . . You have to take care of them, make sure they eat and go to school. But you also have to give them hope and make sure that they are loved and that they grow up to be good people.

In other words, the intense self-exploitation for women involved in provisioning the household is justified precisely because what is at stake is more than an income or a job. It is the economic, social, and emotional well-being of the entire household (González de la Rocha 1994, 2001).

For the forty-two women and men who eventually joined Génesis, the initial stages of this unpaid work were not exactly glamorous. They spent the majority of each workday hacking away at weeds, cleaning up trash, and clearing space under the shade of a large guanacaste tree on a small plot of land that would host the future factory. There, they sat on stacks of concrete blocks and held organizational meetings with nothing more than a small whiteboard warped by rain and humidity. To an outsider such as myself, the meetings seemed lengthy and meandering, often lasting three to four hours at a time. Yet, as I came to understand, the performance was much more significant than rote bureaucracy.

Working together, for these women and men, meant being together. Meetings covered issues as abstract as the meaning of democracy and as prosaic as the schedule for the next day. Through the process of discussing each and every one of them, the members of Génesis practiced what anthropologist David Graeber calls "prefigurative politics" (2001a). What they discussed, and the conclusions to which they came, mattered at least as much as the relationships they built in the process. In this case, they came to think about their cooperative as a community in which it was the responsibility of each member to "align oneself with the spirit of cooperativism" (*alinearse con el espíritu de cooperativismo*), particularly the values of equality, respect, and transparency (Fisher 2010). María, who ran a small stall in the local market before coming to Génesis, reflected:

> Being in a cooperative means that we must always act with respect toward one another because we are all in this together. Although we are not yet getting paid for our work, it is still like a job, like owning and running your own business. We decide how things are run *together*, and no one has the right to tell the others what to do.

Moreover, for those who had spent so much of their time around the house, the act of clearing the land, creating a space for themselves, was a socially and symbolically significant act, if for no other reason than it gave them somewhere to be each day. Literally and figuratively, *la oficina* (the office)—the space underneath the guanacaste tree—was a place for being together and for doing the important work of building a future in the present.

In the same year that Génesis broke ground on their project, I began conducting long-term ethnographic research in Nicaragua. My timing was felicitous in that I was not only able to witness the early organizational phases of the cooperative but was also asked to serve as the technical director of a well-known, large-scale employment generation workshop called the Organization Workshop (OW). The goal of that workshop was twofold. The first focused on unemployment in the Ciudad Sandino community. As a model, the OW targets a community's surplus of unemployed and gives them a framework within which they may come together, pool resources, and develop creative solutions (including new enterprises) to address their own unemployment. The second focused on Génesis itself. According to the workshop's sponsor, a Managua-based NGO called Vientos de Paz, an effective organizational culture is crucial to the success of a producer cooperative. Thus, the other purpose of the OW was to provide Génesis cooperative members a means for developing a "culture of productivity" that would allow them to succeed in a competitive marketplace (Porter 2000, 25).

Very briefly, the OW was first developed in the 1960s in Brazil by scholar-activist Clodomir Santos de Morais (de Morais 1969, 1987). De Morais believed that unemployment was the most pressing issue in the developing world, and he conceived of his workshop as the job-creating equivalent of Paulo Freire's famous literacy workshops. (The two men were close friends, having shared a prison cell during the 1964 coup.) According to de Morais, most development projects are inscribed in highly unequal relations of hierarchical power such that a privileged class ("technicians," "specialists," or other "experts") are regarded as possessing knowledge, skills, or resources and as transmitting them to designated "target populations." In so doing, de Morais argues, they do not end up empowering those target populations at all. Quite the opposite, they inadvertently disempower them by depriving them of control over the instruments of *their own* development (e.g., Carmen 1996). The OW sets itself apart by striving to empower target populations to wield the tools of their own development by taking full control of the workshop. Participants critically engage the conditions of their own lives and democratically define, as a group, their development goals. They run the workshop themselves and learn the necessary skills for managing a large enterprise. In so doing, they transform the way they think about "work," moving from an independent, voluntaristic "artisan consciousness" (in the language of the workshop) to a more complex and collaborative "organizational consciousness"—the difference being the difference between small-scale change and large-scale, sustainable change (Carmen and Sobrado 2000).[5] While in that sense it might appear that the OW is a highly experimental or radical project, it has in fact had remarkable exposure among leading development agencies. Since its origins in Brazil, the workshop has been implemented hundreds of times on five continents by entities as large as the UN Development Programme and the International Labor Organization (ILO). In Latin America alone, the OW has assisted members of the Brazilian Landless Workers Movement in establishing enterprises and formalizing land seizures (in accordance with the demands of Brazilian law). It has helped unemployed workers set up well-known cooperatives in Colombia, Venezuela, Costa Rica, and Honduras. And it has aided *ejido* communities in Mexico in organizing common resources and in developing community infrastructure (see Carmen and Sobrado 2000).

One might think that the radical democratic method might lighten the workload of someone in a director position, and it did in a technical sense, but at the same time it added significantly to the political work of mediating conflicts. However, it was precisely that dimension of my position within the OW that led to some of my most important insights. That is, the Ciudad Sandino OW of 2007 was formally led by the forty-two members of Génesis. Its conceptual center was the land that they had cleared for themselves. And yet it drew on more than two hundred unemployed residents of the local community. The geography of the workshop, in other words, revealed a basic inequality: those who led (and performed the esteemed "organizational" work) and those who didn't. Leaders of the Génesis cooperative became *de facto* leaders of the OW and, in so doing, learned to manage significantly larger and more capital-intensive projects than those to which they were hitherto accustomed. It was the same group who chose to hire, nepotistically, at a rate of 200 dollars over four weeks, family, friends, neighbors, and other acquaintances in order to develop and implement a wide range of job-training classes: from brick-making, welding, carpentry, and electricity to cooking, accounting, cosmetology, jewelry-making, accounting, computing, and English.

Remarkably, as the OW intended, in nearly all aspects of the workshop participants did not rely on the charity of professional expertise of distant others (NGOs or otherwise). They drew almost exclusively on the resources of their own community. By the time the workshop concluded forty days later, many participants testified that they had gained valuable job skills, which in turn provided them with new opportunities, enabled them to transition into new career paths, and even gave them the means to build their own enterprises. One group launched a *comedor*, an informal dining establishment typically run out of one's home. Another launched a small internet café and video game parlor, run out of one participant's home, in which they set up desktop computers, a PlayStation, an Xbox, and a Super Nintendo for rent at a low hourly cost. Yet another group started an informal construction, plumbing, and welding business. Of course, some of these enterprises failed to survive beyond the first year—an important fact that points to broader structural challenges, like access to capital or credit. But the impact of the OW on the lives of participants from the Ciudad Sandino community was nevertheless lasting and significant, if only because, as a social exercise, it instilled a spirit of cooperation and collaboration. Even when projects failed, OW participants started approaching their neighbors with the question, *What can we do together?* Thus, as I wrote in my final report, the OW fails to address key structural issues, but it also offers an important lesson in community economics. Corporations and business magnates are not the only "job creators" in any given economy. Given minimal autonomy in terms of land and basic resources, we must acknowledge that even those most lacking in resources are job creators in the important context of their own communities.

As for the workshop's impacts on the "culture of productivity" of Génesis, successes and failures are still a matter of debate (see Fisher 2010). The truth is that cooperatives are not "productive" organizations in any strictly economic sense. Cooperatives are complex social and cultural organizations composed of complex and dynamic human relationships, the nature of which can never be ascertained *a priori*. Génesis had developed its own organizational "style," if you will, well before the OW arrived. But quite unlike the OW and its emphasis on productivity and efficiency, theirs was organized not around "productivity" *per se* but other values like equality, respect, and transparency. In that respect, the Ciudad Sandino OW had some unintentional and not entirely positive effects. The sudden injection of funds and the push for productivity and efficiency, combined with the empowerment of a select group to manage and disperse those funds with little oversight, fomented new and unanticipated frictions. By the end of the forty days, in fact, interpersonal frictions had turned into widespread accusations of fraud and theft against the co-op leadership. While most were unfounded, in my assessment, they are nevertheless illustrative of the fragility of the collective trust, those small rifts that have the potential for flaring up into much bigger divisions. In Génesis, the effects of those divisions were permanent. In the months following the workshop, the general membership voted to oust the co-op's leadership, many of whom decided to depart from the co-op permanently.

Nevertheless, it is safe to say that for Génesis those disputes tempered the co-op's resolve and resulted in a stronger community, a fact that would prove especially important in the difficult years to come. When the financial collapse hit in 2008, financial institutions scaled back lending worldwide, hurting potential homeowners in the United States, state welfare recipients in Greece, and the entirety of the aid and development industry (UNIDO 2009). Fortunately, CSD was partly shielded from the worst consequences of the global recession because they had tended to finance projects like Génesis through small grants and individual donations—more than 60 percent of which were pledges of less than $100 at a time, rather than loans or large grants. Even so, donations for their projects in Nicaragua fell significantly as a generalized economic anxiety rose in the United States. Donors, in other words, became increasingly worried about their own pocketbooks and were soberly reluctant to spend much at all on idealistic projects like Génesis. The construction of the cotton-spinning plant, which had started at precisely the time that the stock markets crashed, continued, but in a significantly slower and more halting manner, its progress interrupted each time the meager resources wore thin. In the end, the co-op was financed by a scattershot fundraising campaign that CSD called "Making Stone Soup." The title was a reference to a folk story from Western Europe in which a group of travelers, starting with a mere stone, persuade a community to contribute whatever ingredients they can to help them make a cauldron of rich soup to be shared by the whole community.

Once funds eventually started trickling in, the tight budget meant that the actual work of laying the foundation, even raising the structure itself, was left to co-op members. Notably, for the two years that Génesis members worked on this construction project, they were not remunerated for their labor. Rather, in accordance with the Mondragón cooperative model in Spain (see Kasmir 1996), they received "sweat equity" or "social capital." In the case of Génesis, members were credited 50 cents per hour for their labor, which was deposited in their individual accounts within the cooperative (*caja laboral*); the funds would become accessible only if they left the co-op. Despite the intensity of the work and the many difficulties involved in effectively working without pay, the worker-owners of Génesis approached their task with a great deal of hope and enthusiasm. Indeed, even as they remained technically unemployed two to three years into the project, their work was by definition *an investment in the future*. As Giselle, a co-op member with a university degree in economics from the University of Central America, calculated: "Right now we're all unemployed, we're no different from everyone else in Ciudad Sandino. But the difference is that in a few years, we will be our own bosses! We are investing in our future. In a few years, I'm going to be driving my own little truck to work every day."

Of course, working without pay was an onerous task. Those with the weakest support networks outside of the co-op had the most difficulty participating in the project. Several ended up dropping out because of the immediacy of their responsibilities to kin and family. On the other hand, those who had kin willing to support them in the endeavor by providing financial, social, and emotional support—daughters and sons, sisters and brothers, or mothers and fathers—tended to fare better. Even with that support, however, as year after year passed with still no income forthcoming, those support networks also faltered. Family who were once supportive eventually demanded that the member "get a real job." For the women, the strain of participating in the project (thus taking time away from provisioning the household) provoked domestic violence or the breakup of unions. In still other cases, co-op members dropped out voluntarily when guilt about the burden they placed on family, whether financial or otherwise, became unbearable. Things became especially difficult when the cost of supporting a nonworking person in Nicaragua rose to unprecedented levels during a highly destructive market phenomenon termed "the world food crisis" in the United States, understood by economists as a market "correction" and among most Nicaraguans as further evidence of an unfair system (Gilbert 2010; Headey and Fan 2008). Within a year, in any case, prices of basic foodstuffs like rice and beans in Nicaragua nearly doubled.

In response to the diminished support outside of the co-op, Génesis members started developing support mechanisms *within* the cooperative. In 2009, they began to collect fruits (mangos, limes, bananas) from surrounding trees. Then they planted a sizable community garden (*huerto*) on co-op grounds—leaving just enough room for male members to continue to play baseball. There, they grew melons, pipian, and chayote (types of squash) and spices like cilantro. Then, when other staples ran low in their households, the co-op petitioned CSD for economic support. CSD found support in their own networks from a Rotarian club in Oregon, who matched the sweat equity inputs of members to establish a common fund with which members could buy bulk quantities of staples like rice, beans, and cooking oil. Then, to generate cash for other necessities like soap or bus fare, co-op members also experimented with some of the skills acquired during the OW and set up small enterprises of their own. One group of women started a small, rather informal bakery (briefly called "*Panadería Génesis*") but eventually found little profit in the endeavor. So they transitioned to crafting jewelry items like necklaces, bracelets, and earrings. They sold these to visiting delegations of college students, church groups, and civic organizations from the United States, who were hosted on a predictable monthly basis by CSD, usually for a week at a time, and who came with the idea of "helping out"—which conceivably meant purchasing mementos of their service trip.

In the long shot, the diverse strategies Génesis members employed during this time of difficulty illustrate the broad potential for cooperative responses to unemployment. Cooperatives provide semiautonomous spaces within which groups may work together. They are not only spaces for *getting by* in a material sense, they are also spaces for supporting one another socially and emotionally, or for simply being together. In the case of Génesis, these values of cooperativism proved instrumental when, in coming years, the project hit another brick wall.

The Lawsuit

In February of 2010, Génesis completed the construction of the cotton-spinning plant: a fifteen-thousand-square-foot factory with twenty-foot walls and hand-poured, six-foot-deep concrete floors. In celebration, they gathered up all of the scrap metal left lying around, sold it to a local merchant (*chatarrero*), and threw themselves a party with fried chicken, sodas, and piñatas filled with candy for the kids. Meanwhile, in fields around Nicaragua, the agricultural cooperative COPROEXNIC was planting cotton in anticipation of the fact that, by the time the crops were mature, Génesis would be open for business. The "seeds of a hope"—*las semillas de la esperanza*—they imagined, were already in the ground.

Of course, the final missing puzzle piece was the cotton-spinning machinery, the equipment that actually transforms cotton into workable yarn or thread by preparing the cotton, processing it into workable fiber, and spinning and weaving or spooling it into thread, yarn, or cloth. CSD had exhausted its meager funds completing the construction of the factory. Aware of the hardships co-op members had already suffered, they elected to take out a loan of approximately $250,000 from a Dutch development bank to purchase the machinery from a

U.S.-based machinery trading company called AAC International. Doing so was a tremendous risk to their organization, as the loan would be backed with substantial personal collateral, including their land, their offices, and—as they unanimously voted—a substantial portion of their personal retirement funds.

According to staff members at CSD, in late October of 2009, AAC requested a $150,000 deposit with the contractual stipulation that the business load and ship the machinery in early January of 2010. However, several months after Génesis celebrated the opening of their plant, the twelve containers of machinery had still to arrive. In August of 2010, CSD learned from the original owners of the equipment, a Venezuelan company, that they had yet to be paid for the equipment. The owner of AAC never denied this point, nor did he provide receipts to the contrary. He simply ignored CSD's increasingly desperate emails and phone calls. By October of 2010, CSD realized that they had been taken for a ride, and they began to talk to their lawyers in the United States. In one moment of sheer desperation, the NGO broadcast an SOS to its extensive network of supporters that included church-goers, college students, and civic groups—of all ages and political stripes—many of whom rushed to the NGO's aid. In a matter of days, they flooded AAC's mailboxes with thousands of personal notes that contained pleas like:

> As a long-time supporter of CSD in Nicaragua, we are appalled to learn of your unconscionable treatment of the hardworking women and men they support. Please act with honesty and integrity and immediately fulfill your contractual obligations with CSD and the Génesis coopera-tive by immediately delivering the agreed-upon spinning equipment.

Local college students and churchgoers also staged a three-day protest in the name of Génesis in front of the offices of AAC International in South Carolina, where the story gained exposure on local news. Thousands more rushed to support Génesis itself by providing them with funds to buy more fish, rice, beans, and vegetables. It was an extraordinary demonstration of the power of transna-tional networks.

Meanwhile, the first cotton harvests were coming in. Forty-two farmers (including two women's cooperatives) had planted thirty-four acres of organic and fair trade–certified cotton for a total of around six hundred thousand pounds of seed cotton. This was processed by COPROEXNIC's own cotton gin, an antique dating from the early 1960s. Unfortunately, while Génesis' fifteen-thousand-foot facility was full of organic and fair trade–certified cotton ready for processing, they had no machinery to do it with. All they could do was earn a meager sum inspecting the cotton for contaminants, like the stray piece of plastic here and there that had somehow made its way into the mix. It was a far cry from the work that they had envisioned for themselves so many years earlier.

In November of 2010, CSD was surprised to discover that four containers of equipment had arrived in Nicaragua in their organization's name, each of which was now incurring daily fines at customs. Thousands of dollars in fees later, the NGO realized that, although the serial numbers appeared to be correct, the machinery was nowhere near the quality they had been promised and would have cost more than their worth to make operational. CSD filed suit against AAC International, only to find that they were not the only ones seeking retribution from the beleaguered company. AAC had apparently experienced serious financial trouble during the recent economic downturn and had filed for bankruptcy protection. CSD was therefore last on a long list of plaintiffs, each of whom had some claim against AAC's remaining funds. Periodically, AAC extended some settlement "offer"—for example, that the machines would be delivered once the balance due was paid, that they could go to Venezuela themselves and get the equipment—if it happened to still be there—but each offer was rescinded as quickly as the NGO could respond.

If the process was frustrating for CSD, it was maddening for Génesis. The group of men and women felt helpless in the face of the pending lawsuit, a situation made worse by their feelings of powerlessness in the U.S. court system. They suffered even more knowing that, so close to the finish line, they had to continue to seek out family members for still more financial and emotional support. Though CSD tried to get them some work as they continued to wait, co-op members were so focused on the goal of running their own spinning plant that the very thought was excruciating. In response, Génesis rallied together and stepped up the performance of being in a cooperative. With no work to do, members came to work every weekday for more than eight months to replant the community garden, to debate, to strategize, or just to converse about ongoing events.

In the end, frustration overwhelmed Génesis. Although CSD's lawyers had succeeded in upgrading the suit from a civil case to a criminal case—thanks to internal evidence that the serial number plates had been intentionally switched—their fate and the fate of the cotton-spinning project continued to lay in the hands of a fickle U.S. court system. Moreover, from their perspective, it continued to be difficult to discern truth from falsehood in their affairs with the North American NGO, and so once it came to light that, for all their hard work, they were yet again denied their just desserts, CSD was the natural target for their anger. CSD had attempted to include the cooperative in the conversation by forwarding a copy of the written suit and all the legal details (written in English) as well as by setting up meetings between the co-op and their lawyer. Still, conspiracy theories circulated widely. Some theorized that the NGO had been manipulating them from the start, that they had tricked them into building a factory for them, and that they still continued to profit from the poor co-op by selling their tragic story to donors.

In February of 2012, those tensions reached a breaking point. A faction of thirteen Génesis members staged a lockout in the spinning plant building and refused to give CSD or COPROEXNIC, the agricultural cooperative, access to the hundreds of thousands of pounds of organic cotton, effectively shutting down the entire production process and putting at risk several pending business deals. By the end of the third day of occupation, the group called the media outlets. On national television, they accused CSD of defrauding them by cooking up a story of a fake lawsuit. The next day, having gotten wind of the kerfuffle, representatives of the National Workers' Front (Frente Nacional de los Trabajadores, FNT)—the largest of Nicaragua's workers' syndicates—arrived to show their support for the Génesis cooperative. They put up FNT flags around the perimeter of the property, constructed handmade protest signs with messages like *Somos los desocupados de Génesis, respeta nuestro derecho al trabajo* ("We are the unemployed of Génesis, respect our right to work"), and they staged demonstrations outside CSD's gates. Then, as soon as it seemed tensions couldn't escalate further, the conflict turned violent. The FNT flags attracted a group of young men from the local community, undoubtedly embittered by their own job situation in Ciudad Sandino. The men brought with them homemade rum and mortars, a combination often used in protests and celebrations in Nicaragua. However, they pointed the mortars at CSD's offices. In the ensuing chaos, one CSD staff member was physically assaulted as she tried to take photographs of the offenders.

While CSD did not ultimately press charges against the Génesis members who had participated in the sit-in, the NGO did use the conflict to argue for legal mediation between the two groups. In those meetings, Génesis agreed to withdraw from the project in return for receiving two thousand dollars apiece for their five years of work as well as being listed as a claimant in the pending suit against AAC.

Remarkably, although many in the NGO's circle have since come to call the cooperative experiment a "failure," Génesis members still do not think so. Even today, the unemployed cooperative continues to hold meetings on the grounds of a local elementary school. They tote their own chairs from home, and they arrange them in a circle around the same whiteboard, warped by rain, that they used five years previous. Of course, their collective unemployment is still their primary concern, but now they pin much of their collective hopes on the suit against AAC, which as of this writing, remains unresolved but is pending in a South Carolina courtroom. I sat in on one of Génesis' many meetings during the summer of 2012. After years of working with the co-op, both in a professional capacity and as friends and colleagues, what I perceived most keenly was that their work in this cooperative was not just about jobs. Being in the cooperative was a good in, of, and for itself. We spoke for nearly six hours. We talked not just about the financial implications of unemployment but also about the "collapse of a dream" (*el fracaso de un sueño*), as María put it, and the other damage that had resulted. The cooperative—indeed, all of the work that they had done creating community gardens, jewelry, and other crafts and also buying into direct selling schemes—turned out not to be a simple economic input, a way to make ends meet. It was a space of possibility, opportunity, and emergence. And yet, even with the most promising of those endeavors now gone—the idea that they would someday be the owners of their own business—the basic community infrastructure persisted. The cooperative is a place to come and talk, to socialize, to commiserate, to support one another, or simply to be together. María continues, "We are still a cooperative, and we will survive together."

Conclusions

What compels a person to go to work for five years without pay? What compels the same person to continue to show up for work even after everything appears to be lost? The answer, I argue, drives to the core of what is at stake in employment—socially, culturally, emotionally, psychologically, as well as financially—and how different communities respond to the manifold damages of systematic unemployment.

Perhaps the first lesson is that, in order to understand the stakes of unemployment, it is imperative to understand the meaning and purpose of work. In the case of Génesis, work is not just about receiving money in exchange for time and effort. Indeed, work in the Génesis co-op was not particularly lucrative in that respect. Rather, working in the co-op gave members a sense of purpose, pride, self-satisfaction, belonging, and hope for the future. Work, from an anthropological perspective, needs to be decoupled from pay. It needs to be understood as part of a larger vision of human well-being. Although that is almost never considered in modern labor economics, such a perspective has a long philosophical history. Long ago, Aristotle speculated that *good work* consisted in the unity of conception (*noesis*, a person's ability to envision an outcome) and execution and production (*poiesis*, a person's ability to carry it out). Such ideas about work also persist in recent treatises. Echoes abound particularly in Karl Marx's analysis of capitalism. Of course, Marx is well known for addressing questions of ownership, distribution, and exploitation, but for him, too, work is also a matter of the basic capacities of human beings. As Murphy summarizes, "What gives skilled work its dignity . . . is that a worker first constructs in thought what he then embodies in matter; conversely, what makes unskilled work sordid is that one man executes the will of another" (1994, 8).[6]

In this chapter, I have focused on the non-economic entanglements of economic phenomena. Along with Gomberg (2007), I have argued that "contributive justice"—what people are rightly expected or allowed to contribute to many spheres of social life—is at stake in unemployment in addition to a person's ability to make ends meet. To be sure, whether a person can make ends meet is closely tied into his or her sense of dignity and self-worth. Dignity, respect, and one's ability to make ends meet follow entangled paths (Bourgois 1995). This, I think, is also the lesson of the Génesis cooperative. One of the unassailable good aspects of work, even unpaid work, is the process, rather than the end product, of going to work, making decisions, negotiating differences, and coming home satisfied, if tired, for having accomplished something. The work of unemployment, as it were, is valued in part for its meaning as part of larger schematics of action—as a matter of self-determination and the efflux of the human will.

The second and related lesson is that, as inchoate community economies and community responses to unemployment, cooperatives need not always be organized around core principles of productivity, efficiency, profit, or even subsistence. Since the early cooperative experiments of the nineteenth century, cooperatives have played an important role in response to the systematic unemployment of capitalism (Cohen 1998; MacLeod 1997; Staber 1993). Indeed, Marx thought them precursors to socialism not because they revolutionized the technical dimensions of production *per se* but because they demanded new social relations: "an association of free men, working with the means of production held in common, and expending their many different forms of labor-power in full self-awareness as one single labor force" (Marx 1977 [1867], 169–171). But as Génesis demonstrates, cooperatives are not just "productive" organizations made possible by specific sets of social relations. They are social and cultural organizations, indeterminate community economies that may serve any number of different economic or non-economic goals. In this case, to work in the cooperative is to be part of a community that values efficiency, transparency, and equality. It means being part of a community that, even in the absence of paid work, is supportive of one another socially, emotionally, and psychologically. It is to participate in a collective endeavor organized around basic principles of sociality, solidarity, and autonomy. These are not necessarily means to an end—productivity, profit, or employment. They are ends in, of, and for themselves.

For anthropologists, then, and for the societies from which we come and about which we write, the pressing task at hand is to recover from a century or more of economistic discourses on *labor* a sense of what work *means* as well as how unemployment, an apparent law of the capitalist system, strips the lives of human beings of something far more profound than money. That is, we must ask: What is work as a meaningful, emotional, and ethical practice? What happens to a person's dignity, self-worth, or social status when they are unemployed? What does it mean to be a contributing member of a family, a community, or society in general, and what happens when a person is denied that right? And to what ends will a person go to find work, to cope with the manifold consequences of unemployment, to fill up one's day, or to devise new and imaginative alternatives? Quite unlike the reigning conception of labor as something to be simply calculated, measured, and exchanged, work, or the lack thereof, needs to be placed within the meaningful and multidimensional contexts of everyday life.

RETHINKING THE VALUE OF WORK AND UNEMPLOYMENT

Caitrin Lynch and Daniel Mains

Introduction: Swan Song for Unpaid Work

Every January or so, college students in the United States begin to explore possibilities for summer employment. Searching the listings in the campus career center, networking via contacts and internet postings, working all social media angles, the question is soon to arise: "Should I take an unpaid internship?" This question may become less common, for the legal status of unpaid internships is under active consideration in several U.S. courts. In the most high-profile case, a June 2013 New York federal court ruled in favor of two unpaid interns who worked on the film *Black Swan* and sued Fox Searchlight Pictures for violating the state's minimum wage laws. These interns claimed that they should have been paid for the work they did as unpaid interns, work that included taking lunch orders, answering phones, and assembling office furniture. The judge ruled that unpaid internships are only valid in specific circumstances, noting that they "should not be to the immediate advantage of the employer, the work must be similar to vocational training given in an educational environment, the experience must be for the benefit of the intern and the intern's work must not displace that of regular employees."[1] However, in July 2015 a judge overturned this ruling (especially for cases in which students receive school credit), and court observers anticipate that the case may make its way to the Supreme Court (Welkowitz 2015). There have been many such recent cases along similar lines, including class-action lawsuits. Ensuing discussions among employers, interns, and potential interns have revealed the complexity for students of charting career paths in a tight jobs economy where students might strategically choose unpaid internships in order to get a foot in the door of a company and to gain experiences that are required in an environment where there no longer seem to be entry-level job openings.[2]

Although some economically privileged students may accept unpaid internships because the money is immaterial to them, more commonly students may be willing to take the risk of no pay because of what literary critic Lauren Berlant (2011) has called "cruel optimism." Cruel optimism is their unfounded and precarious understanding that unpaid work is a step that will put them on the road to success. In the United States, there is a belief that one can more quickly access the American Dream if one enters into ventures with a perceived delayed payoff. Internships are often a path to a very specific form of the American Dream. As in the *Black Swan* case, even when in practice jobs entail an abundance of mundane photocopying and running errands, they are frequently associated with creative activity in writing, theater, entertainment, and design. In this sense internships are not simply a step toward a lucrative career; they also allow young people to preserve the dream of finding *meaningful* employment—work that is important and valued because of its creative nature.

Debates concerning internships in the United States resonate with a key theme from the chapters in this volume—the intersections among multiple forms of value, unemployment, and work. These studies examine value both in the quantifiable sense of income and material wealth, and in the more qualitative sense that anthropologist David Graeber describes as "what is ultimately good, proper, or desirable in human life" (2001b, 1). Work and unemployment provide particularly useful sites for exploring the complex interrelationships among multiple forms of value. In this volume, from garbage pickers in Argentina (see also Millar 2014) to high-tech job seekers in Texas and striking autoworkers in Korea, we see that work, and its absence, are sites for narrating lives, finding value, and asserting personhood. In his 1975 book *Working*, journalist Studs Terkel wrote that work "is about a search . . . for daily meaning as well as daily bread, for recognition as well as cash, for astonishment rather than torpor; in short, for a sort of life rather than a Monday through Friday sort of dying" (Terkel 1997 [1975]). While work is often an obvious practical means to an end, it may at the same time be experienced and lived as much more than that. The same may be said for the day-to-day struggles to find work, access alternative sources of income, and simply pass the time that are associated with the experience of unemployment. This volume provides rich ethnographic examples of the variety of ways people experience work and unemployment as a search for meaning, recognition, and economic support and livelihood. The authors help us to understand the varied meanings of work and unemployment in the contemporary world. In this epilogue we tease out underlying themes across the variety of cases and places that show the analytical power of anthropological methods and theories to tell us something new about work and unemployment in social and economic life. We leverage our individual ethnographic research on work among youth and among older adults—bookend periods of working life in the United States—and organize our discussion in sections on economic change, the life course, and social relationships.

The essays in this volume concretely demonstrate the strength of anthropology in analyzing how people experience unemployment in vastly different contexts. In many settings worldwide, today and in the past, work has provided people with much more than a paycheck, and the workplace has served as more than a place to earn a wage. What do we gain analytically when we understand that work may, in some cases, enable social engagement, provide a sense of contribution, and offer a respite from domestic troubles? Or that having a job may provide a young man (and others around him) a sense of accomplishment for ascending a ladder of expected life-course phases? To be even more specific, let's consider that for many people in the United States today, paid work is integral to one's sense of self-worth and value. And because of this, many nonworking adults struggle to develop a sense of value that counters the cultural and economic norm. "What do you do?" is a question commonly posed in social settings in the United States. But how do you respond if you have no conventionally recognized work—even if you are industriously engaged as a "stay-at-home mom" or a careworker for aging parents; or if you are unable to or do not wish to find or retain work; or if you self-identify as a person who is unemployed, retired, or on disability support? And how do the answers to the question "What do you do?" vary depending on context?

We seek to build on critiques in this volume of overly economistic perspectives on unemployment. The chapters in this book demonstrate that a rigid dichotomy between unemployment and employment is often problematic. Although the distinction has some analytical utility in categorizing people on the basis of their involvement in paid labor, it does little to describe people's lived experiences. For example, many of the former white-collar workers that Carrie Lane describes are working for money, but they consider themselves to be unemployed because they are not in the field of their choice. In Joshua Fisher's study, Nicaraguan cooperative members are classified as unemployed even though they are often very busy with activities that in many contexts would constitute paid work. And David Karjanen offers a compelling lesson in how conventional labor economists exhibit a "blind spot" in regard to the informal economy, such that they are largely unable to understand the relationships between informal work and the labor market. Furthermore, via the story of Mario, Karjanen shows how, *contra* economic assumptions, attributes of the employee *do* make a difference in the wage an employee receives. In breaking down the unemployment/employment dichotomy, many of the authors suggest that it is necessary to rethink the meaning of work. What might this rethinking entail? How can we best classify and understand work, paid or otherwise? In what follows we focus specifically on the meaning of work and unemployment in relation to changing economic structures, social relationships, and the life course.

Economic Change and the Changing Meaning of Work

In 1995, anthropologist Philippe Bourgois published his book *In Search of Respect* (1995), examining social marginalization in the urban United States, profiling the efforts expended by street-level drug dealers in East Harlem to gain and retain respectability in their communities. Bourgois's gritty description of the efforts of men like Primo and Levi to find respectable work in the deindustrialized city includes analysis of why they sell crack—an illegal and dangerous job that is nevertheless reliable and earns them respect. Technically "unemployed" in formal accounting, these are people who have found income and meaning in work. In his 2009 study, with Jeff Schonberg, *Righteous Dopefiend*, Bourgois focused on the clients of the dealers in the earlier book. As he explained in an interview, *Righteous Dopefiend* is about

> how structural forces beyond our control, historical forces, shifts in the economy, shifts in the political organization of public policy, come crashing down on vulnerable sectors of the population and basically shove them around in very unpleasant ways. These are the people who weren't able to recover from the downsizing of the industrial sector in the United States. A bunch of other types of industries arose in place of that, but those people who aren't able to make that adjustment, those people who don't have the education to shift from being a factory worker to being an information technology processor, are people who fall into indigent poverty. The guys that we studied—their parents were the people who lost their jobs working on the docks of San Francisco, working in the steel mills, working in the warehouses that were serving the active factory sector of San Francisco as a port industrial city. (Davis 2009)

Here Bourgois is describing a world of work and unemployment profoundly changed in the second half of the twentieth century and beginning decade of the twenty-first. Much of the world has experienced declining opportunity and changing expectations about work, so much so, that in 2014 *New York Times* reporter Thomas Friedman described the need for young job seekers to *invent their own jobs*, whereas Friedman (born in 1953) and many of his peers could have rightly expected to work for the same company their entire lives. Referring to his daughters who are in their twenties, he said in an interview, "When I graduated from college, I got to *find* a job. My girls will have to *invent* a job. . . . You no longer think of yourself as having a job—I think you have to think of yourself as an income entrepreneur." He further explained that successful job seekers must go to an employer and say: "I can create value. No boss wants to take a chance on you anymore. They want to know that you didn't just graduate high school 'college-ready.' That you graduated 'innovation-ready.' Every single boss is looking for people who are relentlessly entrepreneurial."[3] Friedman is not alone in effectively mandating entrepreneurship and creation of value (see Lane's contribution in this volume); these expectations pervade the education and work landscape in 2014 and are the wider context for the internship economy in which today's U.S. college students live and study. This volume shows us how people are making sense of their own aspirations in this new economy.

In Lynch's long-term research on a needle factory in the Boston suburbs, the median age of the employees is seventy-four and the oldest worker stopped working in 2013 a week before she turned a hundred and one (see Lynch 2012). Lynch focused on workers born around World War II, mostly white Christian men who profited from the postwar economic prosperity in the United States. The anthropologist Jane Guyer has described the "predictable solidity of this architecture of life" in that era: "pensions, insurance, 30-year mortgages, unemployment and disability benefits, student loans for career development, and so on, that produced personal security at a new level" (Guyer n.d.). But the men in Lynch's study gradually saw this architecture crumble in front of them. One worker named Grant worked twenty-seven years building cars at the General Motors plant in Framingham, Massachusetts—until the plant closed down to relocate operations in Mexico, chasing after cheaper production costs in so-called fresher fields. Grant was raised in the era of "Fordism," which the historian Victoria de Grazia describes as "the eponymous manufacturing system designed to spew out standardized, low-cost goods and afford its workers decent enough wages to buy them" (Grazia 2005). In this era, Americans often heard the phrase "What was good for our country was good for General Motors, and vice versa. The difference did not exist" (Bose, Lyons, and Newfield 2010, 3).[4] Social theorist David Harvey contrasts this Fordist phase with a "flexible regime of accumulation" that began roughly with the 1974 recession (Harvey 1991, 147). This new phase is characterized by flexible labor and capital, with corporations moving operations internationally by aid of globally connected communications and financial systems. The ability for workers to afford the commodities they produce is the exception rather than the rule, and lifetime pensions and affordable benefits are elusive to many. Instead, the new norm consists of part-time workers ineligible for health and retirement benefits.

The needle factory workers of typical retirement age value flexibility: They seek something profoundly different out of work today than they did when they were raising families and paying off mortgages—and their current work allows them to clock out when they like and pick up more or less work. Such unprecedented options are the topic of *positive* policy and scholarly assessment of the ways in which flexible employment policies can benefit employers but also employees who seek to balance their work and family lives. We hear of job sharing, of women's reentry into the workforce after having children, of paternity leave, of phased-in retirement. Flexibility is a central focus for policy analysis of elder employment. The Center on Aging and Work at Boston College, a national leader in elder employment policy studies, highlights workplace flexibility for older workers, whereby "employees and their supervisors have some choice and control over when, where, how work gets done, and what work tasks are assumed by which employees/work teams."[5] This center has conducted many studies that show the importance of flexible hours, tasks, and scheduling to retirees and to the masses of baby boomers as they prepare to retire.

But flexible labor is the subject of considerable *critical* analysis by labor activists and scholars who are concerned with businesses' increasing reliance on flexible labor forces, people who can be hired part-time or temporarily, who are easily fired, and who therefore cannot rely on regular work and are not eligible for benefits and certain labor rights—all in a context of weakening union power.[6] There is ample documentation of the downside of flexible labor policies that frequently put workers at a disadvantage because they cannot rely on consistent wages and find themselves at the mercy of employers who may change employment policies or, worse still, shut down operations to relocate to locations more advantageous to the business. Given criticism of the combination of low pay and high workload, as well as the unreliability of work under flexible regimes, these labor practices are a key target of activism on behalf of workers considered exploited by and vulnerable in the capitalist marketplace. Ann Kingsolver's chapter in this volume urgently directs our attention to South Carolina, where, building on a long history of racial discrimination and inequality in labor practices, the state government aggressively markets its high rate of rural unemployment as an attractive feature to prospective investors. Kingsolver writes that from the perspective of the government, "rural labor is characterized as not very mobile, wage-competitive, or organized." The state government offers up its docile non-union workers as part of an incentive package designed to attract international corporations, in the process creating and re-creating structures of racialized poverty, underemployment, and food insecurity. These concerns about flexible and unreliable labor, self-employment, dwindling unions, lack of benefits, and other structural changes are an important context for making sense of the many cases in this volume.

As the nature of work has changed in the previous decades, so have opportunities for performing valued gender identities. Bourgois examines both the structural issues and the more symbolic dynamics of work. Increasing unemployment and precarity shift the symbolic landscape of work, simultaneously opening and closing different opportunities for creating identities through unemployment. Bourgois and others have noted the decline of masculine labor. How have these structural changes under flexible accumulation impacted women's access to work, the meanings they and their communities make of their labor, and their ability to express femininity? In their respective studies of women working in offshore informatics in Barbados (processing airline tickets, medical claims, and more) and in the garment industry in Sri Lanka, anthropologist Carla Freeman and Lynch have shown how the entry into global labor processes is accompanied by shifts in gendered self-definition and creative redefinitions of how to be a respectable, good woman (Freeman 1998, 2000; Lynch 2007). Lynch examines how the Sri Lankan women demonstrate ambivalence about garment work, which is stigmatized by associations with sexual promiscuity and accompanied by everyday forms of paternalistic managerial control. And yet, this work provides women access to a desired modern lifestyle. Freeman has demonstrated how young women in informatics processing are willing to tolerate employer-mandated flexibility and low wages because of the higher "pink-collar" class status that these jobs offer by comparison with others: "They feel adequately compensated, in spite of their low wages, by the status implied in more fashionable work wear and travel benefits" (Susser and Chatterjee 1998, describing Freeman 1998; see also Freeman 2000). Fran Rothstein's chapter in this volume brings understandings of masculinity and femininity to the fore in analyzing transnational migration: Differing roles of men and women in building social capital contribute to community decisions about who should stay in New Jersey and who should return to Mexico in an uncertain labor market.

Flexibility and the rise of the service sector have only increased since Harvey examined flexible accumulation in 1991. This development corresponds with the rise of discourses promoting freedom and individuality in relation to work. Cardboard picking, food service work, and entrepreneurial activities more generally are jobs that emerge in this context, and bureaucratic enumerators may conceive of all of these as underemployment. We have seen a decrease in state employment, welfare, and other social services and a rise of NGOs (see Fisher and Murphy in this volume). At the same time we have witnessed a general increase in insecurity and uncertainty about the future. In some cases the meaning of work changes in a sort of adaptation or reaction to changing circumstances, for instance, in some cases volunteering or interning might be considered a form of work. As Lane writes in this volume:

> Ultimately I concluded that just as the structure of white-collar work has changed over the previous decades, so too have cultural understandings of what it means to be employed, what it means to be unemployed, and how individual workers feel about both. Specifically, studies of white-collar unemployment to date have, nearly unanimously, presumed a norm—that of secure, long-term employment at a single company—and defined unemployment in opposition to that norm. Yet that "normal career"—in both its real and idealized forms—has changed, and thus our understanding of its alleged opposite, unemployment, must also change.

Lane demonstrates that interpretations of the "normal career" vary with gender and class. The chapters by Strauss and Perelman depict conscious and unconscious attempts to control narrative. In general we see insecurity and flexibility forcing a redefinition of quality work, expectations concerning progress in one's life/relationships, and even a broader shift in worldview (in Claudia Strauss's chapter on positive thinking). Lane, Strauss, and John Murphy all hint at the role of changing expectations in relation to the reproduction of inequality: As expectations regarding the responsibilities of the state and private employers change, inequalities are naturalized.

Taken together, the chapters in this volume examine the relationship between the socially constructed meaning of unemployment and changing economic structure. However, the relationship between constructions of meaning and the shift from Fordism to flexibility varies dramatically as we move from Argentina to France to South Korea to Ethiopia. For example, Perelman's analysis of trash pickers demonstrates that in many parts of the world, an increase in insecurity is not necessarily new. The government jobs sought by young men in Mains's study of urban Ethiopia certainly represent a form of stability, but these jobs are quite different than the private sector employment associated with Fordism in the United States. As we discuss in the following section, a key source of variation in the relationship between meaning-making and economic structure is the particular importance of social relationships for unemployment and work.

Work and Social Relationships

Returning to debates concerning internships, when we consider how the signifi-cant structural shifts of the past forty years have impacted the meanings that people invest in work, it is conspicuous that unpaid internships have risen in prevalence during this same period (see Spradlin 2009; Bacon 2011). The unpaid intern is often an essential part of a creative and media-based economy. Academic departments tell students that unpaid internships are the most important thing on their résumés, and many college programs have the structure to accommodate this need: Students can pay the university to enroll in an internship class in which the students work for free for a semester. Though faculty tell students it will help them get a job, it is worth asking whether this is in fact the case. In many cases there is an expectation that what students lose in income, they will gain in social relationships, a dynamic often encapsulated under the term *experience*. In other words, students invest their time in the cultivation of social relationships with the expectation that these relationships will generate value in the future—value in terms of accessing lucrative work and employment that actualizes their desire for a meaningful life. The trade-off between relationships and income is one of the many ways that work and employment intersect with social relationships.

The chapters in this volume demonstrate that the significance of unemploy-ment depends on the meanings that one invests in work, and these meanings are inseparable from how one is positioned within social relationships. In each case unemployment and work are not experienced so much in terms of changes in income but as shifts in one's social relationships. This insight is a reminder that a lack of economic resources is clearly an important aspect of unemployment, but money in itself is not necessarily the most salient aspect. More important is how access to resources positions one in relation to others. Of course scholars influ-enced by Karl Marx have long theorized work in terms of social relationships, particularly the relations between owners of capital and workers. The potentially exploitative relationship between owner and worker is certainly important for many of the studies in this volume, but the authors make it clear that this is not the only relevant social relationship—and Lynch's own work with elderly needle workers shows the value of membership for people's assessment of the role of work in their lives. Furthermore, it is difficult to apply Marxian under-standings of exploitation and creation of surplus value to many of these studies. For example, where are the exploitative relationships located in the Nicaraguan cooperative that Fisher describes?

Many of the studies in this volume build on Max Weber's classic insight that with the rise of modernity, labor and employment are increasingly associated with self-actualization. As Jong Bum Kwon explains, for South Korean factory workers, labor provided a sense of identity, and the loss of this labor was experienced in a profoundly *physical* manner. We could imagine Marx agreeing that work *should* be about meaning-making, but the meaning that workers find in work is often used as an excuse not to pay for labor—and thus are inequality, power, and exploitation legitimated. This logic dictates that interns, for example, do not need to be paid because they are getting career-building experience and that child care workers can be paid low wages because it is a labor of love. But why does work have to be *either* meaningful and self-actualizing *or* well compensated? The authors in this volume combine Weberian and Marxist approaches in order to examine the complex interactions between meaning-making and material inequality. Lane and Strauss, for example, present the narratives of the long-term unemployed in the United States with a focus on the shifting expectations of employers in terms of maintaining the welfare of employees. An ideological shift that minimizes the responsibilities of employers thereby naturalizes owners' ability to maintain control over greater and greater amounts of surplus value. As important as this dynamic is, the case studies in this volume force us to consider other types of social relationships in relation to work.

Differences in one's day-to-day interactions and relationships are key to understanding the qualitative experience of unemployment. Importantly, these relationships do not necessarily depend on whether or not a person is engaged in paid work. Like in their previous jobs, the cardboard pickers that Perelman describes continued to earn money from their daily activities, however due to the nature of their work, their position within social relationships changed drastically; Perelman emphasizes the sense of shame associated with their work. Mains describes young urban Ethiopians who prefer to remain unemployed rather than engage in work that is not respected by their peers and family. For these young men, decisions about employment are largely based on how work positions them in day-to-day interactions. Young men avoid jobs that require them to subordinate themselves to others outside of the context of a long-term relationship. The meaning of work depends on the activities that fill a person's day. If these activities allow a person to interact with others in a way that is valued socially, work may be evaluated positively, regardless of how one is materially compensated for one's time.

Day-to-day activities that are unpaid are equally important in shaping one's social relationships. Murphy traces the connections that are built between outer-city French youth as they pass time together and share cigarettes and phone cards. Despite the claims of outer-city youth that everyone is on his or her own, they engage in a constant process of exchanging assistance that is essential in maintaining and cultivating relationships. In Fisher's chapter, in the absence of paid employment, Nicaraguan cooperative members work together on day-to-day tasks that are essential to the formation of relationships. As they make decisions together, it is partially an imagined eventual access to resources that supports plans for a shared life in the future. Although these activities are unpaid, they still involve economic decision making through exchanges of time and resources.

Economic dynamics are also highly important for relations of dependency. On one hand employment opportunities are evaluated in terms of their utility in allowing one to support others. On the other hand, one's dependence on others shapes the experience of unemployment and available economic opportunities. As Perelman explains, the shame associated with *cirujeo* is not simply that the work itself is stigmatized and places one in a subordinate position in day-to-day interactions. Perhaps more important is the inability to support one's family because of the significant reduction in one's income. Income is certainly important here, but not because money is intrinsically valued. Rather, the primary issue is how money enables a shift in social position from dependence, to independence, to supporting others and accumulating dependents. Rothstein's study of migration between Mexico and the United States offers a perspective on the importance of dependence and kin for unemployment and the meaning of work. It is the presence of supportive kin relationships and the kinship work done by women that draws men to return to Mexico. In other words, the possibility of depending on others to meet certain socially defined needs enables a greater sense of choice in regards to work.

A more individualized perspective on the meaning of work is present in some of the studies in this volume. Particularly for Lane and Strauss, it is important that the experience of unemployment is defined largely by expectations for oneself. In regards to a former white-collar worker who had found work as a waiter, Lane explains, "For him, as it was for many others, his interim job was not 'real,' because it was not commensurate with his education, experience, and previous pay and status levels. Waiting tables did not line up with his sense of who he is and what he does, so he took comfort in embracing a flexible ideal in which he was not a single kind of worker but an ever-shifting bundle of marketable attributes." In this explanation there is no reference to the man's position in relation to others. Rather, the key point is how he defines success and his own identity, which in this case consists of a list of qualities and experiences that are specific to himself. These cases demonstrate the variation in the importance of social relationships in different contexts. When the self is defined primarily in terms of one's relationship with others, as in the case of urban Ethiopia, the experience of unemployment is largely shaped by issues of dependence, shame, and solidarity. To be clear, the cases described by Lane and Strauss are certainly not completely divorced from social relationships. Strauss, for example, describes the difficulty of maintaining a positive self-image in the face of criticism from one's family. The distinction between evaluating one's work or unemployment in terms of relationships with others versus an individualized sense of self is one of degree. However, these differences, even when subtle, are quite important for understanding how people negotiate their struggles with work.

Life-Course Perspectives

The importance of work in situating oneself in relations of dependence with kin and others is important not only in the present but with the passage of time as well. These chapters allow us to explore these dynamics of unemployment, work, and the life course. Mains's (2012) research focus has been on youth and Lynch's on retirement. Partially because of the importance of social relationships, the experience of (un)employment is highly dependent on how one is positioned within the life course. In the case of the young Ethiopian men that Mains studied, a failure to achieve progress within their social relationships was so important because it represented their inability to attain a desirable future. Similarly, the young people described by Murphy are generally first-time job seekers. Employment represents a bridge between the present and the future. In many contexts, it is an essential step in the process of becoming an adult. And it is a crucial marker for *retaining* adulthood for retirees, or for people forced to retire early due to layoffs; commonly people speak in the United States of feeling less like a person as one ages, that is, of becoming invisible. Maintaining work allows one to retain a sense of personhood. Indeed, U.S. retirees often ask each other, "What did you do in *real* life?"

Mains's chapter advances a common theme in anthropological studies of African urban youth—in a context of extremely limited economic opportunity, many young people are stuck in the social category of youth, unable to take on the responsibilities of adults (Cole 2005; Hansen 2005; Ralph 2008; Weiss 2002, 2004). The concept of *galère*, or living hand to mouth, that Murphy describes among young people in the outer cities of France has also been noted in studies of African youth. For example, in Mains's research young men in urban Ethiopia contrasted a life of living hand-to-mouth, in which each day is the same as the previous day, with a life that involves continual progress and improvement. This may be compared with the U.S. retiree experiences where there is an idealized image of being beholden to no schedules or clocks. So-called "retirement wall clocks," which are commonly presented to retirees as gifts at retirement parties, have the days of the week on them instead of hours or else the integers representing the hours are piled up on the bottom of the clock face—an obvious indication of changing notions of time. Along with greeting cards that feature blank or torn-up "to do" lists, the retirement phase is pervaded by changing notions of time and reassessments of what is needed for life in the future. And yet, as Lynch (2012) found in her research, many people reject that ideal and find the transition to retirement to be a struggle: How can I go from days that felt productive and headed somewhere to days that are all the same in which *nobody* is expecting me to do *anything*?

The experiences of unemployed youth and working retirees raise questions that reveal the interlinkages between financial and social concerns. Even in cases of extremely high unemployment, what may seem like a financial or economic problem of survival is much more than that: The ways in which people are impacted by and make sense of unemployment are at once social, cultural, economic, and political. To make sense of high unemployment in Nigeria (with an unemployment rate of 38 percent),[7] a 2011 BBC article by a Nigerian job recruiter posited that "over-parenting" may be "partly to blame" for so many youths being out of work (Wale-Adegbite 2011). The author, Funmi Wale-Adegbite, suggested that "over-parenting" contributes to a lack of motivation for finding work among youth. She writes:

> Over-parenting is in my opinion the greatest evil handicapping Nigerian youth. It is at the root of our national malaise. Parents, you are practically loving your child to death. Whether you are poor or rich in Nigeria, the culture expects you to nurture your child continuously. The way our culture is, you look at your child as a child forever, and you almost treat them child as a child forever.

The author lamented that stifling and overindulgent parents prevent children from being able to grow up. Her critique of parents resonates with discussions in the United States about the challenges for "accordion families," to use anthropologist Katherine Newman's phrase, that contract and expand to accommodate youth labor market fluctuations (Newman 2012). Media discussions of middle-class adult children who "fail to grow up" and return home as "boomerang children" expose the implicit cultural expectations about how entering the workforce is a rite of passage for its material rewards and a range of social relationships (Parsons 2012). Wale-Adegbite continues:

> Parents sustain their children, they pay them pocket money—sometimes into their 30s. So you can have a 30-something-year-old man and the parents refers to him as a "child." And that person, that adult, behaves like a child, because he gets pocket money, and he gets a driver to take him round. There is no pressure on that "child" to get out and do something—they are comfortable. So a high-proportion of unemployment is due to parents not

cutting the cord, and not leaving that young man or that young woman to make something of themselves. In the UK, an 18 year old is almost a young adult, but in Nigeria that person is a child. (Wale-Adegbite 2011)

Although it is likely that Wale-Adegbite exaggerates the number of Nigerians who are comfortably supported by their parents and provided with a driver, the situation in Nigeria clearly demonstrates that unemployment cannot be understood only in terms of supply and demand of labor and employment opportunities. Expectations and understandings about class and gender, local understandings of the life course and expectations regarding family relationships all shape experiences of unemployment. In Nigeria, as in many places in the world, the markers of transitioning to adulthood have drastically changed as school, marriage, and children have become out of reach for young adults. Whereas life-course transitions such as graduations and marriages may have once been a clear marker of adulthood, how do children attain adulthood when those markers do not exist? Sociologist Michael Kimmel has suggested that in the United States in the late 1990s and early 2000s markers of transition have become more psychological. He argues that boys instead become "guys" for a good decade before they become "men" (2008).

We can compare the struggles of youth and retirees to the aspirations for work at other life stages. For young people, the absence of desirable paid work is particularly important because it stalls the process of social maturation. Importantly, many young people have not yet established a clear and stable identity in relation to their occupation. Although they may envision a specific job in their future, they have not yet performed occupational roles like welder, teacher, or postal worker. For example, many of the people in Lane's chapter are working in food service or other jobs that are decidedly not white-collar jobs, but it is their previous professional employment that forms a key point of reference in their lives and causes them to self-identify as unemployed despite participating in paid work. It is unclear if and when their identity as a "white-collar" will shift to reflect the types of work they are actually performing. To some degree, for the young people that Murphy examines, their parents' class may influence their expectations for the future, but their relation to unemployment and work is clearly very different than adults. Anthropologist Jennifer Cole argues that people of different ages are shaped by selective and simplified narratives of what a "generation" should be and hopes to be doing with their lives (Cole 2013). The frustration and disappointment of reconciling a present that does not cohere with one's past (see the chapters by Strauss, Lane, Perelman, and Kwon) is not relevant for youth. Rather, their key point of struggle concerns accessing imagined futures.

The absence of a prior occupational identity makes the day-to-day activities of youth all the more significant. The shame associated with certain types of employment for Ethiopian youth is doubly important because it potentially establishes a semi-permanent identity. In contrast to the pickers described by Perelman who may refer back to a previous occupation, Ethiopian youth feared placing themselves within an undesirable social category from which it is difficult to escape. Similarly, anthropologist Jane Guyer and sociologist Kabiru Salami discuss the life course of indebtedness in Nigeria as well as how much people do or don't think about the futures in regards to debt (Guyer and Salami 2013).

In Lynch's research on older factory workers near Boston, the mostly white male workers exemplify a range of personalities and class backgrounds and a diversity of reasons for working. Even those who work out of financial need also seek social engagement and purpose. Indeed, workers often invoke the health risks of idle retirement and claim that "working here keeps me alive." The production workers at Vita Needle are all part-time, and none receive medical or retirement benefits—the employer is well aware of such employees' eligibility for funds from Medicare and Social Security. The employer claims to be providing a social service to people otherwise unlikely to find paid work, and he admits to the financial savviness of the model. For their part, Vita workers want to be in control of their time, and they want to be able to clock out in a moment of frustration or when a grandchild needs them—and the production manager has expertly designed the production process to allow that (a surprising feature in an assembly facility). As Grant, a former General Motors line worker, once said to Lynch, "It's a win-win. For them, for us, and I get a little extra money, and I don't use up all my time." These notions of time in the retirement life phase are vastly different than in the Sri Lankan garment factories to which Lynch was first accustomed, in an earlier study, where employees devoted all their time to work and had a very limited ability to take time off. Many Vita workers argue vehemently that they are willing to pay for their flexibility—they will sacrifice higher wages and other benefits if they can maintain a lifestyle where work is qualitatively different than it used to be for them. Whereas we might engage in a debate about whether this is an exploitative work arrangement, more relevant is the observation that the meanings attached to pay, time, and social camaraderie are not static in people's lives. They may become more salient at different points in the life course.

Similarly, as we can see from cases in this volume, work flexibility means something entirely different for those who are supporting children and for whom high income and benefits are likely to be far more important than flexibility. For the middle-aged, unemployment strikes at the core of their identity in a way that is highly gendered. Kwon describes unemployed factory workers who have been separated from the place and activities that they feel have made them men. In Rothstein's chapter, migration and return migration are inseparable from the life course. Particularly for men, it is only at a certain point in the life course that return migration makes sense, both socially and financially. Taken together, these chapters help us to see that work and nonwork look different, experientially and materially, at different life stages.

Conclusion: An Anthropology of Unemployment

Following the 2013 *Black Swan* internships ruling in favor of the interns, *New York Times* commentator Ross Perlin called for an "effective internship culture." He noted that with their efforts to receive pay for work, interns were simply demanding "respect for their work"—and that a paycheck would convey that they deserved respect. Perlin seemed to be optimistic that interns would now get the pay they deserve (culturally and legally) and that respect will bring the end of the negative connotations attached to the role: "For too many people, internships have become slightly shameful, with overtones of menial work, immaturity, parental dependence and being stuck." Perlin added: "For better or worse, pay is the fundamental currency of respect in every modern economy." Perlin's liberal rights attitude toward work as deserving of and generative of respect reveals deep-seated American and Western capitalist attitudes about work and money as well as underlying assumptions about the utility and value of both. And his perspective is silently underlined by assumptions about what the experiences of nonwork, or unrecognized work without pay, must mean for people. Perlin is confident that meanings hold true across the board, or at least "in every modern economy" (Perlin 2013).

Anthropologists have long critiqued overly economistic analyses of work, but the authors in this volume go further than this. In contrast to Perlin, they demonstrate that respect is not always linked to a paycheck. These chapters force a rethinking of the internship debate through increased attention to macro-level economic change, social relationships, and the life course. An anthropological approach considers how internships are part of a broader economic shift in which flexible forms of creative labor are particularly prevalent. Although the question of payment for interns is certainly important, equally relevant for an anthropological analysis is how the intern is situated within social relationships, both in the present and in the past. Finally, as we have argued in this epilogue, the meaning of work and unemployment varies significantly with a person's position in the life course. An unpaid internship has dramatically different implications for the identity of a recent college graduate than an adult who is responsible for multiple children.

Stories of work and unemployment abound in traditional mass media and in social media. At any given moment, Facebook and Twitter pulsate with recurring memes on Wall Street executives' indulgences, the struggles of the working poor, advice on how to retire early and happy, infographics about Walmart workers relying on food stamps and other forms of government poverty-related assistance, or tips from two-career couples on finding that elusive work-life balance. As this volume evinces, anthropologists have much to analyze in these popular representations of work and unemployment. Specifically, ethnographic research provides insights into the lived experience of work and its absence. Attention to the complexity and variation of day-to-day life demonstrates that unemployment is experienced simultaneously as a financial and social problem, and the two dynamics are inextricable. This approach enables the authors in this volume to explore how social personhood is connected to earning an income, how decisions about employment are shaped by understandings of what it means to lead a good life, and how the day-to-day struggle to get by is shaped by gender, age, class, and race.

Notes

INTRODUCTION

1. See 2012 report of the U.S. Bureau of Labor Statistics, "The Recession of 2007–2009." www.bls.gov/spotlight/2012/recession/pdf/recession_bls_spotlight.pdf.

2. "Long-term unemployment experience of the jobless," *Issues in Labor Statistics*, www.bls.gov/opub/ils/ summary_10_05/long_term_unemployment.htm.

3. The numbers are stunning but also deceptive. Employment numbers have acquired the aura of a fetish. We eagerly await each monthly report for an augury of economic recovery. However, as the trajectory of the official figures indicate, employment has to some degree been disassociated from the economy. Furthermore, there is deception in the measure of unemployment (a proportion of the active labor force), which conceals those "discouraged" individuals who have opted out of the formal labor market and those who are only marginally attached to the labor market (not having sought active employment in the previous four weeks).

4. During this most recent recession people laid bare their suffering and struggles with unemployment in extended newspaper series (for example, "Help Wanted: Stories of the Unemployment" in *The Washington Post*, September 2011) and popular blog postings (for example, "Unemployment Stories" at Gawker.com, which spanned forty weekly volumes in 2012 and 2013; reader stories of unemployment in the Careers section of About.com).

5. For examples of the complicated relationship between autonomy and subordination in industrial settings, see Kim 1997; Lynch 2007; Ong 1987; Ngai 2005; Rofel 1999; and Wolf 1994; in non-industrial settings, see Allison 1994; Dewey 2011; Gunewardena and Kingsolver 2008; Kang 2010; and Freeman 2000.

6. Our attention is often drawn to the increasingly expansive public cultures of consumption as the primary locations of contemporary self-fashioning, belying the social-cultural productivity of work and employment, even when experienced as loss (unemployment). One of the primary ideological obfuscations of neoliberalism, as pointed out by the Comaroffs (2001), is the erasure of work and employment as productive sites of personhood and social relationships. Kathi Weeks (2011) also observes the surprising lack of attention paid to work and employment in political theory, despite their centrality in modern social and political life.

7. A striking example is the illegal drug trade. Philippe Bourgois's influential 1995 ethnographic study of crack dealers in El Barrio (New York City) offers a portrait of drug dealing that mirrors the structures and relations of legal retail, including customer relations, commissions, labor-management tensions, and the promise of promotion.

8. Hereafter, *unemployment* will also refer to underemployment (including temporary and contingent work) as well as various forms of informal economic activity unrecorded by official measures. The decision was made not for stylistic convenience alone. As we argue in this volume, unemployment does not precisely capture the various and emergent ways that people who are excluded from formal stable employment cobble together livelihoods or the ways that employment is experienced as intermittent. In addition, even those with full-time formal employment live lives stretched thin by insecurity and declining wages and benefits.

9. For a clear and succinct history and explanation of neoliberalism, see Ganti 2014; Hackworth 2007; Harvey 2005; and Steger and Roy 2010. This part of the introduction is guided by their work.

10. For examples of ethnographic work on the adoption of neoliberal governance in NGOs, see Adams 2013; Elyachar 2005; Karim 2011; and Song 2009. In education, see Lipman 2011 and Urciuoli 2008. In the American political context, one prominent domain in which choice is vehemently challenged is women's reproductive rights. Feminist cultural critics Lisa Duggan (2004) and Wendy Brown (2003) have written incisively about the co-production of antidemocratic impulses and neoliberal ideology in contemporary American politics. Under conditions of heightened economic insecurity, neoliberal ideologies of individual freedom and responsibility articulate powerfully with gendered and racial discourses of defending "American" identity and way of life.

11. Our analysis is influenced by recent research on post-Fordist affect, most notably Muehlebach and Shoshan 2012; Molé 2012; Berlant 2007.

12. The term *precarity*, as noted by Millar (2014, 34), first came to prominence among social movement activists in North America, Europe, and Japan, countries where Fordist industrial production and attendant expectations for secure middle-class employment had taken strong hold (see also Allison 2012; Neilson and Rossiter 2005).

CHAPTER 1: THE LIMITS OF LIMINALITY

1. Newman is of course referencing anthropologist Victor Turner's (1967) well-known work on the disorderly liminal, or intermediary, phase of rites of passage, wherein participants are "betwixt and between" statuses, temporarily standing outside of existing hierarchies and social structures.

2. Well into the twenty-first century, popular films like *In Good Company* (2004), *Up in the Air* (2009), and *The Company Men* (2010) continued to depict layoffs as entirely unprecedented and unexpected events for male white-collar workers.

3. Of the seventy-five interviewees, approximately 30 percent were women; over 80 percent were white; nearly 11 percent were Japanese American, Chinese American, or Indian American; 3 percent were African American; and 4 percent were Hispanic.

4. For an analysis of such moments of tension, when job seekers veer from their usual optimistic, individualistic narratives, see Lane 2016.

5. The figures for jobseekers in this study are slightly higher than those found in another study of laid-off high-tech workers in North Dallas, which found that 46.6 percent of respondents had been laid off more than once (Virick 2003). This discrepancy might be attributed to my informant recruitment methods. Individuals who have been laid off in the past tend to champion the importance of networking, which leads them to the kind of events where I recruited many of my participants. Jobseekers with previous layoff experience are also perhaps more likely to feel comfortable speaking about job loss and unemployment than those experiencing it for the first time.

6. There are of course those who challenge this understanding of frequent job change as a social or individual good or even as a morally neutral phenomenon. Richard Sennett (1998), for instance, argues that frequent job change erodes the narratives people use to organize their identities and corrodes the principles of trust, loyalty, and mutual commitment that comprise individual (and communal) character.

7. As Clark Davis (2001) explains, employers would not have had to fight so hard for these employees had they not artificially limited their own labor supply by excluding women, racial minorities, and most immigrants from all but the most menial positions in their organizations.

8. For the authoritative account of the rise and impact of neoliberal thought and governance, see Harvey 2005.

9. The human, social, and economic costs of insecure employment have been well documented in works such as Fraser 2002; Moore 1996; Rogers 2000; Ross 2009; Sennett 1998; Smith 2001; Uchitelle 2006.

10. The shelves of any bookstore business section testify to this perspective's popularity in recent years. To select just a few from among dozens of representative titles, such books include: *Managing Brand You* (Wilson and Blumenthal 2008); *Me 2.0: Building a Powerful Brand to Achieve Career Success* (Schwabel 2009); *Self Marketing Power: Branding Yourself as a Business of One* (Beals 2008); *The Start-up of You* (Hoffman and Casnocha 2012); *You Are a Brand* (Kaputa 2010); and *You, Inc.: The Art of Selling Yourself* (Beckwith and Beckwith 2007). Barbara Ehrenreich incisively critiques this commodification of the self in *Bait and Switch* (2005), her undercover journey into the work of white-collar job seeking.

11. This reimagining of secure employment as a form of dependence represents a new chapter in the shifting, cyclical genealogy of the term *dependency* in American discourse around work and unemployment (Fraser and Gordon 1994).

12. Other scholars who have studied networking groups for the unemployed identify similar tendencies (Smith 2001; Torres 1996).

13. Layne goes on to suggest other models for job loss rituals might include rituals of birth, death, or collective healing (2000, 503). She also rightly suggests that talking more about job loss and downward mobility, both in person and in the media, will help reduce the stigma associated with such events and increase awareness and support.

CHAPTER 3: OCCUPATION

1. The police issued warrants for many of the high-ranking union leaders after the failed occupation of the factory in February 2001. The leaders escaped the police assault and found refuge at a nearby Catholic Church.

2. During the height of the crisis nearly 20 percent (two million people) were unemployed. At prestigious *chaebŏl* 236,000 workers, blue- and white-collar, lost jobs between 1997 and 2002 (Chun 2009, 78). As Pirie notes, "over 90 percent of all new jobs created between 1998 and 2002 were non-permanent" (2008, 184), and temporary work in the service industry remains the fastest-growing economic sector (Chun 2009).

3. In 1997, at companies with over five hundred employees, workers enjoyed wages 72.3 percent higher than those at companies with between ten and twenty-nine employees. As the wage premium increased to 99.2 percent by 2005, the number of core workers was significantly diminished (Pirie 2008, 184).

4. While the focus of this article is on these core workers, it needs to be made clear that the most precarious were and remain those employed in small companies. It is, in fact, the intensification of exploitation of the least secure that has most enabled increased labor flexibility and increased labor productivity. Women, especially, were vulnerable to labor restructuring. Because of longstanding institutionalized gender discrimination, the majority of women were employed as temporary workers, often at wages less than one-half the wages of men. Even women in permanent positions at large companies were at increased risk of dismissal, commonly pressured to leave "voluntarily" in order to preserve jobs for men during economic downturns (see Chun 2009).

Although the numbers of permanent male workers in large companies are shrinking due to layoffs and inducements for early and "honorary" retirement combined with their replacement by short-term contract workers and subcontracting, they are still some of the most secure workers in the world. From 1997 to 2002, the proportion of all workers employed in large-scale manufacturing fell from 30.7 percent to 20.6 percent (Pirie 2008, 183).

5. It is clear that cultural notions and practices of masculinity are important dimensions in the formation and experience of these factory workers' bodies; unfortunately,

due to the specific thematic focus of this article, I will not be able to elaborate upon the theme. Nevertheless, it should be emphasized that masculinity was structured according to economic productivity. It should also be noted that all of the wives I interviewed revealed that they did not work outside the home, depending financially on their husbands. They saw themselves primarily as "housewives," a social status bespeaking relative prestige and economic stability. Although women's social and economic contributions to family life are far more substantial and complex, the gendered division of public and private domains is an ideological bulwark sustaining masculine and class privilege (Kim 1993; Nelson 2000; Yi 1998). Furthermore, not a few of the older men, who began work at the factory at the height of Korea's industrial development in the 1980s, identified as "industrial soldiers," acknowledging the association of industrial production with national duty. The able-bodied male industrial worker, while lacking the status of the white-collar company man, ambivalently symbolized the masculine discipline of Korea's modernization. As Moon (2005) demonstrates, masculinity, militarism, modernization, and nationalism were powerful intersecting fields of discourse in Korea's modernity.

6. Notable examples include Ong's *Spirit of Resistance and Capitalist Discipline* (1987) and Ngai's *Made in China* (2005), which illustrate the mortification of gendered moral bodily selves by harsh, authoritarian factory discipline.

7. This symptom of feeling unmoored is not uncommon among the unemployed (Newman 1988) and those who have been socially and politically dislocated (Kleinman and Kleinman 1994, 714–715).

CHAPTER 4: THE RISE OF THE PRECARIAT?

1. A return to normalcy was declared based on the observation that roughly "only" one hundred cars had been burned in a single night—a figure close to the national daily average in 2005.

2. I use the term "outer city" for the French word *banlieue*. Without context, *banlieue* simply means suburb. Although there certainly are affluent suburbs in France (Paris's western periphery is a well-known example), the term *banlieue* more readily calls to mind the large-scale, architecturally monotonous, and often rundown housing projects that ring many French cities, as well as the problems—academic failure, juvenile delinquency, unemployment, and drug abuse, to name just a few—linked to them. Because this negative understanding of the word *banlieue* has far more in common with the American notion of inner city than that of suburb, which, by contrast, tends to evoke visions of middle-class stability, "outer city" seems a better translation. There are, however, important differences. Disputing recent claims of American-like "ghettoization" in France (e.g., Maurin 2004), a number of scholars (e.g., Lepoutre 1997; Vieillard-Baron 1998; Wacquant 2008) have, for example, underscored the racial and ethnic diversity of France's urban peripheries. Furthermore, thanks to the elaborate safety net of France's social welfare system, most outer cities have been the beneficiaries of substantial support, even if state aid has wavered over the years, with transitions between left-wing and right-wing administrations. Finally, unlike what tends to be the case in the United States, public housing in France has historically accommodated workers and lower-level salaried staff as well as the very poor, even if such middle-income earners have increasingly sought private home ownership (Noiriel 1990). In 2005 in Limoges, a three-member family (two adults and one child) with a combined annual income of 34,000 euros qualified for public housing. For purposes of comparison, in 2005, 34,000 euros was the equivalent of 41,000 American dollars, roughly 2.5 times the poverty threshold for a household of three ($15,720), as defined by the U.S. Census service.

3. Subsequently, the expression "social exclusion" was popularized by René Lenoir (1974) in his essay "Les Exclus, un Français sur dix."

4. The term *précarité*, like that of social exclusion, was first used in the 1950s and 1960s in discussions about those individuals who for various reasons were not benefiting from the country's rapid modernization.

5. In fact, Limoges is the birthplace of the Confédération Générale du Travail (CGT), one of France's most important labor unions, long affiliated with the once-powerful French Communist Party.

6. Three *grands ensembles* (large-scale public apartment complexes) stand on the edge of Limoges: Le Val de l'Aurence (3,964 apartments), La Bastide (1,916 apartments), and Beaubreuil (1,974 apartments). I worked primarily in these three neighborhoods.

7. I use the adjective "blue-collar" to translate the French notion of *populaire*, even if this word does not quite convey the same meaning. Whereas "blue-collar" tends to be used to designate manual laborers in such fields as manufacturing, mining, or construction, *populaire* has a broader sense, capturing the idea of the "people" or the "masses"—in other words, those individuals located toward the bottom of a social hierarchy, including, but not limited to, manual laborers.

8. Youth living in the city center hardly made out any better. Whereas in 1990 37.2 percent of city-center dwellers aged twenty-five and under had short-term work contracts, by 1999 this percentage had jumped to 51.9 percent (Duplouy 2003, 21).

9. Although this age bracket is approximate (some of the youth I came to know were younger and others older), I chose it because, at the time of my research, sixteen was the minimum age when minors, with the approval of their parents, could leave school to work, whereas twenty-four was the last year of ineligibility for the RMI, a form of state welfare for the long-term unemployed.

10. In France, it is illegal to collect racial or ethnic statistics. These figures therefore represent actual immigrants, not their French-born children.

11. I have used pseudonyms throughout this chapter in an effort to protect the privacy of my interlocutors.

12. For a more developed analysis of my interlocutors' perspectives on the riots, see Murphy 2011b.

13. Some news commentators made a similar observation. Noting that the majority of the destruction occurred in the very neighborhoods where the rioters lived, they argued that it would have made far more sense had it occurred in the bastions of bourgeois or official Paris. At least then it could have been explained in terms of class struggle or perceptions of social injustice.

14. Limoges, like most other French cities, witnessed a flurry of activity during the CPE protests. On February 7, the first of the major rallies, organized by labor unions, political parties on the Left, and high school and university students, brought together an estimated 5,000 demonstrators. This first demonstration was followed by a number of others, each attracting more supporters than the previous one. According to local newspaper estimates, between 10,000 and 15,000 people turned out for a demonstration on March 7; another 15,000 to 20,000 protestors took to the streets on March 18; approximately 30,000 people participated in protests on March 28; and upwards of 40,000 Limougeauds clamored against the CPE on April 4.

15. The word *galère* originally refers to the galley ships propelled by oarsmen—usually prisoners or slaves—from ancient times through the eighteenth century. In popular contemporary usage, the noun and corresponding verb *galérer* have retained some of this original meaning, indicating a particularly difficult albeit usually temporary situation. "Quelle galère!" for example, might translate as "What a hassle!" or "What a headache!" This was not, however, how my interlocutors used the term. For them, as I have explained above, *galérer* was above all about the deleterious consequences of chronic unemployment.

16. In 2005–2006, one euro traded for about US$1.25.

17. In reality, I could have signed up for a pay-as-you-go plan as soon as I arrived in France, but preferred instead to wait for my residency card to purchase a contract and thus benefit from the cost savings this scheme offered.

18. Jennifer Patico (2008), in her work on post-Soviet Russia, notes a similar emphasis on the exchange of nonessentials as a way of promoting sociability in a shortage economy.

19. Anecdotally, after a presentation of an earlier version of this paper a fellow panelist suggested that I had overlooked "religion" when discussing outer-city life. This comment reflects an inclination in certain quarters (both American and French) to see "outer-city youth," "immigrant," and "Muslim" as virtually synonymous. Although some of my interlocutors in Limoges's outer city identified as Muslim, certainly not all of them did, and being Muslim had no bearing, as far as I observed, on participation in the kind of sociality I describe here.

20. For a discussion of how my interlocutors perceived and used the notion of race, see Murphy 2011a.

21. Whether or not they ever could is an important question that exceeds the scope of this paper.

CHAPTER 5: CONTESTING UNEMPLOYMENT

1. In fact, the devaluation of 2001 and 2002 was part of a process that started with the implementation of neoliberal policies during the bloody civil-military dictatorship (1976–1983) and continued during democracy, especially during Carlos Menem's governments (1989–1999). In Argentina during the 1990s, unemployment rates rose dramatically. In just over ten years, the portion of people without a job rose from about 5 percent to about 20 percent.

2. Since it is a native category with its own history and meanings that have social implications, I have decided to maintain the term in the original language.

3. In Spanish it is possible to distinguish between *ser* and *estar*. This copulative expression (that in English can only be translated as "to be") has two alternatives: *ser* desempleado and *estar* desempleado. While the first one refers to a permanent property, the second one refers to a transitory property: in other words, in Spanish "to be unemployed" may mean a permanent condition or a momentary condition. The transition between *estar* and *ser* can indicate an important subjective change in the self.

4. Theoretically it is possible to distinguish between labor and work. Nevertheless in Spanish there is not a different word to establish this distinction. The distinctions that actors made between the notion of "labor" or the notion of "work" must be established exclusively by the context.

5. There is an extended literature analyzing the way in which the Argentine welfare state was de-articulated by a series of political and neoliberal discourses (see Villarreal 1985; Basualdo 2001; Grassi 2003b; Beccaria 2001).

6. A second implication of the *cirujas*' visibility is, in some ways, utilitarian: They are seen as poor by the middle classes, so they received—along with the bags of trash—clothes, food, and other donated goods.

7. "In critical contexts women become protagonists who worked to ensure family survival, primarily within the community [. . .] In times of crisis the neighborhood and their homes constituted not only areas of 'extra-domestic domesticity,' but revealed scenarios that allowed women to leave their homes and settle as public subjects by using their knowledge and domestic skills" (Cross and Ullivarri 2013, 15).

8. As seen in Sutton (2008), embodying neoliberalism is critical to understand economic forces as *lived* processes that involve core aspects of individuals' existence. Women's narratives offer a valuable lens through which to learn about embodied "social suffering," resiliency, and resistance in the age of globalization.

9. According to the INDEC, the unemployment rate decreased from 20 percent in 2003 to 7.9 percent in 2010. See www.indec.gov.ar/.

10. As legitimating notions are performed in the public sphere, it is important to consider the dialogical factor that recognition has. Actors appeal to public and legitimated discourses to construct themselves as people doing something worthy. These notions are the ones that are negotiated publicly by subaltern actors (see Cardoso de Oliveira and Cardoso de Oliveira 1996; Cardoso de Oliveira 2004; Taylor 1996; Perelman 2011b).

11. He is referring to the annual Exhibition of Livestock, Agriculture, and Industry of the Argentine Rural Society (Sociedad Rural Argentina) that usually coincides with the school winter break.

12. As developed in a previous work (Perelman 2011b), lack of employment and hunger are conditions, but they do not explain why people see in the *cirujeo* a chance for survival. The structural distance to the formal activity—paraphrasing the idea of Evans-Pritchard (1987)—of the trajectories of people leads to the construction of desirable lifestyles.

13. The idea that *cirujas* are part of the recycling system is a recent one, giving them additional arguments to constitute themselves as workers.

14. In this section, I will not center the analysis on the different appropriations or on the power relations in which these relations are produced and re-produced. In the interactions I describe there is an unequal appropriation of benefits. For an analysis of these differences and of the way domination constructs stability, see Perelman 2011a.

15. "Plan" has become the native category for referring to various, multiple, and different "social programs" implemented by the state at different levels. During the 1990s and especially after the 2001 crisis, "plans" were widespread. As Quirós (2011, 23) remarked in her study of a neighborhood in suburban Buenos Aires, "Plans were not only revealed as a widespread livelihood, but also as a collective language handled and understood by all [. . .] something similar happened in relation to food programs." Many of the plans from the mid-1990s are Conditional Cash (or income) Transfer Programs, based on the theory that receiving cash (or even food) involved an "obligation" or compensation for work hours or community work. These plans are designed for the unemployed. These types of policies were part of the state's "Human Development" based on neoliberal ideas and were promoted by multilateral credit agencies. The plans were negotiated and managed by social organizations or individuals with relationships to local political power through relationships characterized as clientelism.

16. It is interesting to consider the idea of loyalty as a value in relation to a company. Lane (2011) demonstrates that employees of technology companies, unlike those in other jobs and at other times, do not think of loyalty as a value. The question that arises is how loyalty is constructed and what kind of relationship and moral debts it creates. See for example Sigaud 1996; Perelman 2011b.

17. On the notion of debt, see Mauss 1979; Bourdieu 1996; Godelier 1998.

CHAPTER 7: YOUTH UNEMPLOYMENT, PROGRESS, AND SHAME IN URBAN ETHIOPIA

1. Unemployment rates among urban young men declined after the early 2000s (Broussard and Tekleselassie 2012). However, there has been little change in unemployment rates for urban young women. Based on follow-up interviews with the young people who were involved in my research from 2003 to 2005, I believe that expanded opportunities for higher education and state-sponsored job creation programs have reduced unemployment rates for young men, but for the most part young women have not benefited from these changes.

2. I use *progress* in place of the Amharic word *lewt*, which is sometimes used to imply simple change but often indicates linear improvement that occurs over time. *Idget*, meaning "growth," was sometimes used to convey notions of progress as well.

3. An extensive literature exists concerning similar stigmatized occupation groups in West Africa (Dilley 2004; Herbert 1993; McNaughton 1993). Dena Freeman (2003)

uses ethnographic material from Ethiopia to make an interesting intervention into this literature. She argues that the roots of occupational stigma are to be found in local movements of people and relations of dominance rather than the symbolic qualities of production and transformation that have been associated with blacksmithing and other artisan occupations.

4. The importance of money for social relations was changing, and extremely wealthy individuals were able to access status (Ellison 2006, 2009). Nevertheless, in the early 2000s although working youth often had more access to money than their unemployed peers, their greater purchasing power did not appear to bring them respect at the community level.

5. In contrast to the status of traditional artisans, the stigmas attached to working in lower occupations were very flexible at the time of my research. Stories of the shoeshine who became a powerful business owner were common. Also, how one treated workers in lower occupations varied with the quality of one's relationships with them. James Ellison (2006) argues that occupational status groups have not been historically rigid, and I observed that status is particularly flexible in a contemporary urban setting.

6. At the lowest end of the economic scale, many unemployed young men lived with their single mothers, who earned a meager living baking bread or brewing beer. Although in comparison with middle-class youth, it was more common for young men from poor families to engage in low-status work, many remained unemployed for long periods of time.

7. The increase in the number of students advancing to the university is one of the reasons why urban unemployment has begun to decrease during the past ten years, especially among men. The number of students entering the university increased by a factor of nearly ten between 2003 and 2013. It remains to be seen if the majority of these new university graduates will be able to find work in their field of study.

8. This is not a new phenomenon in Ethiopia, and Donald Levine (1965) describes educated youth who, unable to find employment and unwilling to work in the traditional agricultural sector, migrated to cities in search of opportunities that were largely unavailable. The drastic increase in the number of educated youth without a corresponding increase in government employment, however, has created a far larger and more visible population of unemployed youth.

CHAPTER 8: LABOR ON THE MOVE

1. I am grateful to the Wenner-Gren Foundation for Anthropological Research and to Montclair State University for financial support of the recent research on migrants and return migrants presented in this paper.

2. Interviewees were located initially by talking with migrants and return migrants whom I knew from previous research in New Jersey and Mazatecochco. Additional interviewees were located through informal snowball sampling.

3. For a fuller discussion of the approach used here, see Rothstein 2007, ch. 1.

4. See, for example, Sassen 1988; Gledhill 1998; Canales 2003, 2012.

5. I am not suggesting that women's kin work is not without its abuses. For a discussion of gender inequality in kin work, see Rothstein 2015.

6. See Hirsch 2002, Malkin 2004, 2007, Boehm 2008 for important exceptions.

7. For a discussion of some of the problems with studies of networks and employment, see Rothstein 2015.

8. Unfortunately, the underemployment statistics by gender are not available. Discussions with women migrants suggest that although their hours were sometimes cut, domestic work was not as badly affected by the recession as construction and other men's work.

9. For a discussion of some of the ways *comerciantes* (merchants) have survived, for example by selling their garments in more distant markets such as Guanajuato or Chiapas or diversifying their investments in such activities as textile stores, trucking, and real estate, see Montiel Torres 2014.

10. In 2012 an order of one *chile en nogada* was selling for 50 pesos (what a worker earned for a half a day in a garment workshop); one had to place an order earlier in the week because they usually sold out.

11. I am grateful to Jaime Xicohtencatl Corte for analyzing the INEGI data.

12. See, for example, Greenwood 1969; Mattingly 1999; Menjívar 2000; Aguilar and Massey 2002; Aguilar 2003; Amuedo-Durantes and Mandra 2007.

13. Women are approximately 44 percent of U.S. immigrants from Mexico (Donato et al. 2011).

14. For discussions of how San Cosmeros/as have used kinship and social networks to help their children get ahead when economic opportunities were expanding in the 1960s and 1970s and to deal with job loss in the 1980s, see Rothstein 1999 and 2007 (chs. 3 and 4).

15. For a discussion of gender inequality in caring work, see Rothstein 2015.

16. Although some married men do form unions in the United States, most do not.

17. For similar examples, see Alicea 1997; Ariza 2002; Hellman 2007.

CHAPTER 9: POSITIVE THINKING ABOUT BEING OUT OF WORK IN SOUTHERN CALIFORNIA AFTER THE GREAT RECESSION

I am grateful for the very helpful comments of the editors of this volume, Carrie Lane and Jong Bum Kwon, as well as the feedback from "Carl Mathews," "Lisa Rose," and the audiences who listened to earlier versions of this paper at meetings of the American Anthropological Society, Society for Psychological Anthropology, and American Ethnological Society. This research was funded by the National Science Foundation under Grant Number 1230534 and the Wenner-Gren Foundation.

1. There is a large ethnographic and theoretical literature on hope at present (e.g., Ahmed 2010, Crapanzano 2003, Hage 2003, Mains 2012, and Miyazaki 2004, 2006, 2010), a reflection of prevalent worries about loss of hope.

2. At a conference in Europe, he was told that this way of telling a life story seems very American (McAdams 2006, 5).

3. The new studies focus on white-collar job seekers rather than displaced factory workers. Perhaps positive thinking when they look for work is reinforced by the attitudes expected in their service, managerial, and sales jobs.

4. He also rules out national culture as an explanation, because he did not see the same emphasis on chemistry for blue-collar job seekers in the United States. By contrast, I found positive thinking ideology among both blue-collar and white-collar job seekers in my study.

5. In Foucauldian terms, positive thinking could be considered a "technology of the self" "through which human beings are urged and incited to become ethical beings, to define and regulate themselves according to a moral code, to establish precepts for conducting or judging their lives" (Rose 1992, 148). However, I hesitate to use the Foucauldian terminology because it highlights the importance of expert knowledges and practices. While these certainly contribute to positive thinking in the contemporary U.S. setting, so do vernacular conventional discourses.

6. Later I added one more, bringing my total to sixty-four interviewees.

7. The worst city in terms of numbers of job seekers for every opening at that time was Miami.

8. Some of those who volunteered to participate in my research did not fit the prototype of someone who was unemployed and looking for work. My sample included a young

woman who had cobbled together more than forty hours a week of work from part-time jobs but wanted something better. At the other end I had a few participants who were unemployed but not looking, like a male engineer in his late fifties who had been laid off in 2009 and had come to the conclusion that it was futile to keep searching, so he was relying on his wife's income and help from their parents. But if I included him, should I exclude two housewives who looked for work only while their husbands were unemployed? And what about the woman who was on disability because of her bad knees? Although none of them are quoted in this paper, all of these marginal cases are included in the totals reported here. See also Lane's chapter on the difficulties of defining unemployment in this volume.

9. Another problem is that responses to a two-part question ("What do you think of your situation in general? How would you say you are feeling?") can be difficult to interpret.

10. Lane quotes a job seeker who commented, "'you discipline yourself to be happy'" (Clines 2009, quoted in Lane 2011, 162).

11. My transcription conventions are as follows: [. . .] = deletion; . . . = pause; *italics* = speaker's emphasis; [*italics*] = added by the author for clarification.

12. My use of *self-care* overlaps but differs in emphasis from that of Brown (2006), who takes it to be neoliberal subjects' capacity "to provide for their own needs and service their own ambitions, whether as welfare recipients, medical patients, consumers of pharmaceuticals, university students, or workers in ephemeral occupations" (694).

13. Ehrenreich (2005) found that unemployed white-collar workers were advised to exercise regularly. Unlike Sharone's (2014, 55) interviewees, mine did not feel they had to confine exercise to nonworking hours.

14. This advice came in the religious second half of his lecture, in which he claimed he was happier after he cancelled his subscription to the *Wall Street Journal*, although in the secular first half of his lecture he cited recent *Wall Street Journal* articles.

15. Lisa Rose's comment reinforces the point that positivity is expected for the employed, not just the unemployed. For further examples of what look like "blessing in disguise" narratives, see Druckerman (2012, 9) and Lane (2011, 148).

16. New Age has been defined as "an eclectic group of cultural attitudes arising in late 20th century Western society that are adapted from those of a variety of ancient and modern cultures, that emphasize beliefs (as reincarnation, holism, pantheism, and occultism) outside the mainstream, and that advance alternative approaches to spirituality, right living, and health" (Merriam-Webster online, accessed June 17, 2013). The only interviewee who used this term did so apologetically: "I mean, not to sound too New Age-y, but. . . ."

17. Unlike other versions of Buddhism in which one strives for non-attachment to worldly desires, "Nichiren Daishonin's Buddhism emphasizes obtaining 'actual proof' of the teaching's power" through results in the here and now (www.sgi-usa.org/newmembers/dailypractice.php).

18. See, for example, www.christianbiblereference.org/faq_prayer.htm.

19. On Americans' tendency toward self-enhancement instead of self-criticism, see also Kitayama et al. (1997).

20. One career counselor estimated that in this recession the job search was taking two and a half months for every ten thousand dollars of one's former salary; the higher one's former income, the longer one can expect to be out of work.

21. She was reacting in particular to the view expressed by other interviewees that God had a plan for them.

CHAPTER 10: THE UNEMPLOYED COOPERATIVE

1. Further examples can be found in the troubled job market of academia. The "Academic Jobs Wikis" (www.academicjobs.wikia.com), for example, serve not only as

a common resource for those who want to find out about new jobs and whether they meet the selection criteria; these sites also serve as a forum for tracking searches, seeking advice, and even commiserating with the hundreds of others who are hoping to land the increasingly scarce jobs.

2. Roberto Somoza (former mayor of Ciudad Sandino), personal communication, August 15, 2008.

3. Alex Nading (2014) provides an excellent overview of the many "entanglements" of nature, culture, and politics in the formation of Ciudad Sandino, "the city of emergencies."

4. Pseudonyms are used throughout the text.

5. While "artisan consciousness" refers to the individualistic, voluntaristic, and self-sufficient mentalities that often shut down larger-scale coordination and cooperation among the poor, "organizational consciousness" invokes all of the communicative, technical, social, and organizational mentalities (that is, the "culture of productivity") necessary for successfully running collective enterprises.

6. Or as Marx writes: "A spider conducts operations that resemble those of a weaver, and a bee puts to shame many an architect in the construction of her cells. But what distinguishes the worst architect from the best of bees is this, that the architect raises his structure in the imagination before he erects it in reality" (Marx 1977[1867], 178).

EPILOGUE: RETHINKING THE VALUE OF WORK AND UNEMPLOYMENT

Thanks to Elizabeth Ferry, Jong Bum Kwon, Sarah Lamb, Carrie Lane, Smitha Radhakrishnan, and Cinzia Solari for comments on an earlier draft, and to Shannon Ward for research assistance.

1. Reporter Steven Greenhouse, referring to the Department of Labor criteria (Greenhouse 2013, n.p.). See also http://unpaidinternslawsuit.com/.

2. U.S. Jobless rate data available at www.tradingeconomics.com/united-states/unemployment-rate.

3. "Tom Friedman: I Got it Wrong," Innovation Hub, WGBH radio, available at http://blogs.wgbh.org/innovation-hub/2014/5/1/tom-friedman-i-got-it-wrong/, emphasis added. The quotation about being an "income entrepreneur" begins at 15:07.

4. The source quotes Charles E. Wilson, secretary of defense under Dwight Eisenhower and a former GM executive, in 1953.

5. See the Center on Aging and Work at Boston College, available at http://bc.edu/research/agingandwork/about/workFlexibility.html.

6. On critiques of flexible labor, see, e.g., Susser and Chatterjee 1998; Freeman 1998; Patterson 1998. On the decline of unions, see Durrenberger and Reichart 2011; Fletcher and Gapasin 2008.

7. This article refers to a 2011 World Bank study that found a 38 percent youth unemployment rate in Nigeria: see http://businessdayonline.com/2013/11/addressing-youth-unemployment-in-nigeria/#.U3TIOq1dWSQ.

Bibliography

Abelmann, Nancy, So Jin Part, and Hyunhee Kim. 2009. "College Rank and Neo-liberal Subjectivity in South Korea: The Burden of Self-development." *Inter-Asia Cultural Studies* 10, no. 2: 229–247.

Adams, Susan. 2011. "America's Worst Cities for Finding a Job," *Forbes*, November 23. Accessed September 26, 2015. Available at www.forbes.com/sites/susanadams/2011/11/23/americas-worst-cities-for-finding-a-job/.

Adams, Vincanne. 2013. *Markets of Sorrow, Labors of Faith: New Orleans in the Wake of Katrina*. Durham: Duke University Press.

Adida, Claire L., David D. Laitin, and Marie-Anne Valfort. 2010. "Identifying Barriers to Muslim Integration in France." *Proceedings of the National Aacdemy of Sciences of the United States of America* 107, no. 52:22384-22390.

Agamben, Giorgio. 1998. *Homo Sacer: Sovereign Power and Bare Life*. Stanford, California: Meridian.

AFL-CIO. 2009. South Carolina, Health Care. Accessed March 14, 2009. www.aflcio.org/issues/factsstats/factsstats.cfm.

Aguilar, Michael Bernabé. 2003. "The Impact of the Worker: How Social Capital and Human Capital Influence the Job Tenure of Former Undocumented Mexican Immigrants." *Sociological Inquiry* 73, no. 1:52–82.

Aguilar, Michael Bernabé, and Douglas Massey. 2002. "Social Capital and the Wages of Mexican Immigrants: New Hypotheses and Tests." Working Paper. Department of Sociology. Rice University, Houston, Texas.

Ahmed, Sara. 2010. *The Promise of Happiness*. Durham: Duke University Press.

Alba, Francisco. 2008. "Mexico: A Crucial Crossroads." Migration Information Source. Accessed January 18, 2013. Available at www.migrationinformation.org/feature/display.cfm?ID=772.

Allison, Anne. 1994. *Nightwork: Sexuality, Pleasure, and Corporate Masculinity in a Tokyo Hostess Club*. Chicago: University of Chicago Press.

———. 2012. "Ordinary Refugees: Social Precarity and Soul in 21st Century Japan." *Anthropological Quarterly* 85, no. 2:345–370.

———. 2013. *Precarious Japan (Chronicles of the New World Encounter)*. Durham: Duke University Press.

Amuedo-Durantes, Catalina, and Kusum Mandra. 2007. "Social Networks and Their Impact on the Earnings of Mexican Immigrants." *Demography* 44, no. 4: 849–863.

Ansley, Fran, and Anne Lewis. 2011. "Going South, Coming North: Migration and Union Organizing in Morristown, Tennessee." *Southern Spaces*, May 19. Accessed January 11, 2015. Available at http://southernspaces.org/2011/going-south-coming-north-migration-and-union-organizing-morristown-tennessee.

Applebaum, Herbert. 1995. "The Concept of Work in Western Thought," In *Meanings of Work: Considerations for the Twenty-First Century*, edited by Frederick Gamst, 46–78. Albany: State University of New York Press.

Arellano, Jorge Eduardo. 2009. "La Nueva Gramática de la Lengua Española y el gentilicio de Ciudad Sandino." *El Nuevo Diario* (Managua, Nicaragua). Accessed September 27, 2015. Available at www.elnuevodiario.com.ni/opinion/63780-nueva-gramatica-lengua-espanola-gentilicio-ciudad-/.

Ariza, M. 2002. "Migracion y transnacionalidad en el contexto de la globalizacion: algunos puntos de reflexion." *Revista Mexicana Sociologia* 64, no. 4:53–84.

Arrighi, Giovanni. 2002. "The African Crisis: World Systemic and Regional Analysis." *New Left Review* 15:5–36.

Autain, Clémentine. 2012. *Le Retour du peuple: de la classe ouvrière au précariat.* Paris: Stock.

Autor, David H., and David Scarborough. 2008. "Does Job Testing Harm Minority Workers? Evidence from Retail Establishments." *Quarterly Journal of Economics* 123, no. 1:219–277.

Avendaño, José Carlos. 2014. "Informa la Setyde que 11 empresas están en proceso de instalación o ampliación a la fecha." *La Jornada*, July 22, p. 5.

Babb, Florence E. 2001. *After Revolution: Mapping Gender and Cultural Politics in Neoliberal Nicaragua.* Austin: University of Texas Press.

Bacon, Natalie. 2011. "Unpaid Internships: The History, Policy, and Future Implications of 'Fact Sheet #71.'" *Ohio State Entrepreneurial Business Law Journal* 6, no. 1:67–96. Available at http://moritzlaw.osu.edu/students/groups/oseblj/files/2013/04/6-3.pdf.

Bakke, E. Wight. 1934. *The Unemployed Man: A Social Study.* New York: E.P. Dutton and Co.

———. 1940. *The Unemployed Worker: A Study of the Task of Making a Living without a Job.* New Haven, CT: Institute of Human Relations.

Barbeito, Alberto, and Rubén Lo Vuolo. 1992. *La Modernización Excluyente: Transformación Económica Y Estado de Bienestar En Argentina.* Buenos Aires: CIEPP/UNICEF/Losada.

Barley, Stephen, and Gideon Kunda. 2004. *Gurus, Hired Guns, and Warm Bodies: Itinerant Experts in a Knowledge Economy.* Princeton, NJ: Princeton University Press.

Barret, Christophe, Florence Ryk, and Noémie Volle. 2014. *Enquête 2013 auprès de la Génération 2010. Face à la crise, le fossé se creuse entre niveaux de diplôme.* Marseille: Centre d'Études et de Recherches sur les Qualifications.

Basker, Emek. 2007. "The Causes and Consequences of Wal-Mart's Growth." *Journal of Economic Perspectives* 21, no. 3:177–198.

Basualdo, Eduardo. 2001. *Sistema Político Y Modelo de Acumulación En La Argentina. Notas Sobre El Transformismo Argentino Durante La Valorización Financiera (1976–2001).* Bernal, Argentina: Universidad Nacional de Quilmes.

Baudrillard, Jean. 1981. *For a Critique of the Political Economy of the Sign.* Translated by Charles Levin. St. Louis: Telos Press.

Bauman, Zygmunt. 1998. *Work, Consumerism, and the New Poor.* Buckingham: Open University Press.

———. 2004. *Wasted Lives: Modernity and Its Outcasts.* Cambridge: Polity.

Beals, Stephen. 2008. *Self Marketing Power: Branding Yourself as a Business of One.* Omaha, NE: Keynote Publishing.

Beaud, Stéphane, and Michel Pialoux. 1999. *Retour sur la condition ouvrière: enquête aux usines Peugeot de Sochaux-Montbéliard.* Paris: Fayard.

Beccaria, Luis. 2001. *Empleo E Integración Social.* Buenos Aires: Fondo de Cultura Económica.

Beccaria, Luis, and Néstor López. 1997. "El Debilitamiento de Los Mecanismos de Integración Social." In *Sin Trabajo. Las Características Del Desempleo Y Sus Efectos En La Sociedad Argentina,* edited by Luis Beccaria and Néstor López. Buenos Aires: Losada.

Becker, Gary S. 1962. "Investment in Human Capital: A Theoretical Analysis." *Journal of Political Economy* 70, no. 5:9–49.

Beckwith, Harry, and Christine Clifford Beckwith. 2007. *You, Inc.: The Art of Selling Yourself.* New York: Business Plus.

Béland, Daniel. 2009. "Back to Bourgeois? French Social Policy and the Idea of Solidarity." *International Journal of Sociology and Social Policy* 29, no. 9/10:445–456.

Berlant, Lauren. 2007. "Nearly Utopian, Nearly Normal: Post-Fordist Affect in La Promesse and Rosetta." *Public Culture* 19, no. 2:273–301.

———. 2011. *Cruel Optimism*. Durham: Duke University Press.

Bernhardt, Annette. 1999. "The Future of Low-Wage Jobs: Case Studies in the Retail Industry." Institute on Education and the Economy Working Paper No. 10. New York: Columbia University Teachers College.

Berry, Sara. 1985. *Fathers Work for Their Sons: Accumulation, Mobility, and Class Formation in an Extended Yoruba Community*. Berkeley: University of California Press.

Besteman, Catherine, and Hugh Gusterson. 2009. *The Insecure American: How We Got Here and What We Should Do About It*, edited by Hugh Gusterson and Catherine Besteman, 1–23. Introduction. Berkeley: University of California Press.

Blackman, Lisa. 2008. *The Body: Key Concepts*. New York: Berg.

BLS (Bureau of Labor Statistics). 2009. "Ranks of Discouraged Workers and Others Marginally Attached to the Labor Force Rise During Recession." *Issues in Labor Statistics* (April).

———. 2012. "Numbers of Jobs Held, Labor Market Activity, and Earnings Growth among Younger Baby Boomers: Results from More Than Two Decades of a Longitudinal Survey." BLS Press Release, July 25. Accessed April 2, 2013. Available at www.bls.gov/news.release/pdf/nlsoy.pdf.

Boccagni, Paolo, and Francesca Lagomarsino. 2011. "Migration and the Global Crisis: New Prospects for Return? The Case of Ecuadorians in Europe." *Bulletin of Latin American Research* 30, no. 3:282–297.

Boehm, Deborah. 2008. "'Now I Am a Man and a Woman!' Gendered Moves and Migration in a Transnational Community." *Latin American Perspectives* 35, no. 1:16–30.

Boëldieu, Julien, and Catherine Borrel. 2000. *Recensement de la population 1999: la proportion d'immigrés est stable depuis 25 ans*. Paris: INSEE.

Borgetto, Michel. 1993. *La notion de fraternité en droit public français: le passé, le présent et l'avenir*. Paris: Librairie Générale de Droit et de Jurisprudence.

Bose, Purnima, Laura E. Lyons, and Christopher Newfield. 2010. *Cultural Critique and the Global Corporation*. Bloomington: Indiana University Press.

Bourdieu, Pierre. 1984. *Distinction: A Social Critique of the Judgement of Taste*. Translated by Richard Nice. Cambridge, MA: Harvard University Press.

———. 1992. *The Logic of Practice*. Stanford: Stanford University Press.

———. 1996. "Marginalia: Algumas Notas Adicionais Sobre o Dom." *Mana* 2, no. 2: 7–20.

Bourgeois, Léon. 1902 [1896]. "Solidarité," 3rd edition. Paris: Armand Colin.

Bourgnon, Yves. 2006. "Toutes les générations se dressent face à 'l'institutionnalisation de la précarité.'" *Le Populaire du Centre*, February 8.

Bourgois, Philippe. 1995. *In Search of Respect: Selling Crack in El Barrio (Structural Analysis in the Social Sciences)*. New York: Cambridge University Press.

Bourgois, Philippe, and Jeff Schonberg. 2009. *Righteous Dopefiend*. Berkeley: University of California Press.

Brady, Michelle. 2014. "Ethnographies of Neoliberal Governmentalities: From the Neoliberal Apparatus to Neoliberalism and Governmental Assemblages." *Foucault Studies* 18:11–33.

Braverman, Harry. 1974. *Labor and Monopoly Capital*. New York: Monthly Review Press.

Brodkin, Evelyn Z., and Gregory Marston, eds. 2013. *Work and the Welfare State: Street-Level Organizations and Workfare Politics*. Washington, DC: Georgetown University Press.

Broussard, Nzinga, and Tsegay Gebrekidan Tekleselassie. 2012. "Youth Unemployment: Ethiopia Country Study." Working Paper 12/0592. London: International Growth Centre.

Brown, Wendy. 2003. "Neo-Liberalism and the End of Liberal Democracy." *Theory and Event* 7, no. 1:1–19.

———. 2006. "American Nightmare: Neoliberalism, Neoconservativism, and De-Democratization." *Political Theory* 34, no. 6:690–714.

Budd, John W. 2011. *The Thought of Work*. Ithaca: ILR Press.

Busso, Mariana, and Débora Gorbán. 2004. "Trabajando En El Espacio Urbano: La Calle Como Lugar de Construcciones Y Resignificaciones Identitarias." In *El Trabajo Frente Al Espejo. Rupturas Y Continuidades En Los Procesos Identitarios de Los Trabajadores*, edited by Osvaldo R. Battistini, 235–268. Buenos Aires: Prometeo.

Byrne, Rhonda. 2006. *The Secret*. New York: Atria.

Cameron, Jenny, and Katherine Gibson. 2005. "Alternative Pathways to Community and Economic Development: The Latrobe Valley Community Partnering Project." *Geographical Research* 43, no. 3:274–285.

Canales, Alejandro. 2003. "Mexican Labour Migration to the United States in the Age of Globalization." *Journal of Ethnic and Migration Studies* 29, no. 4:741–761.

———. 2012. "La Migracíon Mexicana Frente a la Crisis Económia Actual. Crónica de un Retorno Moderado." *Revista Interdisciplinar da Mobilidade Humana* 20, no. 39:117.

Cardoso de Oliveira, Luís R. 2004. "Honor, Dignidad Y Reciprocidad." *Cuadernos de Antropología Social* 20:25–39.

Cardoso de Oliveira, Roberto, and Luís Cardoso de Oliveira. 1996. *Ensaios antropológicos sobre moral e ética*. Rio de Janeiro: Tempo Brasileiro.

Carmen, Raff. 1996. *Autonomous Development: Humanizing the Landscape*. London: Zed Books.

Carmen, Raff, and Miguel Sobrado, eds. 2000. *A Future for the Excluded: Job Creation and Income Generation by the Poor*. New York: Zed Books.

Carnevale, Anthony P., Tamara Jayasundera, and Dmitri Repnikov. 2014. *Understanding Online Jobs Data: A Technical Report*. Washington D.C.: Georgetown University Center for Education and the Workforce.

Casanova, Erynn Mase De. 2011. *Making Up the Difference: Women, Beauty, and Direct Selling in Ecuador*. Austin: University of Texas Press.

Cassarino, Jean-Pierre. 2004. "Theorising Return Migration: The Conceptual Approach to Return Migration Revisited." *International Journal of Multicultural Societies* 6, no. 2:253–279.

Castel, Robert. 2007. *La Discrimination négative, citoyens ou indigènes?* Paris: Seuil.

———. 2011. "Les Ambiguïtés de la promotion de l'individu." In *Refaire société*, edited by Pierre Rosanvallon, 13–25. Paris: Seuil.

Castillo, Seydi. 2012. "Creación de empleo: demanda prioritaria." *El Nuevo Diario* (Managua, Nicaragua).

Castles, Stephen. 2010. "Understanding Global Migration: A Social Transformation Perspective." *Journal of Ethnic and Migration Studies* 36, no. 10:1565–1586.

———. 2011. "Migration, Crisis, and the Global Labour Market." *Globalizations* 8, no. 3:311–324.

Catalog of Federal Domestic Assistance. 2015. "Foreign-Trade Zones in the United States." Accessed January 11, 2015. Available at www.cfda.gov/index?s=program&mode=form&tab=core&id=5eb2b1a06998d59eb179a8e7fd76c173.

Catus, Bertrand. 2006. "La Jeunesse répond: 'résistance!'" *L'Écho de la Haute Vienne*, February 2.

Cave, Damien. 2011. "Better Lives for Mexicans Cut Allure of Going North." *New York Times*. July 6: A1, A8–9.

Central Statistical Authority. 1999. *The 1994 Population and Housing Census of Ethiopia.* Addis Ababa: Central Statistical Authority.

Cesari, Jocelyne. 2005. "Ethnicity, Islam, and *les Banlieues*: Confusing the Issues." Accessed August 12, 2014. Available at http://riotsfrance.ssrc.org/Cesari/.

Chabanet, Didier, Pascale Dufour, and Frédéric Royall, eds. 2012. *Les Mobilisations sociales à l'heure du précariat.* Rennes, France: École des Hautes Études en Santé Publique.

Chalfin, Brenda. 2010. *Neoliberal Frontiers: An Ethnography of Sovereignty in West Africa (Chicago Studies in Practices of Meaning).* Chicago: University of Chicago Press.

Chatterton, Paul. 2004. "Making Autonomous Geographies: Argentina's Popular Uprising and the 'Movimento de Trabajadores Desocupados' (Unemployed Workers Movement)." *Geoforum* 36, no. 5:545–561.

Chibnik, Michael. 2010. *Crafting Tradition: The Making and Marketing of Oaxacan Wood Carvings.* Austin: University of Texas Press.

Choi, Jung-ah. 2005. "New Generation's Career Aspirations and New Ways of Marginalization in a Postindustrial Economy." *British Journal of Sociology of Education* 26, no. 2:269–283.

Choi, Kyeong-Hee. 2001. "Impaired Body as Colonial Trope: Kang Kyoong'ae's 'Underground Village.'" *Public Culture* 13, no. 3:431–458.

Chun, Jennifer Jihye. 2009. *Organizing at the Margins: The Symbolic Politics of Labor in South Korea and the United States.* Ithaca: Cornell University Press.

Clines, Francis X. 2009. "Are They Depressed? Nowhere Near." *New York Times*, March 15.

Clough, Patricia Ticeneto. 2007. *The Affective Turn: Theorizing the Social*, edited by Patricia Ticeneto Clough, and Jean Halley, 1–33. Introduction. Durham: Duke University Press.

Cobo, Salvador, Silvia Giorguli, and Francisco Alba. 2010. "La Movilidad de los migrantes de retorno: un analysis comparative entre paises latinoamericanos." In *Salvando Fronteras: Migración Internacional en America Latina y el Caribe*, edited by Katharine M. Donato et al., 249–280. Mexico: Porrua.

Cohen, Jeffrey H. 1998. "Craft Production and the Challenge of the Global Market: An Artisans' Cooperative in Oaxaca, Mexico." *Human Organization* 57:74–82.

Cole, Jennifer. 2004. "Fresh Contact in Tamatave, Madagascar: Sex, Money, and Intergenerational Transformation." *American Ethnologist* 31, no. 4:573–588.

———. 2005. "The Jaombilo of Tamatave (Madagascar), 1992–2004: Reflections on Youth and Globalization." *Journal of Social History* 38, no. 4:891–914.

———. 2013. "Afterword: On Generations and Aging: 'Fresh Contact' of a Different Sort." In *Transitions and Transformations: Cultural Perspectives on Aging and the Life Course*, edited by Caitrin Lynch and Jason Danely. New York: Berghahn Books.

Collins, Jane. 2003. *Threads: Gender, Labor, and Power in the Global Apparel Industry.* Chicago: University of Chicago Press.

Comaroff, Jean, and John Comaroff. 1992. "The Madman and the Migrant." *Ethnography and the Historical Imagination.* Boulder, CO: Westview Press.

———. 2001. "Millennial Capitalism: First Thoughts on a Second Coming." In *Millennial Capitalism and the Culture of Neoliberalism*, edited by Jean Comaroff and John L. Comaroff. Durham: Duke University Press.

———. 2005. "Children and Youth in a Global Era: Reflections on Youth from the Past to the Postcolony." In *Makers and Breakers: Children and Youth in Postcolonial Africa*, edited by Alcinda Honwana and Filip De Boeck, 19–30. Oxford: James Currey.

Comaroff, Jean, and John Comaroff, eds. 2001. *Millennial Capitalism and the Culture of Neoliberalism.* Durham, NC: Duke University Press.

CONAPO (Consejo Naciónal de Población). 2011. *La Situación Démografica de México.* Mexico City, Mexico: Consejo Naciónal.

Cook, Bernard A., and James R. Watson. 1985. *Louisiana Labor: From Slavery to "Right to Work."* New York: University Press of America.

Corbin, Alain. 1975. *Archaïsme et modernité en Limousin au XIXe siècle, 1845–1880.* Paris: Marcel Rivière.

Cottle, Thomas J. 2003. *Hardest Times: The Trauma of Long-Term Unemployment.* Amherst: University of Massachusetts Press.

Couch, Kenneth A., and Robert Fairlie. 2010. "Last Hired Last Fired? Black-White Unemployment and the Business Cycle." *Demography* 47, no. 1:227–247.

Covell, Maureen. 1987. *Madagascar: Politics, Economics, and Society.* London: F. Pinter.

Crapanzano, Vincent. 2003. "Reflections on Hope as a Category of Social and Psychological Analysis." *Cultural Anthropology* 18, no. 1:3–32.

Cross, Cecilia, and María Ullivarri. 2013. "Mujeres Pobres Y Cuestión Social En La Crisis Del 30 Y a Fines de Los 90: Un Estudio Interdisciplinario En Buenos Aires Y Tucumán." *Jornadas Interescuelas/Departamentos de Historia* 14:1–19.

Darity, William, and Patrick Mason. 1998. "Evidence on Discrimination in Employment: Codes of Color, Codes of Gender." *Journal of Economic Perspectives* 12, no. 2:63–90.

D'Aubeterre Buznego, Maria Eugenia. 2002. "Genero, Parentesco y Redes Migratorias Femeninas." *Alteridades* 12, no. 24:51–60.

Davis, Clark. 2001. *Company Men: White-Collar Life and Corporate Cultures in Los Angeles, 1892–1941.* Baltimore: John Hopkins University Press.

Davis, Heather A. 2009. "On the Streets." Penn Compact 2020, Office of the President, University of Pennsylvania. Accessed May 15, 2014. Available at www.upenn.edu/president/penn-compact/on-the-streets.

Davoine, Jérôme. 2006. "Vent de solidarité rue de la Préfecture." *L'Écho de la Haute Vienne*, March 31.

De Boeck, Filip. 1999. "Domesticating Diamonds and Dollars: Identity, Expenditure and Sharing in Southwestern Zaire (1984–1997)." In *Globalization and Identity: Dialectics of Flow and Closure*, edited by Birgit Meyer and Peter Geschiere, 177–210. Oxford: Blackwell.

de Gaulejac, Vincent. 1996. *Les Sources de la honte.* Paris: Desclée de Brouwer.

de Grazia, Victoria. 2005. *Irresistible Empire: America's Advance through Twentieth-Century Europe.* Cambridge, MA: Harvard University Press.

de Morais, Clodomir Santos. 1969. *Algunas Consideraciones en Torno a las Organizaciones Campesinas en Latinoamerica.* Geneva: ILO.

———. 1987. Condiciones Objetivas y Factores Subjetivos de la Incorporación de las Masas Rurales en el Proceso de Desarollo Progresista de la Agricultura en Centroamerica. No. E10 M827c. Washington, DC: World Bank.

Denning, Michael. 2010. "Wageless Life." *New Left Review* 66:79–97.

Desbordes, Chantal. 2004. *Atlas des populations immigrées en Limousin.* Paris: INSEE.

Devine, Theresa J., and Nicolas M. Kiefer. 1991. *Empirical Labor Economics: The Search Approach.* New York: Oxford University Press.

Dewey, Susan. 2011. *Neon Wasteland: On Love, Motherhood, and Sex Work in a Rust Belt Town.* Berkeley: University of California Press.

Didier, Emmanuel. 2007. "Do Statistics 'Perform' the Economy?" In *Do Economists Make Markets? On the Performativity of Economics*, edited by Donald MacKenzie, Fabian Muniesa, and Lucia Siu, 276–310. Princeton: Princeton University Press.

di Leonardo, Micaela. 1992. *The Varieties of Ethnic Experience: Kinship, Class, and Gender among California Italian-Americans.* Ithaca: Cornell University Press.

Dilley, Roy. 2004. *Islamic and Caste Knowledge Practices among Haalpulaar'en in Senegal.* Edinburgh: Edinburgh University Press.

Dimarco, Sabina. 2005. "Experiencias de Autoorganización En Cartoneros: Un Acercamiento a La Configuración de Vínculos Laborales, Sociales Y Políticos En Contextos de Exclusión Social." Informe Final el Concurso. Programa Regional de Becas. Beunos Aires: CLACSO.

Dinerstein, Ana C. 2001. "A Silent Revolution: The Unemployed Workers Movement in Argentina and the New Internationalism." *Labour Capital and Society/Travail, Capital et Société* 34:166–183.

Donaldson, Mike. 1991. *Time of Our Lives: Labour and Love in the Working Class.* Sydney: Allen and Unwin.

Donato, Katherine. 2010. "U.S. Migration Patterns from Latin America: Gendered Patterns and Shifts." *Annals of the American Academy of Political Sciences* 630:78–92.

Donato, Katherine, Joseph Alexander, Donna Gabaccia, and Johanna Leinonen. 2011. "Variations in the Gender Composition of Immigrant Populations: How They Matter." *International Migration Review* 45, no. 3:496–526.

Donham, Donald. 1986. "Old Abyssinia and the New Ethiopian Empire: Themes in Social History." In *The Southern Marches of Imperial Ethiopia: Essays in History and Social Anthropology,* edited by Donald Donham and Wendy James, 3–48. Cambridge: Cambridge University Press.

———. 1999. *Marxist Modern: An Ethnographic History of the Ethiopian Revolution.* Berkeley: University of California Press.

Donzelot, Jacques. 1994 [1984]. *L'invention du social: essai sur le déclin des passions politiques.* Paris: Seuil.

Dore, Ronald. 1976. *The Diploma Disease: Education, Qualification, and Development.* London: George Allen and Unwin.

Druckerman, Pamela. 2012. *Bringing Up Bébé: One American Mother Discovers the Wisdom of French Parenting.* New York: Penguin Press.

Dubet, François. 1987. *La galère: jeunes en survie.* Paris: Fayard.

Dudley, Katherine M. 1994. *The End of the Line: Lost Jobs, New Lives in Postindustrial America.* Chicago: University of Chicago Press.

Duggan, Lisa. 2004. *The Twilight of Equality? Neoliberalism, Cultural Politics, and the Attack on Democracy.* Boston: Beacon Press.

Duguet, Emmanuel, Noam Leandri, Yannick L'Horty, and Pascal Petit. 2007. *Discriminations à l'embauche. Un testing sur les jeunes des banlieues d'Île-de-France.* Paris: Centre d'analyse stratégique.

Dunk, Thomas W. 2003. *It's a Working Man's Town: Male Working-Class Culture.* Montreal: McGill-Queens University Press.

Duplouy, Bérangère. 2003. *Portrait des quartiers de Limoges.* Paris: INSEE.

Durand, Jean-Pierre, and Nicolas Hatzfeld. 2003. *Living Labour: Life on the Line at Peugeot France.* Basingstoke, U.K.: Palgrave Macmillan.

Durand, Jorge. 2010. "Los Inmigrantes tambien Emigran: La Migracion de Retorno domo Corolorio del Proceso." *Revista Interdisciplinar de Modilidad* 14, nos. 26–27:168–189.

Durkheim, Emile. 1984 [1893]. *The Division of Labor in Society.* New York: Free Press.

Durrenberger, E. Paul, and Karaleah S. Reichart. 2011. *Anthropology of Labor Unions.* 1st ed. Boulder: University Press of Colorado.

Ehrenreich, Barbara. 2005. *Bait and Switch: The (Futile) Pursuit of the American Dream.* New York: Holt.

———. 2009a. *Bright-Sided: How Positive Thinking is Undermining America.* New York: Henry Holt.

——. 2009b. "Trying To Find a Job Is Not a Job." *Los Angeles Times*, May 3, 2009. Accessed June 18, 2009. Available at http://articles.latimes.com/2009/may/03/opinion/oe-ehrenreich3.

Ellison, James. 2006. "'Everyone Can Do as He Wants': Economic Liberalization and Emergent Forms of Antipathy in Southern Ethiopia." *American Ethnologist* 33, no. 4:665–686.

——. 2009. "Governmentality and the Family: Neoliberal Choices and Emergent Kin Relations in Southern Ethiopia." *American Anthropologist* 111, no. 1:81–92.

El Sol de Tlaxcala. 2012. "Fincadas las Bases de Desarrollo: Informe del Gobierno." January 15. Accessed January 15, 2012. Available at www.oem.com.mx/elsoldetlaxcala/.

——. 2014. "Bajo en junio la tasa de desempleo en México." July 18. Accessed July 18, 2014. Available at www.oem.com.mx/elsoldetlaxcala/notas/.

Elyachar, Julia. 2005. *Markets of Dispossession: NGOs, Economic Development, and the State in Cairo (Politics, History, and Culture)*. Durham: Duke University Press.

Erem, Suzan, and E. Paul Durrenberger. 2008. *On the Global Waterfront: The Fight to Free the Charleston 5*. New York: Monthly Review Press.

Evans-Pritchard, Edward E. 1987. *Los Nuer*. Barcelona: Anagrama.

Fang, Lee. 2013. "How Private Prisons Game the Immigration System." *The Nation*, February 27.

Farrigan, Tracey L., and Amy K. Glasmeier. n.d. "Living Wage and Job Gap Study." Accessed March 14, 2009. Available at www.povertyinamerica.psu.edu/products/publications/beaufort_living_wage.

Ferguson, James. 1990. *The Anti-Politics Machine: "Development," Depoliticization, and Bureaucratic Power in Lesotho*. Cambridge: Cambridge University Press.

——. 2006. *Global Shadow: Africa in the Neoliberal World Order*. Durham: Duke University Press.

——. 2009. "The Uses of Neoliberalism." *Antipode* 41, no. 1:166–184.

Ferillo, Bud. 2005. *Corridor of Shame: The Neglect of South Carolina's Rural Schools*. Produced and directed by Bud Ferillo. First shown on South Carolina Educational Television.

Fernández Álvarez, Maria Inés. 2007. "'En Defensa de La Fuente de Trabajo': Demandas Y Prácticas de Movilización En Una Empresa Recuperada de Buenos Aires." *Avá* 11:63–86.

Fernández Álvarez, Maria Inés, and Virginia Manzano. 2007. "Desempleo, Acción Estatal Y Movilización Social En Argentina." *Política Y Cultura* 27:143–166.

Fisher, Josh. 2010. "Building Consciousness: The Organization Workshop Comes to a Nicaraguan Cooperative." *Anthropology of Work Review* 31:71–82.

——. 2013. "Fair or Balanced? The Other Side of Fair Trade in a Nicaragua Cooperative." *Anthropological Quarterly* 86, no. 2:527–558.

Fletcher, Bill Jr., and Fernando Gapasin. 2008. *Solidarity Divided: The Crisis in Organized Labor and a New Path toward Social Justice*. 1st ed. Berkeley: University of California Press.

Food Research and Action Center. 2008. "Poverty 2008." Accessed July 31, 2009. Available at http://frac.org/pdf/poverty08.pdf.

Forrest, Alan. 1981. *The French Revolution and the Poor*. New York: St. Martin's Press.

Foucault, Michel. 1969. *L'archéologie du Savoir*. Paris: Gallimard.

——. 1979. *Discipline and Punish: The Birth of the Prison*. New York: Vintage Books.

——. 2009. *Security, Territory, Population: Lectures at the Collège De France 1977–1978*. Translated by Graham Burchell. New York: Picador.

Foucault, Michel, and Graham Burchell. 2010. *The Birth of Biopolitics: Lectures at the College De France, 1978–1979*. New York: Picador.

Fraser, Jill Andresky. 2002. *White-Collar Sweatshop: The Deterioration of Work and Its Rewards in Corporate America*. New York: W.W. Norton.

Fraser, Nancy, and Linda Gordon. 1994. "A Genealogy of 'Dependency': Tracing a Keyword of the U.S. Welfare State." *Signs* 19, no. 2:309–336.

Freeman, Carla. 1998. "Femininity and Flexible Labor: Fashioning Class through Gender on the Global Assembly Line." *Critique of Anthropology* 18:245–262.

———. 2000. *High Tech and High Heels in the Global Economy: Women, Work, and Pink-Collar Identities*. Durham: Duke University Press.

Freeman, Dena. 2003. "Conclusion I: Understanding Marginalisation in Ethiopia." In *Peripheral People: The Excluded Minorities of Ethiopia*, edited by Dena Freeman and Alula Pankhurst, 301–333. Lawrenceville, NJ: Red Sea Press.

Friedman, Jonathan. 1994. *Cultural Identity and Global Processes*. London: Sage Publications.

Friedman, Milton. 1977. "Nobel Lecture: Inflation and Unemployment." *Journal of Political Economy* 85, no. 3:451–472.

Gallie, Duncan, Serge Paugam, and Shelia Jacobs. 2003. "Unemployment, Poverty and Social Isolation: Is There a Vicious Circle of Social Exclusion?" *European Societies* 5, no. 1:1–32.

Game, Ann. 2001. "Riding: Embodying the Centaur." *Body and Society* 7, no. 4:1–12.

Ganti, Tejaswini. 2014. "Neoliberalism." *Annual Review of Anthropology* 43:89–104.

Gibson-Graham, J. K. 1996. *The End of Capitalism (As We Knew It): A Feminist Critique of Political Economy*. Minneapolis: University of Minnesota Press.

———. 2006. *A Postcapitalist Politics*. Minneapolis: University of Minnesota Press.

Gilbert, Christopher L. 2010. "How to Understand High Food Prices." *Journal of Agricultural Economics* 61, no. 2:398–425.

Gledhill, John. 1998. "The Mexican Contribution to the Restructuring of U.S. Capitalism: NAFTA as an Instrument of Flexible Accumulation." *Critique of Anthropology* 18, no. 3:279–296.

Godelier, Maurice. 1998. *El Enigma del Don*. Barcelona: Paidós.

Goffman, Erving. 2009. *Internados. Ensayos sobre la Situación Social de los Enfermos Mentales*. Buenos Aires: Amorrortu.

Gomberg, Paul. 2007. *How to Make Opportunity Equal: Race and Contributive Justice*. New York: Wiley Blackwell.

Gondola, Didier. 1999. "Dream and Drama: The Search for Elegance among Congolese Youth." *African Studies Review* 42, no. 1:23–48.

González de la Rocha, Mercedes. 1994. *The Resources of Poverty: Women and Survival in a Mexican City*. Cambridge, MA: Blackwell.

———. 2001. "From The Resources of Poverty to the Poverty of Resources? The Erosion of a Survival Model." *Latin American Perspectives* 28, no. 4:72–100.

Gorbán, Débora. 2004. "Reflexiones Alrededor de Los Procesos de Cambio Social En Argentina. El Caso de Los Cartoneros." *E-L@tina, Revista Electrónica de Estudios Latinoamericanos* 8:3–16.

———. 2006. "Trabajo Y Cotidianeidad. El Barrio Como Espacio de Trabajo de Los Cartoneros Del Tren Blanco." *Trabajo Y Sociedad* 7, no. 8:1–23.

———. 2009. "La Construcción Social Del Espacio Y La Movilización Colectiva. Las Formas de Organización Espacial de Los Sectores Populares En Buenos Aires. (Salir a Cartonear, Desentrañando Prácticas Y Sentidos Del Trabajo Entre Quienes Se Dedican a La Recolección de Materiales Recuperables)." Doctoral thesis in social science, Universidad de Buenos Aires, Argentina.

Gould, Jens. 2011. "Mexico's Economy Taking Off with U.S. Boost." *Bloomberg News*, February 22. Accessed September 26, 2015. Available at http://embamex.sre.gob.mx/

canada_eng/index.php/component/content/article/241-tuesday-february-22-
2011/2228-mexicos-economy-taking-off-with-us-boost-the-globe-and-mail.
Gould, W. T. S. 1993. *People and Education in the Third World.* Harlow, U.K.: Longman
Scientific and Technical.
Graeber, David. 2001a. "The New Anarchists." *New Left Review* 13:61–73.
———. 2001b. *Towards an Anthropology of Value: The False Coin of Our Own Dreams.* New
York: Palgrave.
———. 2013. "On the Phenomenon of Bullshit Jobs." *Strike! Magazine,* August 17, 2013.
Accessed February 10, 2016. Available at http://www.strikemag.org/bullshit-jobs/.
Grassi, Estela. 2000. "Procesos Politico-Culturales En Torno Del Trabajo. Acerca de La
Problematización de La Cuestión Social En La Década de Los 90 Y El Sentido
de Las 'Soluciones' Propuestas: Un Repaso Para Pensar El Futuro." *Sociedad*
16:49–81.
———. 2003a. "Condiciones de Trabajo Y Exclusión Social. Más Allá Del Empleo Y La
Sobrevivencia." *Socialis, Revista Latinoamericana de Política Social* 7:137–142.
———. 2003b. *Políticas y problemas sociales en la sociedad neoliberal: la otra década infame.*
Buenos Aires: Espacio.
Grassi, Estela, Susana Hintze, and María Rosa Neufeld. 1994. *Políticas sociales, crisis y
ajuste estructural: un análisis del sistema educativo, de obras sociales y de las
políticas alimentarias.* Buenos Aires: Espacio Editorial.
Greenberg, Edward S., Leon Grunberg, Sarah Moore, and Patricia B. Sikura. 2010.
Turbulence: Boeing and the State of American Workers and Managers. New
Haven: Yale University Press.
Greenhouse, Steven. 2013. "Judge Rules That Movie Studio Should Have Been Paying
Interns." *New York Times,* June 11. Accessed May 15, 2014. Available at www.nytimes.
com/2013/06/12/business/judge-rules-for-interns-who-sued-fox-searchlight.html.
Gregory, Chris A. 1989. *Observing the Economy.* New York: Routledge.
Grimes, Kimberly, and Lynne Milgram, eds. 2000. *Artisans and Cooperatives: Developing
Alternate Trade for the Global Economy.* Tucson: University of Arizona Press.
Gunewardena, Nandini, and Ann E. Kingsolver, eds. 2008. *The Gender of Globalization:
Women Navigating Cultural and Economic Marginalities.* Santa Fe: School for
Advanced Research.
Gutiérrez, Pablo. 2005. "Recuperadores Urbanos de Materiales Reciclables." In *Los
Nuevos Rostros de La Marginalidad. La Supervivencia de Los Desplazados,* edited by
Fortunato Mallimaci and Agustín Salvia. Buenos Aires: IIGG-UBA/Biblos.
Gutmann, Matthew. 2006. *The Meanings of Macho: Being a Man in Mexico City.*
Berkeley: University of California Press.
Guyer, Jane. 2010. Preface to "The Life Cycle as a Rational Proposition, or 'The Arc of
Intermediate Links,'" presented October 2010, for Cultures of Finance Group,
Institute for Public Knowledge. Version without preface available at http://
anthropology.jhu.edu/Jane_Guyer/CultureMonetarism.
Guyer, Jane, and Kabiru K. Salami. 2013. "Life Courses of Indebtedness in Rural Nigeria."
In *Transitions and Transformations: Cultural Perspectives on Aging and the Life
Course,* edited by Caitrin Lynch and Jason Danely. New York: Berghahn Books.
Hackworth, Jason. 2007. *The Neoliberal City: Governance, Ideology, and Development in
American Urbanism.* Ithaca: Cornell University Press.
Hadass, Yael, S. 2004. "The Effect of Internet Recruiting on the Matching of Workers and
Employers." *Social Science Research Network,* February 10. Accessed September 20.
2015. Available at http://dx.doi.org/10.2139/ssrn.497262.
Hagan, John. 1993. "The Social Embeddedness of Crime and Unemployment."
Criminology 31, no. 4:465–491.

Hage, Ghassan. 2003. *Against Paranoid Nationalism: Searching for Hope in a Shrinking Society*. Annandale, Australia: Pluto Press Australia.

Hall, Douglas T. 1976. *Careers in Organizations*. Glenview, IL: Scott Foresman.

Hananel, Sam. 2014. "Union Membership Holds Steady at 11.3 Percent." Associated Press. *The Post and Courier*, January 27.

Hansen, Karen Tranberg. 2000. "Gender and Difference: Youth, Bodies, and Clothing in Zambia." In *Gender, Agency, and Change: An Anthropological Perspective*, edited by Victoria Goddard, 32–55. London: Routledge.

———. 2005. "Getting Stuck in the Compound: Some Odds against Social Adulthood in Lusaka." *Africa Today* 51, no. 4:2–17.

Harrington, Brad. 2001. "Protean Careers: A Conversation with Tim Hall." *Sloan Work and Family Research Network Newsletter*, 3, no. 2.

The Harvest. 2009. "Extra Mile Campaign Needs to Raise 7,000,000 Pounds of Food." *The Harvest* 24, no. 1:1, 3. Columbia, SC: Harvest Hope Food Bank.

Harvey, David. 1990. *The Condition of Postmodernity*. Oxford: Blackwell.

———. 1991. *The Condition of Postmodernity: An Enquiry into the Origins of Cultural Change*. Reprint. Oxford, U.K.: Wiley-Blackwell.

———. 2005. *A Brief History of Neoliberalism*. New York: Oxford University Press.

Hayward, J. E. S. 1961. "The Official Social Philosophy of the French Third Republic: Léon Bourgeois and Solidarism." *International Review of Social History* 6:19–48.

Headey, Derek, and Shenggen Fan. 2008. "Anatomy of a Crisis: The Causes and Consequences of Surging Food Prices." *Agricultural Economics* 39:375–391.

Heckman, James J. 1998. "Detecting Discrimination." *Journal of Economic Perspectives* 12, no. 2:101–116.

Heelas, Paul. 1996. *The New Age Movement: The Celebration of the Self and the Sacralization of Modernity*. Oxford: Blackwell.

Heelas, Paul, and Paul Morris, eds. 1992. *The Values of the Enterprise Culture: The Moral Debate*. London: Routledge.

Heinonen, Paula. 2011. *Youth Gangs and Street Children: Culture, Nurture, and Masculinity in Ethiopia*. New York: Berghahn Books.

Hellman, Judith A. 2007. *The World of Mexican Migrants: The Rock and the Hard Place*. New York: New Press.

Herbert, Eugenia. 1993. *Iron, Gender, and Power: Rituals of Transformation in African Societies*. Bloomington: Indiana University Press.

Hill, Napoleon. 1937. *Think and Grow Rich*. Meriden, CT: Ralston Society.

Hoben, Allan. 1970. "Social Stratification in Traditional Amhara Society." In *Social Stratification in Africa*, edited by Arthur Tuden and Leonard Plotnicov, 187–223. New York: Free Press.

Hochschild, Arlie Russell. 2003 [1983]. *The Managed Heart: Commercialization of Human Feeling*. Berkeley: University of California Press.

Hoffman, Reid, and Ben Casnocha. 2012. *The Start-Up of You: Adapt to the Future, Invest in Yourself, and Transform Your Career*. New York: Crown Business.

Holzer, Harry J., Stephen Raphael, and Michael A. Stoll. 2003. *Employment Barriers Facing Ex-Offenders*. Washington, D.C.: Urban Institute.

———. 2006. "Perceived Criminality, Criminal Background Checks, and the Racial Hiring Practices of Employers." *Journal of Law and Economics* 49, no. 2:451–480.

Hutchinson, Sharon. 1996. *Nuer Dilemmas: Coping with Money, War, and the State*. Berkeley: University of California Press.

INA (Institut national de l'audiovisuel). 2005. "20 Heures le Journal: émission du 14 novembre 2005." Accessed August 12, 2013. Available at www.ina.fr/video/2964529001.

INEGI (Instituto Nacional de Estadística Y Geografía). 2010. "Principales resultados del censo de población y vivienda." Tlaxcala: INEGI. Accessed September 26, 2015. Available at www.inegi.gob.mx/prod_serv/contenidos/espanol/bvinegi/productos/censos/poblacion/2010/princi_result/cpv2010_principales_resultadosI.pdf.

INIDE (Instituto Nacional de Información de Desarrollo). 2008. *Ciudad Sandino En Cifras*. Managua: Instituto Nacional de Información de Desarrollo.

INSEE (Institut national de la statistique et des études économiques). 2013. "Taux de chômage localisé par région: Limousin." Accessed March 8, 2013. Available at www.insee.fr/fr/bases-de-donnees/bsweb/serie.asp?idbank=001515859.

Jackson, Michael. 1996. *Things as They Are: New Directions in Phenomenological Anthropology*. Bloomington: Indiana University Press.

James, Daniel. 2006. *Resistencia e integración: el peronismo y la clase trabajadora argentina, 1946–1976*. Buenos Aires: Siglo Veintiuno Editores.

Jeffrey, Craig. 2010. *Timepass: Youth, Class, and the Politics of Waiting in India*. Stanford: Stanford University Press.

Jiménez Guillén, Raul. 2012. "Tlaxcala 5.1, México 3.9. La economía local crece por arriba de la media nacional: INEGI." *La Jornada*, July 30, p. 3.

Kang, Miliann. 2010. *The Managed Hand: Race, Gender, and the Body in Beauty Service Work*. Berkeley: University of California Press.

Kaputa, Catherine. 2010. *You Are a Brand! How Smart People Brand Themselves for Business Success*. Boston: Nicholas Brealey Publishing.

Karim, Lamia. 2011. *Microfinance and Its Discontents: Women in Debt in Bangladesh*. Minneapolis: University of Minnesota Press.

Karjanen, David. 2008. "Gender, Race, and Nation in the Making of Mexican Migrant Labor in the United States." *Latin American Perspectives* 35, no. 1:51–63.

Kasmir, Sharryn. 1996. *The Myth of Mondragón: Cooperatives, Politics, and Working-Class Life in a Basque Town*. Albany: State University of New York Press.

Kessler, Ronald C., Blake Turner, and James S. House. 1988. "Effects of Unemployment on Health in a Community Survey: Main, Modifying, and Mediating Effects." *Journal of Social Issues* 44, no. 4:69–85.

Keynes, John Maynard. 1936. *The General Theory of Employment, Interest, and Money*. New York: Harcourt, Brace, and Co.

Kibria, Nazli. 1994. "Household Structure and Family Ideologies: The Dynamics of Immigrant Economic Adaptation among Vietnamese Refugees." *Social Problems* 41, no. 1:81–96.

Kim, Joo Hee. 1981. "P'umasi: Patterns of Interpersonal Relationships in a Korean Village." Ph.D. diss., Northwestern University.

Kim, Myung-Hye. 1993. "Transformation of Family Ideology in Upper-Middle-Class Families in Urban South Korea." *Ethnology* 32, no. 1:69–85.

Kim, Seung-kyung. 1997. *Class Struggle or Family Struggle? The Lives of Women Factory Workers in South Korea*. New York: Cambridge University Press.

Kimmel, Michael. 2008. *Guyland: The Perilous World Where Boys Become Men*. New York: HarperCollins.

Kingsolver, Ann E. 2001. *NAFTA Stories: Fears and Hopes in Mexico and the United States*. Boulder, CO: Lynne Rienner Publishers.

——. 2006. "Strategic Alterity and Silence in the Promotion of California's Proposition 187 and of the Confederate Battle Flag in South Carolina." In *Silence: The Currency of Power*, edited by Maria-Luisa Achino-Loeb, 73–91. New York: Berghahn Books.

——. 2008. "'As We Forgive our Debtors': Mexico's *El Barzón* Movement, Bankruptcy Policy in the U.S., and Ethnography of Neoliberal Logic and Practice." *Rethinking Marxism* 20, no. 1:13–27.

——. 2010a. "Living Wage Considerations in the Right-to-Work State of South Carolina." *Anthropology of Work Review* 31, no. 1:30–41.

——. 2010b. "Talk of 'Broken Borders' and Stone Walls: Anti-Immigration Discourse and Legislation from California to South Carolina." *Southern Anthropologist* 35, no. 1:21–40.

——. 2011. *Tobacco Town Futures: Global Encounters in Rural Kentucky.* Long Grove, IL: Waveland Press.

——. 2012. "Neoliberal Governance and Faith-Based Initiatives: Agentive Cracks in the Logic Informing Homeless Sheltering in South Carolina's Capital." *Rethinking Marxism* 24, no. 2:202–214.

Kingsolver, Ann, and Sasikumar Balasundaram with Vijayakumar Sugumaran, Jennifer Engel, Timothy Gerber, Craig Spurrier, Colin Townsend, and Kristen Wolf. 2010. "Collaborative Research on Food Security in the U.S. and Sri Lanka." *Practicing Anthropology* 32, no. 4:24–28.

Kirmayer, Laurence J. 1992. "The Body's Insistence on Meaning: Metaphor as Presentation and Representation in Illness Experience." *Medical Anthropology Quarterly* 6, no. 4:323–346.

Kitayama, Shinobu, Hazel Rose Markus, Hisaya Matsumoto, and Vinai Norasakkunkit. 1997. "Individual and Collective Processes in the Construction of the Self: Self-enhancement in the United States and Self-criticism in Japan." *Journal of Personality and Social Psychology* 72:1245–1267.

Kleinman, Arthur, and Joan Kleinman. 1994. "How Bodies Remember: Social Memory and Bodily Experience of Criticism, Resistance, and Delegitimation following China's Cultural Revolution." *New Literary History* 25, no. 3:707–723.

Koehs, Jessica. 2005. "Cuando La Ciudadanía Apremia. La 'ley Cartonera' Y La Emergencia Del Cartonero Como Actor Público." In *Ciudadanía Y Territorio*, edited by Gabriela Delamata. Buenos Aires: Espacio Editorial.

——. 2007. "El Empowerment de Los Cartoneros de Buenos Aires Y Su Emergencia Como Actores Sociales Durante La Crisis Argentina de 2002." In *Recicloscopio, Miradas Sobre Recuperadores Urbanos de Residuos En América Latina*, edited by Pablo Schamber and Francisco Suárez, 185–206. Buenos Aires: UNLa-UNGS-Prometeo.

Koo, Hagen. 2000. "The Dilemmas of Empowered Labor in Korea: Korean Workers in the Face of Global Capitalism." *Asian Survey* 40, no. 2:227–250.

Koselleck, Reinhart. 1985 [1979]. *Futures Past: On the Semantics of Historical Time.* Translated by Keith Tribe. Cambridge, MA: MIT Press.

Kunda, Gideon, and John Van Maanen. 1999. "Changing Scripts at Work: Managers and Professionals." *Annals of the American Academy of Political and Social Science* 561:64–80.

Lagrange, Hugues. 2010. *Le déni des cultures.* Paris: Seuil.

Lamont, Michèle. 2000. *The Dignity of Working Men: Morality and the Boundaries of Race, Class, and Immigration.* Cambridge: Harvard University Press.

Lane, Carrie. 2011. *A Company of One: Insecurity, Independence, and the New World of White-Collar Unemployment.* Ithaca: Cornell University Press.

——. 2016. "Unemployed Tech Workers' Ambivalent Embrace of the Flexible Ideal." In *Beyond the Cubicle: Insecurity Culture and the Flexible Self*, edited by Allison Pugh. Cambridge: Oxford University Press.

Lane, Carrie, and Jong Bum Kwon. 2012. Abstract for Session, "Anthropologies of Unemployment: Disciplinary Borders and Crossings in the Study of Unemployment." Annual Meeting of the American Anthropological Association. San Francisco.

Lang, Kevin, and Jee-Yeon K. Lehman. 2011. "Racial Discrimination in the Labor Market: Theory and Empirics." NBER Working Paper Series. Cambridge, MA: National Bureau of Economic Research.

Lapeyronnie, Didier. 2009. "Primitive Rebellion in the French *Banlieues*: On the Fall 2005 Riots," In *Frenchness and the African Diaspora: Identity and Uprising in Contemporary France*, edited by Charles Tshimanga, Didier Gondola, and Peter J. Bloom, 21–46. Bloomington: Indiana University Press.

Largen, Stephen. 2013. "Democrats: Haley Declaring War on Rural S.C. with Unemployment Office Moves." *The Post and Courier*, February 6.

Latour, Bruno. 2004. "How to Talk About the Body? The Normative Dimension of Science Studies." *Body and Society* 10, nos. 2–3:205–229.

Lavaud, Catherine, and Geneviève Simonneau. 2010. *Le Limousin peine à retenir ses jeunes diplômés*. Paris: INSEE.

Layne, Linda. 2000. "The Cultural Fix: An Anthropological Contribution to Science and Technology Studies." *Science, Technology, and Human Values* 25, no. 4:492–519.

Le Monde. 2005. "Le Ministre de l'Emploi fait de la polygamie une 'cause possible' des violences urbaines." November 16.

Lee, Don. 2014. "Long-term Unemployed Still at Record Levels." *Los Angeles Times*, September 10. Accessed September 26, 2015. Available at www.latimes.com/business/la-fi-longterm-jobless-20140910-story.html#page=1.

Lenoir, René. 1974. *Les Exclus: un Français sur dix*. Paris: Seuil.

Lepoutre, David. 1997. *Cœur de banlieue: codes, rites et langages*. Paris: Odile Jacob.

Letkemann, Paul G. 2005. "Learning and Knowledge in an Office Workplace: Perceptions of the Recently Unemployed." *Anthropology of Work Review* 26, no. 2:8–11.

Levine, Donald. 1965. *Wax and Gold: Tradition and Innovation in Ethiopian Culture*. Chicago: University of Chicago Press.

——. 1974. *Greater Ethiopia: The Evolution of a Multiethnic Society*. Chicago: University of Chicago Press.

Limoges Municipal Council. 2007. *Un PLU pour aujourd'hui et pour demain*.

Lindenboim, Javier. 2008. "Auge y declinación del trabajo y los ingresos en el siglo corto de la Argentina." In *Trabajo, ingresos y políticas en Argentina: contribuciones para pensar el siglo XXI*, edited by Javier Lindenboim, 23–67. Buenos Aires: Eudeba.

Lindstrom, David. 1996. "Economic Opportunity in Mexico and Return Migration from the United States." *Demography* 33, no. 3:357–374.

Lipman, Pauline. 2011. *The New Political Economy of Urban Education: Neoliberalism, Race, and the Right to the City (Critical Social Thought)*. New York: Routledge.

Lippman, Steven A., and John J. McCall. 1976. "The Economics of Job Search: A Survey." *Economic Inquiry* 14, no. 2:115–189.

Lowrey, Annie. 2013. "Caught in a Revolving Door of Unemployment." *New York Times*, November 17. Accessed November 17, 2013. Available at www.nytimes.com/2013/11/17/business/caught-in-unemployments-revolving-door.html.

Luhrmann, Tanya M. 2012. *When God Talks Back: Understanding the American Evangelical Relationship with God*. New York: Vintage.

Lutz, Catherine. 1986. "Emotion, Thoughts, and Estrangement: Emotion as a Cultural Category." *Cultural Anthropology* 1, no. 3: 287–309.

Lynch, Caitrin. 2007. *Juki Girls, Good Girls: Gender and Cultural Politics in Sri Lanka's Global Garment Industry*. Ithaca: Cornell University Press.

——. 2012. *Retirement on the Line: Age, Work, and Value in an American Factory*. Ithaca: Cornell University Press.

MacGaffey, Janet, and Remy Bazenguissa-Ganga. 2000. *Congo-Paris: Transnational Traders on the Margins of the Law*. Oxford: James Currey.

MacLeod, Greg. 1997. *From Mondragón to America: Experiments in Community Economic Development*. Sydney, Canada: Cape Breton University Press.

Mains, Daniel. 2007. "Neoliberal Times: Progress, Boredom, and Shame among Young Men in Urban Ethiopia." *American Ethnologist* 34, no. 4:659–673.

———. 2012. *Hope Is Cut: Youth, Unemployment, and the Future in Urban Ethiopia*. Philadelphia: Temple University Press.

Malkin, Elisabeth, and Simon Romero. 2012. "World Leaders Meet in a Mexico Now Giving Brazil a Run for Its Money." *New York Times*, June 17, p. C3.

Malkin, Victoria. 2004. "We Go to Get Ahead: Gender and Status in Two Mexican Migrant Communities." *Latin American Perspectives* 31, no. 5:75–99.

———. 2007. "Reproduction of Gender Relations in the Mexican Community of New Rochelle, New York." In *Women and Migration in the U.S.-Mexico Borderlands*, edited by Denise Segura and Patricia Zavella, 415–437. Durham: Duke University Press.

Marcus, George, and Michael Fischer. 1986. *Anthropology as Cultural Critique: An Experimental Moment in the Human Sciences*. Chicago: University of Chicago Press.

Marsac, Annette, and Vincent Brousse. 2005. "Les lieux de l'immigration ouvrière en Limousin," In *Un siècle militant. Engagement(s), résistance(s) et mémoire(s) au XXe siècle en Limousin*, edited by Vincent Brousse and Philippe Grandcoing, 147–186. Limoges, France: Presses Universitaires de Limoges.

Marschall, Daniel. 2012. *The Company We Keep: Occupational Community in the High-Tech Network Society*. Philadelphia: Temple University Press.

Martin, Emily. 1995. *Flexible Bodies: The Role of Immunity in American Culture from the Days of Polio to the Age of AIDS*. Boston: Beacon Press.

Marx, Karl. 1977 [1867]. *Capital*. Vol. 1. London: Vintage.

Masferrer, Claudia, and Bryan Roberts. 2012. "Going Back Home? Changing Demography and Geography of Mexican Return Migration." *Population Research Policy Review* 31:465–496.

Mattingly, Doreen. 1999. "Job Search, Networks, and Local Labor Dynamics." *Urban Geography* 20, no. 1:46–74.

Maurin, Éric. 2004. *Le ghetto français*. Paris: Seuil.

Mauss, Marcel. 1979. *Sociología y Antropología*. Madrid: Tecnos.

Mayer, Gerald. 2010. *The Trend in Long-Term Unemployment and Characteristics of Workers Unemployed for More than 99 Weeks*. Washington, D.C.: Congressional Research Service.

McAdams, Dan P. 2006. *The Redemptive Self: Stories Americans Live By*. New York: Oxford.

McNaughton, Patrick. 1993. *The Mande Blacksmiths: Knowledge, Power, and Art in West Africa*. Bloomington: Indiana University Press.

Mdembe, Achille. 2009a. "Figures of Multiplicity: Can France Reinvent Its Identity." In *Frenchness and the African Diaspora: Identity and Uprising in Contemporary France*, edited by Charles Tshimanga, Didier Gondola, and Peter J. Bloom, 55–69. Bloomington: Indiana University Press.

———. 2009b. "The Republic and Its Beats: On the Riots in the French *Banlieues*." In *Frenchness and the African Diaspora: Identity and Uprising in Contemporary France*, edited by Charles Tshimanga, Didier Gondola, and Peter J. Bloom, 47–54. Bloomington: Indiana University Press.

Meda, Dominique. 1995. *Le Travail, une valeur en voie de disparition?* Paris: Alto/Aubier.

Meister, Jeanne. 2012. "Job Hopping Is the 'New Normal' for Millennials: Three Ways to Prevent a Human Resource Nightmare." *Forbes*, August 14. Accessed April 2, 2013. Available at www.forbes.com/sites/jeannemeister/2012/08/14/job-hopping-is-the-new-normal-for-millennials-three-ways-to-prevent-a-human-resource-nightmare/.

Méndez, Jennifer Bickham. 2005. *From Revolution to Maquiladoras: Gender, Labor, and Globalization in Nicaragua*. Durham: Duke University Press.

Menjívar, Cecilia. 2000. *Fragmented Ties: Salvadoran Immigrant Networks in America*. Berkeley: University of California Press.

Merriman, John M. 1985. *The Red City: Limoges and the French Nineteenth Century*. New York: Oxford University Press.

Metcalfe, A. W. 1990. "The Demonology of Class: The Iconography of the Coalminer and the Symbolic Construction of Political Boundaries." *Critique of Anthropology* 10, no. 1:39–63.

Millar, Kathleen M. 2014. "The Precarious Present: Wageless Labor and Disrupted Life in Rio De Janeiro, Brazil." *Cultural Anthropology* 29, no. 1:32–53.

Mirowski, Philip. 1989. *More Heat Than Light: Economics as Social Physics, Physics as Nature's Economics*. Cambridge: Cambridge University Press.

Mishel, Lawrence, Jared Bernstein, and Heather Boushey. 2003. *The State of Working America, 2002–03*. Washington, D.C.: Economic Policy Institute.

Mitchell, Timothy. 1998. "Fixing the Economy." *Cultural Studies* 12:82–101.

Miyazaki, Hirokazu. 2004. *The Method of Hope: Anthropology, Philosophy, and Fijian Knowledge*. Stanford: Stanford University Press.

———. 2006. "Economy of Dreams: Hope in Global Capitalism and Its Critiques." *Cultural Anthropology* 21, no. 2:147–172.

———. 2010. "The Temporality of No Hope." In *Ethnographies of Neoliberalism*, edited by Carol J. Greenhouse, 238–250. Philadelphia: University of Pennsylvania Press.

Molé, Noelle J. 2012. "Hauntings of Solidarity in Post-Fordist Italy." *Anthropological Quarterly* 85, no. 2:371–396.

Montiel Torres, Marco Antonio. 2014. "Sobrevivir a la Crisis: Los comerciantes de ropa de la región Puebla-Tlaxcala en el contexto de lacrisis económica de 2008." Ph.D. diss. Centro de Investigaciones y Estudios Superiores.

Moon, Seungsook. 2005. "Trouble with Conscription, Entertaining Soldiers: Popular Culture and the Politics of Militarized Masculinity in South Korea." *Men and Masculinities* 8, no. 1:64–92.

Moore, Thomas. 1996. *The Disposable Work Force*. New York: Aldine.

Moss, Philip, and Chris Tilly. 2001. *Stories Employers Tell*. New York: Russell Sage Foundation.

Mossberger, Karen, Caroline J. Tolbert, and Mary Stansbury. 2003. *Virtual Inequality: Beyond the Digital Divide*. Washington, D.C.: Georgetown University Press.

Muehlebach, Andrea and Nitzan Shoshan. 2012. "Introduction (A Special Collection: Post-Fordist Affect)." *Anthropological Quarterly* 85, no. 2:317–344.

Mulinari, Diana. 1995. *Motherwork and Politics in Revolutionary Nicaragua*. Lund, Sweden: Bokbox Publications.

Munck, Ronaldo, Carl Schierup, and Raul Delgado Wise. 2011. "Migration, Work, and Citizenship in the New World Order." *Globalizations* 8, no. 3:249–260.

Murphy, James Bernard. 1994. *The Moral Economy of Labor*. New Haven: Yale University Press.

Murphy, John P. 2011a. "Baguettes, Berets, and Burning Cars: The 2005 Riots and the Question of Race in Contemporary France." *French Cultural Studies* 22, no. 1:33–49.

———. 2011b. "Protest or Riot? Interpreting Collective Action in Contemporary France." *Anthropological Quarterly* 84, no. 4:977–1008.

Nading, Alex. 2014. *Mosquito Trails: Ecology, Health, and the Politics of Entanglement*. Berkeley: University of California Press.

Nash, June, ed. 1993. *Crafts in the World Market: The Impact of Global Exchange on Middle American Artisans*. Albany: State University of New York Press.

National Bureau of Economic Research. 2010. Business Cycle Dating Committee Report, September. Cambridge, Massachusetts: National Bureau of Economic Research. Accessed August 27, 2013. Available at www.nber.org/cycles/sept2010.html.

Ndiaye, Pap. 2008. *La condition noire. Essai sur une minorité française.* Paris: Calmann-Lévy.

Negash, Tekeste. 1996. *Rethinking Education in Ethiopia.* Uppsala, Sweden: Nordiska Afrikainstitutet.

Neilson, Brett, and Ned Rossiter. 2005. "From Precarity to Precariousness and Back Again: Labour, Life, and Unstable Networks." *Fibreculture Journal* 5. Available at http://five.fibreculturejournal.org/fcj-022-from-precarity-to-precariousness-and-back-again-labour-life-and-unstable-networks/.

——. 2008. "Precarity as a Political Concept, or, Fordism as Exception." *Theory, Culture, and Society* 25, nos. 7–8:51–72.

Nelson, Laura C. 2000. *Measured Excess: Status, Gender, and Consumer Nationalism in South Korea.* New York: Columbia University Press.

Newell, Sasha. 2005. "Migratory Modernity and the Cosmology of Consumption in Cote d'Ivoire." In *Migration and Economy: Global and Local Dynamics*, edited by Lillian Trager, 163–190. Walnut Creek, CA: Altamira Press.

Newman, Katherine. 1988. *Falling from Grace: Downward Mobility in the Age of Affluence.* Berkeley: University of California Press.

——. 1993. *Declining Fortunes: The Withering of the American Dream.* New York: Basic Books.

——. 2012. *The Accordion Family: Boomerang Kids, Anxious Parents, and the Private Toll of Global Competition.* Boston: Beacon Press.

Ngai, Pun. 2005. *Made in China: Women Factory Workers in a Global Workplace.* Durham: Duke University Press.

Nicole-Drancourt, Chantal. 1992. "L'idée de précarité revisitée." *Travail et emploi* 52:57–70.

Noiriel, Gérard. 1990. *Workers in French Society in the Nineteenth and Twentieth Centuries.* New York: Berg.

Olavarría, José. 2003. "Men at Home? Child Rearing and Housekeeping among Chilean Working-Class Fathers." In *Changing Men and Masculinities in Latin America*, edited by M. C. Gutmann, 333–350. Durham: Duke University Press.

Omi, Michael, and Howard Winant. 1994. *Racial Formation in the United States: From the 1960s to the 1990s.* New York: Routledge.

Ong, Aihwa. 1987. *Spirits of Resistance and Capitalist Discipline: Factory Women in Malaysia.* Albany: State University of New York Press.

——. 2006. *Neoliberalism as Exception: Mutations in Citizenship and Sovereignty.* Durham: Duke University Press.

Orenstein, Dara. 2011. "Foreign-Trade Zones and the Cultural Logic of Frictionless Production." *Radical History Review* 109:36–61.

Osnowitz, Debra. 2010. *Freelancing Expertise: Contract Professionals in the New Economy.* Ithaca: Cornell University Press.

Pager, Deborah, Roland Fryer, and Jorg Spenkuch. 2011. "Racial Disparities in Job Finding and Offered Wages." National Bureau of Economic Research Working Paper 17462. Available at www.nber.org/papers/w17462.

Pager, Deborah, Bruce Western, and Bart Bonikowski. 2009. "Discrimination in a Low Wage Labor Market: A Field Experiment." *American Sociological Review* 74:777–799.

Paiva, Verónica. 2006. "El Cirujeo. Un Camino Informal de Recuperación de Residuos. Buenos Aires. 2002–2003." *Estudios Demograficos Y Urbanos* 21, no. 1:189–210.

———. 2007. "Cooperativas de Recuperadores de Residuos Del Area Metropolitana de Buenos Aires." *Recicloscopio. Miradas Sobre Recuperadores Urbanos de Residuos de América Latina.* Buenos Aires: UNLa-UNGS-Prometeo.

———. 2008. *Cartoneros y cooperativas de recuperadores: una mirada sobre la recolección informal de residuos. Área Metropolitana de Buenos Aires, 1999–2007.* Buenos Aires: Prometeo Libros.

Pankhurst, Alula. 2003. "Introduction: Dimensions and Conceptions of Marginalisation." In *Peripheral People: The Excluded Minorities of Ethiopia*, edited by Dena Freeman and Alula Pankhurst, 1–26. Lawrenceville, NJ: Red Sea Press.

Pankhurst, Alula, and Dena Freeman. 2003. "Conclusion II: Change and Development: Lessons from the Twentieth Century." In *Peripheral People: The Excluded Minorities of Ethiopia*, edited by Dena Freeman and Alula Pankhurst, 334–366. Lawrenceville, NJ: Red Sea Press.

Pappas, Gregory. 1989. *The Magic City: Unemployment in a Working-Class Community.* Ithaca: Cornell University Press.

Parsons, Sandra. 2012. "Why So Many 20-Year-Olds Are Failing to Grow Up." *Daily Mail.* July 31. Accessed May 15, 2014. Available at www.dailymail.co.uk/debate/article-2181789/Why-20-year-olds-failing-grow-up.html.

Passel, Jeffrey, D. Cohn, and A. Gonzalez-Barrera. 2012. "Net Migration from Mexico Falls to Zero—and Perhaps Less." Washington, D.C.: Pew Hispanic Center. Accessed November, 3, 2012. Available at www.pewhispanic.org/2014/09/03/as-growth-stalls-unauthorized-immigrant-population-becomes-more-settled/.

Patico, Jennifer. 2008. *Consumption and Social Change in a Post-Soviet Middle Class.* Stanford: Stanford University Press.

Patterson, Thomas C. 1998. "Flexible Accumulation, Flexible Labor, and their Consequences." *Critique of Anthropology* 18:317–319.

Paugam, Serge. 2000. "L'exclusion, usages sociaux et apports de la recherche." In *La sociologie française contemporaine*, edited by Jean-Michel Berthelot, 155–171. Paris: Presses Universitaires de France.

Paugam, Serge, and Helen Russell. 2000. "The Effects of Employment Precarity and Unemployment on Social Isolation." In *Welfare Regimes and the Experience of Unemployment in Europe*, edited by Duncan Gallie and Serge Paugam, 243–264. Oxford: Oxford University Press.

Peale, Norman Vincent. 1952. *The Power of Positive Thinking.* New York: Prentice-Hall.

Peck, Jamie, and Nik Theodore. 2007. "Flexible Recession: The Temporary Staffing Industry and Mediated Work in the United States." *Cambridge Journal of Economics* 31, no. 2:171–192.

Perelman, Mariano D. 2007a. "El Cirujeo ¿rebusque O Trabajo? Un Análisis a Partir de Las Transformaciones de La Actividad En La Ciudad de Buenos Aires." In *Recicloscopio. Miradas Sobre Recolectores Urbanos de Residuos En Amércia Latina*, edited by Pablo Schamber and Francisco Suárez, 245–267. Buenos Aires: UNLa-UNGS-Prometeo.

———. 2007b. "Theorizing Unemployment: Toward an Argentine Anthropology of Work." *Anthropology of Work Review* 28, no. 1:8–13.

———. 2010. "Memórias de La Quema. O Cirujeo Em Buenos Aires Trinta Anos Depois." *Mana* 16, no. 2:375–399.

———. 2011a. "La estabilización en el cirujeo de la ciudad de Buenos Aires. Una aproximación desde la antropología." *Desarrollo Económico. Revista de Ciencias Sociales* 51, no. 201: 35–57.

———. 2011b. "La Construcción de La Idea de Trabajo Digno En Los Cirujas de La Ciudad de Buenos Aires." *Intersecciones En Antropología* 12, no. 1:69–81.

———. 2012. "Caracterizando La Recolección Informal En La Ciudad de Buenos Aires." *Latin American Reseach Review* 47 (Special Issue).

Perlin. Ross. 2013. "Unpaid Interns: Silent No More." *New York Times*, July 20. Accessed May 15, 2014. Available at www.nytimes.com/2013/07/21/jobs/unpaid-interns-silent-no-more.html.

Petras, James. 2002. "The Unemployed Workers Movement in Argentina." *Monthly Review* 53, no. 8. Accessed September 29, 2015. Available at http://monthlyreview.org/2002/01/01/the-unemployed-workers-movement-in-argentina/.

Piot, Charles. 2005. "Border Practices: Playing the U.S. Diversity Visa Lottery." Paper presented at the African Studies Association Annual Meeting, Washington, D.C., November 17–20.

———. 2010. *Nostalgia for the Future: West Africa after the Cold War*. Chicago: Chicago University Press.

Pirie, Iain. 2008. *The Korean Developmental State: From Dirigisme to Neo-Liberalism*. New York: Routledge.

Plumer, Brad. 2012. "How Worrisome is the Rise of Involuntary Part-Time Workers?" *Washington Post*, October 9. Accessed April 8, 2013. Available at www.washingtonpost.com/blogs/wonkblog/wp/2012/10/09/who-are-americas-part-time-workers.

Polanyi, Karl. 1957. *The Great Transformation*. New York: Rinehart.

Poluha, Eva. 2004. *The Power of Continuity: Ethiopia through the Eyes of Its Children*. Uppsala, Sweden: Nordiska Afrikainstitutet.

Porter, Michael E. 2000. "Attitudes, Values, Beliefs, and the Microeconomics of Prosperity." In *Culture Matters: How Values Shape Human Progress*, edited by L. E. Harrison and S. P. Huntington, 14–28. New York: Basic Books.

Preston, Julia. 2012. "Mexican Immigration to U.S. Slowed Significantly, Report Says." *New York Times*, April 23. Accessed September 26, 2015. Available at www.nytimes.com/2012/04/24/us/mexican-immigration-to-united-states-slows.html.

Quirós, Julieta. 2011. *El Porqué de Los Que van: Peronistas Y Piqueteros En El Gran Buenos Aires: Una Antropología de La Política Vivida*. 1st. ed. Buenos Aires: Editorial Antropofagia.

Ralph, Michael. 2008. "Killing Time." *Social Text 97* 26, no. 4:1–29.

Rampell, Catherine. 2011. "The Help-Wanted Sign Comes with a Frustrating Asterisk." *New York Times*, July 25. Accessed September 26, 2015. Available at www.nytimes.com/2011/07/26/business/help-wanted-ads-exclude-the-long-term-jobless.html.

Rancière, Jacques, John Drury, Corinne Oster, and Andrew Parker. 2004. *The Philosopher and His Poor*. Durham: Duke University Press.

Renahy, Nicolas. 2005. *Les gars du coin: enquête sur une jeunesse rurale*. Paris: La Découverte.

Rendall, Michael S., Peter Brownell, and Sarah Kups. 2011. "Declining Return Migration from the United States to Mexico in the Late-2000s Recession: A Research Note." *Demography* 48:1049–1058.

Reyes, Belinda. 1997. *Dynamics of Immigration: Return Migration to Western Mexico*. San Francisco: Public Policy Institute of California.

Reynals, Cristina. 2002. "De Cartoneros a Recuperadores Urbanos." *Respuestas de La Sociedad Civil a La Emergencia Social: Brasil Y Argentina Comparten Experiencias*. San Pablo: Postgrado en Organizaciones sin Fines de Lucro y el Centro de Emprendorismo Social e Administração em Terceiro Sector, Facultad de Economia, Administração e Contabilidade, Universidad de San Pablo, Brasil.

Richardson, Tyrone. 2014. "South Carolina to Overhaul Unemployment Benefit System." *The Post and Courier*, January 8.

Rivlin, Gary. 2013. "The Long Shadow of Bad Credit in a Job Search." *New York Times*, May 11.

Roberman, Sveta. 2013. "All That Is Just Ersatz: The Meaning of Work in the Life of Immigrant Newcomers." *Ethos* 41, no. 1:1–23.

Rofel, Lisa. 1999. *Other Modernities: Gendered Yearnings in China After Socialism.* Berkeley: University of California Press.

———. 2007. *Desiring China: Experiments in Neoliberalism, Sexuality, and Public Culture.* Berkeley: University of California Press.

Rogers, Ali. 2009. "Recession, Vulnerable Workers and Migration." Working Paper. Oxford: COMPAS. Accessed February 3, 2012. Available at www.compas.ox.ac.uk/fileadmin/files/Publications/Research_projects/Labour_markets/Labour%20Mrkt%20and%20Recession%20Full%20Report.pdf.

Rogers, Jackie Krasas. 2000. *Temps: The Many Faces of the Changing Workplace.* Ithaca: Cornell University Press.

Rose, Nikolas. 1992. "Governing the Enterprising Self." In *The Values of the Enterprise Culture: The Moral Debate*, edited by Paul Heelas and Paul Morris, 141–164. London: Routledge.

Rose, Dina R., and Todd R. Clear. 1998. "Incarceration, Social Capital, and Crime: Implications for Social Disorganization Theory." *Criminology* 36, no. 3:441–480.

Ross, Andrew. 2003. *No-Collar: The Humane Workplace and its Hidden Costs.* Philadelphia: Temple University Press.

———. 2009. *Nice Work If You Can Get It: Life and Labor in Precarious Times.* New York: New York University Press.

Rothstein, Frances Abrahamer. 1982. *Three Different Worlds: Women, Men, and Children in an Industrializing Community.* Westport, CT: Greenwood Press.

———. 1999. "Declining Odds: Kinship, Women's Employment, and Political Economy in Rural Mexico." *American Anthropologist* 101:579–593.

———. 2007. *Globalization in Rural Mexico: Three Decades of Change.* Austin: University of Texas Press.

———. 2010. "New Migrants in a New Age: Globalization, Networks and Gender in Rural Mexico." In *Class, Contention, and a World in Motion*, edited by Winnie Lem and Pauline Gardiner Barber. London: Berghahn Books.

———. 2012. "Not Just Migrants: Men and Women on the Move in Rural Mexico." Paper presented at the Annual Meeting of the American Ethnological Society, New York, NY, April 20.

———. 2014. "Kinship Networks and Caring among Mexicans at Home and in the United States." Paper presented at the Annual Meeting of the American Anthropological Association, Washington, D.C., November 19.

———. 2015. "'Porque Las Raizes No Se Olvidan': Continuity and Change among Mexican Migrants in New Jersey." *Bulletin of Latin American Research* 34, no. 1:85–98.

———. 2016. *Mexicans on the Move: Migration and Return Migration.* New York: Palgrave Macmillan.

Roy, Olivier. 2005. "The Nature of the French Riots." Accessed August 12, 2014. Available at http://riotsfrance.ssrc.org/Roy/.

Royster, Deidre. 2003. *Race and the Invisible Hand.* Berkeley: University of California Press.

Sanford, Mark. 2009. "Governor Sanford Welcomes Boeing to South Carolina." Press release from the Office of Gov. Mark Sanford. Benjamin D. Fox, communications director. Columbia, SC: October 28.

Sassen, Saskia. 1988. *The Mobility of Labor and Capital: A Study of International Investment and Labor Flow.* Cambridge: Cambridge University Press.

Scarry, Elaine. 1994. *Resisting Representation.* New York: Oxford University Press.

Schamber, Pablo. 2008. *De Los Desechos a Las Mercancías: Una Etnografía de Los Cartoneros.* Buenos Aires: SB.

Schamber, Pablo, and Francisco Suárez, eds. 2007. *Recicloscopio. Miradas Sobre Recolectores Urbanos de Residuos En Amércia Latina*. Buenos Aires: UNLa-UNGS-Prometeo.

Schawbel, Dan. 2009. *Me 2.0: Building a Powerful Brand to Achieve Career Success*. New York: Kaplan Publishing.

Scheper-Hughes, Nancy. 1992. *Death without Weeping: The Violence of Everyday Life in Brazil*. Berkeley: University of California Press.

Schmalzbauer, Leah, Alice Verghese, and Meenu Vadera. 2007. "Caring for Survival: Motherwork and Sustainable Feminisms." *Advances in Gender Research*, vol. 11, edited by Sonita Sarker, 43–56.

Schwartz, Olivier. 1990. *Le monde privé des ouvriers: hommes et femmes du Nord*. Paris: Presses Universitaires de France.

Screpanti, Ernesto. 2001. *The Fundamental Institutions of Capitalism*. London: Routledge.

Seery, Emma, and Ana Caistor Arendar. 2014. *Even It Up: Time to End Extreme Inequality*. Oxford: Oxfam International.

Segall, Jordan. 2011. "Mass Incarceration, Ex-Felon Discrimination, and Black Labor Market Disadvantage." *University of Pennsylvania Journal of Law and Social Change* 14:159–182.

Seigworth, Gregory J., and Melissa Gregg. 2010. "An Inventory of Shimmers." In *The Affect Theory Reader*, edited by Melissa Gregg and Gregory Seigworth, 1–51. Durham: Duke University Press.

Seligman, Martin E. P. 1990. *Learned Optimism: How to Change Your Mind and Your Life*. New York: A. A. Knopf.

Sennett, Richard. 1998. *The Corrosion of Character: The Personal Consequences of Work in the New Capitalism*. New York: W. W. Norton & Co.

Seo, Dongjin. 2011. "The Will to Self-Managing, the Will to Freedom: The Self-Managing Ethic and the Spirit of Flexible Capitalism in South Korea." In *Millennium South Korea: Neoliberal Capitalism and Transnational Movements*, edited by Jesook Song, 84–100. New York: Routledge.

Serneels, Pieter. 2004. *The Nature of Unemployment in Ethiopia*. Oxford: Center for the Study of African Economies.

Sewell, William H. 1980. *Work and Revolution in France: The Language of Labor from the Old Regime to 1848*. Cambridge: Cambridge University Press.

Sharone, Ofer. 2014. *Flawed System/Flawed Self: Job Searching and Unemployment Experiences*. Chicago: University of Chicago Press.

Sharp, Lesley. 2002. *The Sacrificed Generation: Youth, History, and the Colonized Mind in Madagascar*. Berkeley: University of California Press.

Shierholz, Heidi, and Lawrence Mishel. 2009. "Highest Unemployment Rate since 1983." June 16. Accessed March 26, 2010. Available at www.epi.org/publications/entry/jobspict_2009_july_preview/.

Sigaud, Lygia. 1996. "Direito E Coerção Moral No Mundo Dos Engenhos." *Estudos Históricos* 9, no. 18:361–388.

Simmel, Georg. 1978. *The Philosophy of Money*. London: Routledge.

Smith, Aaron. 2015. The Internet and Job Seeking. Report. Pew Research Center. Accessed February 10, 2015. Available at www.pewinternet.org/2015/11/19/1-the-internet-and-job-seeking/.

Smith, Joan, and Immanuel Wallerstein. 1992. *Creating and Transforming Households: The Constraints of the World-Economy*. Thousand Oaks, CA: Sage.

Smith, Joan, Immanuel Wallerstein, and Hans-Deiter Evers, eds. 1984. *Households and the World Economy*. Thousand Oaks, CA: Sage.

Smith, Vicki. 2001. *Crossing the Great Divide: Worker Risk and Opportunity in the New Economy*. Ithaca: Cornell University Press.

Song, Jesook. 2009. *South Koreans in the Debt Crisis: The Creation of a Neoliberal Welfare Society*. Durham: Duke University Press.

South Carolina Department of Commerce. 2013. "South Carolina: Just Right." Columbia: South Carolina Department of Commerce.

South Carolina Educational TV. 2012. "The Big Picture. Boeing." Interview with South Carolina Commerce Secretary Bobby Hitt by Beryl Dakers. May 10.

Spradlin, J. Isaac. 2009. "The Evolution of Interns." *Forbes*, April 27. Accessed May 15, 2014. Available at www.forbes.com/2009/04/27/intern-history-apprenticeship-leadership-careers-jobs.html.

Staber, Udo. 1993. "Worker Cooperatives and the Business Cycle: Are Cooperatives the Answer to Unemployment?" *American Journal of Economics and Sociology* 52, no. 2:129–143.

Stack, Carol. 1975. *All Our Kin: Strategies for Surviving in a Black Community*. New York: Basic Books.

———. 1996. *Call to Home: African Americans Reclaiming the Rural South*. New York: Basic Books.

Standing, Guy. 2011. *The Precariat: The New Dangerous Class*. New York: Bloomsbury Academic.

Steger, Manfred B., and Ravi K. Roy. 2010. *Neoliberalism: A Very Short Introduction*. New York: Oxford University Press.

Stephen, Lynn. 2005a. *Zapotec Women: Gender, Class, and Ethnicity in Globalized Oaxaca*. Durham: Duke University Press.

———. 2005b. "Women's Weaving Cooperatives in Oaxaca: An Indigenous Response to Neoliberalism." *Critique of Anthropology* 25:253–278.

Stettner, Andrew, and Jeffrey Wenger. 2003. "The Broad Reach of Long-Term Unemployment." *Economic Policy Institute Issue*. Brief 194. May 15.

Strauss, Claudia. 2002. "Not-So-Rugged Individualists: U.S. Americans' Conflicting Ideas about Poverty." In *Work, Welfare, and Politics: Confronting Poverty in the Wake of Welfare Reform*, edited by Frances Fox Piven, Joan Acker, Margaret Hallock, and Sandra Morgen. Eugene: University of Oregon Press.

———. 2012. *Making Sense of Public Opinion: American Discourses about Immigration and Social Programs*. New York: Cambridge University Press.

Strully, Kate W. 2009. "Job Loss and Health in the U.S. Labor Market." *Demography* 46, no. 2:221–246.

Suárez, Francisco. 1998. "'Que Las Recojan Y Arrojen Fuera de La Ciudad,' Historia de La Gestión de Los Residuos Sólidos (las Basuras) En Buenos Aires." Documento de Trabajo no. 8. Universidad Nacional de General Sarmiento.

———. 2001. *Actores Sociales En La Gestión de Residuos Sólidos de Los Municipios de Malvinas Argentinas Y José C. Paz*. Tesis de Maestría en Políticas Ambientales y Territoriales, Universidad de Buenos Aires.

Susser, Ida, and Nila Chatterjee. 1998. "Critiquing Flexible Labor." *Critique of Anthropology* 18:243–244.

Sutton, Barbara. 2008. "Gendered Bodily Scars of Neoliberal Globalization in Argentina." In *The Gender of Globalization: Women Navigating Cultural and Economic Marginalities*, edited by Ann Kingsolver and Nandini Gunewardena, 147–168. Santa Fe, NM: School for Advanced Research Press.

Suvankulov, Farrukh. 2010. "Job Search on the Internet, E-Recruitment, and Labor Market Outcomes." Ph.D. diss., RAND Graduate School.

Svampa, Maristella. 2005. *La Sociedad Excluyente. La Argentina Bajo El Signo Del Neoliberalismo*. Buenos Aires: Taurus.

Taussig, Michael. 1980. *The Devil and Commodity Fetishism in South America*. Chapel Hill: University of North Carolina Press.

———. 1987. *Shamanism, Colonialism, and the Wild Man: A Study in Terror and Healing*. Chicago: University of Chicago Press.

Taylor, Charles. 1996. *Fuentes del yo. La construcción de la identidad moderna*. Barcelona: Paidós.

Terkel, Studs. 1997 [1975]. *Working: People Talk About What They Do All Day and How They Feel About What They Do*. New York: New Press.

Terrail, Jean-Pierre. 1990. *Destins ouvriers: La fin d'une classe?* Paris: Presses Universitaires de France.

Thompson, E. P. 1963. *The Making of the English Working Class*. New York: Random House.

Torre, Juan Carlos, and Elisa Pastoriza. 2002. "La democratización del bienestar." In *Nueva historia Argentina T. 8, Los años peronistas (1943–1955)*, edited by Juan Carlos Torre, 257–312. Buenos Aires: Editorial Sudamericana.

Torres, Alicia. 1996. "When Weak Ties Fail: Shame, Reciprocity, and Unemployed Professionals." MA thesis, University of California Santa Barbara.

Townsend, Nicholas. 2002. *The Package Deal: Marriage, Work, and Fatherhood in Men's Lives*. Philadelphia: Temple University Press.

Turner, Edgar. 2010. *The Birth of the 787 Dreamliner*. Kansas City: Andrews McMeel Publishing.

Turner, Victor. 1967. *The Forest of Symbols: Aspects of Ndembu Ritual*. Ithaca: Cornell University Press.

Uchitelle, Louis. 2006. *The Disposable American: Layoffs and Their Consequences*. New York: Vintage Books.

UNIDO (United Nations Industrial Development Organization). 2009. *The Global Financial Crisis and the Developing World: Transmission Channels and Fall-Out for Industrial Development*. New York: United Nations Industrial Development Organization.

United Nations DESA (Department of Economic and Social Affairs). 2011. "The Global Social Crisis: Report on the World Social Situation." Available at www.un.org/esa/socdev/rwss/docs/2011/rwss2011.pdf

Urciuoli, Bonnie. 2008. "Skills and Selves in the New Workplace." *American Ethnologist* 35:211–228.

USAID (United States Agency for International Development). 2006. *Central America and Mexico Gang Assessment*. United States Agency for International Development. Accessed September 29, 2015. Available at http://pdf.usaid.gov/pdf_docs/PNADG834.pdf.

Van Hook, Jennifer, and W. Zhang. 2011. "Who Stays? Who Goes? Selective Emigration among the Foreign-Born." *Population Research Policy Review* 30:1–24.

Vieillard-Baron, Hervé. 1998. *Banlieue, ghetto impossible?* Paris: Éditions de l'Aube.

Vigoya, Mara Viveros. 2001. "Contemporary Latin American Perspectives on Masculinity." *Men and Masculinities* 3, no. 3:237–260.

Villarreal, Juan. 1985. "Los Hilos Sociales Del Poder." *Crisis de La Dictadura Argentina. Política Económica Y Cambio Social (1976–1983)*. Buenos Aires: Siglo Veintiuno Editores.

Virick, Meghna. 2003. "Research Report: The Effect of Layoffs in the North Texas Region." Dallas: North Texas Technology Council and University of Texas at Arlington.

Wacquant, Loïc. 1995. "Pugs at Work: Bodily Capital and Bodily Labour among Professional Boxers." *Body and Society* 1, no. 1:65–93.

———. 2008. *Urban Outcasts: A Comparative Sociology of Advanced Marginality*. Cambridge, U.K. and Malden, MA: Polity Press.

Wale-Adegbite, Funmi. 2011. "Young and Unemployed." *BBC News Africa*. July 20. Available at www.bbc.com/news/world-africa-14201223.

Walkerdine, Valerie. 2006. "Workers in the New Economy: Transformation as Border Crossing." *Ethos* 34, no. 1:10–41.

Weeks, Kathi. 2011. *The Problem with Work: Feminism, Marxism, Antiwork Politics, and Postwork Imaginaries*. Durham: Duke University Press.

Weiss, Brad. 2002. "Thug Realism: Inhabiting Fantasy in Urban Tanzania." *Cultural Anthropology* 17, no. 1:93–124.

———. 2004. "Contentious Futures: Past and Present." In *Producing African Futures: Ritual and Reproduction in a Neoliberal Age*, edited by Brad Weiss. Leiden: Brill.

Welkowitz, William D. 2015. "U.S. Supreme Court May Ultimately Have the Final Word on the Future of Unpaid Internships in the Private Sector." 26 October. FLSA Litigation Tracker, Special Report. Available at http://www.unpaidinternslawsuit.com/images/documents/Unpaid-Interns-Special-Report-BNA.pdf.

Welsh, Patrick. 2002. "Los Hombres No Son de Matre: Desapriendiendo el Machismo en Nicaragua." Catholic Institute for International Relations.

Williams, Raymond. 1983. *Keywords: A Vocabulary of Culture and Society*. New York: Oxford University Press.

Wilson, Jerry, and Ira Blumenthal. 2008. *Managing Brand You: Seven Steps to Creating Your Most Successful Self*. New York: American Management Association.

Wise, Warren L. 2013. "South Carolina Governor, Senior Senator Reach out to Boeing." *The Post and Courier*, November 15.

Wolf, Diane Lauren. 1994. *Factory Daughters: Gender, Household Dynamics, and Rural Industrialization in Java*. Berkeley: University of California Press.

Wolf, Eric. 1997. *Europe and the People without History*. Berkeley: University of California Press.

Wolford, Wendy. 2010. *This Land Is Ours Now: Social Mobilization and the Meaning of Land in Brazil*. Durham: Duke University Press.

Wolkowitz, Carol. 2006. *Bodies at Work*. London: Sage.

Wright, Angus, and Wendy Wolford. 2003. *To Inherit the Earth: The Landless Movement and the Struggle for a New Brazil*. London: Food First Books.

Yanarella, Ernest J., and Herbert G. Reid. 1996. "From 'Trained Gorilla' to 'Humanware': Repoliticizing the Body-Machine Complex between Fordism and Post-Fordism." In *The Social and Political Body*, edited by Theodore R. Schatzki and Wolfgang Natter, 181–220. New York: Guilford Press.

Yi, Eunhee Kim. 1998. "Home Is a Place to Rest: Constructing the Meaning of Work, Family, and Gender in the Korean Middle Class." *Korea Journal* 38:168–213.

Zandy, Janet. 2004. *Hands: Physical Labor, Class, and Cultural Work*. New Brunswick, NJ: Rutgers University Press.

Zewde, Bahru. 2002. *A History of Modern Ethiopia, 1855–1991*. Oxford: James Currey.

Notes on Contributors

Josh Fisher is assistant professor of anthropology, director of environmental studies, and anthropology program coordinator at High Point University in High Point, North Carolina, where he teaches cultural anthropology, environmental studies, and women's and gender studies. He researches and writes on the anthropology of development and feminist approaches to politics of value in cooperativism, fair trade, and environmental policy. Additionally, he has worked in development as the technical director of the Organization Workshop in Ciudad Sandino, Nicaragua, and he is currently the assistant treasurer and member of the board of directors for the Center for Development in Central America (CDCA).

David Karjanen is assistant professor of American studies and faculty affiliate with the Center for German and European Studies and the Immigration History Research Center at the University of Minnesota. He was previously a visiting postdoctoral scholar at the Center for Comparative Immigration Studies at the University of California, San Diego and a former Fulbright Fellow to the Slovak Republic. His work on comparative political economy centers on low-wage work, labor migration, and the informal economy.

Ann E. Kingsolver is professor of anthropology at the University of Kentucky. She was President of the Society for the Anthropology of Work, 2007–2010. Her research has focused for thirty years on how variously situated individuals explain capitalist globalization and its effects on livelihoods and identities; she has done ethnographic fieldwork in the United States, Mexico, and Sri Lanka. Her books include *More Than Class: Studying Power in U.S. Workplaces* (editor, State University of New York Press, 1998), *NAFTA Stories: Fears and Hopes in Mexico and the United States* (Lynne Rienner Publishers, 2001), *The Gender of Globalization: Women Navigating Cultural and Economic Marginalities* (coeditor, with Nandini Gunewardena, SAR Press, 2007), and *Tobacco Town Futures: Global Encounters in Rural Kentucky* (Waveland Press, 2011).

Jong Bum Kwon is assistant professor of cultural anthropology at Webster University. He received his doctorate in cultural anthropology from New York University and was President's Postdoctoral Fellow at the University of California. Having authored "Forging a Modern Democratic Imaginary" (*positions: asia* *cultures critique*, 2014), he is currently completing a book-length manuscript examining laid-off autoworkers' bodily-affective experience of homelessness and abandonment at Korea's neoliberal turn.

Carrie M. Lane is professor of American studies at California State University, Fullerton. She is an anthropologist of American culture and teaches courses on work, community, and ethnographic research methods. Lane received her Ph.D. in American studies from Yale University, and a B.A. in cultural anthropology from Princeton University. She is the author of *A Company of One: Insecurity, Independence, and the New World of White-Collar Unemployment* (Cornell University Press, 2011) and is currently writing a book on the growing field of professional organizing.

Caitrin Lynch is professor of anthropology at Olin College and the author of *Retirement on the Line: Age, Work, and Value in an American Factory* (Cornell University Press, 2012, www.retirementontheline.net) and *Juki Girls, Good Girls: Gender and Cultural Politics in Sri Lanka's Global Garment Industry* (Cornell University Press, 2007). She is working on a book about the ebb and flow of manufacturing jobs in the United States through the lens of a sixth-generation-family-owned New England textile factory.

Daniel Mains is assistant professor of anthropology and African studies in the Honors College at the University of Oklahoma. He is the author of *Hope Is Cut: Youth, Unemployment, and the Future in Urban Ethiopia* (Temple University Press) as well as numerous articles concerning youth and employment in urban Ethiopia. Mains is currently working on a new book project tentatively titled *Technologies of Development: Infrastructure and Governance in Urban Ethiopia.*

John P. Murphy is assistant professor of French at Gettysburg College. Holding a joint doctorate in anthropology and French studies from New York University, he teaches courses on social inequality and the representation of difference in contemporary France. Murphy is the author of *Yearning to Labor: Youth, Unemployment, and Social Destiny in a French Outer City* (University of Nebraska Press, forthcoming). His work has also appeared in *Anthropological Quarterly* and *French Cultural Studies*.

Mariano D. Perelman is assistant professor of anthropology at the University of Buenos Aires, having received a Ph.D. in social anthropology from the same institution. He is researcher of the Urban Studies Area of the Gino Germani Institute of the University of Buenos Aires and associate researcher of the Argentinean National Scientific and Technical Research Council (CONICET).

Frances Abrahamer Rothstein is professor of anthropology at Montclair State University. She is the author of *Three Different Worlds: Women, Men, and Children* *in an Industrializing Community* and *Globalization in Rural Mexico: Three Decades of Change* and the coeditor (with Michael Blim) of *Anthropology and the Global Factory: Studies of the New Industrialization in the Late Twentieth Century* and coeditor (with M. Barbara Leons) of *New Directions in Political Economy: An Approach from Anthropology.*

Claudia Strauss is professor of anthropology at Pitzer College. She is the author of *Making Sense of Public Opinion: American Discourses about Immigration and Social Programs* (Cambridge University Press, 2012) and coauthor (with Naomi Quinn) of *A Cognitive Theory of Cultural Meaning* (Cambridge University Press, 1997) as well as numerous articles. A past president of the Society for Psychological Anthropology, she is currently writing a book on the cultural meanings of work and unemployment in the United States after the Great Recession.

Index